BELGIUM

APA PUBLICATIONS L

Part of the Langenscheidt Publishing Group

ABOUT THIS BOOK

Editorial

Project Editor
Michael Ellis
Managing Editor
Cameron Duffy
Editorial Director
Brian Bell

Distribution

UK & Ireland
GeoCenter International Ltd
The Viables Centre
Harrow Way
Basingstoke
Hants RG22 4BJ
Fax: (44) 1256-817988

United States
Langenscheidt Publishers, Inc.
46–35 54th Road
Maspeth, NY 11378
Fax: (718) 784-0640

Worldwide
APA Publications GmbH & Co.
Verlag KG (Singapore branch)
38 Joo Koon Road
Singapore 628990
Tel: (65) 865-1600
Fax: (65) 861-6438

Printing

Insight Print Services (Pte) Ltd
38 Joo Koon Road
Singapore 628990
Tel: (65) 865-1600
Fax: (65) 861-6438

CONTACTING THE EDITORS
Although every effort is made to provide accurate information in this publication, we live in a fast-changing world and would appreciate it if readers would call our attention to any errors or outdated information that may occur by writing to us at: **Insight Guides, P.O. Box 7910, London SE1 8ZB, England. Fax: (44 171) 620-1074. e-mail: insight@apaguide.demon.co.uk**

Belgium is the hidden, and relatively unknown, heart at the centre of Europe. A desire to see what makes this heart beat was the motivation for Insight Guides to produce a book that unravels Belgium's mysteries. This new edition re-assesses Belgium today, particularly in the light of its burgeoning role in the political and cultural life of Europe.

How to use this book

The book is structured to convey an understanding of the state and its culture and to guide readers through its sights and activities:

◆ To understand contemporary Belgium, you need to know something of its past. The first section covers the history and culture of Belgium in a series of lively, authoritative essays.

◆ The main Places section provides a full run-down of the attractions worth seeing. It begins with the capital, Brussels, and continues with the popular and historically fascinating cities of Antwerp, Ghent

and Bruges. From then on, our writers take you on a guided tour of the various and varied regions of Belgium, from the coastal flatlands to the forests of the Ardennes. The main places of interest are coordinated by number with full-colour maps.

◆ The Travel Tips listings section provides a convenient point of reference for information on travel, hotels, restaurants, shops and festivals. Information may be located quickly by using the index printed on the back cover flap – and the flaps are designed to serve as bookmarks.

◆ Photographs are chosen not only to illustrate geography and buildings but also to convey the moods of the country and the everyday activities of its people.

The contributors

This new edition was edited by **Michael Ellis** and builds on the original book produced by **Kristiane Müller**.

For this edition, new sections have been written by travel writer **Lisa Gerard Sharp**, including the introductory chapter "A Bourgeois Paradise", "Two Surrealists", an essay on Magritte and Delvaux, and an overview of eating out in the capital, "Brussels à la Carte". She also wrote the new features on "Beer and Brewing", "Art Nouveau", "Grand-Place" and "Castles and Chateaux", and assisted greatly in the revision of the Brussels chapters. Alongside Lisa, **George McDonald** – a writer who has produced the *Insight Pocket Guide: Brussels* – provided a variety of additional material and interesting information for an update and expansion of the existing chapters.

The history section was largely written by **Kirsten Kehret**, Hamburg-based journalist **Nina Köster** and historian **Susanne Urban**. Susanne's father, **Eberhard Urban**, contributed the chapters on "Flemish Masters" and "Cartoon Culture".

Hartmut Dierks and **Wieland Giebel** wrote the sections on the Ardennes and Hainaut, while **Christopher Wendt** wrote about Flanders, Bruges and Ghent. **Nina Köster** also contributed the chapter on Antwerp.

Map Legend

———··	International Boundary
————	Province Boundary
—·—·—	National Park / Reserve
————	Ferry Route
Ⓜ	Metro
✈	Airport
🚌	Bus Station
Ⓟ	Parking
❶	Tourist Information
✉	Post Office
✝ ✟	Church / Ruins
✝	Monastery
☾	Mosque
✡	Synagogue
🏰	Castle / Ruins
∴	Archaeological Site
∩	Statue/Monument
Ⅰ	Cave
★	Place of Interest

The main places of interest in the Places section are coordinated by number with a full-colour map (e.g. ❶), and a symbol at the top of every right-hand page tells you where to find the map.

CONTENTS

Maps

The Brussels metro map is on the back flap

Gabled
houses on
the Kornlei

Travel Tips

"Derrière les murs..."

Chambre et petit-déjeuner

Sonner ici   En cas d'absence, s'adresser au n° 41
(en face de l'église)

Possibilité de location à la semaine, quinzaine ou mois
086/21.12.71   086/21.26.21

"A BOURGEOIS PARADISE?"

Supremely boring and bourgeois – or subversive, surreal and salacious?
The everyday life of the Belgians confounds the clichés

On one level, Belgium presents a cosy and comfortable picture of domestic propriety and modest aspirations. It is tempting to dismiss this civilised and cosmopolitan culture, bound together by beer and bonhomie, as a bland and listless landscape; even Belgium's very own Jacques Brel (1929–78) sang sombrely of his native land, with "a sky so low that it engenders humility; a sky so grey that it has to be forgiven for it". But no country with a football team called Racing White Daring Molenbeek can be entirely dull, can it? Besides, it is the masochistic Belgians who are the first to mock themselves. The great Leopold II, King of the Belgians, famously referred to his nation as "*petit pays, petites gens*" (small country, small-minded people). Perhaps the Belgian sense of sarcasm and self deprecation is a response to the reality of a divided culture, split by the language border (*see p63*). But Belgian wit rarely travels well; it prospers best in its surreal and subversive native soil.

If internal rivalries abound, the Belgians are surprisingly tolerant of all their neighbours, including the Germans, who invaded them twice this century. Tolerance has its limits, however, and even Francophone Belgians would never wish to be mistaken for the "haughty" French, any more than the Flemish Belgians would wish to be confused with the "puritanical" Dutch. But if Belgium excels as host to the citizens of Europe, this graciousness tends not to extend beyond the continent. Racism is prevalent towards the country's immigrant communities – be they Turkish, Moroccan or from Zaire. It is little consolation for immigrants to know that the greatest racial tensions are between rival Belgian communities.

PRECEDING PAGES: the rooftops of medieval Bruges; a country inn near Montaigne; wrought-iron artistry in Mons; a bicycle outside a bed and breakfast establishment in southern Belgium.
LEFT: carnival being celebrated in the town of Binche.
RIGHT: eating out in the market square of Bruges, the medieval gem of Flanders.

Chip on the shoulder

Away from the football pitch or the kitchen, the Belgians' faint sense of national pride is hard to fathom. This is partly because the citizenry suffers from an inferiority complex, with Belgians so often dismissed as a duller version of their French or Dutch neighbours. As if in

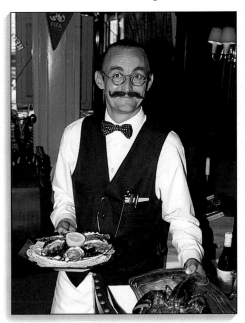

tacit agreement, numerous Belgian icons have been only too eager to escape to fame and fortune in France. Fortunately, when the Belgians do produce someone supremely boring, they often export him: Johnny Halliday, the perennially ageing rocker and French superstar was born plain Belgian Jean-Philippe Smets.

Though Belgian style is outwardly rather nondescript or low-key, Belgians themselves tend to be sharp and self-critical, and internally they frequently harbour a devilish subversive streak. Brussels, in particular, is known for its truculence and irreverence, a cheeky spirit typified by the Mannekin Pis. Magritte, who was perceived as irredemably bourgeois, joined the

Communist Party three times. The great Surrealist painter, a legend in his lifetime, was outwardly conventional to the point of eccentricity. Although his striking images scandalised the bourgeoisie, this clash between conformity and subversion is very Belgian. Ordinary citizens delight in incongruous imagery and secret passions, from penguins to social realist sculpture, to mention only two of the private collections in Brussels. As Magritte said: "If society were not ignorant of the way we are, don't you think it would find us suspect?"

The relationship between the two main communities – the Flemish and the Wallonian –

underlies Belgian life, but can lead to both groups feeling dispossessed or alienated in their own land. Though a single country since 1830, Belgium has never become a single nation, and its cultural identity retains the influence of the French- and Dutch-speaking cultures. At best, Belgian nationalism is negative, resting on a reasonable fear that the centre cannot hold; at worst, it is a nostalgic evocation of a mythical Burgundian "golden age" before the foundation of Belgium. Belgian identity, such as it is, is dogged by bilingualism and prey to separatism. Instead of a fervour for nationhood, there is a passion for Flemish-speaking Flanders or Francophone Wallonia. The "proud to

be Belgian" car sticker has long been banished in the battle between the Walloon cock and the Flemish lion. Today, Belgium is less a country than an administrative entity: the French- and Flemish-speaking regions survive as virtually two federal states. Only foreign policy, the national football team and the comic strip remain unequivocally Belgian.

The Flemish tend to see themselves as industrious, honest, unostentatious and quietly cultured yet view Walloons as sleepy, carefree, indolent, disdainful and slightly incompetent; separatists go further, and dismiss them as degenerate welfare scroungers, subsidised by Flemish profits and taxes. By contrast, the Walloons see themselves as liberal-minded, sociable and good-natured, if latterly threatened by the Flemish ascendancy. In turn, they view their rivals as smug, humourless *paysans flamands* (Flemish peasants), lacking in finesse and undeserving of their economic good fortune. Compared with the dispirited air and neglected facades of Walloon cities, Flanders feels prosperous and well-cared for, with so much renovation that the historic cities are in danger of looking over-restored and museum-like.

Economic milch cows

If the Flemish now consider themselves as the country's economic providers, it was not always so. Wallonia was Belgium's former coal and steel power-house and the bastion of Socialism for almost a century. The Francophones (Walloons) saw themselves as the milch cows of the Belgian state, with their mines, foundries and textile mills supporting Flanders.

However, 19th-century prosperity has given way to decaying heavy industry. As a result, a once radical and reforming region suffers from economic blight, tribalism, old-school trade unionism and a lack of foreign investment. Underworld conspiracies even led to Liège, the spiritual capital of the Walloons, becoming known as Palermo on the Meuse.

Modern Wallonia is eclipsed by the economic might of Flanders, whose post-war recovery continues to blossom. Today, the Flemish see themselves as trapped in a two-speed nation, but in truth it has always been so, with the economic might of the country fluctuating between the rival communities. The Walloons built the heavy industry and the railways; the Flemish built the motorways. In recent years freight has used road more then rail, boosting the Flemish economy whilst starving Wallonia's.

If Flanders flourishes while Wallonia wallows, Brussels is a case apart. Given the presence of the multinationals and international institutions, and thanks to its special status within Europe, Brussels is one of the three richest regions in the European Union. However, the Belgians receive poor governance and social returns for some of the highest taxation in Europe. Partly as a reaction, Belgium, matched by Italy and Greece, enjoys one of the blackest of black economies, representing as much as 20 percent of GDP.

Belgian compromise

Ever since its creation as a buffer state between France and the Netherlands in 1830, Belgium has been in danger of dissolving. *Compromis à la belge*, the process of devolving power to every conceivable minority at every conceivable level, evolved as a way of holding the state together. This separate-but-equal approach came to a head in Leuven in the 1960s when the Francophones were forced out and founded a sister city of Louvain-la-Neuve, taking the French-speaking half of the university.

Since then, segregation has been along linguistic lines, with mutual stereotypes deeply ingrained. Policy-making has gradually passed to the regions, with few powers left for the centre. Antwerp is the Flemish fortress, while Liège is the spiritual capital of the Walloons. Sadly, the quest for linguistic and cultural parity by one side is seen as domination by the other. So, despite its dull, bourgeois image, the present reality of Belgium is that it remains a divided country in terms of race, language, class and income. And the Walloons have seen their historical dominance of national affairs whittled away by their Flemish compatriots.

Virtue and vice

But this is only part of the picture of the complex Belgian psyche. For countering divisions and underhand dealings is a strong sense of civic pride and responsibility, engendered through generations of dutiful burghers, merchants and guildsmen. Such traditions have fostered courtesy, conformity, charity and social decorum –

LEFT: café life in the centre of Brussels.
RIGHT: a riverside scene in Ghent.

virtues that would be rather dry if they were not mixed with the ingredients of creativity and fun that have produced artists and spontaneous revelry in equal quantity.

Indeed, in a country with two languages and two clashing cultures, visual expression is particularly prized. Thus Belgium came to be the greatest producer of comic strip material, as well as the home of Breughel and Rubens.

In recent years, we see both sides of the Belgian coin – vice and virtue – as venality in public life and collusion between police and criminals has caused ordinary Belgians to face the political realities of the 1990s. Although

Catholic society was shaken by the corruption and sex scandals, the country simultaneously experienced an unexpected resurgence of civic spirit, as the public took to the streets.

In such a conservative yet divided society, the sovereign fulfilled his role as a unifying symbol above the complexity of coalition politics. During the scandals, King Albert II appealed for calm, while calling on the ministries and justice system to show humility. He broke ranks with royal protocol and called for "a more humane and responsive system of justice". In this, he was at one with Belgium's "little people", who marched in street protests that united farmers and students, housewives and bureaucrats. The jury is still out on whether the promised openness in public life will ever be delivered. If nothing else, the crisis created a positive sense of unity that transcended the deadlock of communal interests.

Forked tongues

To outsiders, place names can be confusing in Belgium: Gand (Gent); Bruxelles (Brussel); Anvers (Antwerpen); Mons (Bergen); Louvain (Leuven). However, foreigners can be intrigued rather than depressed by the language divide. As one Irish resident says, "I like the difference between French and Flemish speakers; it adds

are not merely the preserve of linguistic balancing; they also extend to gender politics. For example, in 1997 the town of Leuven decided to allocate all new street names to women until parity with "male" streets has been achieved.

Time capsules

In Belgium, appearances can be deceptive. The picturesque cities of Bruges or Ghent resemble medieval tapestries woven around a skein of canals. Yet these twee time capsules of cobblestones, spires and stepped gables are part of the Flemish economic miracle. Far from being frozen in time, Bruges is slickly professional in

a certain friction, a sense of noman's land." Indeed, political sensitivities are such that Belgians from different communities may choose to speak English with one another even if they speak both national languages competently.

Linguistic considerations even seep into the subterranean world of easy listening on the Brussels metro: background music must avoid the human voice. The supplier, the owner of Muzak Corporation, attributes it to political sensitivities: "If one word of Flemish were sung, then French would have to feature. If English were sung, then German, the third official language in Belgium, would have to be included." However, such acts of diplomacy

its packaging of tourism in a medieval carapace. Both cities echo Antwerp in showing the Flemish freewheeling respect for capitalism. "Where Antwerp goes, so the rest of Belgium follows – a few years later" runs a local saying, testament to the progressiveness of the city.

Joie de vivre

The smallest event can become a celebration in Belgium, from students' rag week to the expansive Festival of Flanders, staged in abbeys and castles. Festivals range from religious processions and folkloric displays to military marches and gastronomic feasts. In Antwerp's Rubens market, participants enthusiastically sport the costumes worn in the great painter's day. Food is frequently cause enough for celebration, whether one of the many beer festivals or the quirky butter and cheese festival in Diksmuide, while strolling hordes munching on punnets of chips doused in mayonnaise is part of the pageant of everyday life. Carnival revellers in Aalst celebrate the event by parading in rich costumes and hurling onions from the belfry. Not that any celebration is untinged with criticism. In the Low Countries, there is a long tradition of using carnival as a way of challenging the authorities. Recent parades have caricatured the country's political scandals,

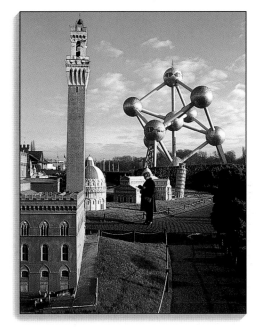

including dubious Government plans to use postmen to snoop on citizens.

Hearty appetites

Placating relatives is a common Belgian pastime, and in such a small country, the family is always close. Belgium has one of the oldest populations in Europe, so lunch with hypochondriac or gastronome grandparents represents a weekend fixture. A warm Sunday sees a bracing family outing to the woods or dunes, with bourgeois Belgians accompanied by preening poodles or *bergers*

LEFT: Ghent is the focal point of the Flemish nationality.
ABOVE: a little piece of Europe in Brussels.

belges, native alsatians. In fact, "The average Belgian takes his Sunday seriously", notes Pamela Readhead, a Brussels-based journalist: "Crusty rolls known as *pistolets* for breakfast; a three-course lunch with Granny at noon, followed by something vaguely healthy, like mushroompicking in the woods, to help the digestion."

Yet resolutely bourgeois Belgium is far from predictable, especially in its attitudes to sex and death. Breughel and the Flemish masters delighted in depicting gory massacres, while modern Belgians cultivate a salacious sexual streak, presented pragmatically rather than poetically. *"On garde un homme par son ventre et son basventre"* (you keep your man by catering for his stomach and what lies below it) is a charming piece of Belgian wisdom. The Surrealists were obsessed by bizarre portrayals of nudes entwined with apples or trains, while detective novelist Georges Simenon boasted that he had slept with 10,000 women. More recently, *The Sexual Life of the Belgians* (1995) was a popular cinematic success, though its subject errs more towards frustration and mishap than sexual celebration. Open prostitution is also common, and Antwerp's red-light district is as lively as Amsterdam's.

As natural bons vivants, Belgians emanate Burgundian warmth rather than French chic. Belgium is a country of mussels and mayonnaise, beer and chocolate, and the people are determined to have their cake and eat it: chips are cut thin (for health reasons) and then fried twice (doubling both the flavour and the cholesterol content). Even Pierre Wynant, Belgium's top chef, always poses the same question to diners: *"C'était suffisant?"* (Did you get enough to eat?). Quantity is as important as quality: the Chimay monks, who make the best brews, proudly quaff their own beer; Trappist vows may cover silence but not abstinence.

Belgian joie de vivre always comes in large portions, from vibrant food markets to voluptuous Rubens nudes and sheer generosity of spirit. Even the heated café terraces lend the wintry cities a seductive Latin air, a world away from cold northern Europe. Winter means good company and hot chocolate in front of a crackling fire in a city inn. In such classic Brussels bars as Le Cirio, permed and proper matrons, accompanied by poodles or pekes, while away the day contemplating life through a succession of Chimay Bleues. ❑

LEO BEL
GICUS

DE   NOORT

ZEE

ANGLIÆ
PARS

GALLIÆ

ZUYDER
ZEE
GER
MA NIÆ
PARS.
Dillenberg
Nassaw
Coblens
Andernach
Engers
Bonn
Godesberg
Trier
Pfaltz
Francfort
Lona flu
Mosella flu
Wesel
Keyserswerd
Dusseldorp
Juliacensis
Colln
Maestricht
Groeningen
Deventer
Utrecht
Palatium Bruxellense
Palatium Comitu Holland
Scala Mili Germanic
Gubernavit Leonem nomine Philippi fratris, ad Annu 1567.
Tertius in gubernando Leone Belgico, obijt Anno 1576. 5. Martij, in Belgio.
Quintus Regis Hispaniæ in Belgio Gubernator, gubernavit ad Annum 1592.
Septimus Regius Belgij Generalis Gubernator gubernavit ad Annum 1621.
Ordinum fœderatorum nomine gubernavit ab Anno 1585 ad Annum 1588.
Ordinum fœderatorum nomine gubernavit ab Anno 1587 ad Annum 1625

Decisive Dates

1st millennium BC: Celtic tribes settle in western Europe.

58 BC: The Belgae, a conglomeration of Celtic tribes living in the northern part of Gaul, fight with great valour against the forces of Julius Caesar, but are forced to surrender in 58 BC.

AD 3rd–5th centuries: The Franks cross the Rhine and settle in Gaul. Christianity spreads.

712: The Bishop of Cambrai dies in what will later become Brussels.

721: Bishopric of Liège established.

800: Charlemagne, a son of Liège, is crowned Emperor of the Romans in Rome.

843: Partition of France. The River Schelde is accepted as the border between Flanders and Wallonia (now a part of Lotharingia).

900: Baldwin, the first count of Flanders, builds a castle at Bruges.

966: The first documented reference to Brussels, then called 'Bruocsella' .

11th and 12th centuries: Development of the cloth trade brings economic prosperity to Flanders. The blossoming trade between the Continent and England results in rapid growth of the cities, including Bruges, which becomes the trading centre for goods from Italy, France, Germany and England.

1302: Poorly armed Flemish peasants and craftsmen defeat an army of French knights in the Battle of the Golden Spurs at Kortrijk.

1308: Henri VII of Luxembourg becomes the Germanic emperor and is crowned Henri IV.

1369: Margaret, the daughter of the last count of Flanders, marries Phillip the Bold of Burgundy. Flanders passes to Burgundian rule.

15th century: Dukes of Burgundy win control of what is now Belgium. The economically powerful areas of the Burgundian empire enjoy a period of cultural enrichment which produces artistic splendour and political prestige. The textile industries, which have developed in the Belgian territories since the 12th century, become the economic mainstay of northwestern Europe.

1425: The university at Leuven is founded by Pope Martin V and develops into the European centre of jurisprudence.

1477: Mary, daughter and heiress of the last Duke of Burgundy, Charles the Bold, marries Maximilian of Austria. As a result , the Low Countries are brought increasingly under the sway of the Habsburg dynasty.

1500: Charles V, grandson of Maximilian and later the German emperor, is born in Ghent.

1521: Erasmus lives in Anderlecht, then a village outside Brussels.

1526: Pieter Brueghel the Elder is born.

1531: Brussels becomes the capital of the Spanish Netherlands.

1541: Mercator draws the first map of Flanders.

1555: Charles V is defeated by the Protestant princes of Germany and is forced to renounce the throne in favour of his son, Phillip II.

1566: Protestant iconoclasts ransack numerous churches. In order to put down the movement, the Spanish Duke of Alba is sent to the Low Countries. As the representative of the Inquisition, he subjects the people to a reign of terror which causes thousands of Protestants to emigrate.

1568: Counts Egmont and Hoorn, the leaders of a revolt against Spanish rule, are beheaded on the Grand-Place in Brussels.

1569: Pieter Brueghel the Elder dies at his home in Brussels.

1579: Under William I of Orange, the seven northern provinces, now called the Netherlands, join forces under the Union of Utrecht and declare their independence in 1581.

1585: In the struggle for recognition of their sovereignty, the Spanish recapture the port of Antwerp and block the River Scheldt. Many merchants and skilled artisans leave Antwerp; Amsterdam replaces Antwerp as the chief trading centre of Europe. From this time onward, the whole of the southern part of the Netherlands recognises Philip II as its sovereign.

1608: Peter Paul Rubens becomes court painter to the Spanish regents; he subsequently paints in France, Spain and England before returning to Antwerp. The artistic achievements of the Flemish school of 17th-century painters, which also includes Anthony Van Dyck and Jacob Jordaens, reflect the commercial and cultural revitalisation of the southern Netherlands.

1648: Treaty of Westphalia, by which Spain recognises the independence of the United Provinces of the north. Belgium remains under Spanish control. The treaty stimulates economic competition among northern European nations.

1667: The French king, Louis XIV, captures large parts of Flanders and Hainaut. Lille falls to France.

1695: Bombardment and destruction of the Grand Place by a French army.

1701–13: The Spanish War of Succession turns Belgium into a battlefield. By the Treaty of Utrecht, which ends the war, the present-day territory comprising Belgium and Luxembourg passes under the authority of the Holy Roman emperor Charles VI and his Habsburg successors.

1795: The French revolutionaries annex Belgium and Luxembourg which remain under French control until the defeat of Napoleon.

1803: Napoleon Bonaparte visits Brussels as First Consul of the Republic.

1815: The Battle of Waterloo and Napoleon's last stand. Eupen and Malmédy annexed by Prussia. Holland and Belgium form the Kingdom of the Netherlands under William I of Orange.

1830–31: Conflicting interests between the north and south concerning religious affairs, economic matters and the authority of the king lead to revolution in Brussels. Belgium achieves independence as a neutral kingdom under Leopold of Saxe-Coburg.

1835: The first Continental railway, from Brussels to Mechelen, is inaugurated.

1881: King Leopold II seizes the Congo and Belgium becomes a colonial power.

1914–18: German troops march into Belgium and Luxembourg. The battles of the Yser are the bloodiest

of the war. The Treaty of Versailles grants Eupen and Malmédy to Belgium.

1929: Hergé's *Adventures of Tintin* are published for the first time.

1940–44: German troops again march into Belgium. The Belgian government seeks exile in London. King Leopold III is deported to Germany. Belgium is liberated by the Allies in 1944.

1948: Customs union agreed between Holland, Belgium and Luxembourg (Benelux Agreement).

1951: King Baudouin I ascends the throne.

1957: Belgium joins the European Economic Community (today the European Union).

1958: The World's Fair at the Heysel in Brussels.

1959: Brussels becomes headquarters of the European Community.

1971 and 1980: Constitutional reform gives both linguistic groups (Flemish and French) more autonomy in economic and cultural matters.

1977: Belgium is divided into three distinct regions: Flanders, Wallonia and the conurbation of Brussels.

1989: In the reorganisation of the Belgian state, Brussels becomes the Capital Region, alongside Flanders and Wallonia.

1993: King Baudouin I dies on 31 July and is succeeded by his brother Albert.

1995: The provinces of Flemish Brabant and Walloon Brabant are created from the old province of Brabant, giving Belgium a total of ten provinces. ❑

PRECEDING PAGES: Leo Belgicus, a powerful symbol of the nation.

LEFT: the 1830 Uprising, which led to the independence of Belgium.

RIGHT: a family portrait by Anthony van Dyck, one of the nation's greatest painters.

FREE TOWNS AND THE AGE OF FEUDALISM

Although the independent state of Belgium has existed only since 1831, the restless history of its territory stretches back much further

Belgium's history begins with Roman invasion, several decades before the birth of Christ. Indeed, Julius Caesar records that the *Belgae*, a conglomeration of Gallo-Celtic tribes, fought with great valour against his forces in 58 BC. Ultimately the *Belgae* lost, however, and Romans remained in the region for almost 500 years, establishing urban living, building roads and developing trade.

Following the collapse of the Western Roman Empire, the power vacuum was filled by the Franks, a loose confederation of Germanic tribes, who did much to spread Christianity throughout western Europe.

During the reign of Charlemagne, born in Liège in 742 and King of the Franks from 768, Belgium became the focal point of European events. Before his reign, invasions from the Barbarian north and Muslim south were eroding Frankish power, but Charlemagne quickly set about rectifying the situation. He subdued the Saxons in northeast Europe and repelled the Lombards in northern Italy. A Spanish March was established south of the Pyrenees "to keep the infidel at bay", while an Eastern March in the Danube basin acted as a buttress against tribes from the east.

Under Charlemagne's rule, the Frankish Empire extended from the Elbe to the Atlantic and from the North Sea to the Mediterranean. For services to Christianity and, in particular, for restoring papal lands in Italy, Charlemagne was crowned the first Holy Roman Emperor by the Pope on Christmas Day 800.

Charlemagne's successors, however, could not retain control over such an enormous territory, and two generations later the Frankish Empire was carved up by the Treaty of Verdun. The territory was split into regions to the east and west of the Scheldt river. Charles the Bald

LEFT: the mighty Charlemagne, King of the Franks from 768 to 814.
RIGHT: the historic city of Bruges.

gained sovereignty to the western section, while Lothair received the majority of the lands to the east. The Scheldt became the natural dividing line between the French and German spheres of influence.

Baldwin the Iron Arm

The inhabitants of these lands concerned themselves less with such divisive affairs, but nevertheless took advantage of the fall of the Frankish Empire to develop extensive independent feudal dynasties.

In Flanders, Baldwin the Iron Arm profited from the weakness of the French throne to become Count of Flanders. He kidnapped the daughter of the French king to make her his wife, and then responded to the indignation of his newly found father-in-law by threatening to enter into an alliance with the Normans. The French king was left with no choice but to concede to the wishes of Baldwin the Iron Arm.

Baldwin's successors soon extended the sovereignty of Flanders to the south as far as the Somme, and in the 11th century, the region controlled by Baldwin V reached eastward beyond the Scheldt. By extending their reign beyond this important river, the Flemish counts, from 1056 onward, became vassals of the German emperor as well as of the French king, further strengthening their already powerful position.

Prosperous trading cities

From the 12th century, cities of commerce developed into important centres of power, especially in Flanders. The blossoming trade between the William of Normandy, the cities of Flanders demanded Dietrich of Alsace as their leader. It is a testament to the power of these trading cities that even the King of France was forced to yield to their wishes.

The reign of the Alsatians began with great promise. Dietrich, and later his son Philip, relied on the support of the cities, as well as a series of arranged marriages, to increase the political importance of Flanders. Philip of Alsace even served for a time as adviser to Philip-August (Philip II of France and grandson of Louis VI), a position which enabled him to control the strings of French politics.

Continent and England resulted in the rapid growth of these cities. Bruges became the trading centre for goods from Italy, France, Germany and England, and merchants from far and wide offered their wares for sale in Flanders. The growing textile industry was also a vital factor in the increasing wealth and prestige of the cities, but this industry relied upon a steady supply of wool from England, a factor that would weigh heavily on later events.

A test of the cities' strength came in the 12th century, after the murder of Charles the Good. Charles, who had fostered relations with the cities, left no heir, and it fell to Louis VI of France to appoint a successor. Although Louis chose

In the year 1181, however, a dispute arose between France and Flanders. In the ensuing conflict, Philip of Alsace overestimated his mortal strength, and died during the siege of St Jean d'Acre. Basing his claims on previously made agreements, Philip II, the first great Capetian king of France, was able to gain control over southern Flanders. Shortly thereafter, in a counter swing of the pendulum that typified the times, fortune once again favoured Flanders, and Baldwin VI, through his alliance with England, was able to reconquer some of the lost territories. But as this historical chapter drew to a close, France proved the ultimate victor, and in 1214 Philip securely established his throne by defeating the Flemish, the English, and emperor Otto IV at the Battle of Bouvines.

In the 13th century, France succeeded in consolidating its position not only in Flanders but also in the German fiefs of Lorraine. It was only owing to the tremendous power of the Flemish cities that the territory of today's Belgium did not entirely come under French rule.

Rebellion of the cities

At the start of the 14th century it looked as if France, under Philip IV (Philip the Fair), would succeed in completing the annexation of Flanders, a task which had been started by Philip II. Guy of Flanders entered into an alliance with England in order to oppose French sovereignty, but still he was unsuccessful. The French felt secure in sending a governor to rule over Flanders, but this confidence was shortlived.

Emotions were at a high pitch within the cities. The craftsmen, under the leadership of the weaver Peter de Coninck, rebelled against the patricians and the French who supported them. The rebellion was suppressed several times, but during the night of 18th May 1302, the rebels overcame the French guards in Bruges. The result was a bloodbath, and in the days that followed, anyone who could not correctly pronounce the Flemish cry "*schild ende vriendt*" (a phrase apparently impossible for a non-Flemish speaker to say correctly) was killed.

Encouraged by the success in Bruges, the common folk all over Flanders reached for their weapons. Armed only with spears, the Flemish craftsmen and peasants faced the French cavalry on the battlefield of Courtrai on 11th July 1302. The French, although confident of an easy victory, were decisively defeated. Not one French soldier survived and, when the fighting had come to an end, the rebels collected 700 golden spurs *(see p230)*.

Philip the Fair eventually yielded to the demands of the rebels and granted Flanders its independence, but the peace treaty did not herald the onset of peaceful times. Years of fighting ensued between the aristocracy and rebellious peasants throughout maritime Flanders. The citizens of Bruges and Ypres had allied themselves with these peasants, but in Ghent, they had, in the main, stayed loyal to the rulers. But at the

end of 1337, this city too became the scene of popular rebellions.

A wolf in sheep's clothing

At the beginning of the Hundred Years' War between France and England, Flanders sided with the French, causing England to boycott delivery of wool to the region. Trade in Flanders came to a complete halt. The people of Ghent – including merchants and craftsmen, rich and poor – were all in agreement about what should be done. In order to get the economy back on its feet, they must rebel against the politics of their rulers and re-establish trade

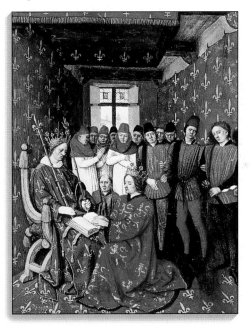

with England. The wool merchant Jacob Van Artevelde was the rebels' leader, and it was under his influence that Edward III of England, who viewed himself as the rightful heir to the French throne by maternal parentage, was proclaimed King of France at the Ghent market in January of 1340.

Alliance with England meant that trade blossomed once again, but with it there returned the old conflicts of interest between merchants and craftsmen. In 1345 the weavers murdered Jacob van Artevelde and usurped power in the cities. Their action was condemned by other craftsmen and a civil war ensued which left Flanders bereft of nearly all the power it had gained. ❏

LEFT: an interior view of Gaasbeek Castle.
RIGHT: Philip the Fair.

GOLDEN AGE OF THE BURGUNDIANS

This was an inflamed period of history, as battles raged throughout Europe.
But, amidst the ravages of war, the arts world of Flanders flourished

The Burgundian Empire came into existence during the period of the Hundred Years' War, a conflict waged spasmodically between France and England from 1337 to 1453. The major point of dispute was the succession to the French throne. The claimant Edward III of England was pitted against the Valois line, which had ascended the French throne when the Capetian dynasty died out in 1328. The war was fought solely on the Continent, and mainly on French soil.

Because of their vacillating position, the Burgundians were again and again drawn into the war. Burgundy basically consisted of two regions, separated from one another geographically. The southern region, in today's eastern France, comprised an area stretching from Dijon to Basle. The other sector, the one of greater strategic importance, consisted of today's Belgium, plus the French territory near the border and a large portion of today's Netherlands. This sector was vital to the Anglo/French dispute, as the seaboard territory offered the best European trade connections.

The Burgundians saw themselves as the potential rulers of France, and to this end their immediate goal was the elimination of French supremacy in Europe. To achieve this aim, they temporarily allied themselves with England.

First of the four great dukes

The Burgundians increased their power and their sphere of influence by means of diplomacy, military endeavours and cleverly arranged marriages. The fortunes of this powerful, though short-lived, empire were moulded by the four "great dukes". These four rulers were in power for barely more than 100 years between them (1364–1477); and yet this was time enough to earn Burgundy an important place in the annals of history.

The great French dynasty of the Capetians expired in 1328 with the death of Charles IV.

LEFT: Philip the Good, Duke of Burgundy.
RIGHT: Philip's wife, Isabella of Portugal.

His successor was Philip VI of Valois, although, as stated, this primacy was disputed by King Edward III of England. Philip was followed by his son, King John II, who was crowned in 1350. The Valois line continued with John's first son, Charles the Wise, who ascended the French throne in 1364. In 1369, Charles deci-

ded that his younger brother Philip – already Duke of Burgundy – should marry Margaret of Flanders, daughter and heiress of the Count of Flanders. Thus in 1385, after the death of the count, Belgian Flanders, Artois and other territories were incorporated into the Burgundian duchy. The Burgundian household now controlled an area comprising today's Netherlands and Belgium.

Insurrections against the nobility

The rulers of the Belgian territory continually underestimated the dissatisfaction of the craftsmen and peasants of Burgundy. The working classes had played no role in the battles for

Civic Splendour

The Burgundian era signalled the beginning of an artistic and architectural flowering in Flanders. The entire Burgundian empire enjoyed a golden age, from vigorous sculpture and architecture in Dijon to the stylised Book of Hours, the exquisite calendar created for the Duke of Berry (*see p85*). The Burgundian court in Bruges patronised distinguished Flemish masters such as Memling and Jan van Eyck. Brussels, in turn, held illuminated manuscripts and altarpieces, Gothic public buildings and noble mansions. Whilst reli-

gious architecture, especially in Brussels, was inspired by French Gothic, civic architecture took a more vernacular Flemish form. Under the aegis of the counts of Flanders and Emperor Charles V, this artistic independence continued.

The power and wealth of the major Flemish cloth towns, Ghent, Bruges and Ypres (Ieper), was essentially a Gothic story. Flemish wealth was literally spun from fine cloth: English wool was transformed into tapestries, furnishings and clothing, thanks to the skill of Flemish weavers. In gratitude and pride, the prosperous burghers and guilds exercised their civic privileges by enriching their cities.

As civic pride burgeoned, the Flemish built town halls and toll-houses, guildhalls and Gothic man-sions, cloth halls and municipal records offices. These major public buildings were clustered around the prestigious main square, the grand-place or grote markt, the finest of which is undoubtedly Brussels' Grand-Place. This was the imposing public face of Brussels, with the city's guilds ensconced in resplendent premises.

Trades and guilds gained their independence in the 14th century and played an important role in shaping Flemish cities. The guilds functioned as protectionist bodies and political forces until the 17th century. The guild halls also acted as social centres and chambers of commerce. Every significant activity was represented, from the guild of bakers, brewers and boatmen to the cabinet-makers and coopers, archers and haberdashers.

A town hall – *hotel de ville* in French, *stadhuis* in Flemish – was the most obvious symbol of civic pride. The Bruges *stadhuis*, dating from 1376, formed the Flemish model for such buildings, inspiring those in Brussels, Leuven and Ghent.

The Low Countries has a tradition of lay women, pious Catholics who nevertheless never took the vow of poverty. They lived in a community known as a béguinage (*begijnhof*), a concept which came into existence in the 13th century. The traditional béguinage consists of low, white-washed cottages set around a central courtyard. Over twenty béguinages remain in northern Belgium, with the main community in Ghent and the most picturesque one inhabited by sisters in Bruges.

During the Burgundian golden age, Flanders was the most celebrated tapestry centre on the Continent: Flemish designs decorated princely palaces, churches and châteaux all over Europe. Weavers and designers worked together to produce harmonious but technically challenging work, as the religious themes of the Middle Ages gave way to historical tableaux, mythological and hunting scenes. The Oudenaarde tapestry industry in Flanders thrived in the 15th and 16th centuries. The skilful technique combined embroidery with weaving, often incorporating silk, gold and silver thread into designs predominantly picked out in blue, yellow and brown, with bursts of red and sections of script. The pictorial scenes were generally based on cartoons of Flemish masters, and inspired by chivalric, courtly, pastoral and religious themes. The tapestries have little sense of perspective and are composed of scenes, packed with incident. ❑

LEFT: *La Vierge à la Soupe au Lait* by Gerard David (1460–1523).

European supremacy, but they had suffered greatly under increasing exploitation of the ruling aristocracy, especially within the flourishing cities. Insurrections had already taken place in several cities long before the death of the Count of Flanders.

The centres of the first revolts (1338–45) were in the cities of Ghent, Bruges and Ypres. The rebels were led by Jacob van Artevelde, elected by the population as Captain of Ghent in 1338. He made a treaty with Edward III of England in 1340 to protect the weaving trade, but when, in 1345, he suggested that Edward III's son, Edward the Black Prince, should become Count

able to stabilise and consolidate the region. In 1385 he signed the Treaty of Tournai, establishing peace with the county of Flanders and the city of Ghent.

When Charles the Wise died in 1380, he was succeeded by his son Charles the Well-beloved (Charles VI of France). Though beloved, Charles suffered increasingly from periods of insanity – resulting in his gaining the new nickname, Mad King Charles – and three of his uncles ruled as regents in his name. However, the ongoing war between France and England drove a wedge between these three uncles and their families. Whereas Charles VI's brother Louis of Orléans

of Flanders, he was killed during the insurrection that ensued. Artevelde's son Philip continued his father's rebellious ways, and in 1382 led the new outbreak of insurgency against the Burgundians, to protect the rights and future prosperity of the craftspeople of Flanders.

Artevelde, together with his followers, managed to capture Bruges but was subsequently defeated. Ultimately the revolts, which lasted almost 35 years, were brutally crushed, and Philip Artevelde met his death in 1382.

With rebellion crushed, Charles the Wise's brother Philip (known as Philip the Bold) was

ABOVE: Philip the Good, Duke of Burgundy.

was interested in continuing the battles against England, his uncle Philip the Bold was eager to enter into a truce. England took advantage of the conflict between the houses of Orléans and Burgundy, a conflict which was to last for the next ten years, despite the death of Philip in 1404.

Philip the Bold was succeeded by his son, John the Fearless. This second Duke of Burgundy remained a foe of Louis of Orléans. John the Fearless made himself not only protector of the peace with England (a peace established by his father independently of Louis of Orléans), but also of the bourgeoisie and the peasants. His aspirations were pitted directly against his uncle Louis and the incalculable Mad King Charles.

Trade Centres and Pilgrim Routes

During the 14th and 15th centuries, Europe was criss-crossed with trade routes, established between major centres of commerce and industry. In northern Europe, Flanders was pivotal to trade between Germany, the Low Countries and Britain. German merchants purchased cloth and fine fabrics from the people of Flanders (textiles being their most important industry) and, in return, sold furs, grain, wood, wax, iron, hemp,

amber and wine. Additionally, the steady stream of traders from further afield – including Italians, Iberians and French – visiting the cities of Bruges and Antwerp offered almost unlimited scope for further trading activities.

During this period, cloth halls and guild halls were integral to the process of trade, and their architectural quality matched the success of the mercantile Flemish cities. Known as a *lakenhalle* in Flemish, the cloth hall was linked to drapers, but also served as a commercial centre, meeting place and, on occasions, place of refuge or political asylum. Some of the finest halls can still be seen, in Ypres (leper) and Bruges; both these cloth halls date from the 13th century.

The commercial hub

Cologne enjoyed the unique position of being located on the two largest trade routes of northern Europe: the Rhine route running between Italy and England, and the Hanseatic route between Novgorod, in Russia, and Bruges. The routes from Cologne to Brabant and Flanders were especially busy, and a mutual dependency arose between the trading cities of Flanders and the commercial crossroads of Cologne.

The merchants controlling trade along the river Meuse transported wine from the Rhine and metal products, gems and luxurious textiles from as far afield as Constantinople, across southern Belgium to the coastal towns. From there they were shipped to England. Every August Meuse merchants from Liège, Huy and Dinant travelled to the trade fair in Cologne, taking samples of their latest metalware.

The artistic achievements of Flanders in the 14th and 15th centuries were underpinned by economic wealth derived from the cloth trade and growth of the guilds, aided by the expanding ports of Bruges and Antwerp. But, by the early 16th century, the cloth towns of Bruges and Ghent fell into decline as the river Zwin, Bruges' outlet to the sea, silted up. This increased the importance of the port of Antwerp, strengthening its link with Cologne and raising its sense of prestige and power.

It wasn't just the merchants who benefited from the movement of goods: wealthy landowners saw it as an opportunity to impose spontaneous taxes on the merchants, and toll houses were set up along the trade routes for this purpose. And if the landowners' taxes weren't deterrent enough, there was always a ready supply of highway robbers.

Pilgrim routes

The route between Cologne, Antwerp and Bruges crossed the Meuse at Maastricht, which, in around 1250 was mentioned as a stopping-off point for pilgrims en route from Münster to Rome. The route continued from Maastricht to Antwerp, and was shared by pilgrims and merchants; all shared the risks of attack, abduction or murder.

The German painter Albrecht Dürer travelled from Antwerp through Mechelen to Brussels in 1520. The diary of his travels throughout the Netherlands is a rich source of information on trading routes: he recorded which routes he took, where he rested and how much money he spent along the way. ❑

LEFT: *The Banker and his Client* by Quentin Matsys, c1520.

John had Louis of Orléans assassinated, defending his action as the necessary removal of a tyrant. A civil war ensued in France, dividing the nation into two camps – those supporting Burgundy and those supporting Orléans. The Belgians remained outside the dispute, preferring to concentrate on their own interests.

Mad King Charles took no clear stand in the dispute either. Without the leadership of Louis of Orléans and with an ineffectual king, opposition to the Duke of Burgundy was limited. Thus, it was not difficult, in the year 1411, for John the Fearless to convince the people of France to side with him and to rebel against Orléans and the French king.

The leader of the revolt was Simon Caboche, a Parisian butcher. However, the actions of Caboche and his followers, the "Cabochians" as they were called, got so out of hand and their blows against the aristocracy became so atrocious that John the Fearless lost complete control over them. He decided to flee Paris and allow the troops of Orléans to conquer the city. The soldiers of Orléans entered Paris, and granted no mercy to the population.

In 1414, John was defeated by his enemies. His allies rescinded their loyalty to him and surrendered to Orléans. John, perhaps for the first time in his life no longer actually worthy of the name fearless, saw no other alternative but to sign a peace treaty in Arras in 1414.

John cooperates with England

Before his defeat, John had approached the English king, hoping for good neighbourly relations and the support of England. A trade agreement between Burgundian Flanders and England had already been signed in 1406. In an attempt to increase England's influence on the Continent, English troops had landed repeatedly in Normandy from 1385 onwards. In 1415 they defeated the French army near Agincourt, not far from Arras. It was after this victory that John, Duke of Burgundy, entered into a secret alliance with King Henry V of England. He supported Henry's claim to the French throne and in return received military support against his lifelong foe, Orléans.

John let the English do his fighting for him and used this short period of time, during which

---

RIGHT: the majestic form of the Gothic Cathedrale St-Michel in Brussels.

his troops were not engaged in any fighting, to gain advantages for himself. He kidnapped the French queen Isabeau in Champagne, carrying her away to Troyes, and formed a new government. Then he found himself faced with a new problem: his English allies were continuing their attempts to capture Paris.

John could not decide whether he should maintain his alliance with England and open the city gates to their troops, or whether he should make peace with his French opponents and fight the English. Both sides noticed his indecision. John delayed too long and in July of 1419, during a conference with representatives

of the Count of Orléans, he was assassinated.

The now precarious Burgundian title was inherited by his son Philip the Good. Philip's first act was to ratify the 1420 Treaty of Troyes, along with France and England. In the treaty, the English king retained the right of succession to the French throne and was granted the French king's daughter, Catherine of Valois, as his wife. The crown prince (Mad King Charles's son) was thus denied his right of succession, and so joined forces with the Count of Orléans to fight against the combined might of Burgundy, England and France.

In 1422, the French king (Mad Charles) died, but the new king, Henry V of England, followed him to the grave soon after. With the despised English successor dead, the disinherited crown prince was able to ascend the French throne, as Charles VII. His reign was accompanied by further battles in and around France, as England disputed his legitimacy – before Henry V's death, his wife Catherine gave birth to a son, and this infant, Henry VI, was next in line to both the French and English thrones.

After several fiercely fought battles, the French managed to push the English out of France, to a large extent thanks to the efforts of Joan of Arc. The Duke of Burgundy (Philip the Good), however, turned her over to the Eng-

king for control of her territory. Her saving strength was her marriage to the Habsburg Maximilian I, an alliance set up by her father. Mary died young, but Maximilian entered into the Treaty of Arras, which granted him sovereignty over the Netherlands as well as Belgium. After many years of fighting between France and Burgundy (now a part of the Habsburg Empire), Maximilian was victorious and was granted control over the entire territory. His daughter, Margaret of Austria, ruled the Burgundian Empire from 1506.

As guardian of Maximilian's grandson, the future Charles V, she prepared him for his royal

lish who famously burned her at the stake in Rouen in 1431.

Belgian Hainaut was added to Burgundian territory in 1433, and a treaty was signed in Arras in 1434 between France and Burgundy, which had by then dissolved its alliance with England. Philip the Good and Charles VII now made peace with one another.

Philip the Good died in 1467. His successor was Charles the Bold, the last "great duke", who was killed in a battle just outside the city gates of Nancy in 1477. Shortly before his death he had added Liège to his duchy.

Mary of Burgundy, the daughter and heir of Charles the Bold, was forced to fight the French

duties. Through the Habsburg line, Charles became the Spanish king in 1516 and German emperor in 1530. But his right to Flanders was still disputed.

When the Habsburg Empire was divided between the Spanish line and the Austrian line in 1556, Philip II, the son of Charles V, was granted sovereignty over the region of Belgium, as well as other territories. Brutal suppression of the Reformation in Belgium continued under Philip II's rule, but the fierce resistance which the Belgians had exercised throughout the centuries of Burgundian rule could not be broken.   ❏

ABOVE: Emperor Charles V on horseback.

Emperor Charles V

When he wasn't standing astride the creaking deck of a sailing ship, Charles V, Holy Roman Emperor and King of Spain would most likely be found in the saddle of a fast horse. His territories were vast, his responsibilities huge and his travels wide. Despite a sickly constitution, the last emperor of the Middle Ages made nine journeys to Germany, seven to Italy, six to Spain, four to France, two to England and two to Africa.

Flanders and Brabant were the nearest thing to home that Charles ever knew. He was born on 20th February 1500 in Ghent, the son of Philip the Handsome, King of Castile, and Joanna the Mad. His father died in 1506, and his mother – called "mad" but in fact a chronic melancholic – was confined for the rest of her life, while her father, Ferdinand the Catholic, took control of Castile.

Charles's childhood was spent in Mechelen under the guardianship of his aunt Archduchess Margaret of Austria. On the death of his maternal grandfather, Ferdinand the Catholic, Charles was ceremonially declared of age in Brussels, being nominated Duke of Brabant and King of Spain (as Charles I) in 1516.

He returned again and again to his native land, and at heart he remained a Netherlander all his life. He shared with his compatriots a love of good food, riotous feasting and fine art. As an old man he referred to the Netherlands in a letter to his son Philip as "Our Father Burgundy".

And yet he never had the chance to settle there. His life of travelling began when he was only 17, shortly after the death of his grandfather. He sailed to Spain in order to take up the reins of government there. Charles had been in Spain for but two years when his paternal grandfather, Maximilian I, died, leaving open the title of Holy Roman Emperor. And so, in the summer of 1520, before he had a chance to win over the proud southerners to his cause, Charles had to return to northern Europe to receive the Holy Roman Emperor's crown. At the age of 20, Charles had become the most powerful monarch in Europe. It wasn't until 1522 that Charles could return to Spain, in an effort to strengthen his hold on a kingdom that had been torn apart by rebellion.

During his lengthy reign, Charles had little chance to settle down. The Spanish and Habsburg empire he had inherited extended across Europe from Spain and the Netherlands to Austria and the Kingdom of Naples, stretching across the Atlantic Ocean to Spanish America. Time and again he was forced to take up arms – to put down his archrival, François I of France or to quash the infidels (Turks and Protestants) within and without his realm.

In the final analysis, he failed on both these counts. By the end of his life he had managed to prevent neither the schism within the Christian church nor the fragmentation of his empire. Charles's fortunes waxed and waned as Henry VIII of England and the popes in Rome transferred their allegiance between his cause and that of François I.

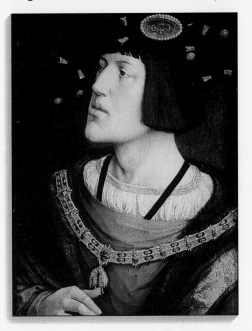

In 1553, old, sick and disillusioned after a lifetime of almost continuous war, he returned to the Netherlands. It was here that he made his last public appearance in October 1555. In a moving speech before the assembled estates of the 17 provinces in the Great Hall of his castle in Brussels, Charles V renounced the throne of the Netherlands in favour of his son Philip.

At the beginning of 1556 he also relinquished the Spanish crown; and shortly after that he abdicated as Holy Roman Emperor in favour of his brother Ferdinand, though this was not recognized until his death. Divested of power, he left the Netherlands for ever, retiring to a Spanish monastery in Estremadura; he died there in 1558. ❑

RIGHT: a portrait of Emperor Charles V.

SQUABBLING OVER A SMALL COUNTRY

During the 17th and 18th centuries, Belgium became a battlefield as empires wrestled for control of its trade routes and industries

The reign of Philip II in the latter half of the 16th century witnessed the separation of the Netherlands as oppositions were polarised between Catholics and Protestants. The Protestant provinces in the north were united by the Union of Utrecht in 1579, and soon declared their independence from the Spanish Netherlands (an area that approximately corresponds to modern Belgium).

The 17th century saw Spain further loosen its grip on the region, as control was wrested from its empire by the United Provinces (formed by the Union of Utrecht), allied with France to the south of the Spanish domain. As the century ended, with the death of Charles II (last of the Spanish Habsburgs), the position of the Spanish Netherlands looked perilous.

Charles had designated as his successor Philip V of Anjou, a Frenchman and grandson of the reigning king of France. Such an heir would have brought together the empires of France and Spain under one ruler, creating a mighty power base. Emperor Leopold I of Austria (a monarch of the Austrian Habsburg line) protested vehemently against such a concentration of strength, and to stake his own claim on the succession sent the Austrian army into battle with France in 1701. The war that ensued, known as the Spanish War of Succession, continued until 1714 and embraced forces from across western Europe.

Austrian realm of power

The peace treaties signed at the end of the war granted sovereignty over the Spanish Netherlands to Austria, it thus becoming the Austrian Netherlands. But, before the dust could settle, a new battle of succession was already brewing.

Emperor Charles VI, who occupied the Austrian throne from 1711 to 1740, also had no male heirs. He did, however, have a daughter, Maria

LEFT: stained glass in the town hall of Bruges.
RIGHT: niche statue at the church of St Carolus Borromeus in Antwerp.

Theresa, and in order to prevent another war, Charles issued a "pragmatic sanction" allowing the crown to pass to Maria. To ensure future peace, Charles appealed to other powers within Europe to sanction his plan, but following his death in 1740, the European powers wasted little time in forgetting their agreement. Maria Theresa wrote of her succession: "I found myself without money, without credit, without an army, without experience and knowledge ..." To defend her inherited lands and right to the throne, she was forced into a war which lasted eight years. In the end, she was victorious and Belgium remained under Austrian rule.

Boom time

Under Maria Theresa, Belgium experienced enormous economic prosperity. Trade and industry were subsidised, and roads were built, linking important cities such as Brussels and

Vienna. But while the Austrian government, Belgian industrialists and city merchants were turning huge profits, the common folk of Belgium fared badly. Low wages, unemployment and social destitution were the lot of a large portion of the population, conditions that would eventually bring about revolts.

But while the sun shone upon the rulers and the wealthy class, their interests developed in the direction of fine arts and crafts. Tournai was a manufacturing centre for porcelain and faïence, and the gold and blue decoration of Belgian porcelain was soon recognised in the finest drawing-rooms of Europe. The fashion

mother having been a devout Roman Catholic), as well as his relatively liberal innovations in education and health were considered despotic by a distrustful public.

In Belgium, Joseph established a strong central bureaucracy in the hope of eliminating regional patriotism. He attempted to bring the Church under the control of the state except in purely spiritual matters – a measure which paved the way for secularised education and civil marriages – and his decree of 1784 made German the official language throughout the empire. Such widespread reforms were seen as unnecessary, and met with an increasing tide

for lace also reached its peak during this period also, and the industry entered one of its most productive periods. Brussels lace *(see page 140)* was worn by anyone in a position of power and wealth. Architecture flourished as well, and Brussels became known for its magnificent buildings and splendid squares.

The distrusted revolutionary

Maria Theresa died in the year 1780 and her son, Joseph II, who had been co-regent since 1765, became her successor. As a student of radical French philosophy, Joseph wished to revolutionise his empire. Curiously, his introduction of freedom of religion (despite his

of resistance within the countries under his rule.

In Belgium, resistance to Joseph II was divided into two very different camps. The followers of the *ancien régime*, who believed in the absolutist form of government, formed the mute opposition. Their leader was the lawyer Henri van der Noot, a radical opponent of enlightenment. The other camp, led by the lawyer Jean Vonck, was opposed to reforms imposed by a single monarch. They demanded a liberal and modern state, and embraced the ideas then emanating from pre-revolutionary France.

Starting in 1788, insurrections broke out in Belgium and a national volunteer army was formed. Van der Noot's conservatives eventually became the dominant revolutionary force, and on 11 January 1790, one month before the death of Joseph II, the "United States of Belgium" was proclaimed.

Every province retained sovereignty over its own territory, but the *Congrès Souverain* (Supreme Congress) exercised control over the areas of foreign affairs, defence and currency. Van der Noot was elected by the *Congrès Souverain* as prime minister, and Prussia, England and Holland finally recognised Belgium as an independent country.

Paradise postponed

This new state of affairs was not to last, however. The new Austrian emperor, Leopold II, sent troops into Belgium to pull the country back into the empire. The fledgling country was quickly defeated and after just one short year of freedom Belgium once again found itself under Austrian rule.

In 1792 the Austrian and Prussian war against revolutionary France broke out and Belgium was drawn into the battle. On 6th November 1792, the French, with the aid of a Belgian legion, defeated the Austrian army near Jemappes. It seemed that Belgium was at last free of the Habsburg Empire.

But, by June 1794 France had taken up occupation of both Belgium and the Netherlands. The two countries were combined and renamed the Batavian Republic. They remained under French dominion for the next 20 years. The French administration proved to be reformist and succeeded in dismantling, piece by piece, the old absolutist system.

The first order of business was to divide the new republic into nine departments, according to the French pattern of government. The possessions of the Church were transferred to the state, and these two main forces of government were officially separated. Inherited titles were abolished, as was the outmoded guild system. A reformed judiciary was pledged to ensure equality for all, as the "Code Napoléon" became the backbone of a new legal system. In this newly created republic, duties levied on peasants became a thing of the past, as did the unjust system of taxation.

LEFT: Belgium prospered through weaving.
RIGHT: Rubens Chapel at the church of St Carolus Borromeus, Antwerp.

Industrial state

The fact that the economy was subsidised by the government helped Belgium develop into the most progressive industrialised state on the Continent. The amount of coal mined increased steadily, and the metal and textile industries flourished, as France became the largest consumer of Belgian goods.

But French domination had its drawbacks. From 1797 Belgians were conscripted to serve in the campaigns of Napoleon. Opposition soon developed into a series of rebellions, from which many liberals and supporters of France sought to distance themselves.

The so-called Holy Alliance, formed by Austria, England, Prussia and Russia, defeated Napoleon once and for all near the Belgian village of Waterloo in 1815 *(see page 159)*. The Batavian Republic was dissolved, but a large number of Belgians were soon to regret the departure of the French, in view of what was decided at the peace conference held in Vienna.

The Congress of Vienna established a new order in Europe. The unification of Belgium and the Netherlands would be perpetuated, but now ruled over by the Dutch House of Orange. The patience of the Belgians was at an end, and 15 years later, the revolution of 1830 was to result in a free and independent Belgium at last. ❑

THE KINGDOM OF BELGIUM

In the early 19th century, independence became the great goal of the Belgian people. Once they obtained it, they established a constitutional monarchy

In Belgium's fight for independence, France became its role model. The ideals of the 1789 Revolution were revived by the French with the July Revolution of 1830. For Belgians this was the signal to rise up against the Dutch House of Orange, and in August 1830 the War of Independence began in Brussels, actively supported by the French government.

By 4 October Belgium had officially declared itself to be an independent country. The provisional government demanded recognition of the new state by other European governments, and on 26 January 1831 the great powers of Europe confirmed their independence and guaranteed its neutrality at the London Conference.

This acceptance of the new nation's autonomy marked the first step along the road towards true independence.

As the next step, the newly created parliamentary monarchy needed a suitable king. In their search for an appropriate sovereign, the political leaders of the country agreed upon Leopold of Saxe-Coburg. By virtue of his blood ties with the English monarchy (he was the uncle of Queen Victoria), his education, his skill in diplomacy and his interest in military matters, Leopold united all the qualities considered to be desirable prerequisites of a representative royal sovereign.

Leopolds I and II

In 1831, the National Congress voted Leopold of Saxe-Coburg King of Belgium, and 21 July was proclaimed a day of national rejoicing. In 1832, Leopold I married Louise, a daughter of King Louis Philippe of France – an act which did much to strengthen the friendly links between the two countries.

Under Leopold I, relations between Belgium and the Netherlands improved considerably and foundations were laid for industrial expansion. Despite such success in international diplomacy, an undercurrent of domestic restlessness at the

LEFT: the city of Ghent as it was at the beginning of the 19th century.
RIGHT: King Leopold II in formal military dress.

continuation of appalling living conditions persisted. From 1840, workers began to rebel, and Leopold found himself unable to live up to the task of mediator and unifier of the Flemish and Walloons. Against a backdrop of language disputes, initially regarded as a secondary problem, violence repeatedly broke out, as Flemish natio-

nalists in the north became increasingly vociferous in their call for independence from the south. On his death in 1865, Leopold bequeathed a range of social problems to his successor, Leopold II.

With scant regard to these problems, the new king soon set about realising his long-cherished dream of colonial power. Through a policy of murder, deception and colonialism, Leopold gained control of the entire Congo basin – a region half the size of western Europe.

Belgium's economic upswing profited greatly from exploitation of the new colony. But in England and within Belgium itself, opposition to the king's private colony was growing. In 1908

Leopold found himself obliged to subordinate his sovereignty over the Congo to the Belgian parliament. This proved to be his last major gesture as monarch, and in 1909 he died.

German invasion

In the first year of World War I, Belgium was defeated by Germany. But at the Treaty of Versailles in 1918, Belgium was able to regain its territory, as well as additional German speaking regions in Eupen-Malmédy.

Albert I, who was the Belgian king during this period, remained so until 1934, when his son rekindled the Leopold name as Leopold III.

1950, however, he abdicated and handed over the throne to his son, Baudouin, then aged 20.

The end of colonialism

The new king was crowned on 17 July 1951. One of Baudouin's most pressing official duties was to supervise the decolonisation of the Belgian Congo. Before that task was achieved, however, there was the more private matter of the king's engagement in 1960 to Doña Fabiola de Mora y Aragon, re-awakening the links between Spain and Belgium.

Whilst the engagement celebrations were taking place in Brussels, in the Congo Belgian

In the face of the increasing threat from Germany, the king was able to have Belgium reinstated as a neutral country in 1936.

Only a few months after the beginning of World War II, German troops invaded Belgium, and Leopold III capitulated in the name of his country on 10 May 1940. The government fled to London, but the king remained at home, interned in Laeken Castle until 1944. As the Allied army advanced, he was moved to Germany, where he remained until his liberation.

When Leopold returned it was not possible to quash all rumours of his collaboration with the Germans, but a referendum as to whether he should continue to reign voted in his favour. In

troops were firing on a population which – despite international protests – had been thrust into independence without any preparation.

The marriage of Baudouin and Fabiola in December 1960 proved childless, so when the king died suddenly in 1993, his brother succeeded him to become Albert II of Belgium, with his Italian-born wife, Paola, as queen. It seems almost certain that Baudouin's eldest nephew Prince Philippe will be next to ascend the throne. Philippe is being prepared for his role in the traditional manner of European monarchs, mixing study with military duty. ❑

ABOVE: Grand-Place, Brussels, photographed in 1908.

The Belgian Congo

For many years Belgium kept out of the race to acquire colonies. In fact, Leopold I, the first King of Belgium, refused to be involved in an official state colonial policy. But after his death in 1865, his son, Leopold II, made up for lost time.

The groundwork was laid by Sir Henry Morton Stanley (1841–1904), the British explorer and journalist. He led an expedition to Central Africa in 1874, having already travelled extensively in America, the Far East and other parts of Africa.

Stanley's first expedition to the River Congo concluded that its wide channel made the river an ideal trading route. In 1878, Leopold II commissioned Stanley to undertake a second trip to the Congo. Following instructions issued by the Belgian monarch, Stanley came to 'agreements' with several of the native tribes.

The basis of these 'agreements' was that the Africans would receive fabric and similar items in return for granting the Europeans property rights to their land. The wording in the contracts was such that the terms could be interpreted as a purchase. In this underhand way, Leopold gained possession of almost the entire area by 1884, renaming it the Congo Free State.

The 19th-century colonial powers soon began to demand a formal agreement on the position of the Congo. A conference, held in Berlin in 1884–85, recognised Belgian authority over the region – with the proviso that henceforth in perpetuity there should be freedom of trade within the country.

At the instigation of Leopold II, the Berlin Conference also passed a resolution repudiating the slave trade. In reality, things were very different. Within Africa, slavery was at its peak. Local inhabitants were unscrupulously sold as cheap labour and porters, or press-ganged as soldiers. Whippings and murder were daily occurrences. Between 1889 and 1890 the "Anti-Slavery Conference" was held in Brussels; once more, lip service was paid to the "noble aims of colonialism".

From 1890 Socialists and Liberals protested with increasing frequency against the king's colonial policy, while the Congolese themselves took up the fight for their own freedom. Between 1895 and 1897 a series of riots was brutally quashed. In 1908 criticism concerning the king's authoritarian

system of exploitation forced the Belgian government to transfer the monarch's power over the Congo to the state. The region became an annexed colony, renamed the Belgian Congo.

Between 1912 and 1918, the determined resistance of the oppressed Congolese led to further unrest. Following the arrest of ringleader Simon Kimbanga, leader of the African National Church and a Congo resident, there was a general strike. The ruling powers replied with machine-gun fire and the internment of freedom fighters.

The outbreak of World War II overshadowed the problem of independence, but after 1945, unrest flared up anew, and the citizens of the Congo de-

manded their independence with increasing vehemence. King Baudouin and the majority of Belgians were disinclined to relinquish the colony, whose minerals, rubber, palm oil and ivory contributed to the national prosperity. But the revolt which erupted after the First African Peoples' Conference in 1958 finally led to the Belgian government's precipitate agreement to independence on 30 June 1960.

Conflict subsequently broke out in the newly independent state, primarily caused by the attempted breakaway of the rich mining province of Katanga (now Shaba). Power struggles continued through the 1960s until elections, held in 1970 awarded the presidency to Colonel Mobutu. The following year the region was renamed the Republic of Zaire. ❏

RIGHT: British explorer and journalist Sir Henry Morton Stanley (1841–1904).

LIFE DURING WARTIME

Belgium's attempted position of neutrality at the outbreak of both world wars

served the country badly, as Germany wilfully ignored its proclamations

On 3 August 1914, the Germans demanded that the Belgian government allow their army passage through Belgian territory; a demand made on the pretext that France was concocting plans to invade Belgium. When the government denied the request, the Germans marched across the border, regardless, instigating their invasion of Belgium. Great Britain, France and Russia all made calls for an immediate retreat of the German forces, but in the meantime the war had already begun. The Belgian army put up a spirited and intense resistance to the invasion, but by the end of 1914 almost the entire country was in German hands.

The fiercest battles were fought in Tirlemont, Liège, Antwerp and Brussels; and these massacres are still remembered in the towns today. Attention then turned to Flanders, close to the French border. The area around Ypres witnessed some of the worst fighting of the entire war, battles often being fought in drenching rain or freezing snow. The trench warfare persisted from 1914 to 1918, with little ground gained by either the Germans or the allies, but with huge loss of life on both sides. Poison gas was used for the first time in Ypres, first chlorine and then in 1917 mustard gas.

One of Germany's biggest defeats came at Langemark, a village near Ypres. The village was considered to be impregnable by the Germans, but on 22–23 October 1914 the army's supreme commanders – quartered securely away from the battlefields – ordered several regiments to attack the village. The regiments, composed mainly of teenage volunteers, stormed blindly onto the "Field of Honour", only to suffer huge losses. A cemetery at Langemark contains the graves of 45,000 soldiers of different nationalities. It serves as a memorial to the victims of this battle – just one of thousands that took place in Flanders.

LEFT: a woodcut by Frans Masereel, part of his *From Black to White* series.

RIGHT: a V1 rocket falls towards Antwerp after the liberation of Belgium by Allied forces in 1944.

Resistance

Even after the Germans were securely entrenched in Belgium, the fighting continued, as the civilian population countered the occupation with a variety of attacks designed to weaken the German position. These included destroying train tracks, telephone lines and telegraph cables in

order to hinder the supply of reinforcements and the transmission of military reports. The German reaction to such tactics was to seize and kill random hostages, or to break the population's resistance by sending Belgian women, teenagers and elderly men to work as forced labourers in Germany.

As the war drew to a close, the fiercest battles were fought in the Ardennes and also on French soil, most notably at the Somme. By the time a ceasefire was declared on 11 November 1918, millions lay dead and years of fighting had turned the Flemish soil into a massive graveyard. Mines, weapons and skeletons are still uncovered in the area to this day.

Between the wars

King Albert I acquired a glorious reputation during World War I. He had become regent in 1909, and personally led the Belgian army in their resistance against the foreign invaders, as well as vociferously encouraging all the country's citizens to do likewise.

After the war, the Treaty of Versailles granted Belgium sovereignty over the German-speaking region of Eupen-Malmédy. The Belgian government abandoned its position of neutrality and moved politically closer to France. In the 1925 Treaty of Locarno, Germany, France and Belgium agreed to recognise their existing borders,

World War II

German troops invaded Poland on 1 September 1939, signalling the start of World War II. After the Third Reich's victory over Poland, Norway and Denmark, it attacked France, the Netherlands, Luxembourg and Belgium on 10 May 1940. The Belgian government fled to London to operate in exile, while King Leopold remained a prisoner in his own country.

The number of collaborators in Belgium is reckoned to have been considerable, and even the king himself was unable to dispel suspicions that he had collaborated with the occupying forces during the conflict. Most collaborators

while Great Britain and Italy served as guarantors of the treaty. Belgium returned to its policy of neutrality in 1936, a move designed to guarantee the country's security and prevent involvement in further war.

Society was also very different after the war. Belgium introduced universal male suffrage (women were not given the vote until 1948) and the right to strike. The economy, badly damaged by the war, was slow to recover. During the Great Depression, unemployment rose rapidly and, as in other countries across the Continent, fascist groups profited from the general unrest.

came from the ranks of the fascist-monarchist movement, a movement which still exists today.

The monarchists, under the leadership of Degrelle, supported the activities of the Nazi occupying forces from 1940 onwards. Later, the infamous SS even boasted two Belgian units, which were composed mainly of Flemish and French-speaking monarchists. These units were sent into action on the eastern front in 1945, where they were almost totally annihilated.

Belgium and northern France were under a common military administration during the war.

BELGIAN SURRENDER

The alacrity of the king's surrender in World War II incensed many Belgians; the move also left allied forces in a perilous state.

Eupen-Malmédy was "reabsorbed" into the German Empire and Flanders was granted special status. Many residents of Flanders belonged to the Flemish movement and enthusiastically supported the German annexation of their land.

Germany thus considered Flanders an "area capable of being resettled". This meant that, after the elimination or deportation of all opposition elements and Jews, Flanders could be recognised a German region.

Many Belgian Jews, in addition to the many German and Austrian Jews who had fled to Belgium in order to escape persecution in their

Liberation

The allied forces landed on the beaches of Normandy on 6 June 1944, and on 25 August Paris was free again. The liberation of Belgium began at the beginning of September, and its success was swift. By 3 September Brussels, Ghent, Bruges and Antwerp had been reached by Allied forces, and one week later Liège was also regained. A final counter-offensive in the Ardennes, known as the Battle of the Bulge, was put down in January 1945. When Germany surrendered on 8 May, Belgium was in ruins; the task of rebuilding the cities and the nation now lay ahead. ❑

own countries, were murdered after the invasion of the Nazis. But some – calculations suggest about half – were hidden by the non-Jewish population.

Many Belgians showed great courage in their commitment to aid the persecuted and become active in the Resistance. People of all ages destroyed transport and communication lines in order to hinder the occupying forces. Socialists, communists, liberals and Christians fought side by side as Belgians and anti-fascists.

LEFT: members of the Resistance, the "Secret Army".
ABOVE: many Jewish girls were hidden by Catholic schools, and so survived the Holocaust.

BELGIUM'S JEWISH POPULATION

From June 1942, Belgian Jews were required to wear the yellow star of David to mark them out from the rest of the population. When called upon to volunteer for the labour camps in the early summer of 1942, many actually did so, tragically believing this was their safest course of action – in this way, thousands unwittingly boarded trains only to perish in the Nazi death camps. Approximately 2,700 Jewish children from Belgium survived, however. Their escape was thanks to the relentless efforts of a unique underground network that hid the children under false names in convents, boarding schools and private families.

POSTWAR BELGIUM

Modern Belgium has been characterised by linguistic and territorial disputes
interwoven into the process of rebuilding the nation

Compared to neighbouring countries, Belgium's economic recovery after the war was quite rapid. The harbour of Antwerp had been spared major damage during the conflict, and the country's energy reserves were adequate to supply all the necessary power.

Reorganisation on the political level, on the other hand, was very slow in coming. In an insecure spirit of conservatism, the country returned to the structures and institutions in place before the war. Parties that had collaborated with the Germans were banned, but other political party changes were slight.

Party politics

The Christian Socialist party, founded in 1945, distanced itself from its forerunner, the Catholic party; it termed itself secular and unitarian, and based itself on individual support as opposed to church affiliation. As was to be seen throughout the political spectrum in Belgium, separate Flemish and Walloon wings were established within the party. In the first elections to be held after the war, in 1946, the Christian Socialists were victorious.

The Socialist party also broadened its political base, turning away from its practice of recruiting members collectively through the trade unions and cooperatives, and began instead to enlist support on a direct basis among individual voters. The Liberal party and the Communist party based their appeal on their existing platforms and programmes. The Communists temporarily replaced the Liberals as the third strongest faction in parliament, but by 1949 the three traditional parties were once again in the forefront of Belgian politics.

The purge of Nazi collaborators, which took place immediately after the war, belong to a depressing chapter in the history of Belgium. Some 53,000 Belgians were judged to have collaborated with the enemy.

LEFT: Brussels' symbol of renewal, the Atomium.
RIGHT: the lights from Belgium's motorways are so bright that they are visible from the moon.

A king in waiting

In May 1945, King Leopold III returned to Belgium from his exile in Germany and the crisis between the king and his ministers turned into an open conflict. The Christian Socialists supported the return of the king, the Socialists and Communists demanded that he abdicate, while

the Liberals were in favour of abolishing the monarchy altogether. The Christian Socialists resigned from the government in protest, but this of course left only opponents of the monarch and of monarchy still represented.

To complicate matters, the Communists then resigned from the coalition, leaving the government unable to function. The Christian Socialists then returned, to form a coalition with the Socialists. Together, they implemented a series of economic reforms, establishing a central economic council, as well as councils for professions and management. Women received the right to vote, and were able to exercise this right for the first time in 1949.

The Christian Socialists gained an absolute majority in this election, and in the following year, 1950, a referendum was held to determine what constitutional rights the monarch should be granted. Throughout Belgium 58 percent of the voters were in favour of allowing the king to return to the throne. But the results demonstrated a regional polarisation. In Flanders, 72 percent of the population favoured the king's return; in Brussels it was only 48 percent, and in Wallonia it was just 42 percent.

In June 1950, new parliamentary elections were held. The Christian Socialists gained the absolute majority again. Parliament voted to

reinstate the king, and, on 22 July 1950, Leopold III returned to Laeken Palace. This resulted in a mighty wave of protest in the Walloon industrial areas. The king announced that he would be willing to abdicate in favour of his son within one year and, on 17 July 1951, Baudouin I was duly crowned.

Regional discontent

It was during this time that the education reform debates between the Catholics and secularists (Socialists, Liberals and Communists) were raised. The Catholics demanded a more autonomous form of education while the anticlerics supported a standard public education.

The same fronts that had formed during the referendum on Leopold III reappeared. On the one side were the Catholics and on the other side the Socialists, Liberals and Communists. It soon became clear that a schism between north and south was a likely possibility and that the only thing which had prevented this from happening so far was the existence of the large national-based parties that could contain regional differences within a broad base of allegiance.

Since the war, there had been differences in the way the Flemish north and Wallonian south had developed and the first regionalist demands were heard. For the time being, however, the federalists and supporters of cultural autonomy were in a minority. The politics of economic and social solidarity practised by successive governments were enough to keep the north and south from drifting too far apart. But by the early 1950s the principal consensus had worn thin, and on 3 December 1953 both the Walloon and the Flemish federalists called for a reform of the centralised state.

Even though the Socialist party was actually in opposition, the three unity parties signed a "schooling pact" on 20 November 1958. This agreement introduced new regulations for the educational system from kindergarten all the way up through high school. It was more democratic, the federal budget included more funds for education, new schools were built and the free religiously affiliated educational institutions were subsidised. A commission was set up to oversee the implementation of the agreement.

While it would be wrong to place the full blame for the ensuing linguistic disputes on this agreement, it is true to say that it stirred up differences within the parties. All parties were now divided on the language question.

The pendulum swings

It was during the 1950s that new economic structures were established, which initially were to favour the Walloons. But by the end of the decade the reverse was increasingly the case. The Walloon mines began to close, related heavy industry suffered setbacks, regional development organisations were established and American industry began to get a stronger foothold on the Continent. Whilst in Flanders these developments were greeted enthusiastically, as the port of Antwerp boomed, in

Wallonia they mapped the beginnings of a cycle of decline.

During this period, the regal presence of King Baudouin was vital to a sustained sense of nationhood. Supported by his queen, Fabiola de Mora y Aragon, the king and his prime ministers, from the Socialist Van Acker to the more recent Christian Socialist Martens, were able to defuse the worst of the country's linguistic problems – formally defining a language border in 1962 – and limit the damage incurred by the disorganised retreat from the Congo (1960), Rwanda (1962) and Burundi (1962). Such international debacles galvanised opposing parties in a common spirit to overcome these crises. And the neutrality of the king gave him in an important unifying role within the country.

Even so, as the new decade began, linguistic disputes and regional economic questions came to the forefront of Belgian domestic politics. The social climate was marked by strikes during the early 1960s. Demonstrations were held to protest against the so-called "law of uniformity" regulating economic development, social progress and the reorganisation of state finances. The strikers demanded federalism and structural reforms. Tensions developed not only between the language groups and different religions, but also within the parties and trade unions. One result was an increase in pluralism. Parties and pressure groups sprouted up throughout the country, their main concern to ensure that they retained their position and their voice in a future regionalised Belgium.

The Golden '60s

However, such political antagonism was taking place against a backdrop of general economic prosperity. The "golden '60s", as they became referred to, in fact lasted for 15 years, until the economic crisis of 1974. Consumer spending and construction boomed. Household appliances, televisions and cars headed the list of consumer goods; department stores and supermarkets proliferated. Belgium was paved with super highways. But the prosperity of some highlighted the poverty of others. Some 900,000 people, a tenth of the entire population, were living on the edge of poverty.

Gradually, reforms began to take place. Both the Flemish population and the Walloons wanted some degree of autonomy, be it cultural, linguistic or territorial. The Walloons sought to pull themselves out of the economic slump through new and more efficient industry, a new division of the territory and the right to administer their own natural resources.

A fractured world

The constitutional revisions of the 1970s and 1980s, and the accompanying legislation, were all designed to preserve the language, culture, lifestyle and spiritual beliefs of the different groups within the country. Since 1970, three

communities and three regions have existed within Belgium: the Flemish-, the French- and the German-speaking communities; the Flemish, the Walloon and the Brussels regions.

In 1980 measures were taken to expand the authority of the regions, which were granted their own rights and institutions. In order to regulate the balance of power between the central organs of the state, the different communities and the regions, a committee of accordance and a disputes court was established. Today Belgium has a complex system of municipalities, provinces and regions as well as a centralised state.

The latest reforms provided for a redistribu-

LEFT: the high-rise face of modern Brussels.
RIGHT: King Baudouin and Queen Fabiola.

tion of authority and finances among the various administrative levels. Currently the state is responsible for about 60 percent of the national budget; local and regional governments must divide the remaining 40 percent between them.

The development of the Brussels region is the latest outcome of the constitutional reform. There are many facilities around Brussels which serve both the Flemish and Walloon communities. The institutional reform has succeeded in bringing a temporary halt to the historic development towards the fragmentation of an entirely federal state.

Many Belgians feel that this policy, known as

education, transport and the environment have all been passed to the regions.

There is growing pressure from Flanders to devolve social security; the Flemish feel they are bearing the brunt by financing the large welfare payments being dished out to the growing numbers of sick, aged and unemployed in Wallonia. Friction between the language groups is exacerbated by an influx of foreigners, particularly the well-heeled Eurocrats who are forcing up house prices.

The rivalry between the language groups is best illustrated by the row which forced the election in November 1991 (the 10th election in

the *compromis à la belge*, attempting to devolve power to every conceivable minority, has got out of hand.

The influence of the European Union over different sectors of communal life is increasing, especially in regional relations. In Belgium, the zones of development recommended by the EU have been imposed on the autonomous Flemish-Walloon regions. European resolutions concerning production capacities for the steel industry have led to added friction.

The central state has authority in national defence, foreign affairs, social issues, agriculture, justice and financial and monetary issues. Policy-making in areas such as the economy,

12 years). When the Flemish refused to grant export licences to two Wallonian arms manufacturers poised to sign a contract with Saudi Arabia on the grounds that Belgium should not be supplying arms to the Middle East, the Walloons retaliated by refusing to sign contracts to provide telephone exchanges to the Middle East, as the lion's share of the contracts were to be handled by Flemish companies.

In 1993, the monarchy changed hands when King Baudouin died. He was succeeded by his brother, Albert II. ❑

ABOVE: comfortable country living; a symbol of the nation's bourgeois aspirations.

Belgium Today

Despite its boring image, contemporary Belgium is a surprisingly volatile country, subject to conspiracy theories, political upheavals and social instability. In 1991, André Cools, the deputy Prime Minister and king-pin of the Socialist Party in Liège, was murdered amidst allegations of financial corruption. Several years later, Willy Claes, the Secretary-General of Nato, was tainted by corruption and forced to resign. In 1998, a series of bank raids saw the death of several security guards; a nationwide security strike led to the freezing of all cashpoints. In response, the government was forced to organize airlifts to transport stocks of money from supermarkets and banks. The strike did little to restore Belgians' battered faith in their institutions.

Nowhere in the European Union do citizens have such little faith in a functioning democracy or in those who govern them. The country has a reputation for clan-like political and judicial systems, with corruption prevalent at the highest levels. The criminal investigation system is open to abuse and rather passive, based as it is on witness statements rather than on systematic investigation and the gathering of hard evidence.

In the 1980s, it was the Brabant supermarket killers, a dangerous attempt to destabilize the government by shadowy right-wing groups. In the 1990s, the pillars of Belgian society were shaken by a paedophile scandal which provoked the largest public protests ever seen in Belgium. A wave of hysteria engulfed the government, with charges of involvement extending right up to the level of the deputy Prime Minister.

The White March

The paedophile case involved the disappearance and rape of six girls and the murder of four. The public viewed it as a conspiracy and cover-up involving the upper echelons of the police, judiciary and government. The 1996 "White March" brought 300,000 people onto the streets of Brussels in protest at police incompetence and a malfunctioning justice system. In Liège, outraged firemen hosed down the Palais de Justice (law courts) to "clean up the legal system". There were reverberations in 1998, in the wake of the farcical escape and recapture of Marc Dutroux, a notorious pae-

RIGHT: cultural disputes take to the streets.

dophile, convicted child rapist and chief suspect in the multiple murder case. The scandal led to further protests, the resignation of ministers and much public breast-beating. The press referred to "the shameful mirror of a nation's soul" but political reform was by no means certain.

United by mutual suspicion

Although Belgium has always been a divided country, it manages to remain unified against the odds. Hitherto, the constitution and the royal family have acted as unifying forces, bolstered by the pivotal role of Brussels as the capital of Europe. Nonetheless, the fragile consensus could yet founder

amidst tensions between the ruling factions. The Flemish community blames the "artificial political construction" of the country for saddling them with an incompetent or corrupt French-speaking police force. In its defence, the (French-speaking) Walloon community accuses the Flemish of using isolated cases of corruption as a pretext for asserting their economic might for political ends. It is not inconceivable that the country will yet divide in much the same way as the Czech and Slovak split.

For now, the linguistic line holds as Belgium prepares for European monetary union. Nonetheless, a Member of Parliament called the situation "surreal and scandalous". Not for nothing is the new Belgian 500-franc note a tribute to René Magritte. ❑

CAROLO ALEXANDRO
LOTH. ET BAAR DUCI, BELGARUM GUBERNATORI, ETC. ETC.
ÆDIBUS EFFICIES TUA QUANTUM AD SIDERA TENDIT
CAROLE TANTUM IMIS CORDIBUS URIT AMOR.
UT QUEM NULLA DIES MEMORI POST EXIMAT ÆVO.
HÆC POSUIT FIDEI PIGNORA CARA SUÆ.
CORPUS BRAXAT. BRUXELL.

1698

BRASSEURS

CAPITAL OF EUROPE

"How many people work in the European Commission?"

"About a third of them." (Belgian joke)

By a convenient quirk of history, Brussels became the capital of Europe. As such, the city is charged with enshrining the European dream (as well as ensuring the protection of the Iberian lynx, French camembert, Belgian chocolate and the great British crisp). The Brussels bureaucrats are the archetypal European bogeymen, residents of a city famous for its faceless image. Behind the mask is a surreal world, more Magritte than Kafka, in which doubting Eurocrats and diplomats are inevitably beguiled. Bland bureaucracy is transformed into an expatriate playground of garden suburbs and gourmet lifestyles.

Brussels remains an anomaly, a French-speaking island in a Flemish-speaking region. Unsurprisingly, a third of the city's population is foreign, mainly European. Apart from being the capital of the European Union, Brussels is the headquarters of Nato and home to over 50 inter-governmental agencies, as well as countless trade associations and many international companies. The Brussels region is prosperous, and in terms of GDP per head, is the third wealthiest in the European Union.

Eurocrats and fat cats

As a capital transformed by institutional wealth, Brussels is a city of corporate lawyers and thrusting lobbyists, Europhiles and Eurosceptics, international agencies and multinationals. The Commission's role as European chief competition watchdog means that lawyers and lobbyists come to study or manipulate the Brussels political machine.

For business and bureaucracy, the lure of this city is great. With such a prestigious international role, numerous foreign companies have chosen to base their European operations here, from IBM and ICI to Bayer and Mitsubishi – Brussels has more office space per head than

any other European capital. Sweeteners such as tax breaks and prime property locations ensure that Brussels finds favour with the multinationals. In particular, the capital prides itself on offering a multilingual, cosmopolitan, highly-skilled labour force and excellent living conditions for foreign inhabitants.

Visually, the European district is something of a disappointment: quartier Leopold, the most fashionable quarter in the 1850s, has disappeared under a dispiriting urban wasteland. As journalist Neil Buckley says, "Visitors to Brussels often expect to see an elegant European Union quarter, Europe's equivalent of Washington DC. They find instead a soulless administrative district where drab office blocks have replaced the 19th-century town houses, dotted with cranes and building sites and criss-crossed by six-lane highways."

The Council of Ministers (metro Schuman) is a sprawling, low-slung building which opened in 1995. Nicknamed the Kremlin, this peach-

---

PREVIOUS PAGES: Triumphal Arch at Cinquantenaire Park, Brussels; the capital's Grand-Place.
LEFT: a view over Brussels' Lower City.
RIGHT: the new European Parliament building.

coloured fortress is already too small, designed for 12 EU members rather than 15. Facing it is Berlaymont, the former, and future, seat of the European Commission, the executive body. Nearby is the European Parliament, Espace Leopold (metro Maalbeek), a glittering blue-green affair resembling a covered city. The lavish public buildings are a sign of European excess or waste, depending on one's point of view. Only Eurocrats are allowed access to the Residence Palace, a fabulous Art Deco apartment block that was saved from destruction expressly for the privilege of plunging into the Pompeiian swimming pool.

much as their counterparts in the Belgian ministries. As well as avoiding punitive Belgian taxes, they can claim an expatriation bonus, child benefit and school subsidies.

Political farce

After the star-shaped 1960s eyesore Berlaymont was found to be contaminated by asbestos in 1991, the Commission's 3000 staff were evacuated to sites all over the city. During the move, over £140 million (US$230 million) of property mysteriously vanished, from cars to computers and carpets. The Eurocrats were outraged at the implication that their flats were fur-

The Commission is a curious constitutional hybrid, part executive body, part policy innovator and proposer of laws. As the European Union's civil service, it is a powerful employer, with 15,000 permanent staff, including a vast number of translators and interpreters. The Commission is only reluctantly practising what it preaches: publicly, it advocates flexible labour forces while privately protecting its own civil servants. These *fonctionnaires* enjoy generous perks and jobs for life. However, the concept of performance-related pay was raised in 1998, much to the horror of the personnel unions and to the delight of the Belgian public. EU civil servants are paid three times as

nished with purloined public property. As a French official retorted, "Have you seen the colour of the textiles? And everything is numbered, even the bland Euro-carpets." After ridding itself of asbestos, Berlaymont is due to re-open by the year 2000. In the meantime, it has become a bizarre landmark in its own right, wrapped in white plastic like a Cristo art work. Ironically, the Commission itself has been slow to implement legislation protecting all European workers from exposure to asbestos.

The new European Parliament is the latest symbol of European unity, set in Espace Leopold, the heart of the Euro-district. It is dubbed Caprice des Dieux, the folly of the gods, after the French cheese whose shape it echoes. The Parliament is paralleled by an equally grandiose European assembly to be unveiled in Strasbourg in 1999. The existence of two follies aims to assuage Gallic pride, and to prevent the French city from being sidelined by Brussels. Given the duplication of parliaments, on average, MEPs spend only two days a week in Brussels. However, as a talking shop and temple to self-aggrandisement, the Parliament has few equals.

Upon completion, this glass and steel behemoth became the biggest building project in Europe. Opened by King Albert II in 1998, the building cost $1.66 billion, and has vast annual running costs. The 626-member body will oversee the new European Central Bank.

At the inauguration of Parliament, French MEPs protested that the Spanish president could not address the King of the Belgians in English. English was originally chosen in order not to inflame the linguistic sensitivities of French and Flemish speakers. However, in a typical Belgian compromise to soothe ruffled feathers, the President gave the speech in four languages – and confirmed that the inauguration plaque on the Parliament wall was in Latin, the only uncontentious lingua franca.

Rampant bureaucracy

Eurosceptics wishing to find fault with Brussels need look no further than this folly: during sessions, there are often more multilingual interpreters than delegates needing translation. Likewise, the hemicycle, the huge debating chamber, holds 1,000 delegates but is used for only two weeks a year. The press delights in reporting stories of rampant bureaucracy within these walls. A recent revelation featured the fitting irony that the capital of bureaucracy lacks its own office supplies: it was only when all fax machines in the Commission ran out of paper that civil servants admitted that supplies were kept in Strasbourg.

For model members of the modern Eurostate, there is little need to visit the outside world. Apart from restaurants and sports facilities, there are 15 conference chambers and countless briefing rooms, offices with bed-

rooms and bathrooms, as well as meditation rooms and a printing plant. Although the main corridors are as wide as motorways, a Dutch MEP has been forbidden from riding his bicycle through the building. More seriously, the Parliament overruled the city by creating a vast underground car park which causes daily gridlock and the asphyxiation of local residents.

After two months, the giant glass monolith required repairs: Belgian birds, attracted to the luxuriant palm trees growing in the atrium, failed to notice the glass ceiling as they hurtled into the corridors of power. This is an apposite image for the Belgian attitude to the European

institutions: an exotic honey-pot from which most native residents feel excluded. Belgian citizens often sense that "the capital of Europe" has little to do with their lives. There are great disparities in wealth between the corps of diplomats and Eurocrats and the average Bruxellois.

For the privileged Eurocrats, the comfort and convenience of life in Brussels transforms Europhobes into Europhiles. In time, both prim British civil servants at the Commission and critical Canadian translators at Nato are accused of "going native" by their compatriots at home. "Going native" in Brussels tends to embrace pro-European views and gourmet cuisine in equal measure.   ❏

LEFT: flags flying high at the new European Parliament building.
RIGHT: a waiter at La Brouette in Brussels.

A BABEL OF TONGUES

The significance of Belgium's two principal languages, Flemish and French, reveals a history of class and economic divisions that have fluctuated through the ages

As a basic rule of thumb, the Flemish-speaking region of Belgium lies in the north of the country and the French-speaking region, Wallonia, lies to the south. In Brussels both languages are spoken, and at Belgium's very eastern extremity German predominates. Provided you always bear in mind that place names are written on road signs in the local language first (Liège/Luik or Brugge/Bruges for instance), you are likely to encounter few insurmountable problems when travelling around the country.

The French dialect spoken by the Walloons of Belgium is a frequent source of amusement to the French. A native of France can seldom suppress a smile when conversing with a French speaker from across the border. The Walloon language has a hard, provincial ring, and it is well known that the French refer to their linguistic partners somewhat disparagingly as *moules-frites* (mussels and chips is of course the national dish of Belgium).

The Flemish-speaking Belgians, in their turn, experience a similar reaction from their Dutch neighbours. Flemish never developed as an independent written language. Instead, it uses Dutch, enriched by Belgian characteristics. This is used in a spoken form by the media, the Church and in schools, although both teachers and pupils revert to a richer, dialectal language after hours.

Early settlers

The quarrel between the two main linguistic groups of Belgium has old and deep roots, stretching back to the earliest inhabitants of the region. The Germanic tribes tended to gravitate towards the north of the country, while settlers from the Romance countries bordering the Moselle and the Mediterranean made their homes primarily in the more remote regions of the Ardennes.

LEFT: happy to be Walloons.
ABOVE: Flemish nationalists take their cultural symbol, the Lion of Flanders, onto the streets.

Foreign rule

It wasn't until the 14th and 15th centuries, when Belgium became part of the Burgundian Empire, that French, as the language of court, gained supremacy. But even then, the simultaneous flourishing of the cloth trade enabled the Flemish provinces of Flanders and Brabant

to win high economic status, and allowed their language to prosper.

During the 16th century, under the Spanish Habsburgs' rule, the Flemish-speaking region was itself divided by an added conflict: religion. The predominantly urban north, who were devoutly Calvinist in the wake of the Reformation, contrasted starkly with the more rural and overwhelmingly Catholic south, and the two factions were unable to unite against their Spanish oppressors.

However, when fighting against the post-revolutionary French troops who began to conquer Belgium in 1794, it was the Flemish-speaking peasants of Flanders who provided the most impassioned resistance. The Flemish language and culture provided a focus and motivating force.

When Belgium was annexed as part of the newly-created Kingdom of the Netherlands in 1815, Dutch was declared the official written language throughout the entire province. However, even the Flemish found the prospect of having their language forced upon them as being boorish. They also regarded their new masters as religious heretics. Consequently the Catholic Flemish and French-speaking liberals united in a revolt against the rulers of the United Netherlands.

language used in public administration, and continued to be regarded as the language of the refined classes. Flemish was considered the language of the man in the street.

The Lion of Flanders

This was the situation when *The Lion of Flanders*, a novel by Hendrik Conscience, was published in 1838. The book fired the imagination of the Flemish, who then began to demand the right not to be forced to use French in their dealings with official bodies. The struggle took many years, but by 1898 both languages were given equal status.

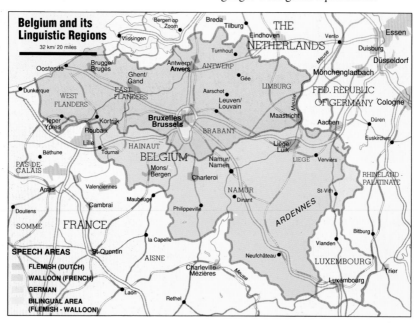

Unequal opportunities

In October 1830 a temporary government proclaimed the newly formed state of Belgium, but controlling the linguistic power struggle in the country proved a delicate balancing act.

The Belgian Constitution of 1831, created in the prevailing spirit of liberalism, called for a strict principle of neutrality regarding the linguistic education of the nation's children. But this clause tended to work to the disadvantage of the Flemish. Their children were mostly instructed in the less well-equipped confessional schools while the more prosperous private schools introduced French as the teaching language. French also became the

A chasm across the land

The language dispute became more acute during the 20th century, a conflict exacerbated by German occupation during the two world wars. While most Belgians remained anti-German, one Flemish group, the "Activists", campaigned for an independent state as a German protectorate, and during World War I collaborated with the forces of occupation.

In 1917, two separate linguistic regions were determined within Belgium. Each one had its own ministries, located in Brussels and Namur. Only a mass demonstration in Brussels in February 1918 prevented total separation. After World War I, everything Flemish was anathema and was despised as being anti-Belgian. In its external policies, Belgium at this stage moved closer to France.

Fighting in class

During the 1920s the language dispute was most heated in the universities. In Ghent, for example, claims for a separate Flemish institute of higher education had been realised during World War I, but were then shelved after the war had ended. Such action frustrated Flemish speakers and led to frequent student unrest.

World War II completely destroyed the status quo once more. However, this time, unlike during World War I, there were collaborators not only within the Flemish communities, but also amongst Walloon monarchists. Under the leadership of Leon Degrelle, the monarchists dreamed of Belgium's belonging to a fascist corporate state. When the war was over, each language group ostracised the other in attempts to find a more appealing concept than peaceful coexistence.

During the 1930s, the nationalist spectrum became polarised. The law's insistence on the use of the local language as the official language in courts and classrooms made Belgium a state with two linguistically homogeneous regions. But a strongly centralist principle continued to dominate in Brussels, where most leading officials were either Walloons or non Flemish-speaking citizens. The French language was entrenched within the machinery of government, making Walloon claims of "cultural superiority" compelling.

ABOVE: the Flemish text is masked out on a car advertisement in a Wallonian town.

Fighting in the streets

During the 1960s, Flemish citizens were forthright in asserting their claims and they were not afraid to use violence: their repeated interruption of French church services and funerals resulted in a series of television reports that shocked the world.

Since July 1966 the governing principle has been one of strict monolinguality in predetermined regions, divided by the "Language Frontier"; Brussels is a bilingual exception. A small number of linguistic enclaves, such as the regions of Eupen-Malmédy, enjoy special status. Since the 1960s, German has been Belgium's third official language. ❑

FESTIVALS AND CELEBRATIONS

Belgian joie de vivre may be a well-kept secret outside the country, but inside it the revelry is often dramatic

Celebrations are almost a daily occurrence of Belgian life, and it is practically impossible to travel through the country without coming across festivities of some kind. The government recognises only 10 official annual public holidays, but these occasions represent only a fraction of the country's countless carnivals and festivals.

A favourite saying maintains that it only takes three Belgians to make a party; in fact, the entire nation loves to celebrate at the drop of a hat. The Belgians' nonchalant approach to life can easily stand comparison with the famous *savoir-vivre* of the neighbouring French. In Belgium you will find a unique combination of popular French, Dutch, and German attitudes and philosophies.

The Belgians are a spontaneous people and are apt to rejoice over almost anything – from a sporting success to a sunny day. Visitors to the provinces may find that simply ordering a beer or coffee leads to their inclusion in a full-scale party. As evening approaches the inns and cafés become busier and busier, and it is not unusual for the local accordion player to strike up a tune. Before long, a gathering will have become a party, complete with singing and dancing. And yet, this may all occur without the formality and fuss of invitation and prior arrangement.

The nation's favourite tipple

In spite of being neighbours of the French, Belgians are not great advocates of wine. Their favourite drink is undoubtedly beer, and almost every type has a specific glass. There are many beer festivals in Belgium, mostly held in the autumn, but the one in Diksmuide is popular enough to rival the Oktoberfest in Munich.

The Belgians' favourite chaser is *jenever* (a fragrant gin). But be warned: it may cause a thundering hangover when drunk in quantity.

LEFT: the Belgians love a chance to dress up.
RIGHT: a springtime festival in Dendermonde, between Antwerp and Ghent.

Festival time

As a rule, the Walloon provinces tend to celebrate carnival with rather less gusto than the Flemish regions, paying more attention to the religious aspects of events. Dancing, however, forms an important part of carnival almost everywhere. In some towns a carnival ball is

held virtually every day during lengthy festivities, and many Belgians wouldn't miss a single one. Usually they are accompanied by traditional Belgian folk music. Strongly influenced by French and Dutch traditions, this is based on wind and percussion instruments, augmented by the accordion.

The annual round of carnival celebrations kicks off in the town of Ronse in East Flanders on 6 January. Its pre-Lenten carnival, known as *bommelfeesten*, is marked by an endless round of celebrations. One of the most spectacular carnivals takes place in Binche, where festivities start a good four weeks before Mardi Gras proper. The revelry reaches a climax on

Shrove Tuesday with the antics of the so-called *Gilles*. Some 1,500 people, colourfully dressed in special costumes, stage a 24-hour display of dancing on the market square, showering the spectators with oranges as they perform.

Malmédy is another town that celebrates carnival with vigour. The local enthusiasm is such that the fun continues well into Lent, when the religiously inclined have started fasting.

Summer celebrations

As summer approaches, the calendar rapidly fills up. The first important celebrations after Easter are the May parades. On 30 May, festivals are held in Hasselt and Genk, where the townsfolk go one step further than the usual maypole dancing by holding a grand procession led by the specially elected May Queen.

On the second Sunday in May, Ypres celebrates its Cats' Festival, in which floats and costumes sport a feline theme. The origin of this festival is, in fact, rather gruesome. It stems from the time when Ypres was an important wool-weaving town. In the winter, cats were encouraged to live in the Weavers' Hall, where the wool was stored, in order to keep the number of mice down. However, when summer arrived, the cats were deemed dispensable and

BELGIUM'S BEST FESTIVALS

Carnival is celebrated widely and wildly in Belgium. Some of the best places to catch the festivities include **Stavelot, Binche** (*see p242*) and **Malmédy** in the Ardennes; **Eupen** in the German-speaking eastern region of the country; and **Aalst** in Flanders, with its Trojan-like horse called Bayard taking pride of place in the proceedings. During the carnival period, Ostend plays host to **The Dead Rats Ball** (*Le Bal des Rats Morts*), which takes place on the first Saturday in March.

In Brussels, one of the year's best festivals is the **Ommegang Procession**. Held on the first Tuesday and Thursday in July, it celebrates the founding of the city with a parade that mixes the civic, military and religious traditions of Brussels. The capital also hosts the **Jazz Marathon**, which makes use of various locations around the city's clubs and cafés.

The **Procession of the Holy Blood** (*see page 207*) in Bruges is one of the most important religious ceremonies in Flanders. It attracts thousands of participants, dressed in costumes that are prepared months in advance, as well as a multitude of onlookers.

The entire region joins in for the **Festival of Flanders**, a series of Classical concerts and cultural events which take place in many of the region's historic towns.

thrown out of the window to meet with certain death at the hands of a gathered crowd. The last of the original, bloodthirsty Cats' Festivals was held in 1817; it was revived in 1938, when cloth cats replaced real animals.

The third weekend in May sees the Windmill Festival at Lembeke in East Flanders, and the exciting Witches' Procession in Nieuwpoort.

The Peasants' Festival during the second weekend in June at Turnhout, in the Antwerp district, is considered a great cause for merry-making, while a fine array of folkloric costumes are paraded on the third Sunday in July in Verviers, near the German border.

Dance Festival in Schoten (Antwerp district) normally held on the second Sunday in July.

There seems no historical justification for the fact that in Baardegem the harvest festival is celebrated as early as the last weekend in July, when the crops are quite clearly still ripening in the fields and a long way off being gathered in. Some think the timing indicates that the festival was originally a fertility cult rather than a festival of thanks. Of course, cynics put it down to being just another case of Belgians seeking any pretext to eat, drink, dance and sing.

The capital, Brussels, provides the site of the Ommegang festival, celebrated on the first

Beer pops up again as a cause for celebration at Oudenaarde in East Flanders. The festival takes place on 30 June, when virtually the entire population of Oudenaarde – translated, the name means "Old Earth" – celebrates the "Adriaen-Brouwer-Feest", dedicated to the many-faceted glory of the national drink. Needless to say, the local beer flows in impressive quantities during the festival – mainly down the throats of its thirsty participants.

Those whose interests are more culturally inclined shouldn't miss the International Folk

Thursday in July. This famous pageant commemorates the arrival of a miraculous statue of the Virgin Mary, and its origins can be traced back to the 14th century. The parade is a spectacular affair and one of the biggest festivals in the entire country. It attracts more than 2,000 participants, all dressed in historical costumes and bearing banners. They assemble on the Grand-Place, while actors dressed in royal attire represent the family of the Emperor Charles V.

Late summer madness

The capital's other big festival celebrates the curious erection of the *meyboom* (maypole) on 9 August (no explanations are offered as to the

LEFT: the Procession of Our Dear Lady in Mechelen.
ABOVE: friendly giants at the Meyboom festival.

reason for a maypole in August). The Giants' Parade begins on the third Sunday in August in Heusden (East Flanders), as does the Heathens Festival in Nassogne. Bruges holds a triennial Canal Festival (August 2001, 2004) and, every five years the Golden Tree Parade (catch it next in the year 2000).

August also sees a number of festivals in honour of the harvests. To confound expectations that the Belgians do not produce wine, or even appreciate it, the festivals in Beaumont and Overijse (in the Hainaut and Brabant districts, respectively) offer glimpses of many a local connoisseur sampling Belgian vintages.

Alternatively, you might like to visit the medieval fair at Franchimont Castle, which takes place at the same time. The castle is situated in the small town of Theux.

To cheer the winter months

Even when the evenings start to draw in with the onset of autumn, there is no let-up in the calendar of events. On the first Sunday in September, a magnificent flower show is held in Ghent as a farewell to the flower-filled summer months. On 3 and 4 September Antwerp celebrates its Feast of Liberation and the Festival of the Guilds. Antwerp's citizens celebrate their cultural history with great gusto.

On the second Sunday in September in nearby Mechelen, the festival of *Op Signoorke* is held. *Op Signoorke* is a giant doll that traditionally symbolised male irresponsibility. Some might say rather fittingly, it also went by the name *vuilen bras* (unfaithful drunkard) and *vuilen bruidegom* (disloyal bridegroom); every year the doll was paraded through the streets and tossed in a sheet. In 1775, however, the doll acquired a new significance when a young man from the rival city of Antwerp tried to steal it. The robber failed in his attempt and was badly beaten, but the outraged citzens of Mechelen decided to rename their doll "*Op Signoorke*", a derisive nickname for the people of Antwerp which stems from the word "signor", and is a rather obscure reference to Antwerp's favoured status under the Spanish.

We have already mentioned the autumn beer festival in Diksmuide, but another popular Oktoberfest is held in the little town of Wieze, in East Flanders. The atmosphere in the marquee, which is large enough to hold 10,000 people, is enlivened by the thigh-slapping music of Bavarian bands. Beer from the local brewery is served until the small hours.

At no other time do the Belgians devote so much attention to their national drink than in autumn. Even small towns and villages are likely to be holding a festival. Visitors are always welcome to join in. Since many Belgians are multilingual you will encounter few problems. A beer festival can be the best place to get to know the Belgians. The relaxed atmosphere of the village festivals is often more conducive to friendship than the more elaborate events staged in the towns.

Finally, before closing this calendar of festivals, mention should be made of the Feast of St Martin on 11 November. The festival is celebrated with great enthusiasm throughout the country. Children receive presents, and many Belgians still observe the tradition of the St Martin's Day bonfire. The eastern town of Eupen celebrates the day with particular panache and a candle-lit procession.

Christmas celebrations in Belgium are rather low key, very much like those in neighbouring France. But after New Year the whole calendar of revelry begins again. ❏

LEFT: drinkers are spoilt for choice.
RIGHT: floats feature highly in Belgian parades.

CYCLING AND OTHER SPORTING PASSIONS

Stereotypes of Belgium don't, usually, conjure up images of its sporting prowess.

But a national passion for cycling has produced sporting stars on wheels

Eddy Merckx, the outstanding racing cyclist of the 1960s and '70s, is one of the few Belgian sporting personalities whose name is familiar abroad. At various stages in his career, Merckx won every major international

cycling race, gaining the coveted Tour de France trophy no fewer than five times.

All in all, however, Belgium does not play a commanding role on the international sporting scene and Merckx is one of the few world-calibre athletes that the country has produced. Even so the majority of Belgians enjoy participating in one or more sporting activities and support their national teams with enthusiasm.

The capital's sports fans are particularly well catered for, with a choice of six stadiums, three horse-racing tracks and several ice rinks. There are top-ranking football teams such as R.S.C. Anderlecht, and an internationally famous athletics meeting (Ivo van Damme Memorial).

In the realm of football, Belgium has always given a good account of itself in international and club competitions within Europe. However, the nation has never won any of the major competitions, such as the World Cup or European Championship. And since 1985 the Belgian capital carries the indelible stain of the catastrophe at Heysel Stadium. This tragedy occurred when supporters of Liverpool and Juventus clashed at the European Cup Final. During the mayhem and disorganised crush of spectators, a wall collapsed costing the lives of 39 Juventus fans; as a result English clubs were banned from European tournaments for several years. The event had a profound effect on the city, though it had very little to do with the everyday reality of sport in Belgium – active or passive – for the average citizen of Brussels.

A passion for pedals

Cycling is without doubt the favourite national sport. It holds a place in the national soul comparable to that of baseball in America, football in Britain, bullfighting in Spain, or ice hockey in Russia and Canada. Cynics maintain that its popularity represents an escape from the boredom of a Belgian Sunday. Whatever the case, hardly a day goes by on which there is no cycling race somewhere or other, and they are always supported by thousands of enthusiastic spectators; a classic cycling race from Liège to Bastogne and back, for instance, will be lined by throngs of spectators all along the route.

But it isn't just the cycling that people come to see. A rally is also a social event. Friends meet, drink a beer together, become carried away by the speed at which the cyclists race past, and enjoy listening to the results on the radio later on. In addition, cycling events are invariably attended by fairs and other attractions appealing to younger family members.

Speculation as to why this enthusiasm for cycling should have grown up in Belgium usually cites the topography of the land. One ideal precondition is without doubt the flatness of the countryside. Except in the hilly eastern provinces, Belgium – like the Netherlands – makes the bicycle the most convenient and inexpensive mode of transport. Children organise impromptu races on the way to school, and farmers' wives use their ancient bone-shakers to reach the nearest village. When national heroes such as grocer's son Eddy Merckx make headline news in the international press, their success fires the enthusiasm of the aspiring youth. The popularity of the sport has little to do with the prospect of monetary gain; apart from the trophies, the prizes are not usually very significant. In a small country like Belgium, the few top sportsmen become role models to a far greater extent than elsewhere.

Although Eddy Merckx is the greatest cyclist Belgium has produced – and indeed the country's most successful sportsman – Rik van Steenbergen also deserves a mention; he won the World Road Race Championship three times between 1949 and 1957. More recently, successes in the cycling world have come mostly in the field of cyclo-cross, where Belgium has had several winners in the World Championships from Eric de Vlaeminck in the 1960s and 1970s to Roland Liboton and Danny de Bie in the 1980s.

Beyond two wheels

Sport in Belgium has a great deal to do with spectacle. The louder and more colourful the event, the better. Motor races are frequent events; many take place through the streets of towns, with all speed limits temporarily lifted (be warned: barriers to protect the spectators are seldom erected). Tens of thousands flock to the races at the Spa-Francorchamps circuit, including the Formula One Belgian Grand Prix, hoping to witness as many hazardous thrills as possible. Celebrations know no bounds when a compatriot wins, and heavy disappointment descends if a Belgian entry is eliminated early on in the race. However, competing is considered the most important thing.

In motor racing, the Belgian Jacky Ickx dom-

BAR BILLIARDS

Belgians with less active inclinations can be found in city bars, indulging in bar billiards, a popular national pastime.

inated the Le Mans 24-hour race from 1969 until 1982, during which he won the race a record breaking six times.

Beyond wheels

Apart from cycling, football and motor racing, the other sports enjoying popularity in Belgium include tennis and golf – both as fashionable here as elsewhere on the Continent. Cross-country skiing is practised in the winter around the hills of the Ardennes; and during the summer months, sailing and surfing are both very popular pastimes

on the English Channel coast between Knokke and De Panne. Rugby is played mainly in the French-speaking provinces, where it is a favourite spectator sport.

Top sportspeople have a difficult time in a small country such as Belgium, and the nation has produced few world-class athletes. However, when successes occur, they produce a spirit of national euphoria to eclipse those of more frequently victorious neighbours. In the 1986 World Cup finals in Mexico, for example, the Belgian football team reached the semifinals. Nobody slept during the quarter final victory night, as the celebrations carried on through until dawn. ❏

LEFT: Eddy Merckx, Belgium's premier sporting hero.
RIGHT: a cycling race gets underway at the Zandpoortvest in Mechelen.

A BELGIAN STEW

Internationally celebrated, the culinary prowess of Belgium ranges from
haute cuisine *to the humble national dish of* moules et frites

Wherever hunger strikes in Belgium's towns and cities, you are bound to be within sight of a friendly inn or a restaurant. And if you only require a quick snack, you are sure to find, close at hand, a chip stand (French: *frites*; Flemish: *frieten*), or a waffle stall and, if you are lucky, a vendor selling snails – a hot, satisfying snack, served wrapped in a fold of paper.

Belgium embraces two regions, each of which has its own language, customs and culinary traditions. But in addition to the culinary traits of the Dutch upon the Flemish and the French upon the Walloons, the discerning diner may also be able to detect influences from Spain and Austria, originating from the time when Belgium was part of the Spanish Netherlands and the Habsburg Empire.

Belgian cuisine is at times light and delicate, and at other times flavoursome and rich. The Walloon cuisine, in particular, tends to be more substantial, more spicy and have more calories than either Flemish or modern French cuisine. But the different provincial cuisines of Belgium are less distinct than they used to be. The country's top chefs have borrowed and combined elements from all regions of the country and the average cook has followed suit.

Specialities

Fish and crustaceans occupy a prominent place in the Flemish cuisine. Mussels are ubiquitous, especially served with chips. The herring is also popular and is cooked in a wide variety of ways; as steamed herring, herring Nieuwpoort-style (marinated herring), fresh herring *bonne femme (*herring in red wine), green herring with spring vegetables, smoked herring in onion sauce or kippers *en papillote*. Lobster, shrimps and oysters round out the Belgian seafood platter. Oysters are usually swallowed raw, but you may also like to try them cooked *au gratin*,

LEFT: waiters at La Civiére d'Or restaurant on the market square in Bruges.
RIGHT: market produce in Brussels.

where the oysters are covered with a crust of breadcrumbs, cheese and fine spices.

All Belgians are fond of a good, hearty soup. It is invariably brought to the table in a huge tureen, from which guests are invited to help themselves. The variety of soups in Belgium is endless, but just some of the local specialities

include carrot soup, cauliflower soup, red cabbage soup, endive soup, cress soup and – more a meal than a soup – a hearty green pea soup with cured pork, potatoes, plenty of vegetables and a slice or two of spicy sausage.

Many regions have their own particular soup – Flemish soup, Ardennes soup, Liège soup and Brabant soup are a few examples. Regions are also proud of their own traditional dishes. Mechelen is famous for its excellent asparagus and chicken; Liège produces fine white sausages, Antwerp has its meat loaves, the province of Luxembourg is renowned for its venison chops and its stuffed goose *à la forestière*. And good food doesn't always have to be *haute cuisine*. The district surrounding Verviers on the edge of the Ardennes, for example, is known for its fried eggs and bacon. Even the local chips, often lovingly prepared, are good enough to win the acclaim of gourmets.

Brussels, the national and provincial capital, the self-styled "Capital of Europe", is also the uncontested culinary capital of the country. Its restaurants rival the top establishments in Paris. One speciality which always features prominently on the menus of all classes of restaurants are *choesels*

GOOD ENOUGH TO EAT

Still-lifes by Flemish artists from Breughel to Snyders have celebrated the region's delight in the hearty food of Flanders.

the best places to eat *moules et frites*, but even the street stall version is excellent.

How this unusual culinary combination came about is uncertain but one unlikely tale attributes its invention to an incident during the time of the Roman invasion. According to the story, when the Belgians unexpectedly turned up in the Roman camp, the soldier in charge of what the Belgians took to be a giant chip pan (in fact, a cauldron of boiling oil to douse the enemy) collapsed like a sack of potatoes. This set the Belgian thinking

(sweetbreads), considered a great delicacy.

Three restaurants in the Brussels area have been awarded the ultimate accolade – the coveted three Michelin stars – and many other restaurants are in the *haute cuisine* bracket (*see Travel Tips section*); but, as in any other major European city, good and inexpensive establishments are plentiful. For those who are on a budget, the best place to head for is the Ilot Sacré, otherwise known as the "Stomach of Brussels".

One of Brussels' favourite specialities is *moules et frites* – mussels and chips – though you will find this dish on menus all over Belgium. *Chez Léon* in Brussels is rated as one of

about the subject of fried potatoes, but his ruminations were interrupted by another battle. During this next encounter, a Gaul named Obélix appeared on the battlefield with planking from a ship, covered with gleaming black mussels. Again this set the mind of the budding Anton Mossiman working, as he pondered on the combination of mussels and chips. And indeed, the marriage of mussels and chips proved so popular with the Belgians that they have been cooking them regularly ever since.

Other keen cooks might like to try their hand at reproducing some of Belgium's specialities at home. Recipes for some of the most popular dishes are given on the next page.

Classic Belgian dishes

In South Belgium, in the area adjoining the French border, the culinary influence of France is very evident. On the Belgian side of the border, however, everything is somewhat spicier and a little richer. Two favourite dishes are ragoût of lamb with chicory and rabbit with prunes and bacon.

To prepare the **ragoût of lamb**, heat some oil in a frying pan and gently fry onions and garlic. When cooked, add the lamb and brown. Add sufficient lamb stock to cover and braise until tender. Fifteen minutes before the meat is cooked, add some chicory and continue to braise until lamb and vegetables are tender. Season with plenty of fresh thyme, salt, pepper, a bay leaf, cloves and parsley. Thicken the sauce slightly with potato flour before serving.

To create **rabbit with prunes and bacon** soak 15 dried prunes in brandy. Cut the rabbit into 6–8 pieces, brown in oil, add some finely chopped onion and soup vegetables and cook in light beer or white wine. Season with salt, pepper, thyme, mustard and a generous pinch of sugar. Add the soaked prunes when tender. Before serving fry 150gm of lean bacon until crisp and add to the rabbit stew.

In order to prepare **anguilles au vert** (green eel) in the Belgian manner, select approximately 1 kg of young, lean eels. Skin and clean them and cut them into pieces approx. 6 cm long. Heat 2 tablespoonfuls of butter in a large frying pan and add 3 coffee cups of chopped fresh herbs, choosing a combination of some or all of the following: parsley, sage, thyme, sorrel, spinach, tarragon, dill, chervil, coriander, lemon balm and cress. Toss the herbs in the butter for a few minutes, then add one cup of dry white wine and bring to the boil. Arrange the eel on the bed of herbs, cover and braise for 10 minutes. Remove the eel and keep warm.

Purée the herbs, thicken the sauce with two egg yolks and season with pepper, salt, a few drops of Tabasco and lemon juice. Stir 3 tablespoonfuls of butter into the sauce, return the eel to the pan and warm through again, taking care not to allow the sauce to come to the boil again to prevent curdling. Allow the eel to cool in the green sauce or serve hot at once. The Flemish name for this dish is *paling in't groen*.

LEFT: seafood features heavily in Belgian dishes.
RIGHT: a seafood display around the Grand-Place.

Waterzooi is a traditional Flemish speciality which translates as "hot water". It is prepared from poultry (usually chicken) or fish (if possible turbot or eel). You will need 1 litre of fish or chicken stock. Flavour the stock with freshly prepared soup vegetables, peppercorns and slices of onion. Add either 1 kg fish, cleaned and cut into cubes approx. 4 x 4 cm, or a whole chicken (approx. 1.2 kg). Simmer until cooked. Remove the fish or poultry (take the chicken meat off the bones, removing and discarding the skin), and cut into pieces.

Pour the soup through a sieve or place in a blender, puréeing the vegetables. In the case of

fish, allow the soup to simmer for at least 30 minutes, then season to taste, and pour over the warm fish. Serve immediately. For the chicken soup, thicken with four egg yolks and 120 ml of *crème fraîche*. Add the chicken pieces and reheat, but do not allow to boil. The addition of the egg yolks will thicken the soup slightly; the stock can also be enriched and flavoured by the addition of white wine.

This is a delicious Flemish speciality; if you sample this "hot water" dish in different regions of Flanders – along the coast and inland in the Brabant region, you will discover that *waterzooi* never tastes the same twice, since each family has its own particular recipe.   ❑

A PASSION FOR CHOCOLATE

The Belgians' love affair with the cocoa bean has turned the production of chocolate into an art form and its consumption into a way of life

Belgian chocolate is widely regarded as the best in the world. Indeed, for Japanese tour groups in particular, Brussels is "chocolate city", and its cream-filled pralines alone often provide reason enough for a trip to Belgium. Chocolates are made, and eaten, on an industrial scale: the average Belgian con-

bean made its transition from South America to the shores of Spain with the return of Cortez in 1520. It rapidly spread a sweet path throughout Europe, allowing Belgians their first taste of the bean for which they would acquire a passion. Anne of Austria, the daughter of Philip of Spain, supposedly popularised cocoa in France and

sumes 8 kilos (18lbs) of best chocolate a year. The cachet of Belgian chocolate comes from its smooth, velvety quality and rich subtlety. Belgian truffles, although made of chocolate, butter, cream and sugar, rarely induce the nausea of over-indulgence associated with inferior brands. As with Belgian beer, the purveyors would have one believe in an absence of lingering after-effects, apart from weight gain.

A dark and rich history

Chocolate was once reserved for the upper echelons of Aztec society, when fruit of the cacao tree was mixed with spices, whisked into a froth and drunk ceremonially. The cacao, or cocoa,

Flanders but chocolate remained a luxury product until the 19th century. In 1815, Kaspar van Houten, an Amsterdammer, successfully discovered the secret of separating cocoa butter and solids and modern chocolate manufacturing began. The Belgian chocolate industry took off in the 1870s, spurred by the gain of the Congo in 1885, with its burgeoning and highly profitable cocoa plantations.

By 1900, Belgium was a major exporter, with manufacturing standards strictly controlled. To meet the increasing demand for high quality chocolates, the best Belgian chocolatiers managed to produce an array of fresh cream fillings on an industrial scale.

A praline paradise

Traditional Belgian chocolates, known as pralines, are filled (*fourrés*) with cream, liqueurs, nuts or ganache, an upmarket dark chocolate. Dark chocolate is made from the best cocoa beans and contains a high proportion of cocoa butter and cocoa solids (around 52 percent). The chocolate coating, *le chocolat de couverture*, should be rich rather than sweet and enhance the flavour of the filling. White chocolate, mainly made of milk and cocoa butter, is especially prized. Die-hard chocaholics like to deliberate and hand-pick their selection, which is seductively packaged in a *ballotin*.

chocolate manufacturers for daring to use the term "chocolate" for their inferior produce, made with vegetable solids.

Purveyors of distinction

Of the *grandes maisons*, Neuhaus rivals Godiva in prestige, as well as competing for possession of the most elaborate window displays. Godiva, on the Grand-Place, claims to be the most exclusive, proudly displaying its royal warrant. Mary, in Rue Royale, supplies the royal family, and is noted for its pure and intensely flavoured dark chocolate. True chocolate connoisseurs swear by the unbridled luxury of these pricey

Pralines are no simple bonbons but the product of jealously guarded secrets, with recipes passed from generation to generation. Belgium is suitably chauvinistic in its support of the local luxury. Given the quality, availability and competitive pricing of good chocolates, a box of pralines is often a more acceptable gift than a bouquet of flowers. In cafés, even a cup of coffee is usually accompanied by a *spéculoos*, a spicy biscuit, or by a chocolate of some kind. Belgians vociferously support the Swiss attacks that have been made in recent years on British

chocolates, which can cost as much as a meal. At the more commercial end of the scale, Léonidas produces the most popular quality pralines, chocolates that are widely available both in Belgium and abroad.

While these chocolates are the most in tune with public taste, other smaller, less commercial chocolatiers still do well. In Planète Chocolat in Brussels, chocaholics can watch Frank Duval, *maître-chocolatier*, model the intricacies of a Gothic church or gabled mansion out of the finest chocolate. In remembrance of Cortez' legacy, he also serves hot chocolate in his tea-rooms: unlike in Aztec times, chocolate is no longer the preserve of the nobilty. ❏

LEFT: a display of pralines in a Brussels shop window.
ABOVE: a customer deliberates.

BELGIAN BEERS AND BREWERIES

The best Belgian beers are treated as reverentially as the finest wines – justly so. From a cloudy wheat beer to a fruity brew, the variety is remarkable

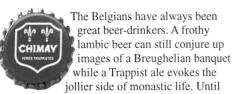

The Belgians have always been great beer-drinkers. A frothy lambic beer can still conjure up images of a Breughelian banquet while a Trappist ale evokes the jollier side of monastic life. Until 1900 each Belgian village had its own brewery, with 3,000 in Wallonia alone. Today, the number of breweries has fallen to 111, but there are still over 500 different beers to choose from, many still produced by the small breweries. Belgian beer enthusiasts can choose the likes of Mort Subite (sudden death) or Verboden Vrucht (forbidden fruit). While Ghent's Stropken (literally "noose") is a tangy brew named after a humiliating event in 1453 when Philip the Good commanded the city burghers to parade with nooses around their necks.

Belgian beers encompass light *bières blanches* or potent Trappist ales, including the renowned Chimay. The tangy flavour of a *blanche* comes from such spicy additions as orange peel and coriander. More of an acquired taste are the cherry-flavoured Kriek and sparkling raspberry-flavoured Framboise – the rosé of beers. Lambic beer has no yeast added, and ferments spontaneously. Belgium is the only place in the world where such fermentation takes place. Gueuze, a Brussels beer made by combining five or six lambics, is a cider-like concoction known as the champagne of beers by connoisseurs.

Peter Crombecq, an expert on the national tipple, explains why the Belgians never seem drunk and disorderly: "We do it gradually: we get drunk around the clock and sober up around the clock."

▽ **SMALL BEER**
Surprisingly, the Belgians are only the fifth largest consumers of beer in Europe, comprehensively beaten by the Germans, Danes, Austrians and Irish.

▽ **WHITE BEER**
Hoegaarden is a *bière blanche* or *witbier*, a milky, light, refreshing wheat beer, often served with a twist of lemon. There's a Hoegaarden brewery in Brussels.

▽ **BOTTLES UP**
There is a strict protocol about serving beer in the correct glass. The choice of glass affects the amount of froth and taste of the beer.

◁ **ABBEY ALE**
Grimbergen, along with similar abbey beers (known as *abdijbier* in Flemish), are commercially produced in the traditional style of Trappist beers.

THE BREWING OF TRAPPIST BEERS

△ BEST-SELLERS
The most popular Belgian beer, Stella Artois, was created in Leuven in 1926 as a special Christmas beer. The name comes from its exceptional stellar clarity.

△ SUDDEN DEATH
The refreshing Kriek beer is made by adding cherries or cherry juice to lambic during final fermentation.

Trappist beers are made by monks and lay brothers who follow the ancient monastic brewing traditions. Only six Cistercian abbeys in the world have the right to term their beer Trappist, and five of these are in Belgium: Orval, Rochefort, Westmalle, Chimay and Westvleteren. Chimay, the "Burgundy of Belgium", is the best-known beer, produced according to a secret monastic recipe in Hainaut and matured in the bottle. At 7% proof Chimay rouge is the least strong of the beers – even so, the monks claim to dilute it before serving it with their daily lunch.

Orval Abbey (*page 271*) is home to 25 contemplative monks who have chosen to live in silence and solitude. Theirs is a fruitier brew than the strong Sint Sixtus Abdij beers from Westvleteren, near Ypres (Ieper).

As for Rochefort, their first brewery was founded in 1595 near Namur, but the current brewery only dates from 1899. It produces a powerful, dark, chocolatey brew. Westmalle Abbey, in Antwerp province, was founded in 1791. The abbey has produced a rich, sweetish, malty beer since 1836.

△ BRUSSELS BREW
The Cantillon Brewery is the sole surviving independent lambic brewery. The beer can only be brewed between October and April.

▷ MONK'S WORK
Chimay produces three distinctive beers: *bleue* is dark and fruity; *rouge* is milder and lighter; and *blanche* is pale and strong.

FLEMISH MASTERS

*Flemish painting is noted for its naturalism and vivacity, for the intensity of its
colours and for the unsurpassed skill in displaying the rich surface of life*

As the Middle Ages gave way to modern times, Gothic art began its transition into the Renaissance. This marked the beginning of a glorious period in Flemish art. The picture on the facing page, *The Betrothal of the Arnolfini* (1434), opened a new chapter in art history. Through the details of the composition, the painter, Jan van Eyck, revealed the minutiae of the subjects' lives and times.

A prosperous burgher and his bride are exchanging marriage vows, in a room that is the epitome of Gothic bourgeois taste. And contrary to what we might imagine, the bride is not in the late stages of pregnancy; her rounded stomach and tiny, tightly-laced breasts correspond to the Gothic ideal of beauty. Her virginity is symbolised by the clear reflection of the mirror, and the presence of Christ as a witness to the betrothal is indicated by the single burning candle. The husband is a member of the bourgeoisie, a fact revealed by the wooden pattens: for while the rich furnishings indicate his wealth, such solid shoes were only worn by those who walked along the dirty streets; the nobility always rode on horseback or in a litter.

The Betrothal of the Arnolfini marked the beginning of the tradition of bourgeois art, as the role of the artist became that of an eyewitness, recording the expression and possessions of a new class of bourgeois patrons.

Jan van Eyck is the artist credited with the invention of oil painting. Although this was not strictly a discovery, the use of oil as a medium for mixing pigments and for applying glazes proved a more malleable and longer lasting medium than egg-based tempera.

Van Eyck also created the Ghent altarpiece, the polyptych of *The Adoration of the Holy Lamb* (1432), which is acclaimed as one of the wonders of Belgium (*see page 189*).

PREVIOUS PAGES: *Samson and Delilah,* circa 1628–30, by Anthony van Dyck.
LEFT: *The Betrothal of the Arnolfini,* 1434, by Jan van Eyck initiated a new chapter in art history.
RIGHT: *Portrait of a Girl,* 1480, by Hans Memling.

Burgundian artistry

Before the advent of panel painting, the only pictures were murals or illustrations in books. The Limbourg brothers were the most famous illustrators of the period, painting the Book of Hours known as the *Très Riches Heures* for the Burgundian Duke of Berry. Burgundian Flanders,

equally noted for its illuminated manuscripts and fine miniatures, provided a fertile ground for 15th-century artists. Whilst not as revolutionary as their Florentine counterparts, the van Eyck brothers (Jan and Hubert), who began as illustrators, used similarly realistic techniques, offering a mirror to reality. In the opinion of Ernst Gombrich, the celebrated art historian: "Jan van Eyck pursued the methods of the brothers Limbourg, and brought them to such a pitch of perfection that he left the ideas of medieval art behind".

Panel painting spread rapidly across Flanders. Artists were highly esteemed (and rewarded), and many became official town painters.

Flemish art

Flemish art transcended the emerging Dutch/Belgian borders of the 16th century, and it is impossible to divide such art by national characteristics. The genius of Flemish art was to move from stylised miniatures and the illusion of reality to the conquest of reality in the works of the so-called Flemish Primitives. Clarity and realism, an acute sense of light, robustly naturalistic native backgrounds, and a gift for portraiture are the hallmarks of Flemish art. The artists' patient powers of observation ensured an accurate portrayal of the texture of cloth, the warmth of flesh, and the vivid surfaces of life.

from Germany to Spain. Unfortunately relatively few of his works remain in Belgium. Hugo van der Goes (1440–82) became a master artist in Ghent and is noted for his melancholy works, expressed with humanism. Dirk Bouts (1415–75) is prized for the luminosity in his rich landscapes: these represented an integral element of his work, no mere decorative detail.

Hans Memling (circa 1433–94) was a mystical innovator in the Flemish school. His travels along the Main and Rhine rivers took him to Cologne. Completing his training under Rogier van der Weyden in Brussels, Memling settled in Bruges, where he personified the spirit of the

Whilst the Florentines excelled at perspective and foreshortening, the Flemish relied on amassing detail upon detail.

Robert Campin (1375–1441), better-known as the anonymous Master of Flémalle, was the talented town painter at Tournai under whom Rogier van der Weyden (circa 1400–1464) studied. If van Eyck was the precursor of Flemish art, van der Weyden continued in the same vein, with realism matched by religious intensity, apparent in his touching *tableaux vivants*. As the town painter of Brussels, van der Weyden exerted considerable influence on Hugo van der Goes, Dirk Bouts and Hans Memling, and on the gamut of European art,

wealthy merchant city. As the most popular Flemish painter under Charles the Bold, his work radiates lyricism and pastoral charm. Memling is generally considered the last representative of the school of Flemish Primitives. Other notable artists in Bruges included Pieter Christus (1410/20–1472/3), a pupil of Jan van Eyck, and Gérard David (1460–1523).

The first industrial painting

Gérard David's influence is much in evidence in the works of Joachim Patinier (1475/85–1524), a Belgium-born landscape specialist, respected by Albrecht Dürer and generally regarded as being the creator of the first industrial landscape painting: *River Landscape with Furnaces.*

Quentin Matsys (1466–1530) learnt the art of realistic portraiture from the works of Dirk Bouts. Matsys used religious subject matter and also painted scenes of commercial activity.

In Antwerp, painting became progressively more stylised. Joos van Cleve (Joos van der Beke, c.1485–1541) stood between the Mannerists and the late Romance artists. Jan Mabuse (Jan Gossaert, 1478–1533/36) was the founder of the new style; he journeyed to Italy with Philip of Burgundy, and became profoundly influenced by artists south of the Alps.

obscene jokes. His haunting representations of evil evoke the fearful demons which plagued medieval minds. In these macabre and grotesque paintings, it is tempting to see Bosch as a precursor of Belgian Surrealism.

Pieter Brueghel the Elder (c.1525–69), who lived in Antwerp and Brussels, began his artistic career inspired by the style of Bosch. In Brussels, he founded a family dynasty of painters who were to become popular and famous. Brueghel was an all-round artist with a philosophical bent, paradoxically the master of vivid allegories and of minutely observed realism. As the first major Flemish landscape painter,

Master of fantasy

Although based in Holland, Hieronymus Bosch (c.1450–1516), had a distinctly Flemish style. He created a world of pictorial fantasy using realistic forms. Some consider him to be the greatest master of fantasy that ever lived. Bosch's world is a mixture of paradise and hell, dominated by sensory impressions, lust and love transformed into sin. Religion and faith are linked with alchemy, arcane erudition and

he could depict a still winter landscape with as much skill as he did the dramatic fall of Icarus. These are genre paintings of a high order, human comedies with Flemish settings, inspired by the Brabant countryside. Despite his sophistication and lofty court connections, Brueghel's talent was for portraying peasant life, scenes of earthy enjoyment and merrymaking.

Pieter Brueghel, widely known as "Peasant Breughel", was the father of two artist sons. Pieter Brueghel the Younger (1564–1638), who frequently copied the works of his father early in his career, became known for his demonic scenes, partly influenced by the works of

LEFT: *Peasant Wedding* c. 1565 by Pieter Brueghel the Elder – a rustic scene.
ABOVE: the hellish vision of his son, Pieter Brueghel the Younger.

Hieronymous Bosch. Such violent images earned Brueghel the Younger the nickname "Hell Brueghel". By contrast, Pieter Brueghel's other son, Jan Brueghel the Elder (1568–1625), was known as "Velvet Brueghel" or "Flower Brueghel" because of his predilection for painting detailed pictures of flower arrangements, set against a background of richly-coloured velvet. He became court painter to the Spanish stadholder and produced a number of works in collaboration with his friend Rubens. In turn, Velvet Brueghel's own son, Jan Brueghel the Younger (1601–78), became a landscape painter in Antwerp.

greatest works. His eclectic range of subjects encompassed mythologies and landscapes as well as dazzling portraits of princes and prelates.

As a court painter, Rubens confirmed the political orthodoxies and was a servant of warring monarchs. Yet as a self-confident citizen, he was inspired by Italian art, notably the works of Caravaggio. Rubens was equally at home with hierarchy, sensuality or mystery: the trappings of success; tumbling figures; fleshy, buxom women; or saints and angels. His art is characterised by intense vitality, robust figures, rich details, bold effects and large-scale canvases. As the most skilled of artists, he had a

Peter, Paul and Rubens

Peter Paul Rubens (1577–1640) was born into a Flemish family in Germany but considered Antwerp his home city. Under Spanish rule, Rubens and an artistic elite presided over a short but sweet Flemish Renaissance in Antwerp. However, as a prolific painter, and the greatest Baroque artist in northern Europe, Rubens carried out commissions for European courts. The vitality and virtuosity of his work was at one with the extravagant Flemish Baroque churches. Fortunately, his works are well-represented in his home city, and visible in ten different locations. Rubens' fame was such that the Flemish tapestry industry prospered on making copies of Rubens'

facility for making his paintings live, with brushstrokes that suggest billowing, palpitating bodily flesh.

Like Rubens, Anthony van Dyck (1599–1641), his pupil and assistant, was a world citizen much in demand as a court painter. His talent for portraying courtly refinement and the dignity of the sitter led him to the English court of Charles I. There, his name was anglicised to Sir Anthony Vandyke and he spent the last nine years of his life. As well as painting numerous equestrian images of Charles I, he inspired the English tradition of landscape painting. Despite his gift for surfaces, whether silk or skin, van Dyck was more than a glorified society painter.

His aim was to match Rubens and the Venetian artists he greatly admired. Certainly, he succeeded in conveying sensitivity and pathos as well as virtuosity. Although best-known as a portraitist, van Dyck was also a landscape artist, an important religious painter from the Counter-Reformation period and a superb engraver, matched for quality only by the genius of Goya and Rembrandt.

Scenes from everyday life

In spite of plunderings by the Spanish, Antwerp remained a conducive artistic environment. Joost de Momper (1564–1635) was a landscape apprenticed to Frans Hals in Haarlem, bridges the gap between Flemish and Dutch art. He returned to Flanders in 1631, and was detained as a suspected spy by the Spaniards in Antwerp, where he remained for the last years of his life. The realistic pictures of David Teniers the Younger (1610–90) reveal the influence of Rubens and Brouwer. In 1651, Teniers became court painter in Brussels and in 1665 founded an Academy of Art in Antwerp.

After a long period of Flemish and Dutch artistic supremacy in Northern Europe, many years were to elapse before their art was to regain its former glory. ❏

painter while Frans Hals (1581/85–1666), a Haarlem-based artist, became a realistic portraitist of the bourgeoisie. Jacob Jordaens (1593–1678), an Antwerp-based follower of Rubens, favoured naturalistic, earthy depictions of everyday life; these were created alongside mythological and Biblical scenes. Adriaen Brouwer (1605–38) also painted scenes from everyday life. Brouwer, born in Flanders but

LEFT: *Christ in the House of the Pharisees* (1464) by Dirk Bouts.

ABOVE: detail of a self-portrait by Peter Paul Rubens, perhaps the most accomplished painter of the Northern Renaissance.

TRACKING DOWN THE TREASURES

Most of the finest Flemish works are concentrated in the major Flemish art cities of Antwerp, Bruges, Brussels and Ghent. Given the greatness of Flemish art and the changing fortunes of the country, it is hardly surprising that some of the most celebrated works are to be found in galleries throughout the world, and particularly in London, Madrid and Vienna. But Belgium has kept enough of its native treasures to satisfy the most eager art-lover. Many artists' homes have been preserved and are open to the public, including those of Brueghel (see *page 131*) and Rubens (*page 177*), and the Memling Museum is another treasure trove (*page 210*).

TWO SURREALISTS

"Of all things ending in -ism, this one was the best. There have been Surrealist paintings, poems, even bistros where Surrealists gathered" (Jacques Prévert)

The Belgian affinity with Surrealism reflects an appreciation for poetic leaps of reason and a penchant for the perverse. Surrealism confounds the distinction between sense and nonsense, conveying the beauty and bizarreness of the world. The Surrealist movement, which began in the 1920s, awakened the sub-

conscious in revolt against rationalism. The movement produced an explosion of striking and subversive images which reflected the avant-garde's wish to scandalise and unsettle. Yet shocking the bourgeoisie was secondary to the desire for a new perception of reality, one forged by poetic distortion or the dissociation of everyday images.

The movement struck a chord in Belgium, a country familiar with Hieronymus Bosch and the murky fears of the medieval mind. In Delvaux's modern visions, the outpourings of his fevered imagination produced skeletons engaged in pedestrian activities, recalling the macabre subject matter of Pieter Breughel the Younger.

René Magritte (1898–1967) was the master of Surrealism, a painter rivalled only by Dali as the pre-eminent painter of the subconscious mind. Magritte realised that the more realistic the image was, the more it supplanted reality. "Magritte was after something more real than reality," states Jacques Meuris, his biographer. Rather like Martian poetry, Magritte stressed the mystery of the everyday object, making the mundane mythical simply by shuffling the cards in the pack.

Born into a petit-bourgeois background, Magritte is seen as a quintessentially Bruxellois artist. Although a legend in his lifetime, this enigmatic artist took pains to be conventional and self-effacing to the point of eccentricity. In his anonymous suburban house, he erected an easel in the dining room and painted subversive works in a business suit. It was a convincing act, both a self-confident statement of bourgeois intent and the subversive's best uniform, a protection against charges of self-aggrandisement or flagrant bohemianism.

Magritte's philosophy was enriched by a literary circle that included the French poet Eluard, who furnished titles for his works. As a painter, Magritte was inspired by De Chirico, particularly admiring in the Italian's work the poetic juxtaposition of everyday elements and unexpected contexts. "Too often, by a twist of thought, we tend to reduce what is strange to what is familiar. I intend to restore the familiar to the strange." In adopting this approach, Magritte ensured that banal objects were imbued with mystery and surprise.

The Dominion of Light provides an initiation to his style. The seductive scene depicts a suburban villa beneath blue summer skies and beside a lake at dusk, with the house warmly glowing in the lamplight against the gathering dark. This mysterious meeting of day and night reflects Magritte's wish "to capture the imaginary in traps of reality".

Unlike many Surrealists, Magritte rejected collective myths and spontaneous dreamscapes. Instead, he placed experience of the world above pictorial experimentation or the tyranny of symbolism. In a neutral, understated style, he "homed in on reality as it was while hoping that it would be sublime" – a comment attributed to his friend Scutenaire.

Magritte also played linguistic games. The celebrated statement "This is not a pipe" (*Ceci n'est pas une pipe*) plays with reality and illusion: a picture of the object cannot be the object; it is merely a picture. By extension: "Magritte is a great painter, Magritte is not a painter." Scutenaire's comment highlights the paradox of a painter who is as much a poet. The treachery of images and names reflects linguistic concerns

and sleeping beauties are lit by gas lamps. According to critic Jacques Sojcher, "he made the world a museum protected by a female custodian, a vestal doomed to perpetual waiting".

Delvaux was born into a wealthy Walloon background and nurtured on the classics, art and architecture. He became a Surrealist in 1934 after seeing De Chirico's strange landscapes and falling for their "simplicity and grandeur". As an introduction to Delvaux's somnambulistic style, travellers can admire the mural of old-fashioned trams at the Bourse metro station in Brussels. While Bohemian beer-drinkers may prefer shrine to Surrealism,

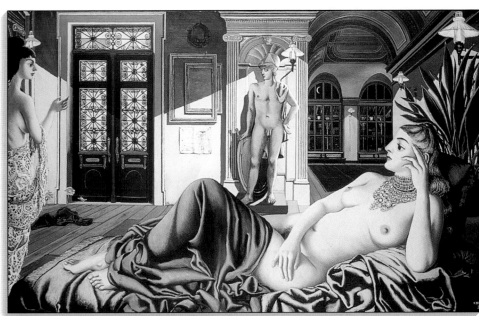

which have intrigued philosophers from Wittgenstein to Foucault. As to the arbitrary nature of names, Magritte said this: "An object is not so attached to its name that another cannot be found for it that suits it better."

Eyes wide shut

Dubbed "a dreamer with his eyes wide shut", Paul Delvaux (1897–1989) rejected the philosophical side of Surrealism in favour of "poetic shock and mystery". Bourgeois interiors meet sombre railway stations on Delvaux's canvases,

La Fleur en Papier Doré, the Brussels café was favoured by Magritte and his fellow chess players (*see page 149*). In keeping with the café's carefree spirit, poets and players devised paradoxical titles to Magritte's paintings.

To celebrate the year of Surrealism in 1998, Belgium launched a series of exhibitions and art trails. Brussels established Surrealist walks in the footsteps of the major painters, while other Surrealist haunts, such as Charleroi and Châtelet responded with their own walks and tours. Brussels tourist office also recommends a "Surrealist Weekend", which incorporates visits to galleries and artists' houses, and offers suggestions for a Surrealist shopping trip. ❑

LEFT: *The Man in the Bowler Hat* by Magritte.
ABOVE: *L'Etage de la Mélancholie* (1948) by Delvaux.

CAPITAL OF ART NOUVEAU

Brussels, along with Barcelona, Vienna, Prague and Glasgow, was a major centre of the new movement that swept Europe in the 1890s

At the turn of the 20th century, Brussels had outgrown its medieval walls and the city was experiencing an economic boom. Prosperity from the Belgian Congo meant an influx of precious materials, from marble to ivory and exotic woods. While Paris opted for sweeping boulevards and mansion blocks set around inner courtyards, the Belgians were less enthusiastic about apartment living. The bourgeoisie preferred individual homes, from small châteaux and villas in the city suburbs to *maisons de maître*, distinguished town houses. While Catholics and conservatives opted for Gothic Revival or Flemish Renaissance styles, free-thinkers chose Art Nouveau, a style that was part of a progressive social movement, with a commitment to public building as well as private commissions.

The main architects of the new style were Victor Horta, Antoine Blérot, Ernest De Lune, Paul Hankar and Henry Van de Velde. Such innovators were generously supported by enlightened patrons, who commissioned architects to create eclectic town houses as "portraits" of their owners.

In Art Nouveau, the line subordinates all other elements, imposing musical rhythms and organic shapes. Architects favoured corner plots as stage sets for experimentation with exuberant facades, bow windows, loggias and intricate balconies. Many facades feature *sgraffito* (incised mural decoration) depicting floral and figurative motifs. The use of "plebeian" materials resulted in iron and glass adorning rich mansions, alongside marble and rare woods.

▽ **TOTAL DESIGN**
Horta pioneered the concept of total design, from overall concept to the smallest detail: "For my house, I drew and created each piece of furniture, each hinge and door latch, the carpets and wall decoration", he declared.

△ **MUSICAL STORE**
Old England (1899) on Place Royale, the newly-restored Art Nouveau department store with its arabesque metalwork.

▷ **ART HOUSE**
Maison de maître, by de Lestre (92 Rue Africaine). Brussels is a city of neighbourhoods, not Parisian-style boulevards.

◁ STAIRWAY TO HEAVEN

Horta's delightful house and studio is now home to the Musée Horta (23 rue Américaine, restored in 1997). Its sinuous stairwell typifies the organic Art Nouveau style.

△ HORTA MUSEUM

In his organic designs, banisters are like tendrils, coat hooks droop like stamens, and floral motifs adorn the walls and stained glass skylights.

▽ POP ART

The Comic Strip Museum was formerly Magasins Waucquez, an elegant department store designed by Victor Horta. Much of the original detail has retained its magnificence.

▽ SLEEPING IN STYLE

Art Nouveau was a movement that aimed to affect the way we lived, by introducing a comprehensive style of elegance into every aspect of our lives.

ARCHITECTURAL LANDMARKS

Musée Horta (*see page 135*) is a capsule of Art Nouveau, designed by Belgium's greatest modern architect. Horta's Maison Tassel (6 rue PE Janson) is considered the manifesto of Art Nouveau (1893), while the Comic Strip Museum (*see page 120*) remains one of his finest works.

The Cinquantenaire and Saint-Gilles neighbourhoods are studded with Art Nouveau mansions (*see page 133*), including works by Horta. In the Brugmann district, Hotel Hannon, 1 Avenue de la Jonction (open Tue–Sun, 1–6pm) displays temporary exhibitions. The frescoed setting (1903) is enhanced by a superb spiral staircase, Tiffany stained glass and mosaics. In the Upper City, Paul Hankar's gorgeous florist's (13 rue Royale) is the only surviving Art Nouveau shop-front (1898) still in use. There's a wonderful contrast between the floral motifs of the graceful ironwork and the fresh flowers within. At number 316 in the same street is De Ultieme Hallucinatie, Hamesse's patrician mansion, and a delightful bar (*see page 127*).

THE CULTURAL SCENE

Belgium draws in the full gamut of international performers to its festivals and venues, but home-grown talent of international standing is still a rarity

Belgian cultural celebrities do not trip off the tongue: they wait to trip you up, to trick, tease and amuse. Tintin, Magritte and Jaques Brel make bizarre, wayward companions, as do Inspector Maigret, Jean-Claude van Damme and Toots Thielemans. These are not so much icons as quirky travelling companions who know their cultural limitations.

The relative isolation of such talents reflects the fragmentation of the Belgian arts scene, in turn a result of the linguistic and political splintering of the country. The rival communities are beset by cultural differences which exacerbate artistic tensions. However, in the year 2000, Brussels will take on the mantle European Capital of Culture, and there are optimistic plans to bring the different communities together under one cultural umbrella. The city plans a series of exhibitions, street carnivals and film festivals to celebrate this year in the cultural limelight.

The written word

Literary Belgium has made few waves beyond its borders. Certainly, the country has suffered from the proximity and cultural dominance of the rich French and Dutch literary traditions. Strictly speaking, Belgian literature has no individual identity of its own; in the north, the Flemish-speaking writers look towards the Netherlands while the French speakers in the south look to France. As a result, even famous Belgian writers are often mistaken for French, a misapprehension which wounds national pride. In the past, Walloon writers have tended to be slow in correcting this impression since many considered themselves to be French writers of Belgian origin.

The previous identification with French culture prompted even Flemish writers to choose French. Charles de Coster (1827–79), wrote his picaresque folk *Legend of Ulenspiegel (see page 219)* in French. Paradoxically, the satirical

work, which describes the Flemish fight for freedom from Spanish domination, helped to establish an independent French school of literature within Belgium. Until then, Walloon literature had been a pale imitation of the French tradition.

In more recent times, Marguerite Yourcenar

(1903–87) has been one of the few Belgian literary and historical novelists to make a name for herself abroad. In 1980, she achieved the distinction of being the first woman to be elected to the Académie Française. Unlike Yourcenar, who could trace her noble lineage back to 14th-century Liège, Georges Simenon (1903–89), her contemporary, came from a petit-bourgeois background in the same region (*see page 254*).

Simenon perfected the detective story, becoming one of the most popular and prolific crime writers of his day. As the creator of Inspector Maigret, he devised one of crime fiction's best-loved and enduring detectives.

LEFT: *Struggles* by Pieter Brueghel the Elder.
RIGHT: a group of musicians while away the night in a Brussels jazz café.

He, and his character Maigret, shared the same motto: "Understand without judging". Curiously, Maigret is rivalled by another fictional Belgian detective: Agatha Christie's Hercule Poirot.

In part, the country's literary low profile has been underscored by the reluctance on the part of international publishers to take risks in translating Flemish works. Nevertheless, Hugo Claus (born 1929), who was born in Bruges, has managed to become the most prominent Flemish writer. He gained international renown for *The Sorrow of Belgium*, a book that denounced the wartime collaboration between his compatriots and the Nazis.

films, where they are shown alongside international productions. Despite its lack of success, Belgium remains a country deeply committed to film as an art form. Given the citizens' linguistic fluency, foreign films are rarely dubbed, but shown with French and Flemish subtitles.

Music

Musically, Belgium has done well for a new nation. The works of César Franck (1822–90), the Liège-born composer of organ concertos, form part of the standard concert repertoire in churches and concert halls. The jazz musician Toots Thielemans (born 1922) and the poetic

Theatre and cinema

Maurice Maeterlinck (1862–1949) was one of few memorable national dramatists. Since then, the Belgian theatre has been sustained by British and American productions (in French, Flemish or English). Recently, there has been a preference for continental playwrights and a slight resurgence of native talent. Brussels, in particular, offers an eclectic range of productions in various languages. As for films, Belgium has a modest cinematic record but Chantal Ackerman, the feminist film director, and Jean-Claude van Damme, Belgium's answer to Schwarzenegger, have made their mark abroad. The Brussels Film Festival is the best forum for small home-grown

singer-songwriter Jaques Brel (1929–78) are two names to conjure with. As a jazz capital, Brussels has had a respectable tradition since the 1920s, and continues to attract the calibre of artists who play in Amsterdam and London. The most famous performer is undoubtedly the harmonica-playing Thielemans, who has worked with such jazz legends as Miles Davis, and created the theme music to *Midnight Cowboy*.

Belgium is most noted for the Flemish Renaissance painters and the Surrealist movement; both these subjects have separate chapters on pages 82–87 and 88–89. ❑

ABOVE: a performance of *Faust* at the Toone Theatre.

Cartoon Culture

It could be argued that the history of the comic strip begins in prehistoric times with the cave paintings in Lascaux and Altamira; that it progressed through the pictorial stories of Ancient Egypt and Assyria and the scenes depicted on Greek and Roman vases; that it developed further via medieval painting and through the largest comic strip of all time, the Bayeux Tapestry. But such a history may be rather fanciful for this unassuming art form that ably thrives on its own merits.

Modern comics evolved in Britain and the United States, where there have been comic cartoons allied with newspapers – the so-called Funnies – for a very long time. Japan and the USA are the super powers of the cartoon world these days, but little Belgium has proved a worthy contender. Any hit-list of world comic figures will be bound to include such stars as Tintin, Lucky Luke, Gaston and the Marsupilami, characters that have established cartoons as the Ninth Art in Belgium.

Hergé (1907–83) – whose pen-name is based on the French pronunciation of the initials of his real name (Georges Rémi) reversed – published his first story about the youthful reporter *Tintin* and his dog *Snowy* in 1930. By 1946, *Tintin*'s adventures were being published in an eponymous comic, *Journal de Tintin*. The two detectives *Blake and Mortimer* also appeared in the first edition of *Tintin*; the characters were created by Edgar-Pierre Jacobs, now a cartoonist equally famous for *The U-Ray* and *The Secret of the Great Pyramid*.

In 1947, Morris (Maurice de Bévère) invented for the comic *Spirou* a hero called *Lucky Luke*. The adventures of the lonesome cowboy were later written by René Goscinny (of *Astérix* fame) and drawn by Morris for the French magazine *Pilote*.

Other founder members of *Pilote* included Albert Uderzo (co-inventor of the most famous Gaulish warrior of all time and his henchman *Obélix*) and the Belgian Jean-Michel Charlier, who had previously worked for *Spirou* and *Journal de Tintin*. Charlier, who died in 1989, was the author of a number of famous series which were then illustrated by great artists: Victor Hubinon drew *Buck Danny* and *The Red Corsair*, Jijé (Joseph Gilain) – who had initially worked as an illustrator for *Spirou* and *Jerry Spring* – drew *Valhardi* and the tales of *Mick Tanguy*

for Charlier. While Gir (Jean Giraud) illustrated the excellent Western cartoon *Blueberry*.

Another famous Belgian story-writer was Greg (Michel Regnier), for whom Hermann (Hermann Hupen) created the character of *Andy Worgan*. Among Hermann's other series were *Comanche*, *Jugurtha* and *Jeremiah*. The emigration of many artists to France led to the establishment of a strong Belgian-French cartoon culture.

The list of Belgian illustrators is still not complete. Bob de Moor created *Barelli* and *The Lions of Flanders*; Jacques Martin was the father of *Alix*, hero of a series of adventures set in ancient Rome. Maurice Tillieux gave fans of all ages *Jeff Jordan*

and *Harry and Platte*; André Franquin created *Gaston* and *Spirou and Fantasio*, the story of a wicked super-monster, the one and only *Marsupilami*.

The number of cartoon characters is still increasing: old favourites have been joined by the *Smurfs* by Peyo (Pierre Gulliford), and *Boule & Bill* by Jean Roba. William Vance (not an American, but a Belgian whose real name is William van Cutsen) was the author of *Bruno Brazil* and *Bruce J. Hawker*. Among Belgium's newest talents are Arthur Piroton (*Jess Long*), François Walthéry (*Little Nickel* and *Natasha*), and Eric Warnauts and Guy Raives (*Congo 40*). One day they will all take their places in the cartoonists' Hall of Fame – the Belgian Comic Museum (*see page 120*). ❑

RIGHT: Tintin, caught in a state of perpetual surprise, his dog Snowy and one of the Thomson twins.

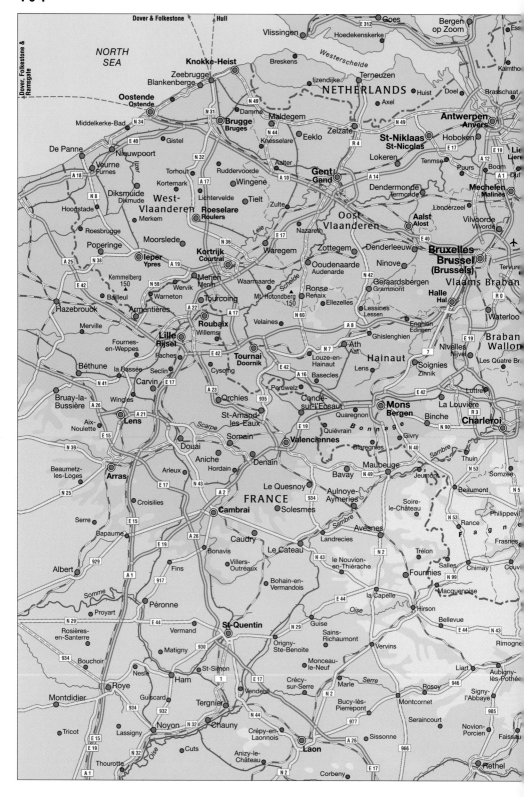

Dover, Folkestone & Ramsgate

Dover & Folkestone

Hull

NORTH SEA

NETHERLANDS

Goes
Bergen op Zoom
Ess
Vlissingen
Hoedekenskerke
Westerschelde
Kalmtho
Breskens
Terneuzen
Ijzendijke
Huist
Doel
Brasschaat
Knokke-Heist
Zeebrugge
Blankenberge
Axel
Oostende
Ostende
Damme
Maldegem
Zelzate
N 49
Antwerpen
Anvers
Lie
Lier
Middelkerke-Bad
N 34
Brugge
Bruges
N 44
Knesselare
Eeklo
St-Niklaas
St-Nicolas
Hoboken
Gistel
Aalter
Lokeren
Tenmse
Puurs
Boom
A 12
Duf
De Panne
E 40
N 31
N 32
Nieuwpoort
A 18
Veurne
Furnes
Torhout
Ruddervoorde
Wingene
A 10
Gent
Gand
Dendermonde
Termonde
Mechelen
Malines
Diksmuide
Dikmude
Kortemark
Lichtervelde
Tielt
A 14
Londerzeel
N 8
West-
Vlaanderen
A 17
Zulte
Oost
Vlaanderen
Aalst
Alost
Vilvoorde
Vilvorde
Hoogstade
Merkem
Roeselare
Roulers
Nazareth
Zottegem
Denderleeuw
E 40
Bruxelles
Brussel
(Brussels)
Tervure
Roesbrugge
Moorslede
Leie
E 17
Ooudenaarde
Audenarde
Ninove
N 42
Poperinge
A 25
N 38
Ieper
Ypres
Kortrijk
Courtrai
A 19
Waregem
Schelde
Geraardsbergen
Grammont
Halle
Hal
Vlaams Braban
R 0
Kemmelberg
150
N 58
Menen
Menin
Waarmaarde
Ronse
Renaix
Ellezelles
Enghien
Edingen
Waterloo
E 42
Bailleul
Wervik
Warneton
Tourcoing
Mt Hotondberg
150
N 60
Lessines
Lessen
Braban
Wallon
Hazebrouck
Armentières
A 22
A 17
Velaines
Ghislenghien
E 19
Merville
Roubaix
Willems
Ath
Aat
Nivelles
Nijvel
Les Quatre Br
Fournes-
en-Weppes
Lille
Rijsel
E 42
Tournai
Doornik
N 7
Louze-en-
Hainaut
Lens
7
Soignies
Zinnik
Luttre
Béthune
Faches
Seclin
Cysoing
E 42
A 16
Basecles
Hainaut
E 42
La Louvière
R 3
la Bassée
Carvin
A 17
Peruwelz
Condé-
sur-l'Escaut
Quaregnon
Mons
Bergen
Binche
Charleroi
Bruay-la-
Bussière
A 26
Wingles
A 21
A 23
Orchies
935
Quiévrain
N 90
Aix-
Noulette
Lens
E 15
St-Amand-
les-Eaux
Blaregnies
Bonnage
Givry
Thuin
N 39
Somain
E 19
Valenciennes
Maubeuge
N 40
Sambre
N 53
Somzée
N 5
Beaumetz-
les-Loges
Douai
Aniche
Denain
Bavay
N 49
Jeumont
Beaumont
N 25
Arras
Arleux
N 43
A 2
Le Quesnoy
Aulnoye-
Aymeries
934
Soire-
le-Château
Rance
N 53
Philippevil
Croisilies
E 17
FRANCE
Solesmes
Sambre
Avesnes
N 2
Frasnes
Serre
E 15
Cambrai
Caudry
Landrecies
Trélon
Chimay
Couv
Bapaume
929
A 26
Bonavis
Le Cateau
N 43
le Nouvion-
en-Thiérache
Salles
N 99
Fournies
Macquenoise
Albert
917
Fins
Villers-
Outréaux
Bohain-en-
Vermandois
E 44
la Capelle
Hirson
Liart
946
Aubigny-
lès-Pothée
Somme
Péronne
Oise
Bellevue
E 44
N 43
Rimogne
N 29
Proyart
St-Quentin
Guise
Sains-
Richaumont
Vervins
Rosières-
en-Santerre
E 44
Vermand
N 29
Signy-
l'Abbaye
934
Bouchoir
Matigny
930
Origny-
Ste-Benoite
Rosoy
Montcornet
985
Nesle
St-Simon
1
Vendeull
Crécy-
sur-Serre
Marle
Serre
N 2
Bucy-lès-
Pierrepont
Seraincourt
Roye
Ham
E 17
977
Novion-
Porcien
Faissau
Montdidier
934
Guiscard
932
Tergnier
N 44
Tricot
E 15
Lassigny
Noyon
N 32
Chauny
Crépy-en-
Laonnois
Laon
966
Rethel
E 19
N 32
Cuts
Anizy-le-
Château
N 2
Sissonne
A 26
Thourotte
A 1
Oise
Corbeny
E 17

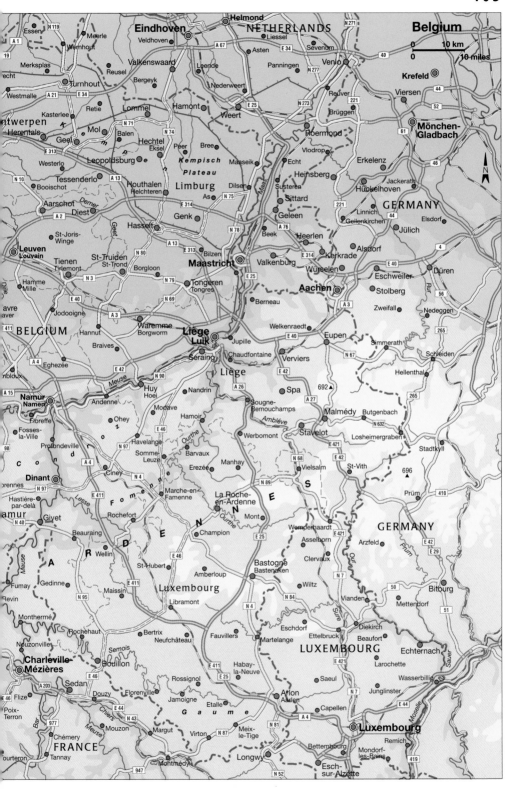

PLACES

A detailed guide to the entire country, with principal sites clearly cross-referenced by number to the maps

Whether you are looking for peace and unspoiled nature, or for art and culture, for festivals and folklore, or beaches and mountains; whether your search is for medieval splendour or modern living, with good food and drink, the 10 provinces of Belgium and their open-minded, friendly inhabitants have much to offer in all respects for a discerning visitor.

Our book begins with the capital city of Brussels, taking you first to the Grand-Place, to sharpen your appetite for the so-called "Stomach of Brussels", domain of some of the world's best chefs. Grand-Place has been described by many as the most beautiful square in the world, and from such a setting we will lead you through the distinctive lower city and the elegant upper city. And if you enjoy raking through markets on your way – whether for kitsch or art, books or flowers, bric-a-brac or exotic spices – you cannot go wrong in Brussels, for every day is market day somewhere in the city.

Those with more than a few days to spare will want to venture further afield. Within easy reach of Brussels lie Terveuren, with its Central African Museum, and Waterloo, site of the historic battle that defeated Napoleon. A trip through Flanders should begin in the medieval cities of Ghent or Bruges. In Bruges, climb the bell tower to get an overall view of this famous trading city, then explore by boat along the canals and Dijver river. Ghent, with more canals and a wealth of ancient architecture, has been compared to Venice by more than a few famous travellers. Take time to explore its nooks and crannies. And whilst in Flanders, follow us along the coast of Belgium, to Ostend, the Deauville of Belgium, and the family-oriented resorts of Knokke-Heist, and their nearby nature reserve.

Antwerp, Belgium's second biggest city, beguiles the visitor with its harbour, its art, and its glittering reputation as a diamond centre. "Antwerp has God to thank for the Scheldt, and the Scheldt to thank for everything else." Does this also apply to Peter Paul Rubens, who created his world-renowned masterpieces in this city?

In the course of a week, the visitor can get to know a great deal about Belgium, including its quieter, wilder spots; the best of its heaths, moors, dunes, forests and lakes lie in the Hautes Fagnes and the Ardennes. ❑

PRECEDING PAGES: a view from the bell tower at Tournai; 15th-century Hotel Ravenstein, Brussels; Waterside delights of Bruges.
LEFT: Groenerei canal in Bruges

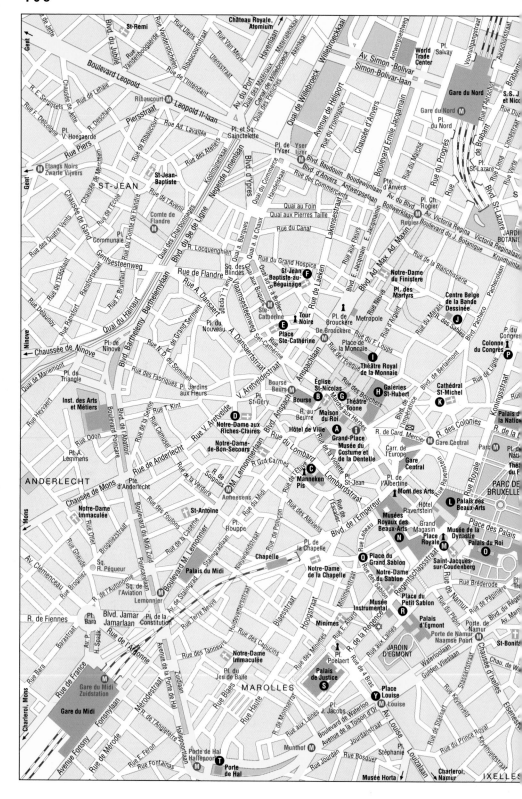

Château Royale

0   300 m

0   300 yds

Brussels

0   300 m

0   300 yds

BRUSSELS

Brussels is often said to lack an identity, but the truth is that it has too many different identities

As a city in search of itself, Brussels befuddles visitors in a host of pleasurable ways, and what it lacks in vibrancy and stunning vistas, it makes up for in conviviality, serendipity and Surrealism. In a contest between conservatism and the avant garde, played out in the museums and on the streets of Brussels, Flemish Old Masters vie with Surrealist Magrittes.

Paradoxes abound in a city that suffers a crisis of identity: provincial backwater or cosmopolitan "Capital of Europe". Brussels strives to be both, but as such is riven with conflicting interests over the protection of its wealth and historic past and investment in the city's future prosperity and burgeoning cultural mix. Bureaucratic failings and political in-fighting have given birth to bruxellisation, a synonym for the destruction of the urban fabric. This is a city that has created and destroyed great art and architecture in equal measure. Historic buildings, from pinnacled gables to Art Nouveau interiors, have been bulldozed in order to create ugly new blocks. Indeed, the "golden bulldozer" award is a teasing sobriquet for the worst excrescences of the genre. Yet behind the bruised or bureaucratic facades hides an understated city full of underrated charms. A new civic spirit coupled with better promotion of the city mean that historic quarters are finally being preserved - and visitors encouraged to look beyond the clichés of lace and chocolate.

Essentially, Brussels is a city of curious quarters and atmospheric trails rather than a city of specific sights. The city comprises a patchwork of 19 distinctive districts, known as communes. A curious feature of the city is that designer neighbourhoods are cheek-by-jowl with bohemian districts or a stone's throw from the bureaucratic business quarter or an African ghetto. In the centre alone, there is the aristocratic Sablon; the working-class Marolles; arty Ixelles; fashionable St Gilles; and the gourmet Ilot Sacré. The city also has its ethnic neighbourhoods, dominated by the African, Turkish and Mediterranean communities. Brussels is surrounded by some of the most beguiling bourgeois suburbs of any European capital city, from historic Waterloo to bohemian Uccle; or royal Laeken to leafy Watermael and Tervuren.

For visitors, the main urban distinction is between the "Upper" and "Lower" city, with the former based on the Grand-Place, and the latter on the Place-Royale and Avenue Louise. The Rue Royale marks the boundary between the two districts, with the prestigious quarter for the francophile upper classes separated from the commercial, historic heart of the city. The historic Lower City is best explored on foot and at a leisurely pace, while the Upper City can also be explored on foot, with the odd tram or metro ride between destinations (*see Travel Tips*). ❑

LEFT: an artist's impression of l'Espace Nord's development since the 1960s.

THE GRAND-PLACE: A SUMPTUOUS STAGE SET

"The grandest stage set in the world", as Jean Cocteau called it, is at the core of Brussels life, representing both civic and commercial traditions

Ideally seen for the first time at night, Grand-Place provides a sumptuous setting for the spectacle of city life. The square is lined by gabled Baroque guildhouses in Flemish Renaissance style, a tribute to the Baroque ideals of balance and harmony. The guilds of haberdashers and archers, coopers and cabinet-makers, brewers and boatmen rivalled one another by producing exuberant status symbols, adorned with gilded facades, scrolled gables and fanciful statuary.

Grand-Place began as a medieval market square, but with the completion of Brussels' Town Hall in 1444, it became the civic heart of the city. This heart was torn out by French bombardment in 1695, with Brussels a casualty of dynastic battles between France and Spain. Only the Gothic Town Hall and several guildhouses were spared, but in a wave of civic pride, the guilds swiftly banded together and rebuilt the square.

From the balcony of the Town Hall, dignitaries have been honoured and ruling dukes have looked down upon festivities; peace has been proclaimed and pardons pronounced. Now guided tours visit the sombre interior, with its 16th-century Council Chamber and array of Flemish tapestries and portraits. The neighbouring mansion, the Maison du Roi, houses the Musée de la Ville. Inside is a display of historical city maps and the bizarre wardrobe of the kitsch bronze talisman, the Mannekin Pis.

▷ **TRADITIONAL PAGEANTRY**
The Ommegang is a medieval pageant of the city guilds, held every July. The first celebration was in honour of Charles V in 1549.

▷ **CIVIC CENTRE**
Taking pride of place on the square is the Town Hall (Hotel de Ville), a Gothic masterpiece, and the finest building of its kind in Belgium. The architect, unhappy with the spire, is reputed to have leapt to his death from the roof.

△ **SWAN SONG**
Le Cygne (The Swan), the butchers' guildhouse, where Marx and Engels planned *The Communist Manifesto* in 1848. Inside is La Maison du Cygne, a celebrated city restaurant.

△ **FACE VALUE**
The gabled facades of guildhouses, including the headquarters of the medieval painters' guild, set on the northeast corner of the square. Competing guilds pushed the boundaries of ornament and decoration.

▷ **FLOWER POWER**
Grand-Place is dressed according to the season, and in the summer on even years, a beautiful floral carpet, the *Tapis des Fleurs*, covers much of the square with 1,860 square metres of begonias.

GUILDHOUSES AND GREAT CAFÉS

Many of the guildhouses on the Grand-Place combine grandeur with conviviality and a Gueuze beer. Most Bruxellois will have a favourite amongst the historic cafés that line the Grand-Place. La Chaloupe d'Or (above), meaning the Golden Galleon, was the headquarters of the tailors' guild. Set on the northern side of the square, and hemmed in by lace and chocolate shops, it is now a welcoming inn. On the west side is the imposing Roy d'Espagne (1696), once the headquarters of the bakers' guild, and now a traditional *estaminet* (inn). The facade is adorned by a bust of Charles V, flanked by Moorish and Indian prisoners. This is the most famous of the bars, with an atmospheric lower storey, and upstairs a fine view of the Grand-Place.

Beside Le Cygne, on the south side of the square, stands La Maison des Brasseurs, the Brewery Museum, and still the headquarters of the brewers' guild, recognized by the hops, ears of wheat and other harvest symbols that decorate its facade.

◁ **FLOWER MARKET**
A colourful, if small-scale, flower market is a daily event on the Grand-Place, adding a sweet fragrance to the morning air. The flowers take a break on Sundays when a bird market replaces the vibrant blooms. But both flowers and twittering birds are overshadowed by the yuletide fair held here.

▽ **ARTISTIC LICENCE**
Avoid the indifferent artists in favour of people-watching from an open-air café, or a *son-et-lumière* or concert here in the summer.

THE LOWER CITY

The Lower City occupies the network of streets that spread out from the Grand-Place. Amidst this old historic core of Brussels you will find many of the city's favourite restaurants and bars

Map on page 108–9

An elegant Upper City and an engaging Lower City: central Brussels is characterised by the contrast between the two. Both uptown and downtown districts are best explored on foot, with the Upper City a short stroll from the Lower City. The Ville Basse (Lower City) encircles the medieval heart of Brussels, entwined around the Grand-Place and the port. This marshy district represented the original settlement of Brussels, with the present stock exchange set close to the site of the first feudal castle. As the pivot of the medieval city, the picturesque Grand-Place signifies the glorification of civic spirit and the guilds. As for the port, unlike most capital cities, Brussels has buried its river underground. Although paved over, the river is still reflected in the city's gabled quaysides and quaint seafood restaurants. At heart, Brussels still feels like a backwater, with its sleepy squares, quiet gardens, underrated art museums and old-fashioned cafés.

The historic core of the city occupies the Ilot Sacré (Holy Isle) around the **Grand-Place A**, the liveliest district in downtown Brussels, especially at mealtimes. The Grand-Place (*see pages 112–113*) makes a welcoming introduction to the city, with its café terraces and melange of market-traders and tourists traipsing over the cobblestones. After a lengthy renovation, the spire has been cleaned and regilded, with the old statue of St Michael (the city's patron) replaced by a new copy.

Close to the Grand-Place is Rue du Marché-aux-Herbes, a narrow street lined by grand mansions that have survived the rigours of more than three centuries, and are now protected by a preservation order. The street was once the link between the city port and the ducal castle on the lofty Place Royale. (Today, it is where you will find the Belgian state tourist office; Brussels city tourist office is on the Grand-Place).

Within easy walking distance of the Grand-Place are several notable museums. Set on the square itself, Maison du Roi (open daily 10am–12.30, 1.30–5pm; weekends, mornings only) covers the city's history and displays the bizarre and kitsch costumes of the Mannekin Pis, the city talisman (*see page 116*). **Album**, Kartuizersstraat 25 (open Wed–Mon 1–7pm) is a new interactive museum covering Belgian history, the royal family, culture and beer. The **Musée de la Dentelle** (Mon–Fri 10am–12.30, 1.30–4pm; Sat & Sun pm only) is a lace museum, with displays of antique and contemporary lace (*see page 140*).

On the side streets adjoining the Grand-Place are a clutch of tempting cafés, confectioners and waffle shops. This distinctly edible district is the place for discovering the perfect chocolate (*see page 78*). One of the most distinctive Belgian biscuit shops is Maison Dandoy (Rue au Beurre). Apart from waffles, the shop

LEFT: Chaloupe D'or on the Grand-Place
BELOW: the cheeky little Manneken Pis.

produces gingerbread figures and *speculoos*, the crisp cinnamon-flavoured biscuits that normally accompany Belgian coffee. Across the street is the tiny **Eglise Saint-Nicolas** (church of St Nicholas, open daily 10am–noon, 2–4pm). Dedicated to the patron saint of shop-keepers, this quaint early Gothic church has a colourful history, dating back to the foundation of the city.

The gloomy interior is panelled and decorated with notable paintings. But more interesting is the sinuous shape of the facade, which follows the line of the paved-over river Senne.

The painting Virgin with Sleeping Child *in Eglise St-Nicolas is attributed to Rubens.*

A stream of consciousness

On Rue de l'Etuve, south-west of the Town Hall, stands the celebrated **Manneken Pis** , the spirit of Brussels incarnated in a bronze fountain in the shape of a naked boy. The sculptor's inspiration is unknown but subject to wild speculation. The best-known theory maintains that during the battle of Ransbeke, Gottfried of Lorraine's son was hung in his cradle from an oak tree to give the soldiers courage. At some stage in the battle, he escaped his cradle unaided and was discovered urinating against the tree. The conclusion drawn from this action is that even as a child, he demonstrated his unswerving courage.

Yet another story tells of a Brussels nobleman's son who, at the age of five, cheekily left a procession in order to relieve himself. One variant has it that a wicked witch put a spell on the child because he dared to urinate against the wall of her house. She turned him to stone, thus condemning him to urinate forever.

The statue escaped damage during the city bombardment in 1695, but it was later stolen on a number of occasions. In 1745, it was captured by the British and two years later by the French. But the Manneken Pis was always recovered.

BELOW: a fire-eater performs in the Grand-Place.

By way of compensation for the French theft, Louis XV, who was in Brussels at the time, presented the statue with a costume of precious gold brocade. The king had the culprits arrested and honoured the Manneken Pis with the title of Knight of St Louis.

In 1817, a newly released convict stole the statue, which was later recast to create the bronze replica. On 6 December 1818, the Manneken Pis was returned to its original site, where it can still be seen today. On holidays, the statue is dressed in extravagant costumes. On 6th April, he sports an American GI's uniform to recall the anniversary of the United States' involvement in World War I. On 3rd September, the Manneken Pis is dressed as a Welsh Guard to celebrate their liberation of Brussels in 1944. On 15 September, the boy becomes a British Royal Air Force pilot, in remembrance of the Battle of Britain during World War II. All in all, the statue possesses 345 uniforms and medals, which are stored in the Municipal Museum on the Grand-Place, but most of the time, the diminutive figure is splendidly free of clothes. In 1985, Belgian feminists demanded a female version, to create an equilibrium in the world of urinating statuary. In a fit of political rectitude, a new statue was duly commissioned.

From here, Rue des Grands Carmes leads to **Notre-Dame-de-Bon-Secours** (Our Lady of Succour). The church was built in 1664 in Italianate Baroque style. The neighbouring **Notre-Dame-aux-Riches-Claires** dates from the same period, with ornate gables in Flemish Renaissance style – a style which is, confusingly, merely a Belgian variant on Baroque.

Close to the Grand-Place, in Rue Henri Maus, stands **La Bourse**, the Brussels Stock Exchange (the most important in the country). The Bourse, founded in 1801, is an eclectic hybrid and proof of past Belgian prosperity. The surrounding streets have been allowed to decline in familiar Brussels fashion. However, there are several landmark cafés to revive one's sinking spirits. **Le Falstaff** (25 Rue Henri Maus) is an Art Nouveau affair (*see page 92*) which was once the haunt of intellectuals and artists, while **Le Cirio** (18 Rue de la Bourse) is a fin-de-siè-cle temple somewhat fraying at the seams.

Streetlife

The Stock Exchange borders Boulevard Anspach, one of the city's busiest commercial thoroughfares. These boulevards, designed in Parisian Haussmann style, were fashionable after the mid-19th century, a time of Belgian self-confidence. Then, the bourgeoisie congregated in the cafés and eclectic palaces designed in Flemish Renaissance style. Today, the uninspiring boulevard is lined with cinemas and specialist shops, including chocolate shops. The avenue opens onto the spacious Place de Brouckère. It was once dominated by the Anspach Monument, a 20 metre (64 ft) high fountain in memory of Jules Anspach, Mayor of Brussels (1863–79), and prime mover behind the construction of the city's broad avenues. The square's grandest landmark is the Métropole, one of the most illustrious historic hotels, which the Belgians refer to as "palaces". The interior, an eclectic mix of Belle Epoque, Art Nouveau and Art Deco, makes a sophisticated spot for a drink or a gourmet meal.

Map on page 108–9

TIP

For a stay of several days, it is worth getting a Tourist Pass from the tourist office on Rue du Marché-aux-Herbes. The pass offers discounts on museum entrance fees and allows one day's free travel.

BELOW: a city view towards the Bourse.

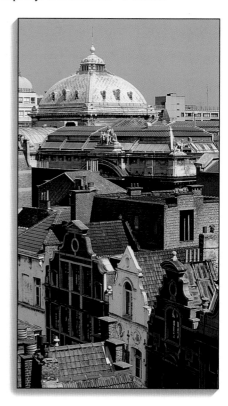

A visitor makes use of binoculars to study the carved detail of a building's facade.

BELOW: the facade of St-Jean-Baptiste-au-Béguinage.

The old port

Not far away is quaint **Place Sainte-Catherine** **ⓔ**, the former port and city fish market. From the 16th century until 1853, Brussels was connected to the sea by means of a canal, with cargoes of bricks and beer unloaded. The church square, covering the former salt and seed quays, was only laid out in 1870 after the basin was filled in. The creation of the metro in the 1970s spelt the final end to the quays. Today, this breezy, endearingly shabby quarter is home to the best seafood restaurants in Brussels (*see page 144*). The square also retains its quayside atmosphere, particularly when bustling with fishmongers and market-traders, their barrows laden with oysters, mussels, snails and pickled herring. Lobster and caricoles, slowly simmered snails, are found in numerous restaurants, including in the renowned **La Belle Maraichère** (11 Place Sainte Catherine).

Only the Baroque tower remains from the original church of Sainte-Catherine but the interior contains a painting of the saint and a Black Madonna dating from the 14th century.

Behind the church stands the **Tour Noire**, the remains of the medieval city wall. Nearby, Flemish Renaissance gables adorn the surviving quaysides of Quai aux Briques and Quai au Bois. Rue St-Catherine and Rue de Flandre display similar dilapidated facades, with the latter home to **Maison de la Bellone**, the grandest Baroque patrician residence in Brussels, now turned into a promising exhibition centre.

Within easy reach is the Rue du Cyprès, which leads to the restored **St-Jean-Baptiste-au-Béguinage** **ⓕ**. Set in a former convent, the exuberant basilica is dedicated to St John the Baptist, and radiates Belgian Rococo style, with onion domes, turrets and rich ornamentation. In accordance with Low Countries tra-

BÉGUINAGES AND BEGIJNHOFS

A *Béguinage*, or *Begijnhof*, often provides an oasis of tranquillity amidst the hurly burly of city life. These enclosed residencies for lay sisterhoods have a tradition stretching back to the 12th century. The word itself is thought to derive from one Lambert le Bègue, a Liège priest who died in 1187. He is believed to have set up the first béguinage in Liège shortly before his death, the sisterhood consisting mainly of widows of dead Crusaders. The sisterhoods enjoyed the support of each other's company and a degree of seclusion, and while the daily life was pious and rules dictated that they dress modestly, the sisters were not bound by religious vows and could, for instance, keep personal possessions and their own money.

Such communities spread throughout Europe, especially in Germany, Belgium and Holland, but during the time of the Reformation many were forcefully disbanded in Protestant countries. In Belgium today, there are about 20 Begijnhofs still surviving, mainly situated in the Flemish region. Some, such as St Amandsberg in Ghent, are still occupied by the Béguine sisterhood, who continue their tradition of charitable work. But in most towns, the small cottages in these walled communities are rented out to the elderly or, in the case of Leuven, to students.

Map
on page
108–9

dition, a béguinage was a community of lay nuns, pious women who never took the vows of chastity, poverty and obedience. (A number of such convents remain in Belgium, including a particularly fine one in Bruges.) In its heyday, the Béguine community in Brussels was home to 1,200 lay nuns, but was dissolved in the 19th century. A Neoclassical hospice now occupies the convent grounds, forming a peaceful and harmonious spot.

Battle of the Bulge

The pedestrianised area between the Grand-Place and the Stock Exchange is known as the **Ilot Sacré**, named after a campaign to preserve it in the 1950s. This "holy isle" is now an island dedicated to profane feasting (*see page 144*). The focus is **Petite Rue des Bouchers**, named after the butcher's shops which were based here in medieval times. As part of a medieval patchwork, this street of stepped gables and decorated doorways connects with the city's elegant galleries. Lined by lively restaurants, the picturesque street is naturally known as the "stomach of Brussels". Vegetarians may turn pale at the array of unskinned rabbits and glassy-eyed fish, but to meat-eaters these are tantalising displays.

A dinner here is worth sampling, if only to experience the cosmopolitan nature of Brussels, capital of Eurospeak and Eurofun. Belgians themselves are quite happy to brave the Eurotrash coach parties and seek out one of the genuine Bruxellois restaurants that remain. Even within this tiny district, there are sections dedicated to Chinese, Greek and Italian cuisines, as well as restaurants to satisfy the native Belgian palate. The main streets essentially offer home-grown fare, however, ranging from classic moules-frites (mussels and chips) at **Chez Léon** to filling Flemish dishes at **Aux Armes de Bruxelles** (*see page 145*).

BELOW: moules et frites at Léon's.

Comic Museum

Bande dessinée, the comic strip, is a cult in Belgium and much of the Continent. Known as the Ninth Art, it is celebrated in comic shops, museums, metro stations and city walls. Fans should enquire about the Comic Strip Route. The tourist office can supply a map of the latest city walls that have been enlivened by comic creations. Recent city policy has encouraged citizens to transform dilapidated gables into visual stories, decorated with comic strip characters.

In particular, the Comic Strip Museum claims to keep children absorbed for hours. However, even sceptical adults will find much to enjoy in the superb building and the skilfully created characters.

The Musée de la Bande Dessinée (20 Rue des Sables; open Tue–Sun 10am–6pm), lies east of bustling Rue Neuve and Place de Brouckère. The building is a stunning example of Art Nouveau architecture by the famous Belgian architect Victor Horta

(1861–1947) (*see page 92*). The appealing Horta Brasserie is graced by patterns of slender columns and exposed girders, and the central courtyard is flooded with light that streams through stained-glass windows.

Known as Magazins Waucquez, the warehouse and shop premises opened in 1906, run by a fabric merchant named Waucquez. Customers entered a fine portal and then mounted the sweeping staircase. Today, these same stairs serve as the launching pad for the red-and-white rocket which Tintin and Snowy used to reach "Destination Moon" long before Neil Armstrong managed the feat.

Tintin, who surpasses the Manneken Pis in fame, is ever-present, usually accompanied by his faithful terrier. Their artist-creator, Hergé (Georges Rémi), first introduced them to the newspaper-reading public in 1930. They are his most popular cartoon characters, followed by the Thomson Twins, Captain Haddock and the absent-minded Professor Calculus. Their adventures have entranced the world ever since.

Incredible though it may seem, the lovely Horta-designed building was once poised for demolition. Fortunately, Magazins Waucquez was saved an untimely death, as artists and architects rallied public opinion with the ingenious idea of turning it into a comic strip museum. The plan was to create a symbiosis between Art Nouveau and the Ninth Art, the comic strip. The experiment has been a clear success, with the museum drawing large crowds ever since it opened a decade ago. Children still enjoy the hands-on exhibits while uninitiated adults can at least focus on the architecture. It is an airy, summery construction that incorporates steel and glass into harmonious designs. Tired children can take advantage of the reading room, comfortably strewn with cushions and comics.

Anything not related to comic characters is related to Horta, and a special exhibition is devoted to his life and times.

A separate exhibition explains how animated cartoons are made, and includes drawings at every stage of development. As a believer in "art for everyone, art in everything", Victor Horta would doubtless have approved of this popular comic vision. ❑

LEFT: cartoon capers.

A narrow cul-de-sac leading off the Petite Rue des Bouchers leads to **Théatre Toone** ⓖ (tel: 511 71 37), a famous traditional puppet theatre. (Folkloric shows are held most evenings in various languages.) The theatre first came to public notice in 1830 under Toone I, who invented the "Woltje", the Little Walloon, both a variant on mocking Mr Punch and the epitome of the cheeky Brussels street urchin. Dressed in a checked jacket and with his cap at a jaunty angle, the puppet acts as the sole narrator, playing all the roles in the irreverent tales.

In 1911 a grim fate befell the puppet-master Toone III: he was discovered hanging dead between his puppets. Today, the seventh generation of Toone family puppeteers has long since lived down this grim family tale.

The puppet theatre also serves as a tiny bar and cosy inn. The standard fare is a sandwich coated in creamy white cheese washed down by a gueuze beer. An antique pianola dominates the entrance; if you put a five-franc piece into the slot, it will tinkle out some old tunes.

The plays are performed in the local Bruxellois (Brusseleer) dialect, which originally evolved in the Marolles, the historic district at the heart of the old city (*see page 131*). Although based on French, it incorporates a mixture of Flemish vocabulary and Spanish expressions adopted from the soldiers of the Duke of Alba. The dialect is used for most performances in the Toone's repertoire.

Shopping in style

From the end of the bustling Petite Rue des Bouchers, it is only a stone's throw to the **Galeries Saint-Hubert** ⓗ. In 1830, the city, embracing its new role as capital of the Kingdom of Belgium, dedicated the exclusive shopping arcades to its new royal family. King Leopold I laid the foundation stone in 1846.

Map on page 108–9

Cartoon culture – an everyday part of street life in Brussels.

BELOW: cafés and shops at the Galleries Saint-Hubert.

Sign above the entrance to the theatre of puppets.

BELOW: Théatre Royal de la Monnaie, Brussels' opera house.

The glass-roofed galleries, lined with shops, comprise the Galerie du Roi, Galerie de la Reine and Galerie des Princes. In its day, the Galeries Saint-Hubert formed the largest shopping arcade in Europe and immediately became the haunt of fashionable society. The exclusive yet old-fashioned shops remain, as well as a several appealing cafes. Just off the galleries, in Rue Montagne-aux-Herbes-Potagères, lurks the nicotine-stained **A La Mort Subite** (*see page 149*), the most authentic and old-fashioned of Brussels' beer halls.

From Galerie du Roi, it is a short stroll to Place de la Monnaie, centred on **Théatre Royal de la Monnaie ❶**, the Brussels opera house. The opera house occupies the site of the former royal mint, which minted coins for the Duchy of Brabant. In August 1830, the Monnaie was the literally the stage for the revolution that led to the country's independence. During a performance of the opera *Masianello*, the audience took their cue from a rousing call to arms within the show, and streamed out of the auditorium with a patriotic fervour to ignite the fuse of revolution. More recently, the handsome opera house was given a facelift in 1985 but is only slowly recovering from the loss of Maurice Béjart's creative ballet company, which left Brussels for Lausanne.

Rue Neuve, leading off Place de la Monnaie, is a bustling, slightly tawdry pedestrian commercial street, lined with department stores and the **City 2** shopping complex (*see page 142*). Tucked behind them is the Baroque Finistère Church. A side street off Rue Neuve leads to the imposing but soulless **Place des Martyrs**, a victim of the Brussels penchant for *façadisme* – blant destruction, concealed by the preservation of the facades. In the middle of the spacious neo-classical square stands a chilling monument dedicated to the 450 heroes of the Revolution of 1830, who died fighting the Dutch.

Nearby, in Rue des Sables, is the more cheery **Centre Belge de la Bande Dessinée** ❶ (Comic Strip Museum, open Tue–Sun, 10am–6pm), set in an Art Nouveau warehouse. The museum is both a testament to the architect Victor Horta (*see page 120*) and a tribute to the Belgian talent for such comic creations as Tintin (*see page 57*). A visit can be followed by a drink in a local comic strip bar: Bar BD (Radisson SAS hotel, Rue du-Fossé-aux-Loups).

The city's cathedral

Cathédral St-Michel ❿ (open daily, 8am–7pm) rises majestically on the hillside between the Upper and Lower City. Although hemmed in by featureless modern buildings, one exception is the futuristic steel home to the Flemish community. The monumental but over-restored Gothic cathedral stands on the site of a Carolingian baptistry, dedicated to the Archangel Michael. After the relics of St Gudula were placed here in 1047, the two saints came to be regarded as the joint patrons of the church.

Although work was begun on the present cathedral at the beginning of the 13th century, it was not completed until the end of the 15th. The building therefore exhibits a number of different architectural styles. Recent excavations have revealed the Romanesque crypt, which can now be seen.

The design and dimensions of the nave are impressive, as is its clarity of form, characterised by 12 round columns and ribbed vaulting. The pillars are formed by Baroque statues of the Twelve Apostles. A typically Belgian Baroque wooden pulpit portrays the banishment of Adam and Eve.

Situated around the high altar are three monumental tombs: two are dedicated to Duke Johann of Brabant and his wife, Margaret of York, who died in 1312 and 1322 respectively. The third commemorates Archduke Ernst of Austria, who died in 1595; as the brother of Emperor Rudolf II, he also acted as Governor-General of the Netherlands. Behind the choir lies the **Chapel of St Mary Magdalene**, built in 1282 but remodelled in Baroque style. The Italian alabaster altar originally stood in the Abbaye de la Cambre, which was destroyed during World War I by German forces.

The stained-glass within the cathedral is particularly fine, and the west window offers a remarkable depiction of *The Last Judgment* from 1528. There are various other windows around the cathedral dating from the 16th century, including a luminous portrait of Emperor Charles V and Isabella of Portugal, which is situated in the north transept. The **Chapel of Our Lady of Redemption** is somewhat later, dating from the mid-17th century. The windows in this chapel portray scenes from the life of the Virgin Mary.

The cathedral, dedicated to St Michael and St Gudula, the twin patron saints of Brussels, is the city's principal place of worship. For centuries it has been the setting for grand state occasions. In 1960 it witnessed the marriage of the late King Baudouin of Belgium to the Spanish Countess Fabiola Fernanda de Mora y Aragon. In 1962 it was officially named St Michael's when it became the seat of the Archbishop of Mechelen. From the cathedral, it is a short, but café-less, stroll to the gracious boulevards of the Upper City. ❑

Map on page 108–9

BELOW: the interior of Cathédral St-Michel.

THE UPPER CITY

*The streets broaden as we move into the Upper City,
the civic district of Brussels, where various and varied
museums border the elegant Parc de Bruxelles*

Map
on page
108–9

The Ville Haute (Upper City) is traditionally associated with the aristocracy and administration, royalty and government. Its monumental squares are joined by classical boulevards, and the district embraces the Belgian parliament, government offices, the official residence of the royal family, and the overweening law courts, the monstrous Palais de Justice, which dominates the scene. Here, too, are the finest museums, the grandest designer shops and the most pretentious cafés.

Yet the Upper City is by no means a cohesive unit: Place Royale is a cold but monumental quarter with excellent museums and the Royal Palace; but, by contrast, the Sablon offers a sophisticated social scene, with chic cafés crammed under the Flemish gables of old Brussels.

From the Grand-Place district, Rue Ravenstein winds up to the royal quarter. Halfway up Rue Ravenstein stands the **Palais des Beaux-Arts L**. This monumental Art Deco palace contains a theatre, concert hall and exhibition space. It was designed (on an off-day) by the famous architect Victor Horta (*see page 92*). Nearby is **Hotel Ravenstein**, one of the grandest of the remaining 15th-century Burgundian mansions, and now a restaurant. However, on foot, the quickest way up to the royal heights is via Monts des Arts, a monumental stairway leading to **Place Royale M**. From the square itself, there is a panoramic view over the Lower City, centred on the soaring spire of the Town Hall on the Grand-Place. In the foreground, the imposing cathedral (*see page 123*) is visible, marking the boundary between the Upper City and Lower City.

For many years Place Royale suffered from benign neglect, but restoration of the neo-classical facades was undertaken in the 1990s. The square is framed by Saint-Jacques-sur-Coudenberg, a graceful neo-classical church inspired by a Roman temple. In its day, it has served as a royal chapel and as a temple of reason during the French Revolution. Bordering Montagne de la Cour and the square is the newly-restored **Old England department store** (*see page 92*). This erstwhile British firm had stylish premises in Brussels at the turn of the century. The intriguing Art Nouveau building is soon to house a musical instruments museum (see below).

Adjoining the square are the **Musées Royaux des Beaux-Arts N** (the Royal Museums of Fine Arts , open Tue–Sun 10am–5pm), Belgium's finest collection of art treasures. The well-designed and interconnected collections are distributed between the **Musée d'Art Ancien** and the **Musée d'Art Moderne**. These two palatial buildings are centred around an impressive museum courtyard which is known as the **Place du Musée**.

LEFT: King Albert I at the approach to Mont des Arts.
BELOW: sculpture garden in Albertinum Square.

The best way of getting around the Upper City is to hop on one of Brussels' yellow and blue trams.

The **Musée d'Art Ancien** (entrance on Rue de la Régence; closed noon–1pm) is a logical starting point, with a superb collection of Flemish masters. On display are works from the 15th to 19th centuries. The great Dutch painters include Rembrandt, Frans Hals, Jacob Jordaens and the landscape artist van Ruysdael. However, the Flemish are particularly well represented, from van Eyck, Roger van der Weyden and Hieronymus Bosch to Pieter Breughel the Elder and Younger. Pieter Breughel's masterpieces include *The Fall of Icarus* and *Winter Landscape with Skaters*. Major artists linked to Antwerp feature strongly, notably Peter Paul Rubens and Anthony van Dyck (*see page 88*).

The **Musée d'Art Moderne** (entrance on Place Royale; closed 1–2pm) contains modern paintings and sculpture from the 19th and 20th centuries. The successful museum, a model of its kind, is centred on a well of light which helps illuminate the eight underground storeys. The collection includes the works of such great artists as Courbet, Gauguin, Delacroix, Corot and Dali. The highlights include masterpieces by the Belgian Surrealists Magritte and Delvaux (*see page 90*), as well as works by Ensor, Permeke and the Flemish Expressionists.

On Place du Palais, just off the square, stands the **Palais du Roi ⊙**, Royal Palace, and adjacent **Parc de Bruxelles**. Although Brussels is one of the greenest capitals, the parks in the city centre are mostly small, sedate, neatly manicured affairs. Laid out with geometrical precision, the Parc de Bruxelles was landscaped in classical style in the 18th century. The park, which served as a royal hunting ground in medieval times, faces the Royal Palace.

The palace occupies the site of the seat of the dukes of Brabant, and was home to such rulers as Philip the Good and Charles V (*see pages 33–5*). In 1731, however, the building burned to the ground. The cause of the blaze has

been linked to the palace cooks, who were too engrosssed in jam-making to notice the spread of the fire. Due to severe winter weather, the city's water supply was frozen, and little was available to quench the flames. In desperation, the citizens vainly attempted to put out the fire with beer. In the 19th century, Leopold II had the palace remodelled in Louis XVI style, combining two patrician mansions. It was further renovated and enlarged at the beginning of this century. Recent excavations on Place Royale have revealed the remains of Philip the Good's palace. (Before the year 2000, a new underground museum on the site should display the excavated finds.)

Although the royal couple spend most of their time in their more alluring palace in Laeken (*see page 137*), this is the official city residence. The dignified but dull building was significantly altered by Leopold II, who was responsible for its imperial feel. The palace houses the Royal Chancellery, as well as state rooms and offices, some of which are open to the public in summer. If the flag is flying, His Majesty is in residence, since this is where King Albert II conducts his official business. A subdued changing of the guard takes place at 2pm. The **Musée de la Dynastie** (Dynasty Museum, open Tue–Sun 10am–4pm), situated behind the Royal Palace, contains an exhibition documenting the history of the royal family.

From the Palace and museum complex, **Rue Royale** provides a puzzling side of the city. The cool neo-classical street leads from the grand Place Royale to the distinctly dubious area of the Botanique and Gare du Nord red-light district. The street itself is generally safe but relentlessly long, so best explored by tram. As always, reasons for breaking one's journey involve individual taste, but along the way look out for **De Ultieme Hallucinatie** (316 Rue Royale), one of the most

Map on page 108–9

TIP

If you fancy giving your feet a break, the Musée du Cinema, adjoining the Palais des Beaux Arts, has daily screenings of old classics and silent flicks from the movie archives.

BELOW: The Palais du Roi at Parc de Bruxelles.

intriguing bars in Brussels. It is indeed a hallucination, an authentic Art Nouveau mansion complete with grotto and winter garden. The patrician mansion, built by Paul Hamesse in 1904, contains a friendly bar and brasserie and a gourmet restaurant. Rue Royale also possesses one of the most old-fashioned hotels in the city, the Edwardian **Pullman-Astoria**, a genteel spot for tea or a weekend classical concert. Diagonally opposite awaits **Confiserie Mary**, a world-famous chocolatier, and confectioners to the Belgian royal family (*see page 79*).

In the same street is a significant but chilling memorial, the **Colonne du Congrès P** (Column of Congress). The monument commemorates the founding of Belgium in 1830, with the names of the heroes of the Revolution inscribed in gold. Enthroned on the top of the column is a statue of the first King of Belgium, Leopold I, a member of the house of Saxe-Coburg-Gotha. The four vast female figures seated at his feet symbolise the human rights that had hitherto been denied Belgians: freedom of education and religion, freedom of the press and freedom of assembly. At the base of the column, an eternal flame burns over the grave of the Unknown Soldier, a memorial to the victims of both world wars.

A gift from the archers

From Place Royale, the monumental Rue de la Régence leads to the **Place du Grand Sablon Q**, arguably the most delightful square in Brussels. The Sablon is graced by the loveliest High Gothic church in Belgium, formally known as **Notre-Dame-des-Victoires** (Our Lady of the Victories). The sumptuous church was commissioned in the 15th century by the Brussels guild of archers. Especially noteworthy are its splendid stained-glass windows, the wall paintings in the choir and the carved wooden chancel. (Entrance to the building is via the

Bilingual street signs, an omnipresent feature of even-handed Brussels.

BELOW: the park and statuary of Place du Petit Sablon.

main portal on the square; open daily 9am–5pm; Sun 1–5.30pm.) The Sablon is particularly inviting in the evening, when the stained-glass windows of the church are illuminated, or during the folkloric Christmas market.

The sloping Sablon square is adorned by the Fountain of Minerva, a gift from the Earl of Aylesbury, who presented it as a token of thanks for the asylum the city granted him during his enforced exile from England. Lining the square are bijou restaurants and antique shops. The square is a popular haunt for after-work drinks or Sunday morning brunch, followed by browsing in the Sablon antiques market. A Sunday morning stroll provides a snapshot of the Belgian bourgeoisie at play: dapper bankers and genteel matrons pop into **Wittamer**, the grandest cake shop, to collect exquisite croissants for breakfast or madeleines for tea. For everyday fare, consider **Le Pain Quotidien** (11 Rue des Sablons), a fashionable but friendly bakery and tea-room. The quaintly cobbled Rue de Rollebeek, leading from the Sablon to the Marolles quarter (*see page 131*) is a popular spot for dining and browsing, given the profusion of picturesque restaurants and antique shops. At the Boulevard de l'Empereur end of the street stand the remains of the city ramparts, including a 13th-century tower.

Facing the Grand Sablon, on the far side of Rue de la Régence, lies the **Place du Petit Sablon** ®. This tiny, well-tended park is surrounded by an intricate wrought-iron grille, adorned with 48 bronze statuettes. Each represents one of the city's ancient guilds. The Art Nouveau railings were designed by Paul Hankar. The harmonious ensemble is dominated by a bronze portraying the dukes Egmont and Hoorn, martyrs of the resistance movement against the merciless Duke of Alba. (The pair were beheaded on the Grand-Place.) Also on the square is the **Musée Instrumental** (Tue–Sat, 10am–4.45pm), the City's Musical Instrument Museum. On display are 5,000 exhibits spanning the history of music. To Belgians, the saxophones are particularly significant since they were invented by a compatriot, Adolphe Saxe. In the year 2000, the museum moves to its new home, the Old England building on Place Royale.

Behind the square stands the **Palais d'Egmont**, a 16th-century mansion remodelled in neo-classical style. Famous past residents of the palace include Louis XV and Voltaire. Today, it is the home of the Belgian Foreign Ministry. It was here in 1972 that Denmark, the United Kingdom and Ireland signed the treaties officially admitting them to the European Economic Community. Only the slightly mournful palace gardens are open to the public, overshadowed by the hulk of the Hilton Hotel.

A judicial colossus

From here, Rue de la Régence and Rue aux Laines lead to the hulking **Palais de Justice** ®.The Palace of Justice, the city's law courts, was commissioned by Leopold II, the most imperial of Belgian kings. The architect, Joseph Poelaert, designed a monument to the Belgian constitution, with the law courts intentionally dwarfing every other building, whether sacred or military. The building was constructed in 1866–83 but Poelaert died, exhausted, before it was completed. In devising this eclectic design, he borrowed from vir-

Map on page 108–9

Although Adolphe Sax is best known for his invention of the saxophone, he also invented three other wind instruments: the sax-horn, sax-tuba and saxtromba. Alas, these three oddities fell into the margins of musical history.

BELOW: the imposing interior of the Palais de Justice.

Map on page 108–9

Brussels' attempt to clean up the streets of canine insolence.

tually every period of Belgian architecture. In the end, the project became a symbol of Belgium's burgeoning industrial and colonial might. However, in recent years, the behemoth has become more a symbol of miscarriages of justice. The paedophile and corruption scandals, in particular, have made the courts a focus for citizens' vocal protests against the ineptitude of the judicial system.

South of the Palais de Justice stands **Porte de Hal** ❼, a former prison and relic of the medieval city fortifications. Despite neo-Gothic turrets, this gate is essentially authentic. Inside is the unremarkable **Musée du Folklore** (open Tue–Sun, 10am–5pm), with displays of carnival traditions, toys and games from the Middle Ages to modern times. The gate leads to the uncompromising immigrant quarter centred on the **Gare du Midi**, home to the Turkish, North African and Spanish-speaking communities.

Instead of visiting Porte de Hal and the souk-like Midi market, consider exploring the **Marolles**, an ancient quarter lying in the shadow of the law courts. Located on the hill where the gallows once stood, the Palace of Justice entailed the demolition of part of the Marolles. Despite its poverty and dilapidation, this neighbourhood is often considered to be the true heart of Brussels. The unique and unmistakable city dialect, a mixture of Flemish, French and Spanish, with smatterings of Hebrew and German, originated here.

However, before delving into the alleys of the Marolles neighbourhood, take sustenance from a café such as **Le Nemrod** (61 Boulevard de Waterloo) to enjoy a final taste of uptown Brussels. The cosy café and mock hunting lodge provides the homely touches expected by bourgeois Belgians: myriad beers; stuffed animals adorning the walls; a blazing fire in winter, and a heated terrace for the spring and summer months. ❑

BELOW: the spiralling stone staircase of Porte de Hal.

The Marolles

The Marolles is the private face of Brussels, a poor but enigmatic quarter whose charm lies in chance discoveries rather than specific sights. The district has few clearly defined boundaries but is rather tucked between the curving boulevards of public Brussels, between the aristocratic Sablon district and Porte de Hal, and beneath the looming presence of the Palais de Justice.

As Brussels' most historic quarter, the Marolles was the birthplace of such personages as Brueghel the Elder (c1525). His house still stands, at 132 Rue Haute, as does the church where he was married, Notre-Dame-de-la-Chapelle – one of the city's loveliest churches, largely Gothic in character, but with Romanesque origins and a disconcerting Baroque bell-tower. As the district developed in the 17th century, it became a residential quarter for craftsmen working on the palatial homes of the Upper City.

It remained a thriving working-class quarter until the 1870s when, with the paving over of the river Senne, the wealthier artisans moved to the suburbs. The district swiftly declined, eventually becoming the preserve of the poor. Today's inhabitants, some 10,000 in all, lead lives largely independent of the outside world. Maghrebis and other immigrants from Mediterranean countries make up half the present population.

Despite the proximity of the Sablon, gentrification has been slow in seeping in. Drab little snack bars still lurk on every corner, hawking mussels, watery stews, soggy chips and thin draught beer.

Nonetheless, immigrants and indigenous traders have been joined by skilled craftsmen and traders who have opened a succession of small boutiques, galleries and brasseries. The patchwork of hilly alleys between Rue des Minimes and Rue Haute has a particular ambience of mystery and neglect. A down-at-heel Turkish café can stand beside a grand gabled town-house, a lute-maker's or a second-hand clothes shop.

Place du Jeu de Balle on Rue Blaes is the setting for the daily **flea market**, surrounded by motley galleries and antiquarian booksellers. The early morning cafés around the Vieux Marché attract a regular clientele, and some do not bother to close at all. The friterie here, and at the adjoining Place de la Chapelle, is supposed to serve the best chips in Brussels.

The district has several of the city's most traditional *estaminets* (brasseries), of which the most colourful is **La Grande Porte** (9 Rue de Notre Seigneur), just off Rue Blaes. **Café Alex** (224 Rue Haute, close to the junction with Rue des Renards) is a stamcafé, a rough and ready bar, and one of the last places to be sure of hearing *brusseleir*, the local patois. Apart from beer and a breezy line in chat, the bar satisfies two other local passions: an authentic Art Deco interior and a wall dedicated to the art of the comic strip. ❏

RIGHT: "Young Turk" – the youth of the diverse and vibrant Marolles district.

THE CINQUANTENAIRE AND LOUISE QUARTERS

Map on page 108–9

Around Parc du Cinquantenaire, and its vast museum complex, are some of the city's most attractive neighbourhoods, displaying wonderful examples of Art Nouveau architecture

To the east of the city centre, beyond the so-called "petit ring" (the wide boulevards that enclose central Brussels) lie some truly intriguing areas. And with such a compact city, they are still easily accessible. The Schuman metro station is close to both the Cinquantenaire and the European quarter, while the Louise metro station leads the way to the elegant district of the same name. The Cinquantenaire is the triumphal district, and is home to a series of prestigious museums, the only rivals to the royal art collections in the Upper City. The Cinquantenaire, surrounded by a superb park, adjoins the "neighbourhood of the squares", an elegant Art Nouveau quarter. Sandwiched between these two districts and the city centre is the European quarter (*see page 59*), the preserve of the Commission, the Council of Ministers and the European Parliament. Compared with the elegance of the Cinquantenaire, the European quarter has been devastated by poor planning. And to the southeast of the "petit ring" is the Louise quarter, the chic commercial heart of the city, with architectural treasures of its own.

Cinquantenaire (metro Schuman or Mérode) is dominated by the **Arc du Triomphe ⓤ**, visible from afar. The bases of the monument are decorated with allegories of the Belgian provinces. As its name suggests, the Cinquantenaire was created in 1880 to celebrate the golden jubilee of the kingdom of Belgium. The prestigious complex, built over a military parade ground, was the jewel in the crown along the triumphal way linking the Royal Park and the royal domain of Tervuren. Leopold II, the builder king, intended the avenue to link the sites connected with the World's Fair of 1897. The surrounding park contains one of the largest museum complexes in Europe, also created by Leopold II.

The **Musées Royaux d'Art et d'Histoire ⓥ** (open Tue–Sun, 9.30am–5pm) are theoretically dedicated to art and history. However, these bombastic museums attempt nothing less than a panoply of human civilisation, from prehistoric times to the present, with the glaring exception of African history. The highlights include 5th-century Syrian mosaics and a bronze of the Roman emperor Septimius Severus, while the section devoted to non-European civilisations is rich in Incan, Mayan and Aztec artefacts. European decorative arts are also well-represented, from medieval furniture to modern ceramics.

The adjacent building houses the **Musée Royal de l'Armée ⓦ** (open Tue–Sun, 9am–noon, 1–4.30pm), which displays weapons and military equipment dating from the 8th century to the present. Exhibits

LEFT: the Arc du Triomphe at the entrance to Parc du Cinquantenaire. **BELOW:** a mosaic floor in the Musées Royaux d'Art et d'Histoire.

include uniforms, sabres and cannon from the Brabant Revolution, as well as weapons used in both world wars. The aviation section covers military aircraft used before and after 1945. The Cinquantenaire complex also contains **Autoworld** (open daily 10am–5pm), an impressive collection of vintage cars. Some 450 top models from 12 different countries make this the finest museum of its kind in the world.

Art Nouveau squares

From Cinquantenaire park, Rue Archimède leads past Eurocrat watering holes to the "neighbourhood of the squares". Dating from the 1870s, the district comprises a symmetrical pattern of avenues centred on Place Ambiorix and Place Marie-Louise. Designed as a prosperous, progressive quarter, it attracted the best architects of the day. Here, Art Nouveau had a brief but brilliant reign.

Place Ambiorix ✪ contains several notable mansions, which are worth seeing for their facades alone, although with the help of the ARAU (*see Travel Tips*) some can be visited with a guide. **Hotel de St-Cyr**, Gustave Strauven's town house at 11 Place Ambiorix, is the most fairytale Art Nouveau house in Brussels, tall, thin and curvaceous. The swirling facade makes use of a filigree effect, centred on a circular window. Strauven's virtuosity is all the more remarkable given his limited resources, which restricted him largely to brick and iron.

At number 4 Avenue Palmerston, between Place Ambiorix and Place Marie-Louise, is the **Van Eetvelde mansion**, a Horta triumph built for the minister for the Belgian Congo. Designed as a showcase for Belgian colonialism, the house is filled from top to bottom with precious materials from the Congo, including mahogany ceilings, mosaics and onyx panelling.

TIP

Tourist service ARAU arranges a variety of themed tours, including one dedicated to the rich legacy of Art Nouveau in Brussels; ARAU can be contacted by calling (32) 219 33 45.

BELOW: the aircraft display in the Musée Royal de l'Armée.

The Louise quarter

A short metro ride west leads to **Place Louise ⓨ**, gateway to one of the city's most diverse districts, offering designer shopping, cinemas and smart cafés in a distinctly uptown setting. Yet this surprising district reveals delightful pockets of Art Nouveau, including the **Musée Horta**, 25 Rue Américaine (open Tue–Sun, 2–5.30pm). The Horta museum is set just off Chaussée de Charleroi, and reached by a 91 or 92 tram from Place Louise to the Janson stop. As Horta's home and studio, the town house is a testament to his style, with an elegant terrace and winter garden and a graceful spiral staircase, surmounted by a glass canopy. The house abounds in exquisite detail, from the stained-glass windows to the original furniture.

Amadeus, a fashionable Art Nouveau bar and brasserie, is in keeping with the artistic mood. The whimsical but welcoming town house was once Rodin's studio and is at 13 Rue Veydt, just off Place Stéphanie. Hungrier and less artistic visitors may opt for **La Quincaillerie**, at 45 Rue du Page, around the corner from the Horta museum.

Rue Defacqz, which leads off Avenue Louise to the west, is the most charming part of the district. The surrounding streets boast exuberant, daring Art Nouveau buildings and a gentrified bohemian ambience. Quirky boutiques and funky galleries are interspersed with Art Nouveau town-houses designed by Paul Hankar. Number 71 Rue Defacqz, Hankar's last home, displays a geometric facade and Japanese decorative influences. In 1897, he designed number 48 as a painter's studio, with its large rounded windows and sgraffito work displaying floral and animal motifs. On the street parallel with Rue Defacqz stands Horta's Hotel Tassel, often considered the manifesto of Art Nouveau. ❑

At 14 Rue Defacqz is a wonderful building designed in an Andalusian Art Deco style, successor to the Art Nouveau mode. The mansion, now the Art-Media Museum (open Tue–Sun 10am–6pm), stages Art Deco exhibitions.

BELOW: the elegant residences of the Louise quarter.

THE GLASS CITY

With rare and wonderful plants, the botanical gardens and greenhouses of the Royal Palace are defining features of the Laeken district, an area that is also home to the distinctive Atomium

Map on page 108–9

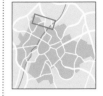

The Royal Domain lies in the outlying district of Laeken, to the north of Brussels. This royal estate both complements and outshines the royal family's official city palace (*see page 126*). The Belgian royal family are not noted city-lovers and infinitely prefer to live in the secluded country setting of Laeken. The magnificent botanical gardens and greenhouses, which rival the English equivalent in Kew, have earned the domain the title of "glass city". As a colonial power, Belgium revelled in the profusion of exotic plants shipped in from the Congo. Apart from the leafy estate itself, Laeken's appeal lies in the exotic oriental constructions and theatrical hot-houses that enliven any visit.

The royal domain revolves around the **Château Royal** (Royal Palace), concealed behind railings on the Parc Royal. Although the palace is not open to the public, the domain is dotted with curious monuments and memorials. The Domain of Laeken was created by Marie-Christine and Albert of Saxe-Teck, the rulers imposed on the country by Emperor Joseph II of Austria. At the end of the 18th century, Laeken was considered to be one of the loveliest estates in Europe. Not that Austria had long to enjoy its new possessions. In 1794, France annexed Belgium and the Austrians left, escaping with their prestigious art collection. This later formed the basis of the famous Albertina collection in Vienna, named after its founder, the Archduke Albert.

The Royal Palace was built by Montoyer during the second half of the 18th century but was remodelled in Louis XVI style under Leopold II (*see page 41*). The occupying French forces planned to turn it into a public hospital. However, in 1804, Napoleon Bonaparte rescued the palace from total ruin, and used it as his residence until his defeat at Waterloo in 1815 (*see page 159*). It was here, in 1812, that Napoleon signed the declaration of war against Russia. William I of Orange-Nassau, the King of the Netherlands, became the next owner but only had a brief period to revel in the splendours of his stately home. A few years later, in 1830, the country gained its independence, and Laeken became the residence of Leopold I, the first King of Belgium, and uncle of the British Queen Victoria (*see page 41*).

Leopold II, the second King of Belgium (1835–1909), was responsible for the creation of the fine park at Tervuren (*see page 154*). However, his impact on Laeken was equally great. The king extended the palace and had magnificent avenues built from the domain to the capital. The park was embellished by two oriental follies, a Chinese Pavilion and a Japanese Pagoda, relics of the Paris World's Fair in 1900. Set on Avenue Van Praet, the Chinese Pavilion and the Japanese Pagoda lend the park an exotic air. The Pavilion houses a priceless collection of 17th and 18th-century oriental porcelain, while the Pagoda dis-

LEFT: the Winter Gardens of the Château Royal.
BELOW: blooming geraniums in the glass city.

plays Japanese art (both open Tue–Sun, 10am–4pm). The king's plans to expand the Domain of Laeken foundered on his death in 1909, with further development halted by the outbreak of World War I. However, Leopold's greatest achievement at Laeken was the creation of the so-called "glass city".

The Royal Greenhouses

The crowning glory was the construction of the Serres Royales, the Royal Greenhouses. This remarkable complex has remained virtually intact since its completion in 1875. Leopold II's predecessors had toyed with more modest schemes. A Chinese tower with adjoining orangery had been built by the ruling Austrian archdukes. Napoleon, too, had entertained grandiose plans for exotic hot-houses, but these came to nothing after his separation from the Empress Josephine. The orangery as it stands today was built under William I of the Netherlands. Leopold I also had a number of lesser greenhouses erected to supply the palace with orchids and pineapples. But nothing was on the scale planned by Leopold II, inspired by his love of grandiose projects and the luxuriant vegetation of the Belgian Congo.

The Royal Greenhouses, one of the best-preserved complexes in Europe, are attributed to Alphonse Balat and the young Victor Horta (*see page 92*). In Leopold's day, the techniques required to build metal-framed glass buildings had reached new heights of sophistication. This permitted the construction of fairy-tale palaces which combined the romantic cult of the exotic with a longing for nature, exemplified by the sinuous forms of the Art Nouveau style. The resulting greenhouses present an architectural treasure that comprises a huge central dome, topped by an ironwork crown and flanked by a secondary chamber, cupolas, turrets and vaulted tunnels of glass.

BELOW: for a few days once a year, the public can enjoy the glorious bloom of the fuchsias.

The interlinked greenhouses allow the visitor to stroll from one end to the other, covering a distance of one kilometre. At its heart, a palm-tree complex meets a series of winter gardens, linked by an airy gallery. The palm-houses include a playful succession of passages and galleries abounding in startling perspectives. The winter gardens, however, are designed according to strictly formal lines: a row of large hot-houses is laid out along a central axis, with the pièce de résistance a vast dome-shaped hot-house.

The plants inside are rare and precious, perfectly in tune with the architecture. Leopold II particularly loved palms, which now curve majestically into the centre of the dome. These were joined by fuschias and figs, geraniums, azaleas and begonias as well as tropical plants and camellias, the king's favourite flowers. Many species are of historical importance: most of the 44 species of orange tree are over 200 years old. Bananas and myriad varieties of palms grow between wall ferns, overshadowed by broad palmyra palms. Ferns and orchids flourish beside camellias which are almost 200 years old, and which formed part of the hot-houses' original Victorian planting. Today, they constitute the most valuable collection of their kind in the world.

It was Leopold II's wish that the greenhouses should be open to the public once a year; and this tradition has been honoured ever since. Each year, in late April and early May, when thousands of flowers bloom in rainbow colours, the royal greenhouses open their doors. A night tour of the greenhouses is often the highlight of a visit to Brussels. The spectacle only lasts a week or so but draws thousands of local citizens who revel in the heady atmosphere of lush palms and exotic blooms. Visitors drift dreamily amidst the steamy fragrances of camellias and orchids, admiring the illuminated patterns of ferns and fuschias. ❑

In the shadow of the Atomium is Mini Europe, a juxtaposition of the most significant buildings of the continent, from Athens' Acropolis to the Georgian town houses of Bath, all scaled down to a fraction of their original size.

Map on page 108–9

BELOW: molecular magnificence – the Atomium.

THE ATOMIUM

Brussels' Atomium is a gigantic model of an iron molecule that dominates the Heysel Plateau, to the northwest of Parc de Laeken. This curious monument was constructed for the World Exhibition in 1958, its dynamic frame symbolising the potential of Belgian industry in the postwar period. Its designer, André Waterkeyn, was a professional engineer, and his conception was to monumentalise one of the fundamental building blocks of matter. To create the Atomium monument, the iron molecule was magnified 165 billion times to reach its 102 metre (326 ft) height. Inside the nine spheres, each representing an atom of the molecule, are the elements of a science museum, and within the connecting tubes are escalators that convey visitors through a disorientating route around the structure. There is also a fast lift that whisks visitors to the uppermost sphere in just 23 seconds.

The Atomium proved such a huge success during the World Exhibition that the locals requested that they be able to hang on to their striking new monument. It has since become a shining symbol for the city, almost as well-loved as the Mannekin Pis. The Atomium is at its spectacular best at night, when a sequence of flashing lights gives the impression that the spheres are revolving.

Map
on page
108–9

Brussels

BRUSSELS LACE

*Now famous the world over, Brussels lace was developed
during the mid-15th century and soon adorned
the collars and cuffs of European nobility*

Brussels lace was particularly sought after by the medieval courts in Paris and London. Queen Elizabeth I reputedly owned 3,000 lace dresses, and it is said that Empress Eugénie of France owned a lace gown which 600 women had toiled over for 10 months using a total of 90,000 bobbins.

By the second half of the 16th century, women throughout Belgium were engaged in the craft and lace was being exported to prosperous families all over Europe. At the end of the century there was scarcely a young girl, even in the most rural areas, who was not employed by the lace merchants.

The labour-intensive industry posed unforeseen problems, namely a shortage of serving maids in the homes of the wealthy. Eventually a decree was passed prohibiting the manufacture of lace by girls of more than 12 years of age. During the 17th century 22,000 women and girls worked as lace makers; during the 19th century, the total reached 50,000. In Brussels alone, the capital of lace production, the figure was some 10,000.

Brussels lace was unsurpassable as regards both the fineness of the thread and the beauty of the motifs, and the capital's churches and museums are still full of examples of the delicate work. The production of large pieces, such as bed covers and entire robes, was only made possible when the technique of lace-

BELOW: *The Lace-maker* 1665 by Jan Vermeer van Delft.

making moved away from the use of a single continuous thread towards knotting, in which individual pieces of lace are almost seamlessly joined together. Until this point it had only been possible to produce small pieces of lace, the size of which was determined by the length of the thread wound on to the bobbin. Following this method of production many women produced the same motif time and time again, often over a period of several years. While the technique allowed for greater versatility in the finished article, the creative aspect of the craft gradually diminished in a sort of mass production.

None of the lacemakers ever became famous or rich. Their reward for their arduous work was determined by the lace merchants, few of whom were generous; the lacemakers were often forced to work in badly lit, damp cellars where the thread would be less likely to break.

Until well into the 18th century, Brussels lace remained a popular symbol of luxury for the rich. Inevitably, however, fashions changed and by the time of the French Revolution lace-making in Belgium was in decline. The craft experienced a brief renaissance during the 19th century but was never able to regain its previous fashionableness or degree of skill.

One of the largest lace merchants in Brussels is the **Manufacture Belge de Dentelles**, whose shop can be found at 6-8 Galerie de la Reine. A wide variety of antique and modern lace is on sale.

Those who prefer simply to look at fine Belgian lace should visit the **Musée du Costume et de la Dentelle** (Costume and Lace Museum) just behind the Town Hall at 6, Rue de la Violette. There is also an excellent lace collection in the **Musées Royaux d'Art et d'Histoire** in the Parc du Cinquantenaire (*see page 131*); the entrance can be found in the Avenue des Nerviens. ❑

Nowadays, few Belgian women want to learn the intricacies of lace-making, and so to satisfy the increasing demand for hand-made lace much of that on sale in Brussels today is actually from China.

BELOW: even expert lacemakers can produce no more than a few inches a day.

Map on page 108–9

Brussels●

WINDOW SHOPPING

Beyond the beer, lace and chocolates, Brussels shopping offers the seduction of antiques and high fashion

BELOW: the
weekend antiques
market on the Place
du Grand Sablon.

The city abounds in the tasteful and the tacky, from traditional chocolate to collectable Euro-tat. Shop windows often reflect the cosy domesticity of much Belgian culture, but – to the surprise of the French – the Belgians are also market-leaders in avant-garde fashion. Designers such as Dries van Noten and Ann Demeulemeester have put Belgium firmly on the fashion map.

Even amongst the conservative Belgian male fashions there are some notable exceptions, such as **Olivier Strelli** (72 Avenue Louise), Belgium's answer to Armani. Female fashion can be far bolder than Parisian style. **Elvis Pompilio** (18 Rue Lombard) is where Madonna buys her hats, a kitsch, outrageous but often stylish collection. For both sexes, Rue Antoine Dansaert (metro Bourse) is the centre of avant-garde design, with **Stijl** (at number 74) the trendy citadel of Belgian fashion, exulting in its self-consciously industrial setting. Nearby is **Kat en Muis** (at number 32), with miniature versions of designer clothes for well-behaved designer children. Belgian fashion is noted for its quality and durability, and prestigious names such as **Delvaux** (for leatherware) carry a similar cachet to the Chanel label.

Chocaholics can make their first stop at the grand chocolatiers on Grand-Place. After soaking up the atmosphere of one of the square's cafés (*see page 113*), it is time to plunge into the galleries. Brussels proudly possesses more shopping arcades than any other city in Europe. The galleries off the Grand-Place are the oldest and best-loved but those in the Upper City are far more fashionable.

The elegant shopping arcades display everything an old-fashioned Brussels bureaucrat might desire, from a bejewelled tie-pin to a lace handkerchief. The **Galeries Saint-Hubert** displays a Renaissance-style motif proclaiming Omnibus omnia, "everything for everyone", but the prices preclude that. Even grander are **Galerie du Roi** (with the exclusive **Corné** chocolatier), **Galerie de la Reine** (with **Neuhaus** chocolates, and, at number 6-8, genuine lace). By contrast, the new galleries off the Grand-Place contain a mixture of youthful tourist tat, street fashion and the odd ethnic exotica. Typical products are jeans, leather goods, jewellery, and unintentionally kitsch souvenirs.

The Lower City

From the Grand-Place, shoppers inexorably drift towards the fashion shops and cafés around La Monnaie, the opera house (*see page 120*) and La Bourse, the Stock Exchange. Neighbouring Rue Neuve has been turned into a tawdry pedestrian zone, which provides minimal atmosphere but mainstream fashion at reasonable prices. **City 2**, also in Rue Neuve, is the main modern shopping centre in the Lower City, catering to the youth market. Brussels department stores are on a par with those in most other European capitals, with **Inno**, in Rue Neuve, the biggest and best, rivalled by the neighbouring British **Marks and Spencer**. Boulevard Anspach, close to the Bourse, is a lively thoroughfare, with the stretch before Place de Brouckère providing a succession of boutiques, newsagents and chocolatiers. Nearby is the surprising Rue Antoine Dansaert, the avant-garde fashion and design centre which offers an intriguing mix of minimalist boutiques and baroque bars.

The Sablon

Sandwiched between the Upper and Lower City, the Sablon is one of the city's most elegant shopping districts. The café-lined square and side streets are also home to the city's main antique dealers and art galleries. Whilst bargains are rare, the quality is generally good and the dealers knowledgeable. The galleries are tucked into discreet shopping arcades leading off the square. Idlers can often slip into the regular *vernissages*, the drink-fuelled openings held by smarter galleries. As for designer shops, **Flamant** (at number 32) sells the best Belgian Royal Boch chinaware, faience in production since 1841. Neighbouring streets, such as Rue de Rollebeek and Rue Lebeau, sell quirky antiques and designer-ware, with **Chinz B** (39 Rue de Rollebeek) specialising in the shabby chic look in home furnishings. By contrast, **Linen House** (10 Rue Bodenbroek) displays Flemish linen to its best advantage.

An elegantly coiffured mannequin.

The Upper City

The best luxury boutiques and jewellers are found along the wide avenues and galleries of the Upper City. Designer boutiques are clustered along Boulevard de Waterloo and Avenue Louise, particularly between Place Louise and Porte de Namur. The galleries also rate among the most elegant and expensive, from Galerie Espace Louise to Galerie Louise and Galeries de la Toison d'Or. The shop **Natan** (158 Avenue Louise) is an upmarket but discreet fashion store favoured by the present Queen Paola. **Delvaux** (27 Boulevard de Waterloo) is an emporium of exclusive hand-crafted luggage, which capitalises on local lore that pronounces every woman entitled to a "Delvaux" once in her life. Apart from designer boutiques, the area has lots of perfumeries and shops devoted to home furnishings. Interior decoration is an art in the capital, with attractive shops in most middle-class districts. However, the adjoining Art Nouveau quarter centred on Rue du Bailli makes a more charming and eclectic place to shop for fashion or home furnishings.

BELOW: copies of the Manneken Pis come in many forms, including these sweet lollipops.

Window-shoppers dismissive of Belgian fashion and design can still find much that is edible or entertaining. Apart from the gourmet delicatessens and chocolate shops, the Belgians excel at florists, with the loveliest in an Art Nouveau setting on Rue Royale. Music-lovers in search of instruments can visit **Azzato** (Rue de la Violette) or **Antoni Jassogne** (21 Rue des Renards), a lute-maker in the Marolles. Before leaving Brussels, fans of Belgian kitsch should visit **La Boutique de Tintin** (13 Rue de la Colline) for comic strip souvenirs or risk the tiger-print lingerie at Champagne et Caviar (40 Galeries du Centre). Belgian shopping need not be boring. ❑

Map on page 108–9

Brussels

BRUSSELS À LA CARTE

As gourmet capital of Europe, the culinary hallmark of Brussels is plentiful, unpretentious cuisine, prepared with knowledge and skill

Although the language and style of Brussels' gastronomy is undeniably French, the Belgians often do it better. And while both nationalities are equally demanding of culinary greatness, the Belgians have never succumbed to faddishness or calorie-counting. Belgian portions tend to be larger, and the Bruxellois delight in long, leisurely meals and gastronomic self-indulgence, taking time to savour the classic cuisine.

In the landscape of Brussels cuisine, fish and seafood compete with stews, fine cheeses and rich sauces, often enriched by the use of beer. The best-known Belgian dish is *moules-frites* (mussels and chips) which can be found equally on street stands or on brasserie menus. Other filling classics are: *stoemp* (hot pot); *chicons au gratin* (endives cooked in a cheese sauce, often with ham); and *waterzooi* (a chunky Flemish stew made with vegetables and either chicken or fish). Such dishes even find their way onto upmarket menus.

Brussels has a colourful and touristy restaurant district in the Ilot Sacré, close to the Grand-Place. More sophisticated is the restaurant-lined square of the Sablon, sandwiched between the Upper City and Lower City, while the most characteristic seafood quarter is centred on Place Sainte-Catherine. For details of world-famous gourmet temples and earthy estaminets (an even cosier version of the Paris bistrot), see Travel Tips, pages 316–18).

BELOW: café life in the heart of Brussels.

Ilot Sacré

This area close to the Grand-Place is Brussels' main restaurant quarter. Most gabled houses have been converted into restaurants adorned by polished antique barrows heaving with wet fish and feathered game. **La Maison du Cygne** (9 Grand-Place) provides an exquisite (expense account) introduction to Brussels. This elegant yet romantic restaurant occupies a perfect location on the city's most famous square. The panelled interior is matched by original coffered ceilings, mellow woodwork, and walls hung with copies of Flemish masters. The cuisine combines French and Belgian influences, with the chef noted for his Belgian beer sauces. Typical entrées are *foie gras* and *huîtres chaudes au tombé de chicons et Vouvray* (oysters with Vouvray wine in a bed of Belgian endives).

Aux Armes de Bruxelles (13 Rue des Bouchers) is a Belgian institution, noted for its reliable cuisine and no-nonsense approach to both customers and cooking. This traditional restaurant has been in the Veulemans family for 75 years. Though there are many tempting restaurants in the Ilot Sacré, this bustling restaurant – famous for its Belgian *moules*, cooked every imaginable way – can be unreservedly recommended. Throughout the restaurant, the rooms offer a variation in ambience and style, from rustic tables and benches to sophisticated touches of art deco design.

The Lower City

The district from the Grand-Place to Sainte-Cathérine has the greatest concentration of restaurants. **L'Alban Chambon** (Hotel Métropole, Place de Brouck-ère) is a gourmet restaurant set in the oldest hotel in Brussels. Decorated in authentic Belle Epoque style, this is one the loveliest dining rooms in the city; the supremely formal setting echoes the elegant Art Nouveau ambience of the hotel. Fortunately, the classic French cuisine is not overshadowed by the splendour of the setting. Dominique Michou, the inventive French chef, is worthy of the task of reviving jaded palates. As a disciple of Escoffier, Michou sees his style as homage to the master. However, this is a modern interpretation and, unlike Belgian cuisine, is a light classic style, although it steers well away from the minimalism of nouvelle cuisine. As well as supplying excellent food, L'Alban Chambon also holds regular musical evenings, which spill over into grand Empire Style reception rooms.

La Belle Maraichère (11 Place Sainte-Cathérine) lies in the heart of Sainte Cathérine, the seafood quarter. Run by two Belgian brothers, Eddy and Freddy Devreker, this award-winning seafood restaurant is set in a gabled Flemish Renaissance town-house. When not too busy, Freddy Devreker, master chef, greets his customers personally before rushing back to the kitchen. The decor is Bruxellois, a cosy bistrot style that is a little at odds with the formality of the cuisine. The rustic downstairs dining room is more appealing than the classic upstairs version. On the menu, Belgian seafood predominates, including *waterzooi de trois poissons* (a chunky fish stew made with three types of fish). As a typical introduction to his cuisine, the chef recommends *terrine de raie et crabe* (skate and crab terrine) followed by half a lobster.

BELOW: seafood served on a bed of ice in Ilot Sacré, the "stomach of Brussels".

The neighbouring **Les Crustacés** (8 Quai aux Briques) lies on Brick Wharf and is as single-mindedly crustacean as it sounds. This shrine to the lobster has been run for more than 30 years by the Van Cauwelaert family. The restaurant – always a hive of activity – is as popular with locals as with visitors, and is the perfect place for a leisurely meal. Set in two rambling town-houses, the seafood restaurant enjoys a Bruxellois decor, sporting a homely clutter and assortment of Flemish paintings. The chef cheerfully suggests that diners dedicate a day to the lobster, starting with *bisque de homard* and followed by the house speciality, *homard à la nage*, lobster cooked in a vegetable broth. Although many diners choose to eat both hot and cold lobster during the same meal, there is, as yet, no lobster sorbet.

The Sea Grill (Radisson Hotel, 47 Rue du Fossé-aux-Loups) is situated on the ground floor of a futuristic hotel, with an Art Deco-inspired facade topped by a bold atrium. Inside, American shopping mall meets Continental kitsch, with glass capsule lifts, an original Romanesque wall and a running brook. The hotel's famous seafood restaurant is justly proud of its two Michelin stars. The Sea Grill is crisp-looking, furnished with Scandinavian simplicity in muted colours, with a glass wall depicting Norwegian fjords, a reminder that the hotel is Scandinavian. The prestigious French chef at this establishment, Jacques Le

The best seafood in Brussels is to be found in the vicinity of Place Sainte Cathérine.

Divellec, trained the current Belgian chef and still maintains a connection with the restaurant. The Sea Grill's popularity is assured by a well-supplied oyster and lobster bar. Brittany lobster is a signature dish, as is *plateau de fruits de mer* (seafood platter), a popular introduction to the Sea Grill.

The Sablon and Marolles

The genteel Sablon square is home to **L'Ecailler du Palais Royal** (18 Rue Bodenbroek, Place du Grand Sablon). Set on the city's most elegant square, this old-fashioned French restaurant serves some of the best seafood in Brussels. Unlike most gourmet haunts, L'Ecailler has a faithful, predominantly Belgian clientele. As the first restaurant dedicated solely to seafood and shellfish, it has pursued excellence for forty years. The intimate setting – best experienced on the cosy ground floor of this 17th-century town house – is in marine mode, with aquatic-coloured tiles and pictures of fish adorning wood-panelled walls. Apart from the popular oyster bar, diners can opt for fishy starters such as caviar, lobster ravioli, smoked salmon and smoked eel. Main courses include red mullet on a bed of spinach, grilled brill or turbot in a wine sauce.

Les Brigittines (5 Place de la Chapelle) lies in the shadow of La Chapelle church, not far from the chic Sablon quarter. Housed in a former post-house, this superior brasserie has a stylish Belle Epoque interior, all gleaming brass and burnished woodwork. The brasserie specialises in *plats du terroir* – earthy local dishes, some of peasant origin – while sole from Zeebrugge is another popular choice. Nearby is **Les Petits Oignons** (13 Rue Notre-Seigneur), set in a shabby but characteristic part of the Marolles. The gabled 17th-century town house is splendidly atmospheric, adorned with plants and bold paintings. In winter, din-

BELOW: the Waterloo Tavern.

Map on page 108–9

ers can enjoy an open fire or dine in the garden in summer. The welcoming service in the split-level restaurant is matched by fine *cuisine française*, with roast lamb, Brittany oysters and lobster salad on the menu.

The Upper City

This is a mixed district, embracing the Place Royale and Avenue Louise, not far from the Sablon. **De Ultieme Hallucinatie** (316 Rue Royale), Flemish for "the ultimate hallucination" is an indicator of the surprises in store. The restaurant, once a Masonic lodge, is a superbly preserved Art Nouveau town house noted for its elaborate ironwork and stained glass, as well as gourmet cuisine. The restaurant, under Flemish management, offers French cuisine with a Flemish flavour. Signature dishes include poached brill, lobster and other seafood, as well as game in season. To appreciate the magical setting, have a drink at the boisterous brasserie at the back, which incorporates original Art Nouveau features, including a grotto and winter garden. The elegant but compact dining room is rather formal, exhibiting the stained glass typical of Art Nouveau. The seats come from decommissioned Belgian third-class railway carriage compartments but are surprisingly comfortable nonetheless.

   Les Salons de l'Atlantide (89 Chaussée de Charleroi) is a theatrical restaurant close to the upmarket Avenue Louise district. Named after the lost city of Atlantis, this Baroque affair occupies a former auction rooms. Surrounded by grand fireplaces, Baroque frescoes, arcane carvings and esoteric signs, the restaurant prepares inventive *cuisine française*, offering strong but pure flavours that make for a memorable meal. The menu includes a variety of steaks and seafood, including monkfish and salmon carpaccio.

BELOW: waiters at a restaurant on the Grand-Place.

Map on page 108–9

Temples of gastronomy

Invidious though it is to choose, **Comme Chez Soi** (23 Place Rouppe) is generally regarded as the temple of Belgian gastronomy. The proud possessor of three Michelin stars is masterminded by Pierre Wynants. Stangely enough, this "temple" is set in a shabby and rather dodgy area, beside one of the scruffiest Belgian bars imaginable. Yet the restaurant's Art Nouveau interior is superb, an authentic display of sculptural curves, splendid stained glass and burnished wood. The elegant salon is a setting for classic *cuisine française* choreographed by balletic waiters. Diners should take the time to sip an apéritif at the sumptous bar. This is inspired French cuisine, albeit with a few nods to Belgian sensibilities. Classic dishes are given a subtle modern twist but remain beautifully balanced. Fairly typical is the *foie de canard au porto et gingembre* (liver paté with port and ginger).

La Villa Lorraine (75 Avenue du Vivier d'Or) rivals Comme Chez Soi, the other pillar of Belgian gastronomy. The restaurant enjoys a splendid setting bordering the wooded park of Bois de la Cambre in Uccle, a desirable residential area in southeast Brussels. The classic *cuisine française* is the work of master chef Freddy Vandecasserie. The menu changes with the seasons, but is perhaps best appreciated in summer, when one can eat in the garden. Signature dishes include oysters in champagne, wild game in season and terrines such as *terrine de légumes au foie gras et aux asperges* (vegetable terrine with foie gras and asparagus). The game is a particular speciality, provided by enthusiastic huntsmen from the Villa Lorraine staff. Despite such giddying gastronomic heights, it is good to remember that local chefs are equally at home in the simplest estaminet or brasserie. ❑

BELOW: the Art Nouveau interior of Le Falstaff is a key to the bar's perennial appeal.

Bars and Cafés

The institutional greyness of Brussels is swiftly banished by the city's homely bars and sumptuous Art Nouveau cafés. Some take on a desolate air during the day but all come to life at night, when even the nicotine-stained bars with wooden booths, surly waiters and wizened Bruxellois have their own odd charm. The Lower City is home to the best estaminets (inns or bistrots) where steaks, salads or crusty cheese sandwiches (*tartines au fromage*) often accompany traditional brews.

The Grand-Place brasseries make an atmospheric start to a Belgian bar crawl. Despite promising sudden death to passive smokers, **A La Mort Subite** (7 Rue des Montagnes-aux-Herbes Potagères) is one of the most engaging of the authentic bars near the Grand-Place. The hatchet-faced waiters were probably the same ones who served the mournful Belgian singer Jacques Brel. **A La Bécasse** (11 Rue de Tabora) is another old-fashioned inn and the place to drink draught lambic or kriek beer served in pitchers and accompanied by *tartines au fromage blanc*.

L'Imaige Nostre-Dame (3 Impasse des Cadeaux, off Rue du Marché-aux-Herbes) is a snug bar decorated like a Dutch kitchen, with stained glass, heavy oak tables and leather banquettes. **La Fleur en Papier Doré** (55 Rue des Aléxiens), once a Surrealist haunt, retains its bohemian air. The quaint 17th-century inn is still lined with yellowing clippings, sketches and poems. Gloomy **Le Cercueil** (12 Rue des Harengs), named after a coffin, has a suitably funereal ambience, underscored by Gregorian chant and the use of coffins as tables.

Close to the Stock Exchange are a couple of celebrated bars: **Le Cirio** (18 Rue de la Bourse), designed in opulent, if faded, fin de siècle style and **Le Falstaff** (19-25 Rue Henri Maus), a rambling and popular Art Nouveau inn, with a heated winter terrace for outdoor dining. **Le Greenwich** (7 Rue des Chartreux) is an Art Nouveau haunt once popular with the Surrealists but now favoured by serious chessplayers. Its mirrored interior, with wood-panelled walls and marble tables, makes a peaceful escape during the day. Near Place Sainte-Cathérine is **L'Archiduc** (6 Rue Antoine Dansaert), decorated in Art Deco ocean-liner style, which offers a mellow ambience.

Towards the Upper City, the Sablon and Louise quarters offer a taste of uptown Brussels. **Le Kartchma** (17 Place du Grand Sablon), arguably the most appealing of the chic sidewalk bars, is the place for people-watching. **Le Wine Bar** (Rue des Pigeons) is a gentrified gabled affair tucked in a neighbouring alley. Set in a brick cellar, it is a refined rendezvous for wine-tasting and sophisticated snacks. Close to Avenue Louise, **L'Amadeus** (13 Rue Veydt), once Rodin's studio, is a romantic yet whimsical Art Nouveau bar and fashionable brasserie. Nearby, **Le Nemrod** (61 Boulevard de Waterloo) is a homely café and mock hunting lodge beloved by bourgeois Bruxellois. By contrast, a stroll downhill takes you to the rough stamcafés in the Marolles, friendly drinking dens noted for their cool beer and heated discussions. ❑

RIGHT: service is generally cheery in the bars of Brussels, and waiters take pride in their work.

AROUND BRUSSELS

Map on page 154

As well as its own sights, Brussels provides an excellent base from which to make day trips to the surrounding countryside, abbeys, parks and historic towns of Brabant

There are a number of worthwhile excursions that can be made from the capital. Just to the north of Brussels lie several attractions that can easily be be combined if you want a breath of fresh air. The **Nationale Plantentuin** (National Botanical Gardens) at the village of Meise (park open daily; greenhouses Easter–Oct, Sun–Thur and pub hols; park free, entrance fee for greenhouses) is a beautiful country estate, the Domein de Bouchout. It's a great place for a walk and has loads of exotic plants and trees, both outdoors and indoors, as well as a castle beside a lake. In summer, the park's Orangerie café is open.

Not far away is **Grimbergen Abbey** ❶, source of the strapping Trappist Grimbergen beers, which are sold in the abbey's café. The abbey was founded in 1128, but the present church dates from the 17th century. It has a particularly fine interior, including delicately chiselled carvings by Antwerp sculptor Hendrik Frans Verbruggen and a number of Flemish old master paintings from the 17th and 18th century. Continuing northwards in the direction of Mechelen is the **Rijksdomein Hofstade** (open daily; free, but beach and parking fees in summer). The artificial beach around the big lake here is considered by many to be an acceptable substitute for the distant beaches of the Flemish coast, and it gets busy in summer. The lake and its surrounding also form a nature reserve that is frequented by many species of birds.

The university town of **Leuven** ❷ (Louvain) lies about 25 km (16 miles) east of Brussels. During the 12th and 13th centuries, the town's weaving industry made it one of the most important cloth manufacturing centres in Europe. The monasteries and churches still bear witness to the tremendous wealth of the Counts of Leuven, who, in 1190, also became Dukes of Brabant.

Leuven's **Stadhuis** (town hall) was built by Mathieu de Layens between 1448 and 1463 for the ruling Duke of Burgundy, Philip the Good. The three-storey building has 10 pointed-arched windows per floor and six exquisitely carved octagonal turrets, making it a masterpiece of Brabant Gothic architecture. The niches in the facade house statues of famous local personalities and reliefs illustrate themes from the Bible.

Within the town hall itself, visitors may tour the jury room, once furnished by paintings by Dirk Bouts, a powerful influence on German 15th-century painting, who died in Leuven in 1475.

Directly opposite the town hall stands the late Gothic **St-Pieterskerk** (church of St Peter). The cruciform basilica with ambulatory and chapels was never finished as the foundations proved unstable.

The exuberantly baroque pulpit, dating from 1742, is adorned with reliefs depicting Peter's denial and the conversion of St Norbert. Three arches completed

PRECEDING PAGES: the Onze Vrouweten Poelkerk middle entrance portal detail. **LEFT:** roof detail on the town hall at Leuven. **BELOW:** the Leuven town hall at night.

in 1488 separate the choir from the nave. The church's most valuable treasures are two triptychs by Dirk Bouts, one illustrating the *Martyrdom of St Erasmus* and the other his c.1464 painting of *The Last Supper*.

The **University of Leuven** was founded in 1425 at the request of Duke Jean IV of Brabant, with 12 teachers summoned from Cologne and Paris by its founding father Pope Martin V. Pope Adrian VI, Erasmus of Rotterdam and Justus Lipsius, who founded the discipline of classical and antiquarian studies, all had close links with the university.

Encounter with Africa

On the eastern fringes of Brussels is the historic town of **Tervuren** ❸. During the 17th and 18th centuries **Tervuren Park**, with an area of more than 200 hectares (500 acres) of gardens and lakes, was the setting for many a glittering court ball. But the palace has long since been demolished, and only a chapel and the stables remain. Nowadays Tervuren is principally famous for the **Royal Museum of Central Africa** (Koninklijk Museum voor Midden-Afrika / Musée Royal de L'Afrique Centrale, open Tue–Sun; fee) on the edge of the spacious gardens. The core of the exhibition was provided by Leopold II's Congo Collection. Exhibits on display include a variety of Central African ivory carvings, dancers' masks, weapons, everyday tools, cult objects and sculptures.

The most popular attraction in the museum is a huge pirogue – a boat carved from a single tree trunk – housed in the right wing. The zoological, geological, mineralogical and botanical sections provide a wealth of information about Central Africa, and children of all ages love the dioramas, displaying stuffed crocodiles, antelopes, water buffaloes, rhinoceroses, zebras, lions, giraffes and

Leuven University produced the first Latin version of Thomas More's Utopia in 1516. During World War I, the university's entire archive, consisting of more than 300,000 books, went up in flames.

BELOW: an elephant stands proud outside the Museum of Central Africa in Tervuren.

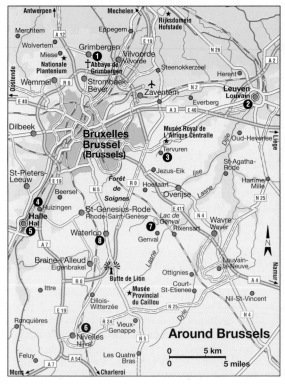

Around Brussels

elephants, all set in mock-ups of their natural habitats. Before leaving the town, it is worth taking a stroll in the **Kapuzinenbos**. Leopold II had a little footpath laid between Tervuren and Jezus-Eik; it's a lovely woodland route, skirting the domain of a former Capuchin monastery. An **Arboretum** was planted here in 1902, harbouring a collection of trees from the temperate zones as well as a number of more exotic specimens.

South of the city

In **Huizingen ❹**, about 15 km (9 miles) southwest of Brussels, there is an extensive park covering an area of 91 hectares (225 acres). It provides an excellent place for recreation, and the magnificent gardens display more than 1,200 species of flowers and plants.

Just south of Huizingen lies the pilgrimage town of **Halle ❺**. The **Basilica of Our Lady**, formerly known as the church of St Martin, is a fine example of Brabant Gothic dating from the 14th century. The tower recalls the fortified towers of many Belgian town halls and weavers' halls. Inside, above the high altar is a wooden statue of Our Lady, carved during the Middle Ages and thought by some to possess miraculous powers. Processions of pilgrims visit the statue of Our Lady at Whitsun and at the beginning of September each year.

Walking country

The region to the south of Brussels is ideal territory for taking extensive country walks. Nestling at the heart of this magnificent landscape lies the town of **Nivelles ❻**, some 35 km (22 miles) from the capital. The town's history is closely linked to that of the **Abbey of St Gertrude**. Founded in the 7th century,

Map on page 154

TIP

If you are interested in the Art Nouveau architecture of Henry van der Velde, his home, Het Nieuwe Huis – built to his own designs – can be found at Albertlaan 3 in Tervuren.

BELOW: the curved and stepped gable roofline on Leuven's Grand-Place.

the abbey is the oldest monastery in Belgium. According to legend, following the death of the Frankish ruler Pepin the Elder, his widow Itta retired with their daughter Gertrude to a villa on the hillside over the Thines valley. After the death of her mother and after an unsuccessful marriage to Dagobert I, Gertrude founded the monastery, at the instigation of Amand, Bishop of Maastricht.

Nowadays, the abbey church is regarded as one of the finest Romanesque church buildings in Belgium. The porch is flanked by two small towers, the "Tour Madame" and the "Tour de Jean de Nivelles". The Tour de Jean de Nivelles contains a bronze statue which has become a symbol of the town and which was donated by the Duke of Burgundy, Charles the Bold.

Inside, a silver reliquary contains the remains of St Gertrude. Each year, on the Sunday following the Feast of St Michael, the bones of St Gertrude are carried in procession along a 12-km (8-mile) route through the town and its immediate surroundings. The tradition has been observed since the 12th century.

The village of Nivelles grew up around the abbey and developed into one of the country's most famous weaving towns. As such, it prospered until well into the 17th century, but fell into economic decline after the Weavers' Uprising and subsequent emigration.

Lake of Dreams

BELOW: St Gertrude's Monastery and church at Nivelles.

A popular weekend outing for the Bruxellois is a stroll around the pleasant **Lac de Genval** ❼ (Genval Lake), combined with a refreshment break at one of the lakeside terraces. It lies southeast of the city on the Wavre road, midway to Louvain-la-Neuve and about a 40-minute journey by train from the Gare Centrale. Genval Lake is not big. You can walk around on Avenue du Lac in about 40 minutes at an easy pace, but the location is idyllic and the lakeside dotted with imposing houses and villas overlooking the water. When the lake, fed by the Argentine stream, was created in 1904, the first villas built replicated famous buildings. For example, the pavilion Rendezvous d'Amour is based on an original at Versailles, while the chalet Le Rütli and the villa Guillaume Tell are based on Swiss buildings associated with William Tell. Swimming is not permitted, although there is boating and fishing, occasionally water-skiing events, and a high fountain, the Genvaloise, that gives the lake the aspect of a miniature Lake Geneva. You continue past Le Blanc Mesnil restaurant, the marina and some waterfront houses, including the villa Guillaume Tell.

Eventually you come to a cluster of restaurants, including Le Caraquin du Lac for Belgian cuisine, and next door Le Shangri-La du Lac, an excellent Chinese restaurant. Just beyond this restaurant, turn right off Avenue du Lac and follow the signs a short distance to the Musée de l'Eau et de la Fontaine (Water and Fountain Museum) (Avenue Hoover 63; open Sat, Sun, pub hols; entrance fee). This is a curious little place, with a collection of fountains, both functional and decorative, as well as old water-pipes, pumps, filters and other hydraulic equipment, plus displays on the problems of water pollution and distribution. Back at the lake, the shoreline is dominated by the

Château du Lac, formerly a Schweppes bottling plant based on the design of an abbey, and now transformed into a 4-star hotel by British brewing magnate John Martin. There is an excellent restaurant, le Trèfle à 4, an amply stocked bar, the Kingfisher Inn, and mineral water from four nearby springs.

Map on page 154

More light relief can be found just outside Wavre, at the Walibi (open Apr–Sep daily; entrance fee) and Aqualibi (open summer daily; winter Tue–Sun; entrance fee) amusement parks. The former is famed for its white-knuckle rides among 40 or so different rides and shows, and the latter is a sub-tropical water theme-park. Beyond Genval, running north across the Wallonia-Flanders line towards Leuven, is the scenic Valley of the River Dijle. Although close to Brussels, it seems almost to be in a different world, a place of attractive little villages, châteaux and farms, with lakes and river views along the way. The road through Sint-Agatha-Rode, Sint-Joris-Weert, 't Zoet Water and Heverlee makes a fine driving or cycling excursion.

Fôret de Soignes

Between Genval, Brussels and Waterloo is the **Fôret de Soignes**, which is more or less a continuation of the city's Bois de la Cambre, except that the forest is much more rugged and such grass as there is is not kept carefully trimmed. There are many paths through the forest and this is a favourite place of escape for the city denizens at weekends and during the summer.

The Fôret de Soignes on the way from Brussels to Waterloo.

One of the most popular attractions in the entire province of Brabant is the battlefield of **Waterloo ❽**, situated some 18 km (11 miles) from the capital. It was here that in June 1815 Napoleon suffered a crushing defeat at the hands of the united forces of Prussia and England (*see pages 159–163*). ❑

BELOW: the Butte de Lion at Waterloo.

WATERLOO

On the battlefield at Waterloo, the combined effort of Anglo-Dutch forces led by Wellington and the Prussian army of Blücher defeated Napoleon, and destroyed his dreams of European domination

Map on page 154

A bout 18 km (11 miles) south of the Belgian capital lies **Waterloo**, where Napoleon, following his period of exile on the island of Elba, attempted to return to the political arena of Europe. He failed dramatically, and in the day-long battle more than 45,000 soldiers were killed or seriously injured and 15,000 horses were slaughtered.

To visit the scene of this epic battle, it is best to begin at the **tourist office** in the centre of Waterloo (Chaussée de Bruxelles 149; open daily). The tourist office hands out free maps of the area, indicating the location of the principal sights, and stocks an array of books describing the events of 18 June 1815. From the tourist office, you can also purchase a ticket that gives access to all the battle-related attractions, such as the Wellington Museum, the Butte de Lion, Napoleon's quarters and the Battle Panorama.

The **Wellington Museum** (Musée Wellington) (open daily; fee) is situated right next door, in the inn in which the Duke stayed on the night preceding the battle. This is well worth a visit, and contains fascinating documents, such as the remarkably courteous messages sent between the Allied commanders and battle plans constructed for the day's military tactics. Opposite the museum is the church of Saint Joseph, which contains memorials to the British soldiers who lost their lives upon the fields of Waterloo.

From the town it is about 3 km (2 miles) to the site of the battle, and there are frequent buses to take you there. Standing proud on the gently sloping fields is the **Butte de Lion** (open daily; fee), which was built in 1826 by the Dutch to commemorate the patch of land where William of Orange was wounded. The butte rises to a height of 45 metres (147 ft), and is surmounted by a 28-tonne lion. The view from the platform just below the paws of this hefty beast is extensive, and most of the tactical sites of the battle can be picked out across the landscape. At the base of the butte is a waxworks museum (Musée de Ceres) and the **Panorama de la Bataille** (open daily; fee), which contains a 360-degree panorama of the battle.

Napoleon spent the night of the 17 June in a farmhouse about 3 km (2 miles) south of the battlefield at Le Caillou. The farmhouse is now a museum, **Musée Provincial du Caillou** (open Tue–Sun; fee). The room that Napoleon used contains a miscellany of mementos relating to the battle and to the Emperor's life, including letters, maps and his bronze death mask.

Battle preparations

The history of the Battle of Waterloo begins on the night of the 14–15 June 1815, as the French army, comprising 125,000 soldiers and 25,000 horses, moved northward towards Brussels. The following

LEFT: a modern-day Napoleon surveys the field of battle.
BELOW: Visitors ascend the Butte de Lion.

The Visitor Centre is at the base of the Butte de Lion, but just next door is the Panorama de la Bataille, which is much more fun.

BELOW: the 360-degree Panorama de la Bataille.

day Napoleon rode through Charleroi. Leaving the town behind him, he rode on to a rise where the road forked left towards Brussels and right towards Fleurus. Here the Emperor came to a standstill. Back on the road, the seemingly endless winding procession was veiled in dust; the heavy tramping sound of thousands of foot soldiers mingled with the rhythmical beating of drums, the shrill blasts of bugles and the echoing cries of *"Vive l'Empéreur!"*

A short time later, Napoleon explained his war strategy to his field marshals and commanders. The English soldiers, under the command of the Duke of Wellington, had stationed themselves around Brussels; the Prussian troops, under Field Marshal Blücher, were approaching from the Rhine. It was vital for Napoleon that these two armies should be prevented from joining forces.

The Battle of Ligny

On Friday, 16 June 1815, Marshal Blücher set up his command post in a windmill at Brye, while Napoleon took up position in a windmill near Fleurus, observing the troop movements of his opponent through a telescope. At 3pm he gave the signal to attack. The Prussian army were dug in at Ligny, hoping that Wellington's troops would reach them during the course of the afternoon. .

Ligny was soon engulfed in a sea of flames under the gunfire of the French. The Prussians waited in vain for reinforcements from the English, and by 10 o'clock that night it was clear that the French, though fewer in number and less well equipped than their opponents, would emerge from the bloodbath victorious. Prussia, having lost the battle but not the war, beat an ordered retreat, marching northward with the intention of joining forces with the English. Wellington and his troops, who had left Brussels the previous night, took up bat-

tle positions on the hill known as Mont St-Jean on the road between Brussels and Charleroi. Their plan was to ward off the French army until Blücher arrived. Wellington himself established his headquarters to the north of his troops, in the village of Waterloo. During the afternoon of 17 June there was a sudden thunderstorm and the ground was turned into a quagmire.

Napoleon reached the Belle Alliance inn, some 9 km (5 miles) south of Waterloo shortly after 6pm. He watched Wellington's troops setting up camp across the valley, then took up quarters himself in the dairy farm called Le Caillou.

The rain looked as if it would never cease. The cavalry soldiers sat huddled in their saddles trying to snatch some sleep. The foot soldiers searched in vain for dry patches in the trampled fields of corn. The camp fires had to be stoked continually with wood. They produced clouds of acrid smoke, but very little warmth. It had been a wasted day, a day for reflection.

Map on page 154

The protagonists

The three leading players in the battle of Waterloo were no strangers to each other. For 20 years, Europe had acted as a stage for their warring. Napoleon Bonaparte, a native of Corsica, was infamous. He had become consul, emperor, ruler of the Continent and beneficiary of the Great Revolution of 1789. But Arthur Wellesley, since 1814 First Duke of Wellington, and Gebhard Leberecht von Blücher, a Pomeranian landowner and field marshal with a pathological hatred of Napoleon, were both revered military men.

Wellington, a tall, slim Irishman, was a typical product of the British aristocracy. He was cool, phlegmatic and a logical tactician. He rarely wore a uniform, and his tailor was considered one of the finest in England.

BELOW: British soldiers march to the field of combat.

*Young visitors
at Waterloo.*

The campaign to defeat Napoleon represented a combined strategy by the Allied Coalition – the seventh formed against France between 1792 and 1815. A total of five armies was involved: an Anglo-Dutch force under Wellington and Blücher's Prussian regiments were to meet near Brussels and converge on France; the Austrians under Karl Philipp von Schwarzenberg were to operate along the Rhine, with the Russians led by Barclay de Tolly in reserve; and an Austro-Italian army commanded by Johann Maria Frimont was to block a retreat from northern Italy.

During the month of June in 1815, the English and Prussian forces spearheaded the attack. Refusing to be discouraged by the defeat at Ligny, during which Blücher was wounded, the Prussians broke camp at Wavre at dawn on 18 June to continue their westward march. Blücher was confident that once they had joined forces with the English army, his soldiers would have little difficulty in defeating Napoleon.

The Battle of Waterloo

Napoleon and his troops also rose early that Sunday morning. The breakfast table was laid before 5am. But, as fate would have it, bad rain impaired visibility and the attack – planned for 9am – was delayed. The gun crews could hardly move the cannon on the muddy ground, even with teams of 15 men and 12 horses per gun. But, despite such unpromising conditions, Napoleon was sure that the final victory would be his: "Gentlemen, if you carry out my orders well, we shall sleep tonight in Brussels," he told them.

At 11.30, from his command post south of the Belle Alliance inn, the emperor gave the signal to attack. The English troops were engulfed in the fire from 120 French cannon. Opposite, in his headquarters at Mont St-Jean, Wellington took shelter under an elm tree, from where he could direct his army.

BELOW: reviving the spirits with a half-time beer.

In the valley between Mont St-Jean and the Belle Alliance lay the ancient manor of Hougoumont to the west and the farmstead of La Haie Sainte to the east, on the road to Brussels; both were occupied by English troops. It was evident that if the French wanted to storm the Mont St-Jean they would need to take both strongholds first.

The attack on Hougoumont had started shortly after 11am; it was a long and bitter battle. At 5pm the French gave up their attempt and retreated. Piled up in front of the manor's perimeter wall was a gruesome heap of corpses – almost 3,000 French soldiers lost their lives in the assault.

In the meantime, at 1pm, Napoleon took a risky decision and ordered his men to attack the centre of the valley. He had already been informed that the Prussian forces were at last approaching, but their imminent arrival did not alter his plan.

The French infantry charged down into the valley in 24 columns – 200 soldiers in each. The English forces waited behind the embrasures of La Haie Sainte or behind the hills. A deadly rain of cannon fire engulfed the manor; to the amazement of the French, thousands of English soldiers suddenly rose up from the crest of the hill and fired their muskets.

The French, even more than their opponents, fought as if in a drunken frenzy. Some of their columns did actually manage to reach the top of the eminence, but the task of killing the enemy became progressively more difficult as the growing mountains of dead soldiers and horses hampered their advance. At 6.30 that evening the French Tricolour was hoisted above La Haie Sainte. Wellington's front at the heart of the Mont St-Jean began to waver. He had no more reserves left. Hopes for the arrival of Blücher and his troops or nightfall were the only comfort he could offer his generals when they demanded fresh supplies.

But Napoleon, too, had only one more reserve battalion when, at about 7.30pm, the first brigades of Prussians reached the battlefield. The emperor sent his personal guard charging down the hill of Belle Alliance, where they were met by the well-aimed fire of the English marksmen. By 8.30pm, Blücher and his entire army had arrived. The French then knew they faced defeat. The cry went up: "Run for your life!", as the Prussians and British careered down the hillside in pursuit of the fleeing soldiers.

At 9.30pm, Wellington and Blücher embraced each other in the courtyard of the Belle Alliance inn. It was a hard-won victory. The Prussian band played "God Save the King" and "*Grosser Gott, wir loben Dich*". In Wellington's words, the outcome of the battle had been "the nearest run thing you ever saw in your life". Just four days afterwards, Napoleon dictated his second abdication in Paris. From there he was sent to the Atlantic island of St Helena.

On 18 June each year, a re-enactment of the battle is played out on the fields of Waterloo. The anniversary of the battle is celebrated with more than 2,000 participants dressed in historical uniforms and carrying muskets. Visitors come from all over the world to witness or take part in this colourful event. ❑

Map on page 154

Whilst writing Les Misérables, *Victor Hugo stayed in Mont St-Jean in order to write his description of the battle.*

BELOW: the French infantry prepare for a last ditch effort.

ANTWERP

Map on page 168

Hugging the eastern bank of the river Scheldt, Antwerp is a lively and amiable city. Its attractions are many and varied, from the diamond life of the gem trade to the artistic legacy of Rubens

By any measure, Antwerp must be one of the most thoroughly underrated cities in Europe, a status that its stint as European Capital of Culture in 1993 did little to alter. Perhaps Antwerp is often overlooked because its identity is split between its many facets. For while Brussels is the European capital, Liège is known as the country's steel centre and Bruges is nicknamed "La Morte" for its museum-like status, Antwerp is many things to many people: a major port, a diamond centre, an industrial nucleus, the city of Rubens, a cultural metropolis, a haven for gourmets and an elegant shopping centre. In Antwerp, medieval charm and modern industry go hand in glove, and if some aspects of life in the city seem somewhat provincial, this tends to be balanced by an insouciant, cosmopolitan air and a healthy degree of tolerance.

The Scheldt has always been Antwerp's lifeline, and the rise and fall of the city's fortunes has followed the tidal rhythm of the river. According to legend, even the name Antwerp is inextricably linked with the river. A giant named Druon Antigon was said to demand high tolls from every ship that passed his castle on the Scheldt. Anyone who refused to pay this fee had a hand chopped off. Eventually, Silvius Brabo, a Roman soldier, mustered the courage to kill the giant. As a final act of good riddance he chopped off Druon Antigon's hand and threw it in the Scheldt. The site where this all took place was called "Antwerpen" – hand-*werpen* (hand-throwing) – by the people of the region. (A modern reminder of the legend is the Brabo Fountain in front of the town hall, erected in 1887.)

In reality, the naming of Antwerp is much more prosaic. The name refers to the city's foundation on an arm of land reaching into the river: *aanworp* or *aanwerpen* means "raised ground".

History

The oldest testimonials about Antwerp date from Gallo-Roman times. Frisians settled on the Scheldt in the 2nd and 3rd centuries AD; Salic Franks followed, building their houses in the north of the city, and in the 7th century, they erected a fortress, which was later destroyed by the Normans in the 9th century. After the fall of France, Antwerp became a possession firstly of Lorraine in 843, and then, in 963, of Germany. At the beginning of the 12th century, the Duke of Brabant took over power in Antwerp.

A wall was then built around the city to protect it from Flanders, which continued to develop its sphere of influence without interference from its French rulers. The Scheldt also acted as a natural barrier against invasion, but neither this nor further fortifications built in the 13th century were able to prevent the city from being annexed by Flanders in 1357.

PRECEDING PAGES: having chopped off the giant's hand, Silvius Brabo threw it into the river. **LEFT:** a delicate operation to restore a monument. **BELOW:** the city's cathedral.

*Carved with pride –
a sign for the city of
Antwerp beneath the
station clock.*

The Flemish had had their eye on Antwerp, which had received its city charter at the end of the 12th century, for a long time. The city on the Scheldt could not hold a candle to Bruges, then at the optimum point of its flowering, but its port was experiencing a new phenomenon – the arrival of increasing numbers of ships from Venice and Genoa. With the birth of the Flemish weaving industry, the city became a vast warehouse for English wool and prospered accordingly. The splendour of the church of Our Lady, which was begun in 1352, reflected the city's pride and sense of well-being. The cathedral, which was finished 170 years later, is one of the largest in the world.

In 1406, under the Dukes of Burgundy, Antwerp was reunified with Brabant and was on its way to becoming the major port of western Europe. Protected by its new rulers, and with the silting up of the port of Bruges benefiting Antwerp still further, the city entered a golden age. By 1560, the city had a population of 100,000. More than 100 ships entered and left the port every day, and over 1,000 foreign businessmen conducted their commercial affairs from Antwerp. Booming trade was reflected in a corresponding growth of industry: textile factories, sugar refineries, soap-makers, breweries, diamond-cutters and book publishers all prospered. In 1532, the city opened a stock exchange. Many guilds built splendid houses on the marketplace to display their wealth and status.

Drawn by Antwerp's wealth, famous artists and scientists also came to settle along the Scheldt. They included Christoph Plantin, the greatest book printer of his time; painters such as Otto Venius, Quentin Massys and Pieter Breughel; Gérard Mercator – the famous Flemish geographer and map-maker – and classicist and humanist Justus Lipsius. The writer Anna Bijns, and sculptors Pieter Coecke van Aalst and Corelis de Vriendt also made their way to Antwerp.

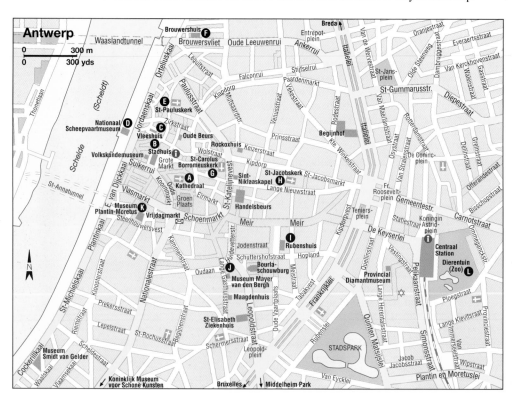

Map on page 168

The new belief

Antwerp's flowering was curtailed by the advent of Protestantism. Under William the Silent the city became the centre of the revolt against the Catholic Church and Spanish political authority. In 1566, the city's cathedral was ransacked by ardent Calvinists, who, with an iconoclastic fervour, destroyed many of the precious works of art housed there. Revenge came ten years later, when Spanish forces under Charles V's fanatical son, Philip II, attacked the city in 1576, killing, looting and burning all around them. The episode, which became known as the "Spanish Mutiny", cost 8,000 lives. The Spanish forces were driven out in the following year, and the public practice of Catholicism was outlawed in Antwerp. But the Spanish returned, and in 1585 Alessandro Farnese forced the city to its knees in a siege which lasted seven months.

The punishments that the Spaniards meted out to adherents of the new belief were so ghastly that the residents of Antwerp left the city in droves. To top it all, the navigation of the river Scheldt fell into the hands of the Dutch, starting a mass exodus from Antwerp. In 1582, there were still 83,700 people living in the city; by 1589, the number had fallen to just 42,000. The city's role as an economic centre of Europe was abruptly terminated.

The city then descended into a long period of depression. James Howell's "Letter to Sir James Crofts, 5th July 1619" described the changed character of Antwerp vividly. "This goodly ancient City methinks looks like a disconsolate Widow, or rather some super-annuated Virgin, that hath lost her Lover, being almost quite bereft of that flourishing Commerce wherewith before the falling off the rest of the Provinces from Spain she abounded to the envy of all other Cities and Marts of Europe."

The Guild of St Luke, founded in the mid-15th century by Philip the Good, is attributed with the birth of the Flemish School, which spawned the rich tradition of painting in the region.

BELOW: the bustle of the city centre.

Various boat trips explore the waterways of the Scheldt and the historic port, offering an insight into the development of Antwerp. Boats sail from the harbour behind the Steen Maritime Museum.

BELOW: Rubenshuis – former home of Peter Paul Rubens and now a museum dedicated to the great painter.

Legendary artists

Despite the economic decline, the fine arts continued to flourish. In the first half of the 17th century, the chief painter of the baroque, **Peter Paul Rubens**, painted his masterpieces in Antwerp. The artist, who managed to achieve fame and fortune in his own lifetime, had a house built for himself on the Wapper. Today the Rubens House, containing paintings by Rubens and a reconstruction of his apartment, is a place of pilgrimage for fans of baroque painting.

As well as Rubens, both **Anthony van Dyck** and **Jakob Jordaens the Elder** lived and worked on the Scheldt. The city has immortalised all three of these artists in stone: Rubens' statue stands on Groen Square, van Dyck's on the Meir, and Jordaens' on the bank of the Scheldt. Two other artists who were inspired by Antwerp's cosmopolitan character were the sculptor **Artus Quellin** and the well-known woodcarver **Christoffel Jegher**. Many of their works can be seen in the churches and museums of Antwerp.

An agreement signed by the Spanish at the end of the Thirty Years War in 1648 effectively ruined Antwerp by cutting off its lifeline: the Scheldt was closed to traffic, and without the blood of trade, the city withered. Economic well-being didn't return to Antwerp until the18th century. The French, who after a brief interval of Austrian rule became masters of the city in 1792, opened up the river Scheldt once more; under Napoleon Bonaparte, the port was built up as a base for the French navy. For Napoleon, Antwerp was a prized possession, "a pistol aimed at the heart of England", as he described it.

The docks and jetties which Napoleon built proved extremely valuable to the city. Antwerp's trade with overseas colonies was stepped up, particularly under the Dutch, who took over from the French.

Map on page 168

The port grows

In 1830, the Belgian Revolution put an end to this economic upswing. Belgium had won its independence, but the mouth of the Scheldt still lay in the hands of the Dutch. Only when the Scheldt Tax was lifted in 1863 was it possible to continue the expansion of the port begun by Napoleon.

In 1881, the former city centre had to give way to the expanding port. More than 800 houses and the old landing-place were demolished. To compensate, brand-new buildings, streets, alleys and squares were erected elsewhere. The Palace of Justice, the National Bank, the Royal Gymnasium and the former City Theatre are examples of the architecture typical of this period. In the course of expansion, Antwerp was provided with running water, gas and electricity.

With this expansion, the city's finances and its fine arts experienced a renaissance. Artists such as Leys, de Keyser, Verlat, Wappers and de Braekeler comprised a famous school of Antwerp painters. Peter Benoit, Jan Blockx and Emiel Wambach gave new impetus to music, while authors such as Willems, van Rijswijck, Snieders and Conscience wrote their greatest works in the city. In 1885 and 1894, Antwerp was the location of major world exhibitions.

During World War I, the Belgian government initially fled to Antwerp from Brussels, but in the face of further German advances they were forced to set sail for Ostend. The two world wars postponed the city's development, but in the postwar period the city experienced another economic boom, as capital from overseas streamed into Antwerp. Today, in the north of the city, refineries, chemical plants, shipbuilders and automobile factories crowd together. The port stretches to the Dutch border. Its half a million inhabitants and 520 sq km (200 sq mile) area make Antwerp Belgium's second largest city.

Antwerp has God to thank for the Scheldt, and the Scheldt to thank for everything else.

— LOCAL SAYING

BELOW: vessels large and small on the broad river Scheldt.

Rubens

Peter Paul Rubens was northern Europe's greatest baroque artist. Having developed a taste for baroque expression during a lengthy stay in Italy, he unleashed his prodigious talent upon the gentry and courts of northern Europe, from his return to Antwerp in 1608 until his death 32 years later.

Rubens was born in Germany in 1577, the son of a successful Antwerp merchant, who as a Protestant was forced to flee from Catholic persecution which had engulfed his native city. Following his father's death, Rubens and his mother returned to Antwerp in 1587, where Peter was raised as a devout Catholic. He studied painting with Otto van Veen, who probably encouraged his young protégé to visit Italy, as he himself had done.

As a new century dawned, Rubens set off on a southward quest to the artistic centres of Italy. There, the young artist devoured his new aesthetic environment, absorbing the major works from the Italian Renaissance.

He studied the works of Leonardo and Michelangelo, Titian and Veronese, as well as the paintings of his near contemporaries Annibale Carracci and Caravaggio.

In Italy, Rubens found a style and a confidence, he excelled in his own work and soon became a match for the best of the Italians. Indeed, he may well have extended his career in Italy, but in 1608 Rubens returned to Antwerp, because of the death of his mother. His stay was to have been brief, but his work received such immediate acclaim in high circles that to leave proved impossible. He also married in 1609, further establishing his ties with Antwerp.

The vitality of Rubens was extraordinary. Physically energetic and intellectually adroit, he mustered a prolific output of paintings across a broad range of themes, completing commissions for courts throughout Europe and for the Catholic Church. The triptych *The Raising of the Cross* (1609–10) within the cathedral in Antwerp was one of his first major commissions back within his home city. In the muscular bodies and dramatic fall of light across the composition one can sense Rubens' empathy with the Italian spirit. But his meticulous rendering of the surrounding greenery and startling clarity of a foreground dog reveal the influence of the Flemish tradition of heightened realism.

To meet the burden of an ever-growing demand for his work, Rubens developed a factory-like studio, with apprentices doing much of the ground work on his paintings once he had sketched out each composition. As such, connoisseurs sometimes favour his drawings and sketches in paint, where the hand of Rubens can be assured throughout. But to deny the finished article, whether largely or partially completed by Rubens, is to neglect his vision for the epic theatre of the large canvas, the passion and vital strength engendered into figures that represent the full intensity of life. In the finished work, we see the romantic heart of Italian baroque, full of drama and bursting with life, married with the studied devotion to the tangible substance of the world, inherent in the northern tradition. Rubens never returned to Italy, arguably his spiritual home, but he frequently signed himself "Pietro Pauolo". ❑

LEFT: Rubens' *Descent from the Cross.*

The city's sights

The city on the Scheldt is a marvellously vibrant place, whose populace is dedicated to living life stylishly and to the full. Antwerp fairly bubbles with energy. As with all Flemish cities, most of the action is around the main square, the Grote Markt, with its 16th-century guildhouses and Flemish Renaissance town hall. The elegant ensemble is overlooked by the soaring (in this case the adjective is not overstated) spire of the Onze-Lieve-Vrouwekathedraal (Cathedral of Our Lady) in nearby Handschoenmarkt. These two squares are ably supported in the old centre by Groenmarkt and Vrijdagmarkt. In and around these focal points, as well as along the Scheldt waterfront which fringes them, there are masses of restaurants, bars and clubs, many of which are both notable and highly individualistic. In good weather they spread the terraces out onto the cobbles, and after dark the whole area glows with bonhomie.

The great harbour begins only a mile or so north of the Grote Markt yet it could just as easily be on another planet for all the visible impact it has inside the city proper. Between the two is a relatively tranquil area, characterised by the Sint-Jacobskerk (Saint James's Church), the University and the old Begijnhof. At the boundary is a line of former harbour warehouses which have been renovated and one of which houses the Museum of Modern Art. Southwards from the centre, at Leopold de Waelplaats, lies the Koninklijke Museum voor Schone Kunsten (Royal Fine Arts Museum). Eastwards, at the end of the Meir and de Keyserlei, is Centraal Station, looking more like a great temple than a railway station, and beside it the world famous Antwerp Zoo. This area also sparkles as the Diamond Quarter, centre of Antwerp's most glittering industry. First-time visitors should begin their sightseeing in the **Old City**. The heart of the historical centre is the **Kathedraal Ⓐ** (cathedral, open Mon–Fri; Sat 1–4pm; Sun 1–9pm; entrance fee) With its seven aisles, 125 pillars and a 123-metre (400-ft) high tower, this cathedral is the largest and most beautiful Gothic church in Belgium. Its construction took from 1352 to 1521, and the finishing touch was the slender tower. On Monday evenings in summer its beloved carillon of bells attracts crowds.

Inside the cathedral, you can see a wealth of masterpieces by Rubens: in the transept, you will find the *Crucifixion* to the left and the *Descent from the Cross* to the right. The altarpiece in the choir depicts the *Assumption of the Virgin*, also by Rubens. Although a fire in 1533, a spate of iconoclasm in 1566, and the French occupation were responsible for the loss of a whole group of irreplaceable ornaments, the cathedral still houses many artistic treasures: as well as valuable paintings, it contains magnificent tombs, marvellous sculptures, fine woodcarvings and impressive examples of stained-glass painting.

The old alleys and squares around the cathedral are interesting places in which to wander. Residents are particularly proud of the **Vlaeykensgang**, an alley and courtyard which has been restored in the style of the 16th century. It can be reached from the **Oude Koornmarkt**, a square containing a wide range of restaurants, pubs and cafés. Gourmets take note: the entire Old City is full of excellent eating establish-

Map on page 168

The golden clock high up on the city's cathedral.

BELOW: detail on a Rubens painting.

An exhibit at the Nationaal Scheepvaartmuseum, the national maritime museum.

ments. Sample the local specialities: mussels, prepared in a number of ways, stewed eel in chervil sauce or meat casserole. You'll find a number of characteristic Antwerp pubs selling good local beers in the **Suikerrui** and on the **Handschoenmarkt**, at the foot of the cathedral.

Creating a strong architectural contrast to the venerable cathedral is the nearby **Torengebouw** bank building, a soaring modern edifice. It is 100 metres (more than 300 ft) and 27 storeys high. Built in the 1920s, it was the first skyscraper in Europe. There is a wonderful view of the city centre from the top floor.

Turning northwest from the church of Our Lady, you'll come to the **Grote Markt** and the Brabo Fountain, town hall and guild houses. The stately Renaissance **Stadhuis** **B** (town hall, open Mon–Sat; guided tours until 3pm; entrance fee) with its marble facade and richly decorated rooms was built between 1561 and 1565, according to plans by Cornelis de Briendt; it combines Flemish and Italian stylistic elements. Most of the guild houses, which have been painstakingly restored over the last few years, also date from this period. With these splendid buildings, influential guilds, such as the archers, grocers, carpenters, and tailors, erected monuments to their respective trades.

On Gildekamersstraat, behind the town hall, you will find the **Museum of Folk Culture** (open Tue–Sun), presenting the customs and traditions of old Flanders. Only a few steps away, the **Vleeshuis** **C** (open Tue–Sun; entrance fee), built as a butcher's market and guild house, today accommodates a museum of arts and crafts and local history. The house of the butchers' guild, its "bacon streaks" of red brick and white sandstone carefully restored to their original glory, is one of the most remarkable secular buildings in all Antwerp. What is particularly notable about its interior is an extensive collection of musical instruments. If you would like to hear what these sound like, investigate the dates of the concerts which regularly take place in the museum.

Southwest of St Paul's church, where the Venetian and Genoese ships once anchored, you'll come upon the oldest building in Antwerp: the Steen. Built in the 12th century, this castle is now the location of the **Nationaal Scheepvaartmuseum** **D** (Steen National Maritime Museum, open Tue–Sun; entrance fee; tel: (03) 232 0850). Here, model ships, old land maps and sea charts, and historical instruments of navigation document Antwerp's centuries-old connection with the sea and shipping.

Right next to the Steen the white excursion steamers of the shipping company Flandria put to sea. Interested visitors can take a tour of the Scheldt of either 50 or 80 minutes' duration. Alternatively you can opt for a two-hour tour of the port or choose one of the various day excursions available. Day trips to the mouth of the Scheldt, to the river Rhine or through the coastal delta are particularly popular, especially as Flandria is well known for its first-class service.

Halfway between Vleeshuis and Brouwershuis stands the magnificent 16th-century **St-Pauluskerk** **E** (church of St Paul's, open May–Sep daily; Oct–Apr a.m. only), in which elements of Gothic, Renaissance (tower) and baroque (interior) are harmoniously juxtaposed. The former Dominican church contains

BELOW: the exterior of the Vleeshuis.

many paintings by Rubens, Jordaens and van Dyck, as well as Artus Quellin's statue of St Rosa of Lima and his wonderful *Stations of the Cross*.

Less centrally located, but no less interesting, is the **Brouwershuis** ❻ (open Tue–Sun; entrance fee) on Adriaan Brouwerstraat, near the port. This was where, in the 16th century, water was drawn for the breweries in the area. In the lowest storey you can still see the horse-mill with the aid of which the complicated machinery was set in motion. Forty metal buckets scooped up water and transported it to the upper storey, from where it was piped to the various breweries. It is worth looking in on the ornately decorated conference room in which the brewers continued to hold their annual meetings until relatively recently.

The old masters

The **Koninklijk Museum voor Schone Kunsten** (Royal Museum of Fine Arts, open Tue–Sun; entrance fee; tel: (03) 238 7809) on Leopold de Waelplaats spans the complete history of art. The collection of Flemish painting takes up a considerable part of the museum. The first floor has over 1,000 works by old masters, including such famous works as *The Adoration of the Magi* by Rubens, the *Entombment of Christ* by Quentin Matsys, and the *Seven Sacraments* by Rogier van der Weyden. With some 20 paintings by Rubens, reflecting virtually every period of his creative output, this museum holds the most remarkable collection of Rubens works in the world.

More recent painting is also well represented in the museum. Some 1,500 paintings and sculptures in the collection date from the 19th and 20th centuries. As well as well-known works by international artists, the surrealistic pictures of the Belgians René Magritte and Paul Delvaux are particularly worthy of note.

Map on page 168

BELOW: Rubens' magnificent altarpiece in St-Carolus Borromeuskerk.

Another jewel in the old city is the **St-Carolus Borromeuskerk ⒼⒼ** (church of St Charles Borromeo, open daily; closed to tourists during services; entrance fee), built between 1614 and 1621 in the so-called Jesuit baroque style after plans by Huyssens and Aguilon. Rubens is said to have been responsible for the design of the main facade. Thirty-nine ceiling paintings by Rubens were destroyed in a fire in this church in 1718. Three of his altar paintings, however, have been preserved, as well as carved-wood confessionals from the 18th century and some magnificent statues of angels. The Chapel of Our Lady also survived unscathed, as did the graceful tower and the facade.

Several hundred metres to the east of the Jesuit church towers the Gothic **St-Jacobskerk Ⓗ** (St Jacob's church, open summer Mon–Sat; winter until noon; entrance fee), where the foremost families of the city buried their loved ones. Rubens is among those buried here. His altar painting of the Holy Family was originally designed for his funereal chapel. Containing as it does paintings by virtually all the great Flemish masters, valuable sculptures and ornate items of gold and brass, the church outdoes even the cathedral in artistic wealth.

Belgium is keen to augment Antwerp's reputation as a diamond centre. Relaxed import and export laws and various tax concessions make the Belgian diamond trade particularly lucrative.

Chips and beer

Proceeding south from St Jacob's church, you'll come to the **Meir**, which divides the old city, surrounded by broad avenues, into two parts. The Meir and **De Keyserlei**, which leads to the main railway station, are Antwerp's two leading shopping streets. The people of Antwerp love to stroll along the "shopping mile", and then relax in one of the streets' excellent cafés. Order a *handje* (sandwich) and one of Antwerp's famous beers: a light Pintje, a strong Bolleke, or a dark, heavy beer.

BELOW: the steady hands of a diamond cutter.

THE GLITTER OF PRECIOUS STONES

Bruges was Belgium's first diamond trading centre. In the 13th century, the precious stones were taken there from Venice, which had exclusive trading rights with India, where the diamonds were mined. By the 15th century, the trade had spread to the city of Antwerp, which soon became the leading economic and diamond centre of Europe. Since then there has been intermittent rivalry with Amsterdam for pole position, but from the 1950s Antwerp has led the world in this glittering trade.

Nowhere else can you find so many different diamond cutters, exchanges and shops in such a small vicinity as in the "Diamond Quarter" of Antwerp, at edge of the old town. Six schools are devoted to teaching the skills of diamond cutting and the High Diamond Council ensures standards of quality, judged upon carat, colour, clarity and cut. Carat is a measure of weight (deriving from carob beans – the original unit of measurement); colour varies from black to pink, but clear stones are the most highly valued; clarity is a measure of purity, and cut is judged on symmetry and the clean intersection of facets. The **Provincial Diamond Museum** (Lange Herentalsstraat 31) and the **Grobbendonk Diamond Museum** (Bovenpad 3a, Grobben-donk) offer a glimpse into the world of hot rocks and diamond cuts.

On the other side of the Meir, you can follow in Rubens' footsteps to the **Rubenshuis** ❶ (open Tue–Sun; entrance fee; tel: (03) 232 4751) on Rubensstraat. The painter had the house built in 1610. It was not acquired by the authorities until the middle of the 20th century, by which time it was virtually derelict. Now it has been turned into a museum devoted to the artist; the studio where he worked and taught and the living apartments have been carefully restored. The apartment in the left wing of the house is soberly decorated in the old Flemish style, but the studio demonstrates the more lively spirit of the baroque. Ten works by Rubens are on display in the house, including *Adam and Eve in Paradise*, a work painted in his youth.

Don't neglect to take a look at the garden. The imposing portico which divides the inner courtyard from the garden makes an appearance in many of Rubens' pictures. It's assumed that the artist designed this portal himself.

You can enjoy more art in the nearby **Museum Mayer van den Bergh** ❶ (open Tue–Sun; entrance fee) on Lange Gasthuisstraat. Located in a former patrician home, the museum bears the name of a wealthy Antwerp citizen who bequeathed his unique art collection to his native city. High points of the collection are two paintings by Pieter Breughel: the *Dulle Griet*, one of his most striking works, and the *Twelve Sayings*, an early piece.

Just next door, you'll find the **Maagdenhuis** (open Tue–Sat), once an orphanage, today a museum with wonderful faience pieces from the 16th century and valuable paintings, sculptures, and other ornaments from the 15th century. A few steps further on, you come to the **St Elisabeth Hospital**, which is supposed to have been founded in the year 1204. If you go a little further down the Lange Gasthuisstraat with its attractive, historical facades, and then bear left, you'll

Map on page 168

TIP

For current information on things to do and places to visit, there are two tourist offices: one at Karel Oomsstraat 11, and the local office at Grote Markt 15.

BELOW: exhibits in the Rubenshuis.

come to the **Oude Vaartplaats**, where Antwerp's most famous market, the **Bird Market**, is held every Sunday morning. Everything from animals and plants to food and clothing and art and kitsch changes hands at this market. In the evening this area is a popular meeting-place: its many cafés, bars and pubs have earned this neighbourhood the nickname of *Quartier Latin*.

The **Beguine Convent**, on Rodestraat, is rarely visited by tourists. But this 16th-century group of alleyways, cottages and gardens is an oasis of peace and quiet amidst the bustling city.

Old books and modern art

Bibliophiles should certainly include in their itinerary the **Museum Plantin-Moretus ⓚ** (open Tue–Sun; entrance fee), a handsome Renaissance building on Vrijdagmarkt, only a few hundred metres from the Steen. The house has been turned into a museum celebrating the golden age of Antwerp. You can see the original printing presses (still functioning) and typesetting equipment, stroll through an old Flemish patrician apartment and browse over old manuscripts and books, copper-plate engravings and woodcuts. Particular gems of the collection are the 13 copies of the 36-line Gutenberg Bible and the *Biblia Regia*. If you schedule your visit to this museum on a Wednesday or Friday, you can also visit the **Friday Market** (Vrijdagmarkt). Twice a week, antiques and knick-knacks are auctioned off to the highest bidder.

Those interested in modern sculpture may find something to their taste in the **Middelheim Park** in the south of the city. Here, some 300 famous works of contemporary sculptors from Rodin to Moore can be viewed in the open air. Every two years, between June and September, this open-air museum is also the

Alongside the arte-facts of early print-ing in the Museum Plantin-Moretus are several portraits of members of the Plantin-Moretus family, several of which are by Rubens.

BELOW: face to face at Antwerp's Museum of Folk Culture.

site of the Sculpture Biennial, which is well regarded in the international art world. Jazz festivals also take place regularly in Middelheim.

If you're in the mood for something completely different after seeing so much art and architecture, a visit to the **Antwerp Zoo** ❶ (open daily; entrance fee; tel: (03) 202 4540), with its aquarium, dolphin house, reptile house and planetarium, could be just what you need to revive. Located next to the main railway station, this zoological garden is one of the most beautiful in the world. More than 6,000 animals of 950 different species live in conditions as near to their natural habitats as possible. The so-called Nocturama, dedicated to nocturnal animals, is of particular interest.

A special Children's Zoo opened in 1984; the antics of the young raccoons, nimble squirrels and other animals seem to divert even the most fractious children. In the winter, the zoo allows visitors to take a look behind the scenes.

East of the main railway station, the **Jewish Quarter** stretches between the Avenue Frankrijklei, the zoo and the Koning Albert Park. Antwerp, which is sometimes nicknamed "the Jerusalem on the Scheldt", has the largest Orthodox Jewish community in Europe. Fifteen thousand Jews in the city live in observance of strict religious laws; there are 22 synagogues in Antwerp. Hasidic jews with long black coats, broad-brimmed hats, long beards and side curls are a common sight on the streets around the railway station. When the sabbath begins on Friday evenings a host of candles illuminate the windows of this district. In Pelikanstraat and the streets around it, there are many small shops which sell kosher groceries, Hebrew books and menorahs. One of Antwerp's four diamond exchanges is also located on **Pelikanstraat**. The Jewish community is extensively involved in Antwerp's diamond trade and industry.   ❑

Map on page 168

A rearing statue in gold balances atop a gabled roof in Antwerp.

BELOW: eating mussels in Antwerp.

Map
on page
181

Brussels●

AROUND ANTWERP

It's well worth exploring outside the densely packed centre of Antwerp. Communities on the outskirts are steeped in history, and close by are interesting towns such as Lier and Mechelen

L ike so many other major cities, Antwerp has expanded its boundaries at the expense of surrounding towns. Today, the city is made up of 10 boroughs which still bear the names of the autonomous communities they once were.

The district of **Hoboken** ❶, to the south of the city, has four admirable palaces, including the rococo castle **Sorgvliedt**, as well as parks and the late Gothic **church of Our Lady**. Hoboken is highly thought of in Japan, apparently, because of the sad little tale of Nello and his faithful dog Patrasche, who drove their milk-cart from Hoboken to Antwerp every day. This children's story – called *A Dog of Flanders* and written by Marie-Louise de la Ramée in 1871 – was a best-seller in Japan long before its discovery and subsequent rise to fame in Belgium. Nello and Patrasche have since been immortalized with their own memorial opposite Hoboken's tourist information centre.

For years residents of **Wilrijk** ❷ have been known as "goatheads", a nickname which sprang from the long tradition of goat-raising in the town. This is not to say that Wilrijk, originally a Roman settlement, is without any architectural interest, however: there is, for example, the magnificent 15th-century **Iepermann Castle** and the Gothic **church of St Bavon's**.

Berchem ❸ is well known far beyond the city limits for the **Zurenborg Quarter**, where, at the turn of the century, art nouveau and all manner of subsequent derivatives originated. One of the main attractions in the town of **Deurne** ❹ is the museum, in which 19th-century workers' apartments have been faithfully reconstructed; but the town is best known for its "giants". Every September, giant puppets are carried through the streets. A similar festival takes place in nearby Borgerhout, where the giants, slightly smaller than those in Deurne, dance to the music of a band.

Geese are the centre of attention during the "goose riding", held during Carnival and on Easter Sunday in **Zandvliet** and **Berendrecht**. The festivities attract thousands of visitors to the two cities, which, despite the continuing expansion of the port, have managed by and large to preserve much of their local character.

Heavenly rainfall

The main sights in **Ekeren** ❺ are a moated castle from the 16th century and the 500-year-old **church of St Lambert** with its towers of white sandstone. Local legend has it that many years ago a heavy hailstorm struck Ekeren and after the storm the hailstones in one area instead of melting remained lying on the ground in the shape of a cross. The population interpreted this as a holy sign and renamed the place "hailcross". Every year a festive parade is held on the site of the miracle, today marked by a stone cross.

BELOW: a riverside view of Lier.

Driving south

On the border of the Kempen, where the Great and Lesser Nete intersect, the town of **Lier** ❻ lies only 17 km (10 miles) away from Antwerp. Local wisdom has it that Lier's residents declined a university in favour of a cattle-market. This story is said to have resulted in their nickname "sheepheads". But Lier isn't devoid of culture. The birthplace of the Flemish author Félix Timmermans, it gained worldwide renown under the pseudonym "Lierke Plezierke". The writer erected a literary monument to this city and to the Flemish way of life in his works. The **Timmermans-Opsomer House** (open Apr–Oct, Tue–Thur, Sat & Sun; Nov–Mar, Sun only; entrance fee) in the old manor of van Geertruyen is dedicated to him and to other artists who were born in Lier.

Opposite this, on the other side of the Lesser Nete, stands the main sightseeing attraction of Lier: the **Zimmer Tower** (open daily; entrance fee), named after the clockmaker and astronomer Louis Zimmer. The tower, which once belonged to the medieval fortifications of the city, has housed the astronomical studio with planetarium and Zimmer's Jubilee Clock since 1930. The clockwork of Zimmer's timepiece is a masterpiece of human precision. Its 13 dials are clearly visible on the building's facade.

Lier became a city as early as 1212. The one-time clothmaking community still retains much of its original plan. Its chief attractions are located close together: the Gothic Saint Gummarus church (1425–1520), with its imposing tower and many artistic treasures; the **Grote Markt** (main square) with its rococo **Stadhuis** (town hall) and the **Bell Tower** from the year 1369; the **Vleeshuis**, from 1418; and the medieval **Beguine Convent**. Founded in the 13th century, expanded in the 17th, and still in an extremely good condition, the

TIP

Try and coordinate a visit to Lier in time to see the clockwork figures on the Zimmer Tower, which come out at midday.

BELOW: the Zimmer Tower in Lier.

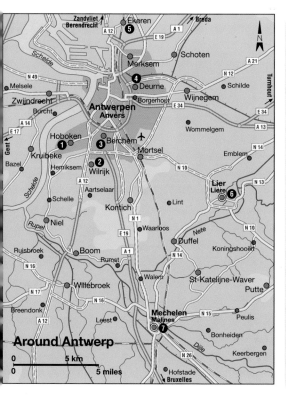

Around Antwerp

0   5 km
0   5 miles

Beguine Convent is a town unto itself. A stroll through its narrow alleyways, past the low houses and picturesque corners, transports the visitor from the modern day to the fictional world of Felix Timmermans.

Tall stories

Only 23 km (14 miles) from the gates of Antwerp lies **Mechelen** ❼ (Malines). Mechelen can look back on a glorious past; today, it is known as the city of the bells and has made a name for itself as a carpet producer and a centre for market gardening. The Emperor Charles V grew up in this city, which was an enclave of the diocese of Liège in the Middle Ages. After 1356, it belonged to Flanders. In 1473, Mechelen became the base of the highest court in the Low Countries, the Great Council; shortly thereafter, it was made the capital of the Burgundian Low Countries, and was the epitome of splendour and glamour. The Emperor Charles's guardian in the Netherlands, Margaret of Austria, resided in Mechelen from 1507 to 1530. In 1559, Mechelen became the religious centre of Belgium. The primate of the Catholic Church resides in Mechelen.

Mechelen's main symbol is the mighty **Saint Rombout's cathedral** (open daily; entrance fee), the construction of which began in the 13th century, but was not completed until 200 years later. The church tower was to have extended to a massive height of 167 metres (546 ft), but in the end, construction stopped at 97 metres (317 ft). Anyone who climbs this tower can enjoy a wonderful view over the city. The citizens' pride in their tower may be responsible for a story that they once tried to reach the moon – their curious aim being to put out its light. Ever since this story came about, the inhabitants of Mechelen have been referred to as *maneblussers* – moon-extinguishers.

BELOW: the cloth hall in the town of Mechelen.
RIGHT: a funfair on Mechelen's market place.

Inside the cathedral you will find a wealth of marble altars, ornate tombs, paintings by Flemish masters – including a *Crucifixion* by van Dyck – and baroque decoration, some of it the work of Artus Quellin. But the church is best known for its carillon. Since 1981 the tower has had two sets of bells; the new carillon, with 49 bells, is not only the heaviest in Europe, it is said to be the richest in tone, as well. You can judge for yourself during the Monday evening concerts in the summer, when the bells of the cathedral, the **church of Our Lady Across the Dyle**, and the **Hof van Busleyden** ring out.

Mechelen is said to be the cradle of the Flemish carillon. In Russian, the word for carillon translates as something like "bells from Mechelen". The Internationaal Hoger Instituut voor Beiaardkunst is the place where would-be bell-ringers from around the world are trained to become masters of their profession. Mechelen's enthusiasm for bell-ringing is such that the city even has a mobile carillon for processions.

The cathedral is not the only souvenir of the city's glory days: there are also several other buildings of note, including the **Palace of Margaret of Austria**, today's Palace of Justice, built in 1520; the old **Assizes** (today the City Archive); the late Gothic Hof van Busleyden, now the city **museum** (open Tue–Sun; entrance fee); and many splendid churches. The city's town hall is located in the former Cloth Hall (14th century) in the **Palace of the Great Council**. Its construction lasted nearly 400 years, until the beginning of the 20th century. A statue of Margaret of Austria stands on a pedestal in the square in front of the building. The impression that she is giving the building the cold shoulder rather than standing sentinel is explained by the fact that the council used to meet on the other side of the marketplace, where the main post office stands today. ❑

Map on page 181

Mechelen's St-Janskerk is also worth a visit, not least because of the Rubens triptych that can be seen there, the Adoration of the Magi, *1619.*

BELOW: Van Dyck's *Christ on the Cross* in St Rombout's cathedral.

GHENT

*Built over the waterways of the Leie and the Scheldt, Ghent's
historical centre of meandering alleyways and elegant buildings
is surrounded by a vibrant city of industry and maritime trade*

Map
on page
188

Ghent (Gent), the capital of the province of East Flanders and harbouring a population of 250,000, has for centuries been the focal point of the Flemish nationality. As is the case with other major Flemish cities, Ghent owes its historical importance to the cloth trade. The city flourished during the Middle Ages, and there was even a period, around the turn of the 14th century, when it was the second largest city north of the Alps; only Paris was then bigger. Today it is the third largest industrial region in Belgium and the country's second largest port; its harbour is connected to the North Sea by canal. The city's economy revolves around the chemical, steel and automobile industries, as well as publishing and banking.

One of the first of many visitors to liken the city to Venice was the diarist John Evelyn. In 1641 he wrote that "the Ley and the Scheld meeting in this vast Citty divide it into 26 Ilands which are united togethere by many bridges somewhat resembling Venice." Thackeray, ever a cynic, was less flattering in 1844, referring disparagingly to the city's "dirty canals and old houses", whilst noting that it possessed "more beershops than any city I ever saw".

PRECEDING PAGES:
cruising on the river
Leie in Ghent.
LEFT: Korenlei from
the bridge by the
Vleeshuis.
BELOW: the
Triomphante Bell,
with the cloth hall
in the background.

The view from on high

On arrival in Ghent, it is a good idea first to ascend the **Belfort ❹** (bell tower, open Tue–Sun; entrance fee) and survey the layout of the city, which spreads over 13 islands at the confluence of the Scheldt, Leie and Lieve rivers. Should your legs not feel up to the 90 metre (300 ft) climb, there is an elevator.

The tower, a symbol of the freedom of the citizens of Ghent, has been crowned with a gilded dragon since the 14th century. In the Middle Ages, the tower represented the power of the city guilds, and its bell (named Klokke Roeland) was said to "send a storm throughout the country" whenever it tolled to call the Ghent citizens to arms. At the foot of the tower is the Triomfante Bell, the 17th-century successor to Klokke Roeland; the Triomfante cracked in 1914.

The Gothic **cloth hall** (open daily; entrance fee) once housed the inspection commission for the cloth weavers who were responsible for Ghent's economic well-being. Today, a visitor to the hall can watch the audiovisual documentary *Ghent and the Emperor Charles V*. The film relates the history of Charles V, who was born and raised in Ghent. With territories in South America captured by his mother, the Infanta of Spain Joanna of Castille, Charles was able to boast that the sun never set on his empire. Despite his Flemish origins, Ghent temporarily rose up against Charles in 1639; only to herald his return to the city with a six-hour triumphal parade the following year.

The bell tower's "Klokke Roeland".

Near the cloth hall, you'll find the 16th-century town hall, the **Stadhuis** Ⓑ (open in the summer for guided tours only, Mon–Fri afternoons; entrance fee; tel: (09) 223 9922) which is built partly in the style of Flemish late Gothic, with additional features in Renaissance style. The building's dark, ornate facade is an impressive sight, embellished as it is with countless sculpted figures and ghoulish ornaments.

However unified the massive block of the town hall may appear from without, its interior is segmented and convoluted, in part as a result of building additions and modifications carried out over the course of the centuries. The loveliest feature of its interior is the rectangular Gothic spiral staircase in the corner between the "Collatiezolder" and the Throne Room. In 1576, the Pacification of Ghent was signed in one of the building's most beautiful rooms; this treaty officially ended the disputes between Catholics and Protestants.

Opposite the town hall, on the **Botermarkt** (the Butter Market), you can find **St-Jorishof** Ⓒ, built in the 13th century and one of the oldest hotels in Europe. In the Middle Ages the archers of Ghent kept their practice ranges here. Both Charles V and Napoleon have been guests in St-Jorishof, but its biggest moment was when it hosted celebrations for the engagement of Maximilian of Austria and Mary of Burgundy.

If you cross Limburgstraat and head south, you pass a modern memorial to the brothers Jan and Hubert van Eyck, and one to Geraard de Duivelsteen. Right by this is the **castle of Gerhard the Devil**, a fortified knight's castle dating from 1245. It is a remarkable building for its age, and it has certainly been well used over the years and centuries that it has stood here, becoming successively an armoury, a school, a mental hospital, a prison, an orphanage and a fire station.

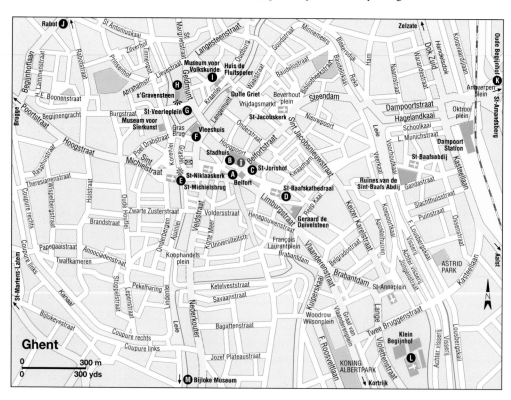

Ghent

Map on page 188

The Ghent Altarpiece

When Albrecht Dürer began his exploration of this "large and wonderful city", he immediately beat a path to Ghent's most important artistic site: the Ghent altarpiece, housed in **St-Baafskathedraal ⑩** (St Bavo's cathedral, open Mon–Sat; Sun pm only for touring; entrance fee, except for the Ghent Altarpiece). From the outside, Ghent's main church, which is also known as St Baaf's, has a somewhat eclectic appearance. Visitors with an interest in art history can trace the development of architectural styles from late Romanesque to late Gothic. But the undisputed highlight of this church, where Emperor Charles V was baptised in 1500, is first and foremost Jan van Eyck's most famous and admired work, the Ghent altarpiece, known as the *Adoration of the Holy Lamb,* located in one of the cathedral's 20 side chapels.

It is not certain whether Jan van Eyck painted this 20-panelled work alone between 1425 and 1432, or whether he collaborated with his brother Hubert; the latter is not mentioned in any documents but is cited in a somewhat enigmatic inscription on the frame of the altarpiece itself. Despite this inscription, many art historians believe it to be the work of one hand only: Jan's.

This altar which, like Hans Memling's *Shrine of St Ursula* in Bruges, belongs to the so-called "Seven Wonders of Belgium", is regarded as the greatest masterpiece of early Flemish art and is one of the most famous paintings in the world. The use of light in the canvas is such that the viewer has the impression that the sunlight from the cathedral's windows is continually illuminating the altarpiece's 284 figures. The work depicts the Adoration of the Lamb of God, an allegorical glorification of the death of Christ. But this masterpiece wasn't always so revered. At the end of the 18th century, Emperor Joseph II of Austria

I can hardly endure to call a place so dignified by such a name.

– DOROTHY WORDSWORTH WRITING ABOUT THE BOTERMARKET

BELOW: the altarpiece in St Bavo's cathedral.

St Bavo's cathedral, home of the Ghent Altarpiece.

took exception to the nakedness of Adam and Eve; as a result, the panel depicting Adam and Eve was replaced by a new painting of two clothed figures and the original panel was hidden away in the sacristy. Today, the original Adam and Eve have been restored to their rightful place in the altarpiece; the panel with the clothed figures hangs near the exit, on the left wall.

During every major European conflict the altarpiece has been looted from Ghent; Napoleon Bonaparte took it to Paris and it was stolen by the Germans during World War II. But it always found its way back to the city – except, alas, for the panel depicting the wise judges, which had to be replaced by a copy after it was stolen in 1934.

The visitor shouldn't forgo a visit to the **Sikkel Complex** situated behind St Bavo's cathedral. Some guidebooks list it as the Hoogpoort Complex. This extensive complex was built as a residence for a patrician family between the 13th and 15th centuries, and continued to be rebuilt and expanded; it is reminiscent of similar establishments in Italy. The buildings are arranged around a central courtyard containing a fountain. The Sikkel family, who commissioned the palace, even included a watchtower in their plans. Sikkel is the Flemish word for "sickle", and you can see the family's emblem, three sickles, on the building's facade. Hoogpoort is the name of the Gothic facade of the complex.

On the banks of the Leie

BELOW: the exterior of St Michael's church.

The most beautiful view across the city's breadth can be appreciated from the vantage of **St Michelsbrug** ❸ (St Michael's Bridge), which spans the Leie. From here, the view extends from 's Gravensteen, the fortress of the Counts of Flanders, across the Romanesque, Gothic and baroque facades of the ware-

houses and guild halls on Korenlei and Graslei, all the way to the towers of St Bavo in the distance and St Nicholas and the bell tower in the foreground.

The rows of houses along **Korenlei** and **Graslei**, the two roads bordering the river Leie between St Michael's Bridge and Gras Bridge, comprise the architectural heart of Ghent. Along the river's banks, you will encounter some of the loveliest residential buildings in the whole of Flanders. Ghent schoolchildren are frequently brought here to draw or paint, even in preference to the bell tower or 's Gravensteen. And while it is undeniable that Bruges offers the more unified image of a medieval city, it cannot match the wealth of ornament and intricacy which these houses of Ghent possess.

Side by side stand centuries of architectural heritage. On one side of the narrow **Customs House** of 1682 is the **House of the Grain Measurer**, a building of red brick and white stone, with decorative stepped gables, built in 1698; while on the other side is the Romanesque **Stockpile House**, built over 550 years earlier in 1130. Closer to St Michael's Bridge is the **House of the Free Boatmen** (1531), with the figure of a ship cast above the doorway. Splendid houses line both sides of the river; richly ornamented with stepped or curving gables, false fronts and lavishly decorated cornices. But Ghent's wealth of elaborate old houses isn't confined only to these two streets. A row of houses in the **Oudtburg** really shouldn't be missed, the most famous of which is the pub "In de Hel" ("In Hell").

Also worth a look is the former house of the spice merchants' guild, called **Klein Turkje** (Little Turk). Klein Turkje is part of a hostelry in which Albrecht Dürer stayed when he visited Ghent. The inn still bears the name it bore then: "The Red Hat". Dorothy Wordsworth, visiting Ghent in 1820, was enchanted by the city's

Map on page 188

TIP

Boat trips offer a wonderful introduction to the sights of Ghent. Boats depart from various locations along both sides of the Leie, along Grasslei and Korenlei.

BELOW: the stepped and curved gables on houses bordering the Leie.

The national flag flies above the rustic form of 's Gravensteen.

BELOW: a traditional toy shop's window in Ghent.

houses: "The buildings, streets, squares, all are picturesque; the houses, green, blue, pink, yellow, with richest ornaments still varying. Strange it is that so many and such strongly contrasted colours should compose an indiscordant whole."

Back to the river

Just north of the Gras Bridge stands the imposing **Vleeshuis ⑥** building. This was the medieval meat market, although its form suggests the castellations of a fortified stronghold. Passing this, and crossing the Vleeshuis Bridge, you will come to the **Dulle Greet**, a cast-iron cannon from the Burgundian epoch.

Around here, or indeed in any one of Ghent's many restaurants, you can sample a speciality of the region: *waaterzoi*, a chicken or fish and vegetable stew. Whilst wandering around the city, you may notice that the dialect spoken in Ghent is much harder and louder than in Bruges, for example, and to the ears of strangers it may even sound inflammatory.

Back in the 17th century, in his study of the Burgundian region, Caspar Merian set Ghent alongside Paris and Liège as one of the European cities most easily incited to revolt; and it is still said that the citizens of Ghent are among the most single-minded in the country. During centuries of conflict, the people of Ghent have risen up more often than most in Flanders. At such times, the **Vrijdagsmarkt** (Friday Market) has often provided the stage for political meetings. Dominating the Vrijdagsmarkt, where the colourful weekly market takes place today, is the statue of the 14th-century Ghent brewer Jacob van Artevelde. He died in a riot after proposing that Edward the Black Prince (the son of Edward III of England) should be made Count of Flanders, when the region was caught in the midst of conflict between the English and the French *(see page 31)*.

Between the Vrijdagsmarkt and the castle gates of 's Gravensteen lies pretty **Veerle Square** . But the square's many beautiful old gabled houses belie a gruesome past. Prior to the late 18th century, the square contained a wheel of torture and a gallows. Murderers and thieves, magicians and witches, forgers and heretics, vagabonds and robbers were strangled, beheaded, hanged, flayed on the wheel or bound and thrown into vast vats of boiling oil.

The Counts' former quarters now house a museum documenting the medieval system of criminal justice. The museum contains a harrowing collection of tools and tales of torture, either to force a confession or to kill the condemned in the grisliest possible manner. It may be with considerable relief that you reach the top level of the castle's main tower, where a cheerier panorama spreads before you. If it weren't for the captivating view from St Michael's Bridge, the tower of the castle would provide the best view of the city.

Gloomy castle

Ghent's other major castle, **Gravensteen** (open daily; entrance fee; tel: (09) 225 9306), is much larger and more important. But this fortress of the Counts of Flanders is perhaps the most gloomy medieval building in Europe. The castle, which is protected on one side by the waters of the Leie, was built on the model of the castles constructed by the Crusaders in Syria and the Holy Land. Philip of Alsace encountered such buildings when he himself undertook a crusade to the Holy Land.

At first, 's Gravensteen served as a residence and a fortress; after the 14th century, however, even the Counts of Flanders themselves became a little uncomfortable in the sinister surroundings, and the building was turned into a dungeon, its inner courtyard used as a place of execution. Even the crypt was used as a torture chamber. Today, these chambers, with their gruesome collection of exhibits, are the most popular of the castle's attractions.

But there was plenty of torture and execution going on outside the walls of the castle, as well; medieval Ghent could boast of many institutions which were empowered to "interrogate painfully" and execute suspects. At the foot of 's Gravensteen, there's a bridge that recalls Ghent's murderous past: **Ondhoofdingbrug** (Bridge of the Beheaded).

A short stroll from 's Gravensteen is the **Old Securities House**, which is worth closer inspection for its interior architecture, and particularly the vaulted ceiling. Located in Abrahamsstraat, the house was founded as a credit institution under the regency of Albert and Isabella of Austria in 1621. It's a perfect example of Flemish Renaissance architecture. For 300 years, the citizens of Ghent were able to borrow money here, albeit at an exorbitant rate of interest.

On the opposite side of 's Gravensteen is the **Museum voor Volkskunde** (folk culture museum, Kraanlei 65; open Apr–Oct daily; Nov–Mar, Tue–Sun; entrance fee), housed in 18 small, typically Flemish houses. The museum conveys a picture of life in Ghent around the year 1900 through the recreation of typical environments, such as a cooper's workshop, a chemist's laboratory and a town inn.

Map on page 188

TIP

During the summer, a walk around Ghent at night can be magical, as many of the city's buildings are floodlit. For the rest of the year, the buildings are only lit on Friday and Saturday evenings.

BELOW: the castle of 's Gravensteen from the river.

A symbol of resistance and pride, the Lion of Flanders.

BELOW: lace for sale in Ghent.

Ancestral ruins

Prinsenhof, the castle where Charles V was born, was once a large castle complex with a well-tended garden, fountains, and 300 rooms. Today, there isn't much left, except for an entrance gate, **Donkere Poort**, and a memorial plaque on a house in Mirabelklostraat – the sole reminder of the room in which Emperor Charles V was born. His birth was celebrated in great style: it was deep winter and the authorities even went to the trouble of flooding the Vrijdagsmarkt so that the children could ice-skate.

Just west of Donkere Poort rises the **Rabot** ❿, one of the few remnants of the medieval city fortifications. Built in 1489, the Rabot is simply a large river-lock, flanked by two round towers. It stands at the place where the canal of Lieve once lapped the former city walls.

No city in Flanders is without its Beguine convent, and Ghent has two: the large and the small Beguine Convents. The large convent, **Oude Begijnhof** ⓚ, located in the eastern suburb of Sint Amandsberg, is fitted out as a museum of the Flemish Beguines. To the east of the city centre, you'll find the small convent, **Klein Begijnhof** ⓛ, which looks like a miniature 17th-century town. Between the two are the remains of St Bavo monastery, founded in the 7th century by St Amandus. Only a few sections remain: the cellar, the refectory and a nave. Today it serves as a location for the **Ghent Stone Museum**, containing mosaics, cobblestones, and old architectural ornamental building elements.

The former monastery of van de Bijloke has been converted into an archaeological museum, the **Bijloke Museum** ⓜ (Godshuizenlaanz; open Tue–Sun; entrance fee), although this name is a little misleading. The former convent, erected in the 14th century and worth a visit for architectural interest, houses

implements of daily life in the Middle Ages: weapons, pieces of clothing, porcelain and glass, as well as a fine collection of Chinese art. An interesting story is attached to the mechanical Jenny-loom. The Mayor of Ghent, Lieven Bauwens, smuggled it out of England (breaking the strict export laws) at the end of the 18th century. With this loom and others modelled upon it, a new era of economic prosperity dawned in the city of Ghent, releasing it from a long period of decline.

Artists' colony

Ghent is a good city to walk around, and most of the notable sights are accessible on foot. You may, however, choose to take a half-hour tour of the city by motor launch; or, for a rather longer journey, a boat tour of several hours up the Leie to **Deurle**. This unusual village is one of the most interesting places in the area surrounding Ghent, and has attracted many craftsmen and artists. Expressionist Flemish painters are particularly well represented. Visit the **Gustaaf de Smeets Museum** (De Smetlaan 1) or the **Dhondt-Daenens Collection** (Museumlaan 14) to see examples of their work.

The neighbouring village of **St-Marterns-Latem** is another area renowned for its artists. The whitewashed houses, bright flower gardens, windmills and the picturesque banks of the Leie provided inspiration for the painters of the Latemer School.

If you have a particular interest in the lives of notable Flemish painters you may fancy stopping off in the Ghent suburb of **St Amandsberg**, or rather, at its cemetery, **Campo Santo**, where many figures from the worlds of art, science and culture are buried. Further along the road to Antwerp is the village of **Lochristi**. On the green outside the village's church there's a monument to

Map on page 188

TIP

If you want to sightsee in style, take a carriage ride through the city. The horsedrawn carriages stand under the bell tower, ready to take on passengers.

BELOW: a fanfare from the long horns at a local festival.

Along with Brussels and Bruges, Ghent was a major centre for the production of lace. Shops are still devoted to the delicate craft today.

Reinaart; the author of the great Netherlands animal epic *Van den Vos Reinaarde* (Reynard the Fox) who set the activities of his animal characters in the area between Ghent and the town of Hulst, which is located in the Netherlands.

Lochristi is also the centre of the flower industry which has come to play such an important role in the economy of East Flanders. From the end of July until well into October, Lochristi is perfumed with the begonias which carpet its vast fields. In 1157, Dietrich of Alsace had his **Castle Laarne** built on land enclosed by a bend in the river Scheldt, only a few miles from Ghent. This was the same Dietrich who brought the Sacred Blood to Bruges (*see page 207*) and who had 's Gravensteen built in Ghent. Laarne Castle, however, shares none of 's Gravensteen's dark air of gloom.

One of the most beautiful castles in East Flanders that is open to the public is **Castle Ooidonk** (open Sun & pub hols Easter–mid-Sep, Sat July & Aug; entrance fee), superbly located in the enchanting Lys Valley. The foundation walls date from the 12th century, when the castle was built as a defensive fortified outpost for the city of Ghent. For nearly 200 years it belonged to the Montmorency family; Philip II of Montmorency spent his youth within its walls. He was to become famous as Count Horn who, together with his father, Count Egmont, was beheaded on the Grand' Place in Brussels at the command of the Duke of Alba.

A visit to **Leeuwerghem Palace**, south of Ghent between Aalst and Oudenaarde, is also strongly recommended. The palace isn't usually open to the public, as it is still privately inhabited; visitors must content themselves with a stroll through the palace grounds, which contain one of the most unusual theatres in Flanders. This park is laid out in the style of Le Nôtre, the famous

BELOW: an enticing town café.

French landscape designer of the 18th century. The theatre has a seating capacity of 1,200 in its two-level balcony, its circle and its orchestra level.

Aalst (Alost), halfway between Ghent and Brussels, on the southwest border of the province of East Flanders, is perhaps not one of the great cities of Flanders, but as the former capital of the county, lying between the Scheldt and Dender, it does possess a number of noteworthy old buildings. In addition, Aalst – which for many years belonged to the province of Hainaut – is interesting in any case from a standpoint of cultural history and population.

The **Schepenhuis**, the Gothic town hall, dominates the old town. In 1469 the bells in the **bell tower** rang out over the Flemish town for the first time. In a corner of the town hall lies the **Beurs van Amsterdam**, or Barbara Chamber, a building from the early baroque period. Richly ornamented, and notable for an arcade on the first floor, this building once housed a rhetoricians' guild, a type of guild common in Flemish cities in the past. In the south transept of **Sint Maartenskerk** (the church of St Martin) you will find Rubens' painting of Christ imbuing St Roch with the gift of healing the victims of plague.

The Walloon influence on the town is especially visible in the annual Carnival, when one of Belgium's most splendid parades takes place. Many of the participants wear high, waving ostrich feathers in their hats, a custom shared by the Carnival in Hainaut.

Aalst, like Poperinge, lies in countryside characterised by its fields of hops. During the hop harvest, the villages of **Moorsel**, **Baardegem**, **Medert** and **Herdegsem** hold harvest festivals, at which plenty of Lambieck (French: *lambic*), a traditional strong beer of Belgium, which is produced according to an extremely specialised process of fermentation, is consumed. ❑

Map on page 188

During Carnival in Aalst, a parade of giants includes the Trojan-like "Bayard" horse, hiding weapon-bearing soldiers who pop up from the horse's back.

BELOW: the trappings of a pious Flemish household.

BRUGES

*The capital of West Flanders is one of Europe's best preserved
medieval cities, with a turbulent history that is concealed
by the serenity of its present-day appearance*

Map
on page
202

Those who speak of Bruges as the "Venice of the North" or "Belgium's Amsterdam", do little service to a city that is simply unique and happy to be itself. This city is not some pale imitation of another, and needs no such false comparisons to illuminate it. Bruges is the pride and joy of Flanders, and right below the smoothly cosmopolitan surface with which it greets its legions of foreign admirers it is Flemish through and through.

In attempting to describe this canal-fretted ensemble of medieval architecture, it is hard to avoid the word "picturesque". As Arnold Bennett said as long ago as 1896: "The difference between Bruges and other cities is that in the latter, you look about for the picturesque, and don't find it easily, while in Bruges, assailed on every side by the picturesque, you look curiously for the unpicturesque, and don't find it easily."

There's an almost unreal quality to just how stagily pretty Bruges can be, as if in the Middle Ages the city had been a place of universal grace and effortless charm instead of the noisy, smelly sink it probably was. Should Bruges have a weak point this is it. A city that looks and feels like a museum can be hard to get close to, however grateful we might be that it has come down to us through the centuries in this pristine condition. After a while you might even get to miss the kind of gritty urban reality that gives cities like Ghent and Antwerp a more fully developed character. But if this is a criticism, it is hardly an onerous one. Certainly no one from Bruges will blame you for setting competing philosophies of urban existence aside and getting on with the business of enjoying your stay.

One of the most remarkable facets of life in Bruges is the almost unfailing politeness and patience of the population. The natives really are friendly here. Considering that they actually have to go about their everyday business in this open-air museum, tripping over hordes of tourists every day of the year, this could hardly be taken for granted, even taking the commercial benefits they derive from tourists into account.

PRECEDING PAGES:
early morning
in Bruges.
LEFT: sunshine
on the Markt
in Bruges.
BELOW: Bruges' Old
Toll House.

Finding your way around

On a warm and sunny day there is no better or easier way to see the city than from a canal boat. A boat tour offers a good overview of the historic centre, allowing you to return to places or areas that appealed without having to walk your socks off in the search. Yet walk you should, as far and as much as possible, to see Bruges at a human pace and to touch the legacy of a thousand years. There is no shortage of restaurants and bars along the way. Restaurants range from fast-food outlets to some seriously gourmand establishments, with a big mid-range of tasteful places to cater

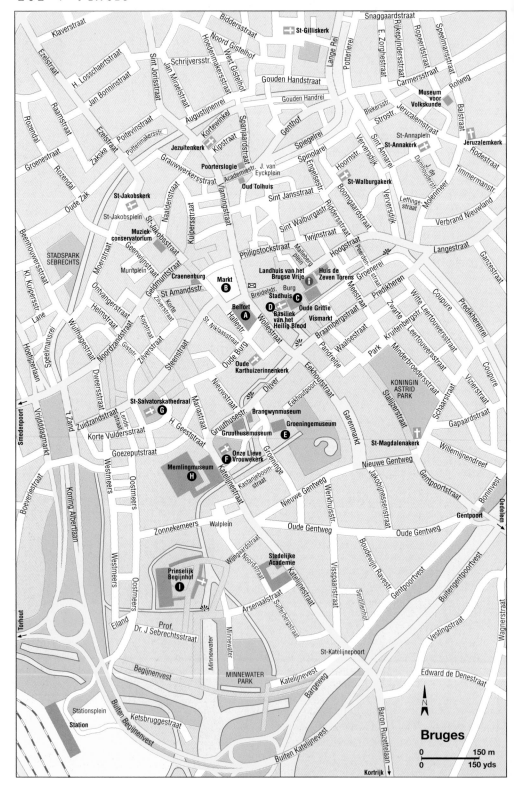

Bruges

0 ___ 150 m
0 ___ 150 yds

for the many visitors that descend upon this historic town (*see* the Travel Tips section for recommendations). Sit on a canalside terrace and drink a Flemish beer, such as Bruges' own Straffe Hendrik. Visit some, if not all, of the museums and churches described in this chapter. You can even save yourself a trip to Italy by seeing a genuine Michelangelo sculpture: a *Madonna and Child* in the Onze-Lieve-Vrouwekerk (church of Our Lady).

Bruges is a small city which discourages cars, so it is pleasant to walk through its old central district. But it is also interesting to get a feel for Bruges outside the centre, where the lucky inhabitants have a historical treasure all to themselves. They just happen to live in it, and without the necessity to dress it up for the benefit of tourists, although it is picture-book pretty almost everywhere. Bruges rewards aimless wanderers as well as itinerary-followers, so just wander around, with your eyes open to make your own discoveries. However, having said that, there are certain sights that shouldn't be missed, and these are described throughout the rest of the chapter.

Historical overview

Despite being a favoured destination for tourists, this city enjoys no more than a shadow of its former glory. In the 14th and 15th centuries, when the grand dukes of Burgundy, the heirs to the Counts of Flanders, held their court in Bruges, it was the last word in pomp and splendour. Some thought it the last really princely court of the Middle Ages. At the time, Charles the Bold was reaching out to grasp a royal crown, to make Burgundy the third major European power after France and Germany. Bruges, his capital, was a radiant nucleus and, since the founding of the guilds, the largest, richest and most powerful merchant city north of the Alps.

Only after seeing Bruges (Brugge), the grande dame of the cities of Flanders, can you understand Flanders, or begin to grasp and recognise the many-faceted heritage which the Burgundians and French, the Austrians and Spanish, the Germans and English have left in this city between the North Sea and the Ardennes. Perhaps this sounds exaggerated, not to say unkind to the other Flemish cities, but whoever has got to know Flanders knows that it's true: Bruges is Flanders. Flanders would be a very different place without this city. It plays host to the most important religious festival of the region, the Holy Blood Procession (*see page 207*), which takes place on Ascension Day, and is proud to celebrate itself in two separate festivals. The Golden Tree Pageant only takes place every five years, but celebrates the grandeur of the city's Burgundian heyday, while the Reiefeest, held on the waterways of Bruges, recreates moments from the city's history a little more frequently – every three years. Both festivals will next take place in 2001.

Part of the city's history includes the legacy of the great painters who have lived or created work in Bruges. The greatest period of artistic activity accompanied the economic prosperity of the Middle Ages, when the likes of Jan and Hubert van Eyck created some of their greatest works. It was in Bruges that the brothers worked on the Ghent Altarpiece, the

Map
on page
202

TIP

Although beautiful in the sunshine, Bruges is thronged with visitors in summer. It is therefore worth making a trip in autumn or spring, when the rain makes the cobbles and brickwork shine with a rich hue.

BELOW: a view of the canal beside St-Janshospitaal.

A horse awaits, ready to transport visitors through the centuries of Bruges' history. Carriages depart from the Burg, by the Basilica of the Holy Blood, throughout the day between March and October.

BELOW: medieval Bruges from the bell tower.

Adoration of the Holy Lamb (*see page 189*), before it was transported to St Bavo's cathedral. Jan van Eyck's pupil Petrus Christus also worked here, and Hans Memling, although born in Germany, is profoundly linked to this city that became his home; many of his great works can still be seen in Bruges.

Physical overview

Because the most exciting first impression of Bruges is to be had from above, our visit to Bruges begins by climbing stairs. Not just a couple of steps down to the waters of the omnipresent Reie, which flows around the old city, criss-crossing it with its canals, but the really difficult, steep flight of stairs up to the **Belfort Ⓐ** (bell tower; open daily; entrance fee). This mighty tower, nearly 88 metres (300 ft) high, is a landmark of the city. It is located next to the medieval **cloth hall**, where the merchants of Bruges used to store their textiles. Bruges' wealth stemmed from fabric production and trade.

The towers of the church of Our Saviour, the church of Our Lady, and the bell tower comprise the triumvirate of Bruges towers which makes the city visible from so far away. There are 366 steps leading to the observation deck; here, one is high enough to get a real perspective on this unique city.

Cut off from the sea

In the midst of the city is the broad marketplace, the **Markt Ⓑ**, with its memorial to the two liberation fighters Jan Breydel and Pieter de Coninck, who distinguished themselves in the Battle of the Golden Spurs in 1302 (*see page 230*). The splendid neo-Gothic edifice of the county administration building dominates the right-hand side of the marketplace; to the left and in the background are

the guild houses, their narrow gables looking as neat as pickets in a fence. Sitting on the terrace of one of the Markt's many restaurants, you can listen to the bells pealing out from the bell tower; folk melodies played on a carillon of 47 bells echo over the city.

One building on the Markt which is particularly worthy of note is the **Cranenburg**, which like so many of the houses here is now a restaurant. This was where, in the Middle Ages, the knights slept and ate with their ladies. The Cranenburg has often played a significant historical role, notably in the 15th century when Maximilian of Austria was incarcerated here for 100 days.

By then the fortunes of Bruges had started to decline. With the silting up of the Zwin, Bruges was cut off from the open sea, and the city was in danger of losing access to its trade routes. Furthermore, the reign of the Dukes of Burgundy had come to an abrupt end through the tragic death in a riding accident of the young Mary of Burgundy in 1482.

The citizens were incensed at certain tax increases which had been forced upon them by their rulers. They captured their sovereign, Mary's widowed husband Maximilian, and locked him up in the Cranenburg. The audacity of incarcerating the Crown Prince of the House of Habsburg, later to become Emperor Maximilian I, called the "last knight", caused a stir across the whole of Europe. Eventually Maximilian's father, Frederick III, demonstrated his imperial power by sending in warships. Maximilian was set free, but not before swearing to respect the rights of the proud burghers of Bruges in the future.

Maximilian paid no attention to his oath and immediately took his revenge on the citizens of Bruges. He moved the Ducal Residence to Ghent, and transferred Bruges' trading privileges to Antwerp. This sealed Bruges' fate; the death

Map on page 202

BELOW: the town hall, a testament to past prosperity.

A stallholder at Bruges' flower market.

BELOW: the strong Catholic influence is manifest in the town's religious processions.

sentence had been pronounced and executed. For nearly 500 years Bruges was "la ville morte", the dead city. Not until the final years of the 19th century was the city, by then badly dilapidated, rediscovered with all its original charms.

Gothic beauty

Today, one has to say that the city's economic death after 1488 was a blessing in disguise. During the ensuing centuries, the city simply couldn't afford to reconstruct or alter its Gothic character. One of the most beautiful parts of the Gothic city lies just under the bell tower: Burg Square with its Stadhuis (town hall), Holy-Blood Chapel, Office of the Town Clerk, and justice buildings. The **Stadhuis** ❻ (open daily; entrance fee) is considered to be the square's tour de force. Built in 1376, it resembles nothing so much as a large stone copy of one of the reliquaries often seen in Flanders' churches. The Stadhuis in Bruges is the oldest and perhaps the most beautiful town hall in Belgium.

Originally, the facade was ornamented with brightly painted statues of important personages, male and female, in the history of Flanders. The painting was the work of the great artist Jan van Eyck, who worked for a period in Bruges. Unfortunately the sculptures were destroyed in the wake of the French Revolution. Replacements for them have gradually been erected over the course of the past few decades, although today's sculptures are a sober white.

Particularly lovely is the figure of the Virgin to the outer left in the bottom row, just where the narrow Blinde-Ezelstraat begins. This is the Madonna of Oudenaarde – also known as the Madonna with the Inkwell. The highlight inside the town hall is the vaulted ceiling, carved entirely of oak. It used to be described as the eighth wonder of the world, and is numbered among Belgium's

own seven wonders. The walls are painted with relatively recent frescoes, dating from the 19th century and depicting important events in the city's history.

The Renaissance edifice next to the town hall is the former Office of the Town Clerk, the **Oude Griffie**; next to this, on the site where the castle of the Counts of Flanders once stood, is the building housing the **Law Courts**. In the jurors' court, you can see a splendid ebony and black marble chimneypiece dating from the Renaissance. The alabaster frieze depicts the victory at Pavia over Francis I of France, and the subsequent Peace of Madrid, in 1529. This treaty was particularly important, as it was through it that Belgium finally managed to separate itself from France.

Holy blood

To the right of the Stadhuis, you'll find the **Basiliek van het Heilig Bloed** ⑩ (Basilica of the Holy Blood, open Apr–Sep daily; Oct–Mar closed Wed pm; basilica free, entrance fee for museum). The lower part houses the Romanesque Basilica of St Basil, while the upper part documents the history of Bruges' veneration of the Holy Blood. Returning from a crusade to the Holy Land in 1149, Count Dietrich of Alsace brought a small phial containing a drop of blood said to have been washed from the body of Christ by Joseph of Arimathea. It was given to him in recognition of his bravery during the Second Crusade. To commemorate the return of the victorious army with the relic, a procession is held every year on Ascension Day; it is the most important festival in Flanders.

The reliquary can be seen in the **Museum of the Holy Blood** in the Holy Blood Chapel; it is one of the finest pieces of medieval goldsmithery in existence. One of the most valuable components of this shrine is a diamond that is

As well as housing the reliquary, the Museum of the Holy Blood also has several fine paintings, including a triptych portraying members of the Brotherhood of the Holy Blood by Pieter Pourbus and an Adoration of the Magi by van Eyck.

BELOW: bearing the cross at the Holy Blood Procession.

HOLY BLOOD PROCESSION

Once a year, on Ascension Day, Bruges plays host to the Holy Blood Procession, the most important religious festival in Flanders. The procession centres around a precious religious relic: a crystal phial, supposedly containing the blood of Christ. While the official story has it that this phial was awarded to Dietrich of Alsace by the Patriarch of Jerusalem for bravery in the Second Crusade against the Saracens, other historians place its origins in Constantinople, and suggest that its presence in Bruges is the result of the ransack of the ancient capital of the Byzantine Empire. Whatever the truth, the phial of blood is a precious relic; as such, it is kept throughout the year in a silver reliquary and venerated every Friday, in the morning and evening.

But for one day a year, the relic is paraded around the streets of the old centre of Bruges in a day-long ceremony. The parade is divided into two parts: in the first a number of biblical scenes are enacted; while the second part re-enacts the return of Dietrich with the relic. Hundreds of inhabitants of Bruges take part in the enactments, which continue a tradition from the Middle Ages – a time when reading was uncommon amongst the peasantry, and visual forms were used to teach Christian tales and beliefs.

A restaurant sign, in the centre of town, with the day's specials chalked-up.

supposed to have belonged to the English queen Mary Stuart. The crown which tops the reliquary once belonged to the young Mary of Burgundy.

The small, narrow Blinde-Ezelstraat leads to the Fish Market. If you like seafood, you should sample the delicious lobster stew in the fish restaurant called De Visserie. A few steps further along, past the delightful Café Mozart, where you can hear good classical music, you come to the Huidevettersplein, which boasts some of the best eating establishments in the city. The view over the waters of the Burgundian Cross is stunning and painters often set up their easels here. Winston Churchill was one of those who painted the scene.

The Dijver, the branch of the Reie which flows from here in the direction of the mighty church of Our Lady, is the place to find water pursuits. Its banks are punctuated by berths for motor launches. The sightseeing tours of the waterfront and canal network of Bruges are highly recommended.

Flemish primitives

Some of the old patrician houses of Dijver still have window panes made of valuable Venetian glass; House No. 7, in particular, is worth noting. Right next to these is Bruges' municipal painting gallery, the **Groeningemuseum E** (open Apr–Sep daily; Oct–Mar Wed–Mon; entrance fee). This gallery, located in a former Augustinian monastery, is small both in terms of physical size and in terms of its collection; yet in terms of the quality of what you can see here, the gallery deserves to be ranked with the Hermitage in Leningrad or the Prado in Madrid. The collection concentrates on the work of the Flemish Primitives, the term used to describe the artistic trend of the 15th century, instigated by Jan van Eyck, for painters to depict real people in their paintings.

BELOW LEFT: local produce at the town market.
BELOW RIGHT: a stallholder at the Wednesday market.

The works of Jan van Eyck feature strongly: they include his famous *Canonicus van der Paele* and a portrait of a woman which is taken to be his wife. Hans Memling is represented with a painting of St Christopher. The works of painters Gérard David, Pieter Pourbus, and Rogier van der Weyden are also displayed in the museum.

The **Gruuthuse Palace** (open Apr–Sep daily; Oct–Mar Wed–Mon; entrance fee), situated next to the Groeninge Museum, dates from the 15th century. Its owners, the Lords of Gruuthuse, had the right to impose a tax upon the grain (gruut) used in the brewing industry: hence the name of the family and their residence. The English kings Edward IV (1471) and Charles II (1656) both found asylum within its walls. Today, the building houses a museum dedicated to life in 16th and 17th-century Bruges.

The **Onze Lieve Vrouwekerk** ❻ (church of Our Lady; open daily except Sun am for visitors; church free, chapel of Charles and Mary entrance fee) close by is the largest Gothic church of the Low Countries; it was built in the 13th century. During the reign of the Grand Dukes it served as Royal Chapel to the Dukes of Burgundy. It was here that the magnificent wedding of the wealthy Burgundian heiress Mary, daughter of Charles the Bold, and the impoverished but handsome Crown Prince of Habsburg, Maximilian of Austria, was held.

Maximilian made a triumphant entry into the city, his armour gleaming in silver gilt, a garland of pearls and precious stones instead of a helmet on his blond head and the black cross of Burgundy emblazoned on his breast-plate. Formal introductions in the ducal palace were inhibited by neither bride nor groom speaking the other's language and by courtiers milling about to witness the Flemish custom of finding a flower concealed on the bride's person.

Map on page 202

BELOW: view of the Onze Lieve Vrouwekerk.

A Benedictine nun in a convent of the Beguine tradition.

The tombs of Mary of Burgundy and her father (which were fully restored only a few years ago) and several Old Master paintings are among the chief highlights of the church; another sight not to miss is the Michelangelo *Madonna and Child*. The sculptor executed this piece for the cathedral of Siena, but when it was completed he found that the cathedral had no money to pay him. Thus the Madonna came to Bruges; it was the only work by Michelangelo that left Italy during his lifetime.

The other major church in Bruges also houses masterpieces from the time of the Burgundians. The Gothic choir stalls in the **St-Salvatorskathedraal** (church of Our Saviour), the city's diocesan church, founded by Saint Elegius in 646, still bear the crest of the Knights of the Golden Fleece. Philip the Good, Mary of Burgundy's grandfather, established this order on the occasion of his marriage to Isabella of Portugal. Jan van Eyck, incidentally, had sued for Isabella's hand by proxy on behalf of his Duke (in such marriages the proxy groom was required to lie next to the bride on a bed with one leg bare). When Isabella came to Bruges, she brought her private secretary. She allowed him to build an enchanting brick house; today, this is home to one of the finest and most atmospheric restaurants of Bruges, the **Vasquez**.

Bruges museums

The **Memlingmuseum** (Mariastraat; open Apr–Sep daily; Oct–Mar closed Wed) has pride of place among Bruges' museums. It is housed in the medieval St-Janshospitaal, built in the 13th century. The only evidence of the museum's former role is the dispensary, which dates from the 15th century, and some wards. The ward nearest the entrance contains a large picture of what the hos-

BELOW: bordering the waters of the canal, St-Janshospitaal.

pital looked like when it was in operation. In the adjoining room, originally where terminal cases were kept, hang some of the most important works of the German-born painter Hans Memling: note in particular the *Marriage of St Catherine* and the *Shrine of St Ursula*. This shrine, on which Memling depicted six scenes from the life of the saint, is numbered among the seven most important art treasures in Belgium.

Map
on page
202

Beguine Convent

One of the most enchanting nooks in Flanders is the **Prinselijk Begijnhof** ❶ (Beguine convent, open daily; free), founded in 1245. The convent incorporates a hatful of architectural styles, starting with Gothic and working forward. Right next to the entrance gate, one of the little cottages is set up as a museum.

The women of the convent are not in fact Beguines any longer, but belong to the order of the Benedictines. The order of the Beguines was founded in the 13th century, to give unmarried or abandoned woman a chance to join a respectable and secure society without having to take the strict holy vows of a monastic order. Although their life was far from comfortable, the Beguines were allowed privileges not granted to bona fide nuns – they were, for example, allowed to have personal property. Traditionally, members of the order devoted themselves to the care of the sick, or earned their bread by making lace; the Benedictine nuns who live here today prepare and maintain the costumes for the participants in the annual Holy Blood procession – all 2,000 of them.

There are few places in Flanders which radiate such an aura of peace as the Beguine Convent in Bruges. Concealed behind white walls, the small houses are arranged over a broad expanse of greensward dotted with poplars. When the

BELOW: Hans Memling's *Altar with the mystical Marriage of St Catherine* c.1475–9.

bells of St Elisabeth's ring out in the morning and evening, the sight is remarkable as the small doors of the cottages open and black-clad sisters scurry over the grass toward the church.

The Beguine Convent lies in the area where lace-making, the most famous craft of Bruges, is still practised. On warm days, you can see old women and young girls sitting in the alleyways around the Beguine Convent, their fingers deftly working the fine threads. You can buy "Kant", the fine lace of Bruges, virtually anywhere in the city. For those especially interested in lace, there's a Lace Centre in Baalstraat, open every afternoon.

Wandering around the streets and alleyways north of the market, you stumble over the past at literally every turn; in the Middle Ages some 35 European cities, countries and republics had business outlets and embassies in Golden Bruges, as it was known in Europe. Spanjardstraat leads to the oldest bridge in the city; there, one sees the Spaanse Looskai, the Oosterlingeplein and the Natiehaus (Nation House) of Genoa. Today, this last building is known as the "Saeyhall" after the serge fabric once traded here. The headquarters of the Florentines were located at the corner of Vlamingstraat and Academiestraat; the Venetian residence was a little further along the street.

Between the Florentines and the Genoese lies a particularly handsome Gothic house, now home to the Bank of Roselare and Westvlaanderen. In 1257, this building belonged to a family of prosperous brokers named Ter Beurse. The businessmen of the city used to meet each other in front of the house, to negotiate their business in the open air; they called this "going Ter Beurse", to the Bourse. "Bourse" (and variations thereupon) is the word for stock exchange in many European languages, and here in Bruges is the source of its derivation.

The swans which glide along the canals of Bruges have a historical precedent. As a penance for having killed the councillor to Maximilian of Austria, the Bruges citizens were ordered to keep swans – a bird that appeared on the councillor's coat-of-arms.

BELOW: the Begijnhof in Bruges.

A few steps down the Academiestraat, you'll find the **Poorterslogie**, the Porters' Club, which was a meeting place for the well-to-do citizenry during the 14th century. The white bear which you can see on the facade outside is the emblem of a jousting club. The jousters used to hold their tourneys (or competitive bouts) in the marketplace.

Diagonally opposite this building is the old **Customs House**, one of the most beautiful and most richly ornamented Gothic buildings of Bruges. Next to this, the Ghent Courtyard contains a memorial to the painter Jan van Eyck; a similar memorial to Hans Memling can be seen in the nearby Woendsdagsmarkt.

Only two important buildings in Bruges fell victim to the troops of the French Revolution. One of these was the cathedral of St Donatus, which stood in Burg Square; all that remains of it today is an outline on the pavement. The other was called Prinsenhof, the residence of the Dukes of Burgundy. Remnants of its walls were incorporated into the building of what is today an old people's home.

Before you leave the medieval city of Bruges, drive along the Reie on the ring road which runs around the city, and look at the medieval city gates: the **Gentpoort**, the **Kruispoort**, the **Ezelpoort** and the **Smedepoort**; these date back to the beginning of the 15th century. And while you pass the Kruispoort, look out for the wonderful old **windmill** which rises above the Kruisvest.

There's only one way to take your leave of a city whose past greatness was based on overseas trade: go out by the Canal Road, which leads you through the countryside along the Bruges-Sluis Canal towards Damme.

If you're lucky, you'll be able to get a seat on one of the small launches which run along the canal between Bruges and Damme. Or you could rent a *fiets* (bicycle) and ride along the canal, lined with fishermen and windmills. ❑

Map on page 202

TIP

Boat trips from Bruges to Damme (approx. 45 minutes) sail along the canal from April to October. Boats leave from a quay to the north of Bruges, which can be reached via a short bus journey from the central Markt.

BELOW: a horse-drawn coach on the Burg in the town centre.

BELGIUM'S COAST AND THE BATTLEFIELDS OF FLANDERS

Map on page 218

Belgium's coast is a pleasant stretch, from the salty flatlands of Het Zin to the dunes of De Panne, but a short distance inland takes you into the historical battlefields of Flanders

Belgium's short coastline is made up of long stretches of sand, punctuated by busy resorts, fishing villages and ports. Beyond the coast, the flatlands of Flanders are dotted with small communities and medieval towns. But Belgium's coast only began to be developed in the mid-19th century. Up until that time, the precarious region, flat and barely above sea level, remained almost a noman's land, midway between the fertile countryside and the salty sea. The coastal dunes have never been enough of a barrier to stop the encroachment of the sea upon the plains of Flanders, and dykes have been used since the 10th century to forestall the influx of tidal waters. These polders, criss-crossed with narrow dykes and wider canals, are one of the defining features of the coastal region, their villages conspicuous against the single line of the horizon. The polder areas along the northern section of the coast, close to the Dutch border, are particularly attractive, and many of the canals are lined with poplars.

It was the events of 1830 that led to the development of the quiet Belgian coast. The new kingdom had a new leader, Leopold I, and he picked Ostend as a royal residence. This decision transformed the small harbour town into a modern, vibrant and fashionable resort, connected to the capital by a new railway line. Its popularity spread, and before long a whole series of smaller resorts stretched along the coast. Leopold II continued the coastal development, creating a tram route to join the resorts and building a series of sea defences. The coastal towns are all rather similar today, but one or two, such as Knokke and De Haan, recall the splendour of their early days.

PRECEDING PAGES: a fishing boat returns to harbour. **LEFT:** Het Zwin nature reserve. **BELOW:** fishing for shrimps.

Damme

Our tour begins a few miles inland at **Damme ❶**, midway between Bruges and the Dutch border. Damme is an enchanting, sleepy village these days, where time seems to have stood still ever since the ship-bearing, life-giving Zwin silted up in the 16th century. During the Middle Ages, however, the town flourished as a harbour of Bruges. The landscape of the area was rather different at the time, and the town was then situated on a dyke – the "dam" from which it gets its name – which lay at the end of a sea inlet. As a trade centre, Damme basked in the reflected glory of Bruges, and even when Philip-Augustus, the King of France, had the town burned to the ground in 1213, it was rebuilt in even greater splendour, and soon began to flourish again. But, when the Zwin became clogged with sand, the harbour choked and the city's fortunes foundered. By 1527 the town had passed its prime and became relegated to a backwater.

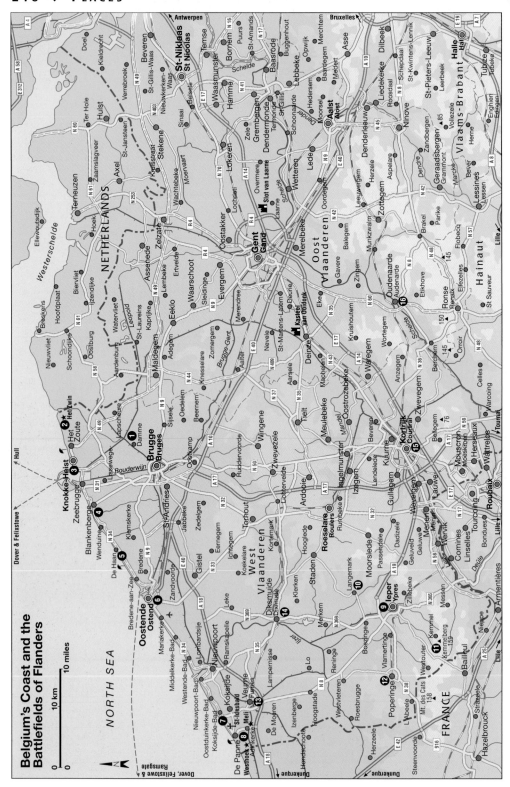

Belgium's Coast and the
Battlefields of Flanders

This sense of a town that has slept for centuries contributes much to Damme's appeal. It has one of the most beautiful marketplaces in Flanders, dominated by the late Gothic town hall, or **stadhuis** (open daily; entrance fee), which is one of the most impressive in the region. Although its style is unmistakably Gothic, the town hall is in fact a far more recent reconstruction, following a fire. But the attention to detail and craftsmanship employed in the reconstruction have ensured that the building remains a telling memorial to the city's glorious past. The statues in the niches of its facade are of the great figures of Flanders and Burgundy, such as Philip of Alsace, the founder of the city; and Charles the Bold. The superb sculpting captures a tenderness in Charles the Bold, as he offers the graciously smiling Margaret of York a wedding ring in his outstretched hand. The wedding of this noble couple took place in the town in 1468, in the house of the ducal administrator, Eustaas Wyts, and the building still exists today. The town hall contains a museum of the city's history, and on the other side of the street, you can see the oldest house in Damme, **De grote Sterre**. This is a charming brick house, built in the 15th century. It now houses the **Ulenspiegel Museum** (open Apr–Sep daily; Oct–Mar Sat & Sun only; entrance fee).

Towering high above Damme is the **church of Our Lady**. In the wake of the town's decline, parts of this church have been dismantled, but it remains huge nevertheless. The church tower, which has been without a spire since 1725, is 45 metres (147 ft) in height. A narrow staircase, with hairpin turns and 206 steps, leads to the top of the tower, and from this vantage point a magnificent view over Damme and the surrounding countryside unfolds. From here, the town looks like a seven pointed star stretched over the land, while beyond its borders, lines of poplars mark the banks of the canals.

> **Map on page 218**

As Damme went into decline, a special tax was enforced on barrels of herrings passing through the port in order to pay for the construction of the original Gothic town hall.

BELOW: a stained-glass tribute to Ulenspiegel in the town of Damme.

ULENSPIEGEL IN DAMME

The roguish character of Tyl Ulenspiegel is one that has jested and laughed his way through folk tales throughout northern Europe since the 16th century. He is a prankster and a mischief maker, the wag who takes everything said literally, attempts to teach a donkey to speak and, as a quack doctor, tries out upon his patients the cure of pure fear. Every tale seems to place him in a different location, but in 1866 the Flemish author Charles de Coster (1827–79) placed Tyl firmly in Flanders with the publication of *The Legend of Tyl Ulenspiegel.*

De Coster's story begins with the words: "In Damme in Flanders, as the May moon opened the flowers of the hawthorn, Ulenspiegel, the son of Claes, was born." With these printed words, Tyl was torn from the timeless, episodic realm of the folk tale and given a specific birthplace and an exact time of birth: 1527, the same year as King Philip, the Infante of Spain and son of Charles V. Thus the story sets up a direct opposition between Philip, as foreign ruler, and Tyl, as liberator and Belgian freedom fighter.

Through the book de Coster inspired confidence and national pride in the newly independent Belgium. Two memorials in Damme pay tribute to the pair: one in the churchyard and one near the water, on the Speystraat.

A sign for the nature reserve and bird sanctuary of Zwin.

The silence of the nuns

Diagonally opposite the Ulenspiegel Museum is **St-Janshospitaal** (open Apr–Sep daily; Oct–Mar Sat & Sun only; entrance fee), which was founded in the 13th century by Margarete of Constantinople. To gain access to this building, which has been converted into a museum, pull the bellrope by the entrance and wait. The sound of shuffling footsteps will announce the approach of a nun, who will silently accompany you on a tour of the museum. It houses a collection of old furniture, documents, and sacred objects.

If a prize were ever awarded for medieval preservation, the town of Damme would offer short odds in the betting stakes. Its tour de force in this respect would have to be the exquisite marketplace, upon which stands a **statue of Jakob van Maerlant**, a 13th-century writer who was the first author to pen his work in Dutch; as such, he has been dubbed the Father of Dutch poetry. The marketplace is lined with restaurants, offering all manner of Flemish culinary delicacies. The Flemish have always known how to eat well – a trait that has been admirably illustrated by the still-lifes of the region's artists, from Pieter Breughel to Felix Timmermanns.

The land beneath the sea

The land between the city of Bruges and the coastal town of Het Zoute was formed less than a millennium ago. In the Middle Ages the waves of the North Sea would have splashed in the inlet of the Zwin, and the waters would have reached right up to the city gates of Bruges. Sailing ships once floated where today low whitewashed farmhouses nestle under their red roofs.

The inlet was created by a terrible storm in the 5th century. But what the ocean gave, it was gradually to take away by depositing increasing quantities of sand. Eventually the Zwin silted up altogether.

However, the salt marshes hereabouts still acknowledges the area's aquatic past. **Het Zwin ②** (open Apr–Sep daily; Oct–Mar Thur–Tue; entrance fee; tel: (050) 607086) is now a reserve for waterfowl and saltwater flora, located on the edge of Knokke, Belgium's most cosmopolitan seaside town.

An imaginative complex of aviaries, open-air enclosures and specially constructed water sites enables visitors to examine a multitude of waterfowl at close range. Children in particular enjoy the reserve's amenities. Visitors can stroll along the dyke and survey the breeding-grounds of thousands of resident and visiting birds, or walk along the narrow paths through the salt marshes, where sheep graze and geese waddle about fearlessly. Guided tours of the reserve are given every Thursday and Saturday between Easter and the end of September.

Het Zwin belongs to the municipality of Knokke-Heist, located on the Belgian seacoast. This coast, over 70 km (44 miles) long, contains Belgium's best loved family resorts. There are plenty of opportunities for safe bathing and sandcastle building. This fact is reflected in the great efforts that are made to cater to children's needs: hotel staff are pleased to set up children's beds in their parents' rooms free of charge and

BELOW: a bronze memorial to the founder of Het Zwin nature reserve, Count Léon Lippens (1911–86).

go to great lengths to provide baby-sitting services and special entertainment. The 15 towns between Het Zoute and De Panne, west and east of Ostend, comprise a holiday zone, better known and more popular than size would indicate.

Map on page 218

The posh resort

Knokke with its suburbs Heist and Het Zoute is the epitome of an elegant, well-kept resort nestling in the dunes. Nearly 12 km (8 miles) long, the beach here bears no traces of the massive hotels and high-rise apartments which mar so many seafronts. Strict zoning regulations forbid any building to be higher than two storeys, so the sun falls evenly everywhere along the beach.

Knokke ❸ has always been a resort for guests with high expectations (and incomes); located near the Belgian-Dutch border, it's the number one bathing resort in Belgium today. Nowhere else in the country, not even in Brussels, are the shops so exclusive.

With its casino, international exhibitions of modern sculpture, annual Cartoonale, an exhibition of caricatures from around the world, and its cosmopolitan beach life, Knokke is up among the most renowned, most elegant beach resorts in Europe, on a par with Deauville or Biarritz. The attractions of Knokke are rounded off by its 18-hole golf course set among the dunes; it is considered to be one of the most beautiful golf courses in Europe.

Things are less pretentious, quieter and more family oriented in the beach resorts lying to the west of Knokke, such as Heist, a suburb of Knokke, Duin-bergen, and **Zeebrugge**. But however peaceful Zeebrugge seems to be as a bathing resort, it's busy in its function as a harbour. It's the second largest fishing town in Belgium and consequently an excellent place to eat freshly caught

An owl looks out from one of Het Zwin's aviaries.

BELOW: coastal breezes at Knokke.

Flemish style – the jagged edge of a stepped gable.

fish (try any one of the little restaurants clustered around the harbour). Visitors to Zeebrugge can also take an exhilarating stroll along the harbour breakwater, which extends for more than one-and-a-half miles into the North Sea.

Blankenberge ❹ is a more traditional bathing spot, which is today known as the Festival Bathing Resort. The most important festivals held here are the Carnival in February, the Harbour Festival in June, the Ocean Festival in July and the large, bright Flower Parade in August. These festivals, like nearly all festivals in Belgium, are rooted in ancient traditions. One of the largest festivals is held on Whit Monday in nearby Wenduine, in which a special blessing is invoked for all those whose livelihoods are connected with the sea.

For a quiet, elegant beach resort with a residential air visit **De Haan** ❺. The dunes of nearby Vosseslag have been incorporated into a splendid 18-hole golf course. These forested dunes are the pride and joy of foresters, who have managed to persuade the sand to support plant life. The tram which trundles along the Belgian coast, the **Kusttram** (Coast Tram), stops in De Haan at one of the most enchanting art nouveau stations in Europe.

On the opposite side of the inlet to the 28 campsites of **Bredene** is the port of **Ostend** ❻, situated right in the middle of Belgium's coast. The city suffered greatly as part of the Spanish Netherlands in the 17th century. It valiantly tried to hold out against the Spanish and won the admiration of Protestants all over Europe. One siege lasted from 5 July 1601 to 15 September 1604. Some 70,000 people lost their lives before the city was eventually stormed.

BELOW: storm clouds gather over Blankenberge pier.

William Beckford, an 18th-century English visitor to Ostend, expressed his dislike for the place in no uncertain terms: "Were I to remain ten days in Ostend I should scarcely have one delightful vision; 'tis so unclassic a place!

Nothing but preposterous Flemish roofs disgust your eyes when you cast them upwards: swaggering Dutchmen and mungrel (*sic*) barbers are the first objects they meet with below."

By the 19th century, however, Ostend was being hailed as the "Queen of the Belgian Coast". Both Leopold I and Leopold II endeavoured to turn the former village into a presentable bathing and health resort for the upper classes of 19th-century Europe.

Ostend is perhaps no longer Belgium's most stylish bathing resort, but it still has a fine sandy beach; the international jetset, or those who would like to be thought of as such, continue to meet in the elegant gaming casino and the spa. The carnival festivities held in the Ostend casino are some of the most spectacular to be held in any part of Belgium.

Visitors with a passion for art may know Ostend as the abode and workplace of the painter and engraver James Sydney Ensor. He was born in Ostend of Anglo-Belgian parentage in 1860, and died here in 1949. Although he trained at the Brussels Academy he rarely left Ostend and, for his coastal reclusion, was neglected by the art world for much of his life. His imaginative, often macabre, carnival paintings of fighting skeletons and masked revellers have led to his being described as the heir of Hieronymus Bosch and Pieter Breughel and a precursor of Expressionism. His fiercest work was probably the *Entry of Christ into Brussels*, painted in 1888.

Ensor's first home, Vlaanderenstraat 27, has been turned into a museum, the **James Ensorhuis** (open Tue–Sun; entrance fee) dedicated to the artist, although the paintings housed here are not originals. To see the genuine articles you must go to the **Museum of Fine Arts** (Wapenplein; open Tue–Sun; entrance fee).

Map on page 218

TIP

The strong breezes along the Belgian coast make it ideal for windsurfing. Ostend, De Panne, Knokke and Nieuwpoort are all good places to give it a go, while Ostend is also noted for ordinary surfing.

BELOW: the harbour at Ostend.

Euro style – blue cloth and gold stars predominate in this Flemish tourist shop.

BELOW: a seaside home for the birds.

Maritime industry and regal leisure

Ostend has a long maritime history. Today it is the most important port for ferries to and from England. Children, and anyone else interested in sailing ships, will probably go aboard the **Mercator** (open Apr–Sep; irregular schedule). Once the ship for the sailing school of the Belgian merchant marine, it now lies at anchor in the harbour of Ostend, and is open to visitors as a floating museum of ships and sailing. Another draw for children is the **North Sea Aquarium** (open Apr–Sep daily; Oct–Mar Sat & Sun only; entrance fee), located in the former auction rooms of the crab fishermen on Visserskai.

The **Royal Villa** is famous far beyond the borders of Flanders. It was originally built on the dyke as a summer residence for Leopold II and commanded an unparalleled view of the beach and the sea. It was destroyed in World War II, but has since been rebuilt by the citizens of Ostend.

The royal couple, however, preferred to holiday in Spain, so the former summer residence of kings was rented out. Today the building has been converted into a hotel and one of the most famous restaurants in Belgium, **Au Vigneron**, famous for its gourmet fish and shellfish dishes. It is said that Leopold II, by all accounts an amorous man, had a tunnel built between the palace and the city so that he could conduct his various affairs undetected.

The neighbouring towns of **Westende** and **Lombardsijde** are known for their folk markets and shrimp fishing, for rustic farm festivals and antique markets; **Nieuwpoort** (Nieuport), on the other hand, is a renowned centre for sailors and sailing craft. Its modern European marina has berths for 2,600 boats. The harbour restaurants are well known for their excellent fish. The Fish Market, held early every morning after the boats return, is an experience worth catching. Even if you don't understand a word of what the auctioneers are shouting, you are bound to enjoy all the bustle and excitement.

Ostduinkerke has preserved a unique Belgian tradition: "shrimp-fishing on horseback". Clad in oilcloth and sou'westers, the fishermen mount their heavy Belgian horses and ride out into the sea to snare shrimp in their trawling nets, just as they have been doing for centuries. When the weather is fine, spectators follow them into the water.

In Nieuwpoort, a visit to the **National Belgian Fishing Museum** (Pastooor Schmitzstraat 5; open daily; fee) presents the visitor with a summary of the development of fishing on the North Sea coast from as early as 700 BC up until the present day. **Koksijde's** main attraction is **St-Idesbald** ❼, more commonly known as the Dune Monastery. In the 12th century, St Idesbald was the most important monastery in Flanders. But the monks who founded it had not reckoned on the destructive force of the shifting dunes.

Eventually the encroaching sands proved invincible and the monastery was buried. St Idesbald was rebuilt, but again the sand destroyed everything and the monks were obliged to move away from St Idesbald. Today, the dunes have been cleared from a section of the ruins and are restrained by a protective wall. The museum here displays artefacts which have been rescued from the shifting sand.

Map on page 218

The claim that one can swim in the North Sea and then, half an hour later, wander through the dunes of the Sahara may seem a bit far-fetched, even in this jet age, but in fact it's perfectly possible in **De Panne ❽** (La Panne), Belgium's westernmost beach resort, a mere 2 km (1 mile) from the French border. The largest dune area in Belgium, located just behind the last apartment houses of De Panne, has been called the Sahara for as long as anyone can remember. So wild and wide are these sand dunes that cinema directors have occasionally used them as a stand-in location for desert scenes.

On 17 June 1831, Belgium's first king, Leopold I, who had been living in England, set foot in his kingdom for the first time in De Panne. Today, this beach is a paradise for beach sailors who enjoy the sport of sand yachting. Their narrow, wind-powered carts reach speeds of no less than 75 miles an hour (120km/h) as they zoom over the broad, firm sands.

De Panne's Sahara is part of a wildlife preserve called **Westhoek** (open permanently; free). The preserve covers 340 hectares (840 acres), stretching from De Panne to the French border. Three km (2 miles) inland is Adinkerke, a town with a family-orientated amusement park called **Meli** (open Apr–Sep daily).

The killing fields

The past begins to take over as soon as you come to the city limits of **Ypres ❾** (Ieper). From a distance, the **Menin Gate** looks like a Roman triumphal arch. In fact, it is a memorial arch to the 54,896 British and Commonwealth soldiers who were listed as missing in action after the battle of Ypres. Some 150 British cemeteries in and around the city are testimony to the bitter, four-year-long struggle for the contested city of Ypres and the devastating losses.

BELOW: rows of small white crosses line the fields of Flanders.

An old soldier's war medals weigh down his jacket.

Contemplating the astonishing death toll represented by the rows of graves, one is inevitably reminded of the words of Rupert Brooke:

> *If I should die, think only this of me:*
> *That there's some corner of a foreign field*
> *That is for ever England. There shall be*
> *In that rich earth a richer dust concealed,*
> *A dust whom England bore, shaped, made aware...*
> *A body of England's, breathing English air,*
> *Washed by the rivers, blest by suns of home.*

Brooke himself died on the Greek island of Skyros, on his way to fight in the Dardanelles in 1915; he was 28.

Today, Ypres is an attractive city with a picturesque marketplace, a **bell tower**, and the **cloth hall** (open Apr–Nov, Tue–Sun; entrance fee) to attract visitors; one part of the 13th-century cloth hall is given over to a **Museum of World War I**. Ypres was, along with Bruges and Ghent, among the most important Flemish weaving centres of Europe's Middle Ages. But none of what you see today is original medieval architecture. When the war was over, not one stone of Ypres was left standing, the city was a complete wasteland. The memory of the worst four years in the history of the little city is kept alive still: every night a policeman stops traffic before the Menin Gate at 8pm and four uniformed firemen on the street perform the bugle call of the Last Post.

BELOW: youngsters remember at the last post in Ypres.

Hill 62 near Ypres bears the great memorial for the fallen soldiers of Canada. The Canadian front line ran along here in 1916. Between this elevation and the nearby English cemetery you can find the **Sanctuary Wood Museum**, one of the many museums dedicated to the war. It contains various relics, including

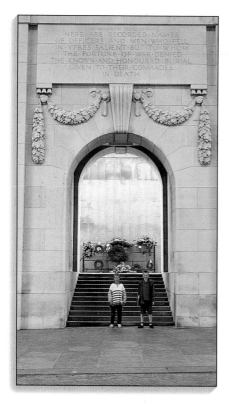

BLOOD-DRENCHED FLANDERS

De Panne's Sahara is part of a large wildlife preserve called Westhoek. This name, which roughly translates as "Western corner", has come to denote the entire western part of the province, the area along the French border. No other area in the country of Belgium, today so peaceful and quiet with its canals and bell towers, its windmills and grazing cows, is as drenched in blood as this one. Westhoek was the most horrible battleground of World War I. Tens of thousands of young men from Britain, Germany, France, Canada and Australia met their deaths here.

Even so long after the event, places such as Ypres and Langemark evoke strong emotions, and not just among the dwindling number of old soldiers who come to relive old memories and pay tribute to dead comrades. It is impossible to hike through the countryside around Kemmelberg without sensing the blood shed upon this land.

Watching the farmers of Poperinge harvesting hops, admiring the stately farmhouses, encountering trucks laden with sugar beets in the autumn, or seeing the facades in the marketplace at Diksmuide that recreate a bygone age, you might be lulled into thinking the area is typical of Belgium – until you see children playing in the abandoned trenches and sheep chewing grass in tumble-down bunkers.

Map
on page
218

bayonets, shells, rifles and bully cans. In front of the small Café Sanctuary Wood, where British, Australian, and Canadian flags wave, you can buy souvenir grenade shells, steel helmets and bayonets. Inevitably the relationship between war memorial and tourist attraction is an uneasy one.

A resting place

Passing through an apparently peaceful landscape, which a painting by Pieter Brueghel (the elder) couldn't have made prettier, you come to the village of **Langemark ❿**. This was the battlefield where tens of thousands of young Germans were killed between 1914 and 1915. The German cemetery bears the inscription which was the battle-cry of so many of these young soldiers: "Germany must live, even if we have to die for it." Commonly known as the Students' Cemetery, it holds the bodies of 44,294 fallen Germans, 25,000 of them in a mass grave. The cemetery of Vladslo contains another 20,000 German graves; at the edge of this graveyard you can see the powerful sculpture *Grieving Parents*, by Käthe Kollwitz, whose own son Peter lies in Vladslo.

On the once infamous **Hill 60**, near Zillebeke, there's a monument at the edge of the road to the fallen Australians. Behind this is a plot of fenced-in land. A few sheep roam among rabbits darting to and from their holes. This field, many acres in area, was created entirely by bombs. Shell crater by shell crater, every cubic centimetre of land here was torn up by exploding shells. Here and there you can see the remains of bunkers, torn apart by the shells. The front of the British cemetery Tyne Cot is almost a mile long. Altogether, 11,856 soldiers are buried here; only some of the 11,856 headstones, arranged in seemingly endless rows, are inscribed with a name; others simply bear the

BELOW:
Grieving Parents, a commemorative work by German artist Käthe Kollwitz.

words: "A soldier of the Great War known unto God". The names of the missing – 34,959 of them – are carved upon the surrounding wall.

The drive along the winding roads of the so-called Flemish Ardennes to **Kemmelberg**  is a pleasure, especially in autumn. Kemmelberg itself was an important strategic site in the Great War. It was captured by Bavarian mountain troops in August, 1918, and held for a total of four days.

The distinctive, tulip-shaped, glass for a Duvel beer.

Today, the crest of the hill is occupied by one of the best restaurants in Flanders (in the woods a little way from the road), which enjoys spectacular views of the Flemish hop-growing country below. Only 100 metres away, a large monument commemorates the many French soldiers who died at Kemmelberg and who were buried in the cemetery at the foot of the hill. There are cemeteries everywhere. Their crosses and headstones are as much a part of the landscape of Westhoek as the 6-metre (20-ft) hop trellises, whose cover helped the little town of Poperinge to escape the death and destruction of neighbouring villages.

Poperinge

Poperinge ⑫ is a pretty little town with a tranquil marketplace which, unusually for towns and villages hereabouts, is the original, old square. One of the village's oldest houses is the **Talbot House** of the British Army. Today this house provides accommodation for a modest charge to any British citizen who travels to Flanders to visit the graves of relations or former comrades.

The three churches of Poperinge are every bit as worthy of note as the **Nationaal Hopmuseum** (Belgian Hops Museum, open Jul & Aug daily; May, Jun & Sep Sun & public holidays only; entrance fee). Poperinge lies in the middle of an extensive hop-growing area. The town's annual Hops Festival

BELOW: gabled houses on the Grote Markt in Veurne.

takes place on the first Sunday in September. A leisurely drive along the Hops Route, through the hop fields, is definitely worthwhile, particularly in summer.

Veurne ⑬ on the river Ijzer is another town that was largely spared in World War I. The little town lies on reclaimed land, some 4 metres (13 ft) below sea level. It is associated with the period in history when Flanders was ruled by the Spanish line of the House of Habsburg, for Veurne served as headquarters of the Spanish officers. The Old Landhouse, the bell tower, the rebuilt meat market and the church of St Walburga in the town centre are worth a quick stop, but the town, which served as the Belgian Army Headquarters in 1914–15 and was the provisional residence of the king, has more to offer.

Of special note are the so-called "new town hall", the **stadhuis**, and the 16th-century inn called **Nobele Roze**. The New Town Hall, which stands on the picturesque marketplace, was built in the 16th century, and contains priceless leather wall-coverings of Spanish origin, while the Nobele Roze was where the Austrian lyric poet Rainer Maria Rilke once stayed.

The city's old town hall, which quartered Spanish officers, is known as the **Spaans Paviljoen** (Spanish Pavilion, open for guided tours only; Apr–Sep daily; Oct–Mar on request; entrance fee). The 17th-century Hoge Wacht at the edge of the marketplace also housed Spaniards for a time.

Veurne's best-known folk festival, the Atonement Procession on the last Sunday in July, hearkens back to Spanish austerity with its cross-bearing participants shrouded in dark hoods and robes.

It's not only Route 14–18 that allows access to the battlefields of Flanders; you can also visit them by boat from Nieuwpoort. Boats sail to Diksmuide along the river Ijzer, whose name was given to one of the war's terrible battles.

Map on page 218

Caught in a terrible storm whilst returning from the Crusades, Count Robert II of Flanders vowed to give a relic of the True Cross to the nearest church if he survived the night. He did survive and the gift was awarded to Veurne, beginning the annual Atonement Procession.

BELOW: the tranquil convent in Kortrijk.

Sculptural detail in Diksmuide – a 20th-century copy of a 13th-century original.

Diksmuide , like Ypres, had to be completely rebuilt after 1918 and it was decided to reconstruct the original village as faithfully as possible. Unfortunately this has resulted in something of a stage-set atmosphere; the houses, facades and gables, the town hall, the copy of the 13th-century Beguine Convent with its idyllic nooks and crannies were all built in the 20th century.

Less beautiful, but impossible to overlook, is the **Cross of Diksmuide** which commemorates the Battle of Ijzer, and its museum of the battle. The cross-shaped building affords a broad view of the countryside around the Ijzer, which was flooded in 1914 when the dykes were opened. This was done to prevent, or at least hinder, the invasion of German troops.

Canvas and lace

There are several paintings from the Rubens school in **St Martin's church** in **Kortrijk Courtrai** , as well as a richly carved tabernacle (1585) by Hendrik Maes. Although it contains many beautiful old buildings and was ranked as one of the great cloth producers of medieval Flanders, this town does not endeavour to present quite the same image of an old Flemish city as Bruges, Ghent or Ypres.

On the **Grote Markt** you'll find the **bell tower**, or as much as remains of it today. The statues on the facade of the high Gothic town hall next door to the bell tower are of the Counts of Flanders – introduced when the building was renovated in 1962. There's a municipal museum of fine art, the **Stedelijk Museum**, (open Tue–Sun; entrance fee) in one of the city's most lovely patrician homes. It contains many fine examples of lace and damask, some 18th-century Delftware and paintings by Roelandt Savery. Nearby are the **Broel Towers**, remnants of the medieval city's fortifications.

BELOW: the rearing Lion of Flanders.

BATTLE OF THE GOLDEN SPURS

Flanders has always been a contested land. And it was a battle – albeit a much more ancient one – which thrust Kortrijk (Courtrai), in the south of West Flanders, to fame. The Battle of the Golden Spurs was fought on 11 July 1302 between a group of Flemish weavers under the leadership of Pieter de Coninck and an army of French knights, led by Robert of Artois. Against all the odds, the Flemish weavers, armed with only pikes and catapults, managed a resounding victory over French knights, who were, by medieval standards, armed to the teeth.

One of the weavers' most cunning battle tactics was to disguise an expanse of marshy ground outside the town with brushwood. The French, anticipating an easy victory over their amateur opponents, failed to take due precautions and fell into the swampy mud. The triumphant Flemish took more than 600 golden spurs from the fallen French, and preserved them in the church of Our Lady, which dates from the 12th century. Unfortunately, these spurs are no longer to be seen, but the church does contain a terrific *Descent from the Cross* by van Dyck.

A monument dedicated to the Battle of the Golden Spurs stands at the site of the encounter, a little way to the east of the town centre in Groeningelaan.

However, the most noteworthy sight in Kortrijk is the **Belgian Flax Museum** (open Mar–Nov Tue–Fri; Sat & Sun pm only; entrance fee). Even today, flax continues to be produced in large quantities in the area around Kortrijk.

Another enchanting sight is a Beguine convent, the **Begijnhof**, the largest of its kind in Belgium. Forty little cottages form a small "town within a town". Its picturesque streets afford a wealth of fascinating insights into this self-chosen world of seclusion and solitude. The Beguine convent was founded in 1241 by Joanna of Constantinople.

On your way to Ghent, it's worth while making a short stop in the small town of **Oudenaarde** ⑯ (Audenarde). In the Middle Ages the town on the upper Scheldt was renowned for two things: for its masons, who worked on the construction of many famous Flemish buildings, such as the town hall in Bruges; and for its tapestry-makers, the weavers who created the beautiful and world-renowned wall tapestries.

The town hall on the Grote Markt is an ornate edifice in the style of Brabant Gothic, built in the 16th century. In the cloth hall, which dates from the 13th century, you can visit the **Museum of Oudenaarde Tapestries** (open Apr–Oct; free). Other noteworthy sights are the **church of Our Lady of Pamele** (open to guided tours only), the **church of St Walburga**, the **Beguine convent** and the **Our Lady Hospital** (also open to guided tours only).

As a young man, Charles V had a love affair with a girl from Oudenaarde, who bore a daughter, in 1522, named Margaret. The king's illegitimate daughter played an important role in the history of Flanders and the Netherlands under the name of Margaret of Parma. In her role as regent of the Low Countries under her half-brother Philip II, Margaret proved an able politician. ❑

Map on page 218

In Lalaing House, across the river from the marketplace, the town's long tradition as a centre for tapestry continues, with the restoration of old tapestries and the production of new designs.

BELOW: a twin gabled café in Oudenaarde.

HAINAUT AND THE SOUTH

The Hainaut region takes in a wide spectrum, from the cultural treasure chest of Tournai to the post-industrial landscapes around Charleroi. Between the two lies the region's capital at Mons

Map on page 236

Brussels

wenty-five kilometres (15 miles) south of Kortrijk, and an equal distance from the French city of Lille, is **Tournai ①** (Doornik; population 70,000), one of Belgium's most important art centres. It is also, along with Tongeren, one of the oldest cities in the country. The original Roman settlement of Turris Nerviorum was home to the Merovingians from 440 to 486, when Clovis, ruler of the Merovingians, overthrew the last Roman governor in Gaul and moved his capital to Soissons. In the 6th century, the town became the seat of a bishopric, and later was known for its porcelain, wall tapestry production and paintings, particularly through the work of Rogier van der Weyden.

Tournai was fought over in the 17th century by the French and the Dutch, but was spared in World War I, as it lay on the westernmost edge of war activity. But in World War II the city centre was destroyed by bombing raids, and nearly 1,300 houses were flattened. Nevertheless, one of the oldest residential houses in Europe (1175) survived, and can be found in the street Barre-St-Brice.

In the 9th century, a new cathedral was built on the site of the earlier Merovingian house of worship; this was, however, destroyed in the wake of Norman pillaging and arson in 881. Its successor didn't last long, either: it caught fire in 1060. Thousands of people made pilgrimages to the image of Mary in the cathedral during the plague epidemic of 1089, praying for protection or salvation from the disease. A procession of relics on 14 September 1090 was dedicated to driving out the plague. The church which we see today dates from the 12th century.

Tournai's cathedral, **Notre Dame** (Place PE Janson; open daily; free, but entrance fee for Treasury), rises up majestically over the roofs of the city. Frequently the accolade "the most beautiful church in Belgium" has been conferred upon this cathedral. The blue granite building is of tremendous proportions: a length of 135 metres (441 ft), with a nave 66 metres (216 ft) wide and a central tower 83 metres (271 ft) high. Each of its five towers – four on the outside and one centrally placed – is shaped differently.

Pilgrims to Our Lady

On the northern, river side of the cathedral, one enters or leaves through the **Porte Mantile**, or Mantilius Portal. Its name refers to the blind Mantilius, whom Saint Eleutherius once miraculously healed at this spot. Near the bell tower, the **Porte de Capitole** (Capital Portal) stands at the church's south entrance. Today somewhat damaged, the door is carved with images of the Last Judgment. One of the images depicts an angel battling with evil at the bedside of a dying man, representing the redemption of the dead. By the main portal, the founders of the cathedral and

PRECEDING PAGES: straddling the river Meuse, industrial Liège. **LEFT:** a woodland statue near the palace at Beloeil. **BELOW:** Notre Dame at Tournai.

The Wallonian sign to indicate a protected monument.

the first Christian community of Tournai, **St Piatus** and **St Eleutherius**, keep watch, the latter holding a model of his church. Between them, "Our Lady of the Sick" is an object of veneration for countless pilgrims every year.

Once inside the cathedral, you'll be overwhelmed at the sight of the immense central nave. Its sides are four storeys high. Because of the daylight streaming in through the many windows, and the light-coloured walls, the interior of the building is unusually bright. Cruciform vaulting from 1640, which spans the nave and the side aisles, has replaced the earlier wooden ceiling. The chapels of Saint John the Baptist and Saint Margaret contain wall paintings from the 13th century, but these chapels can only be visited on special request.

The chancel dates from 1759; here, too, stands the revered **Notre Dame la Brune** (the dark-complexioned), who is borne through the city in an annual procession on the second Sunday in September. In the right side aisle, a chapel is dedicated to Saint Louis. Built in the year 1299, it contains remains of stained-glass paintings from the 14th and 15th centuries, as well as baroque panelling

Hainaut and the South

from the Monastery of St Ghislain, near Mons, which was destroyed in the French Revolution. The original Gothic choir screen was replaced in 1572 by a marble and alabaster rood screen, built by Corneille de Vriendt of Antwerp. Off the aisle, the Chapel of the Blessed Sacrament contains an oil painting by Rubens dating from 1635, depicting the Salvation from the flames of Hell.

Bishop's relics

At the entrance to the **Chapel of the Holy Ghost**, you'll also find the door to the Cathedral Treasury, which contains valuable objects such as two late Romanesque reliquaries. A golden shrine of the Virgin Mary from 1205 is shaped in the form of a house; this ornate work is studded with precious stones and small enamel insets dominated by the colour blue. Another masterpiece of the goldsmith's art, the **Shrine of St Eleutherius**, dates from 1247, and contains the relics of the first Bishop of Tournai. The treasury also includes crosses set with gemstones and tapestries from Tournai. To the south of the cathedral is a monument to the painter Rogier van der Weyden, born in Tournai in 1399.

Immediately adjacent to the cathedral, a 72-metre (235-ft) **bell tower** (open Wed–Mon; entrance fee) rises high over the triangular marketplace. Construction work on the tower commenced in 1187, making this edifice the oldest of its kind in Belgium. Since then, the bell tower has been altered and renovated every bit as often as the cathedral itself.

A Renaissance building from 1610, the **Halle aux Draps** (cloth hall) also stands on the Grand-Place. Located on the south side of the square, the building reflects the flourishing textile industry which was responsible for the city's economic well-being until the 16th century. A bronze statue commemorates

Map on page 236

TIP

River boat excursions can be taken from Tournai between May and August. They depart from Pont des Trous, just within the ring road in the north-east of the city.

BELOW: a fair on the Grand-Place at Tournai .

Flowers from the fields of Wallonia.

Christine de la Laings, under whose leadership the citizens of Tournai were able to defend themselves during the siege of 1581. The **church of St Quentin** stands on the northwest side of the marketplace. Although it originally dates from the 12th century, it has been modified and restored many times since. To the northwest of the marketplace, the **Pont des Trous** (Bridge of Holes) consists of two towers which were part of the original fortifications of 1290.

A short walk southwest of the marketplace (away from the river), and you'll come across the **Musée des Beaux-Arts** (Museum of Fine Art; Rue St-Martin; open Wed–Mon; entrance fee; tel: (069) 222043). Although containing many examples of modern art, the museum also displays paintings by Rogier van der Weyden and Rubens. A famous painting by Louis Gallait of Tournai depicts the plague of 1032. Further paintings by this artist include *The Abdication of Charles V* and *The Severed Heads of Counts Egmont and Horn*.

A boating excursion on the river Escaut (Scheldt) is a wonderful way to get one's first impression of Tournai: the boat trips last approximately one hour.

Little Versailles

About 30 km (20 miles) east of Tournai lies the community of **Beloeil ②**, a little town known for its **palace** (open Apr–Sep daily; entrance fee; grounds open all year round daily; entrance fee), which once belonged to the Princes of Ligne. After a damaging fire in the 19th century, most of the original castle was rebuilt and restored; but its oldest sections date from 1511. At first glance, the building looks like a miniature Versailles. The palace houses an impressive collection of art and artefacts, including paintings from the 15th century to the 19th, an array of tapestries and excellent examples of Rococo furniture. The palace

BELOW: the long trip for the postman at Beloeil Palace.

gardens were laid out in the 18th century by a Parisian designer, and are modelled on the formal gardens of Le Nôtre. Amongst the manicured hedges and carefully bordered lakes is an Orangery with a restaurant. There is also provision for camping within the grounds.

The Giants of Ath

Winding a path 10 km (6 miles) northward along narrow country lanes that pass a handful of villages and several large farmhouses, we come to **Ath ❸**, which lies at the intersection of the two Denders rivers. Baldwin IV, Count of Hainaut, had a fortress erected on the road from Flanders to Burgundy in 1136; today, all that remains of it is the **Tour du Burbant** (Brabant), with walls 3.7 metres (12 ft) thick. Modest though it is, the tower's significance resides in the fact that it is the oldest surviving military fortification in Belgium. The **Grand-Place** has a number of interesting buildings around it, including a stepped-gable house from the 16th century, several buildings from the 17th and 18th centuries and the **town hall**, which was begun in 1614.

During the last weekend in August, the Grand-Place is the site of the so-called "Wedding of Goliath". The highlight of this folkloric festival is the **Procession of the Giants of Ath** which winds through the town. This festival originated in 1390, at which time it was a purely religious event. In the middle of the 15th century, completely secular figures and vehicles began to be included in the procession: farm wagons decorated with flowers, representatives of the guilds and, in particular, giants, who danced in the street to the music of brass bands. In the course of the festivities, the giantess "Madame Gouyasse" (Goliath) weds the giant "Gouyasse", in a ceremony that has been enacted since 1715. The couple are married in front of the Town Hall every year, after pledging their troth before the mayor and the local magistrate. After the wedding, by way of matrimonial celebration, David challenges Goliath to a fight; in the course of the ensuing battle, the giant is felled, and David becomes a hero.

Industry and history

On a slight rise in the landscape 25 km (15 miles) southeast of Ath, we come to **Mons ❹** (Bergen, population 100,000). Warehouses, modern industrial complexes and gleaming shop fronts let you know you're entering the capital of the province of Hainaut. Church towers mingle with factory chimneys in this upright, industrious town.

The city is the centre of the **Borinage**, Belgium's largest coal-mining area. Coal was mined here as early as the 12th century, in one of the first coal mines of Europe. By then the city was already well established, having grown up around a cloister, founded in the 7th century by Waltraud, the daughter of a Count of Hainaut. This cloister developed into a cathedral chapter of canonesses at the centre of what later became the city. Waltraud died in 688; her relics have been preserved and honoured in various buildings. In 1295, Mons became the capital of the County of Hainaut; over the ensuing centuries, it was a key strategic point in numerous wars. The city has been occupied by

Map on page 236

TIP

The tourist information office for Ath and the surrounding area can be found in the town at Rue Nazareth 2.

BELOW: the flower market on the Grand-Place in the town of Mons.

*The tourist informa-
tion office in Mons,
which can be found
just off the Grand-
Place.*

BELOW: the boy
fountain in the
Jardin du Maieur at
Mons.

French, Spanish and Austrians since the 17th century, and has withstood several sieges. The 20th century offered the city no respite from the ravages of war: Mons suffered under bombardment and artillery shelling during World Wars I and II.

However, the **Collégiale Ste-Waudru** (church of St Waudru, open daily; free) has been preserved. Its architect, Mathieu de Lazens, also built the renowned town hall in Leuven. This edifice has long been admired for its beauty and dominating presence. Built between 1450 and 1621 of light grey stone, the domed church of St Waudru was to have had a tower 190 metres (621 ft) high, but only the base of it was ever built. Further construction was forever abandoned in 1669, when the three aisles were roofed over. Twenty-nine chapels surround the church, and an imposing staircase leads to the main portal.

The precious reliquary of St Waltraud is housed in the church, as is, in the foyer, the gilded processional coach (Car d'Or), in which the bones of the saint are borne through the city on the Sunday after Whitsun. This famous procession dates back to the plague of 1348. The church treasury contains gold objects from the 13th to the 19th centuries, including monstrances, communion goblets, reliquaries, censers and liturgical books.

Located above the church, **Place du Château** ❸ was laid out on the site of the former castle of the Counts of Hainaut. All that remains of the castle today is the **Calixtus Chapel**, erected in 1051 by Countess Richilde to house the relics of Pope Calixtus; she had received these as a gift from her Aunt Egberge, the Abbess of Neuss. When Place du Château was constructed, workers uncovered **wall paintings** from the 11th and 12th centuries; these were badly damaged, and eventually disappeared entirely, not to be reconstructed until 1951.

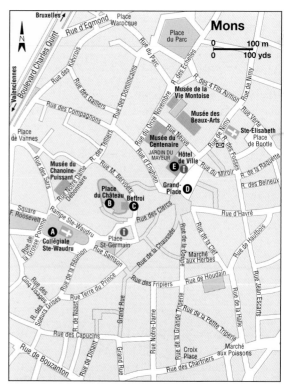

The chapel door is made of heavy oak and the walls are 1.5 metres (5 ft) thick. Three reclining figures are housed in the interior. The first of these is a representation of the Gilles de Chin, a knight who was interred in the monastery of Saint-Ghislain after his death. When this cloister was destroyed in the 18th century, the figure was brought here; but over the years it has become rather badly damaged. The other two figures date from the 14th century and are of Guillaume de Gavre, Lord of Steenkerque and Tongrenelle, Count of the Holy Roman Empire, and his wife, Jeanne de Berlo de Liège, Luxemburg et Westphalie. These were donated to the city of Mons during the 19th century by Baron de Hérissem, who was a city counsellor of Mons from 1849 to 1866.

The seal of Hainaut

To the left of the entrance hang reproductions of significant **charters**, all of which were issued in 1200 by **Baldwin VI** of Hainaut before his departure on the Fourth Crusade. Seals of all the counts and countesses of Hainaut from the 11th to the 14th centuries are displayed in a cabinet on the wall; you can also see the **Seal of Mons** and the seals of the other most important cities of old Hainaut. Casts of two more figures lie in the middle of the crypt. Both of these are of French kings: Philip VI of Valois (1328–59) and Charles V, the Wise (1364–80). The originals are preserved in the Basilica of St-Denis-lès-Paris and in the Louvre in Paris.

Place du Château is a good observation point: the hill lies nearly at the city centre, and commands a panoramic view of Mons and its surroundings. Looming over the square's southwest side is the **beffroi ⊙** (bell tower, open Tue–Sun; entrance fee), built between 1662 and 1672 by the architect Louis Ledoux and

Map on page 240

From 1879 to 1880, Vincent van Gogh lived on Rue du Pavillon in Cuesmes-Mons. The painter assured his friends that the Borinage was every bit as picturesque as old Venice, Arabia or Brittany.

BELOW: springtime in Mons.

the engineer Anthoni. The tower is 87 metres (284 ft) high, and has two ground floors, one on the Rue des Gades and one at the level of Place du Château. In the former guardroom, you'll find large panels explaining the four major battles of World Wars I and II which were fought at Mons. Comprised of 47 bells, of which the heaviest weighs 6,000 kg (13,200 pounds), the carillon was somehow able to survive both world wars. On 11 November 1918 and on 2 September 1944, the same citizen, M. F. Redouté, tolled the mighty bells to announce the liberation of the city.

North of Place du Château is the British war memorial, which Lord Alexander of Tunis had dedicated in 1952. It commemorates the two battles of Mons, which marked the beginning and the end of World War I for the British.

Going along the Rue des Clercs, you'll come to the **Grand-Place D** with its Gothic town hall and its Renaissance and baroque houses. A tranquillity pervades the marketplace, which is devoted mainly to vegetables and flowers. The town hall, or **Hôtel de Ville E**, was built between 1458 and 1467. The two storeys of the facade have 10 pointed window arches and are ornamented with architectural reliefs. To the left of the town hall's main entrance, the **Singe du Grand-Garde**, a little cast-iron monkey, is supposed to bring luck to the unmarried; according to local superstition, anyone who touches him will soon find a partner. The monkey's head has been worn smooth over the years. The main entrance of the town hall leads into the mayor's garden, close to the **Musée du Centenaire** (open Tue–Sun; entrance fee), which exhibits ceramics.

About 20 km (13 miles) eastward along the N90 we come to the little town of **Binche ⑤**, which contains remnants of a 12th-century city wall and whose riotous carnival celebrations are said to have given rise to the English word

There is a monument in the mayor's garden dedicated to Roland de Lassus, better known as Orlando di Lasso, one of the foremost composers of the 16th century. Di Lasso was born in Mons in 1532.

BELOW: the tiled facade of a chemist's shop in Binche.

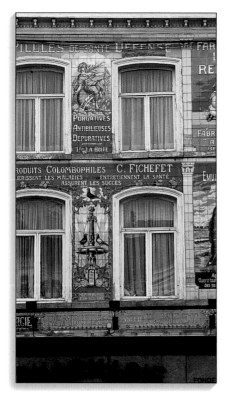

BINGEING IN BINCHE

Binche is well known as Belgium's carnival capital. For three days in spring, the whole town becomes a hive of activity. The festivities follow a centuries-old tradition, with Shrove Tuesday providing the focus for the town's revelry. This is the day when the "Gilles" dominate proceedings. Hundreds of men, born and brought up in Binche, gather at daybreak in costumes made of linen and decorated with heraldic lions. During these early hours, their heads are covered in white hoods, and their faces shielded by grand masks that display a painted moustache and green spectacles. What better to complete this ensemble than clogs upon their feet to dance a slow dance through the streets, maintaining steady rhythm.

In the afternoon, the masks are exchanged for headgear of extravagant white ostrich feathers and the dancers balance a tall basket of oranges on one hand. Then, to the deafening accompaniment of violas, accordions, barrel organs and drums, they dance their way through the streets, transforming the medieval town into a vibrant flow of colour and noise. The origins of this carnival can be traced back to the 14th century, and its importance to Binche is maintained to this day. In the weeks leading up to the carnival, fancy dress balls are held as well.

binge. To the north of Binche is the royal palace and park of **Mariemont** ❻. A wrought-iron fence 3 metres (10 ft) high surrounds this wonderful wooded park; its grounds are so extensive that the park has developed its own micro-climate, perceptibly contrasting to that of its surroundings.

Doubtless because of the region's developing mining and steel industries, whose smoke darkened the skies, the king lost interest in his residence here. Nowadays the ruins of the ornate 16th-century palace are overrun by children.

Industrial legacy

Charleroi ❼ typifies the legacy of industrial decline in this region. Built up during the industrial boom time during the first half of the 20th century, it now struggles for an economic foothold amongst new world markets, its industrial lifeblood reduced to a trickle. Once red, the brick buildings of the former miners' communities are laid out symmetrically around the former mine. Near the entrance to the pits are the directors' villas, and between the two the foremen's houses. The city centre is characterised by plain administrative buildings, but amongst them are two or three museums of interest.

The town's two best museums are the **Musée des Beaux Arts** (Place Charles II; open Tue–Sat; entrance fee), which covers a range of painting, from the sedate portraits of the 18th century to industrial landscapes of 19th-century Charleroi, and into the imaginary landscapes of Paul Delvaux (*see p91*). Nearby on Boulevard Defontaine is the **Musée du Verre** (Glass Museum; open Tue–Sat; entrance fee). The prospect of a museum devoted to glass may fail to raise the pulse of some visitors, but the array of artefacts, from Egyptian jewellery to examples of Chinese, Islamic, Byzantine and Venetian glass is a remarkable sight. ❑

Maps:
Mons 240
Area 236

In the basement of the Musée du Verre in Charleroi is a room devoted to the Roman and Merovingian history of the region. Exhibits reveal the craftsmanship in ceramic production of the time.

BELOW: a quiet day in the centre of Binche.

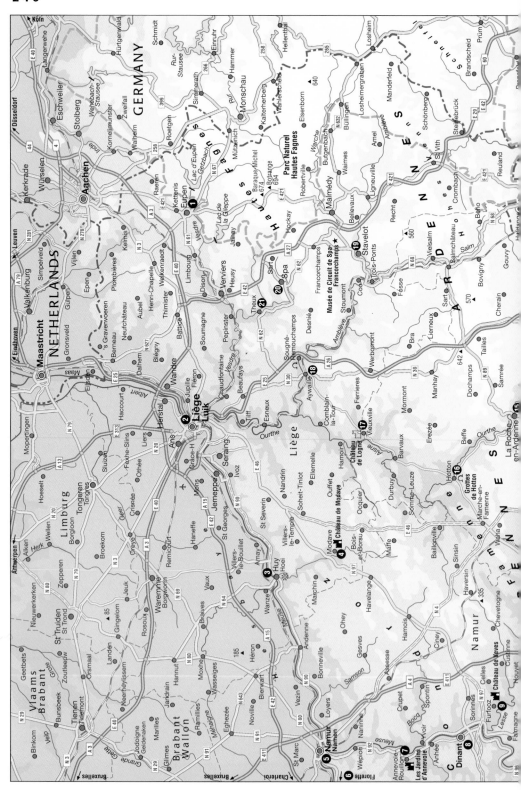

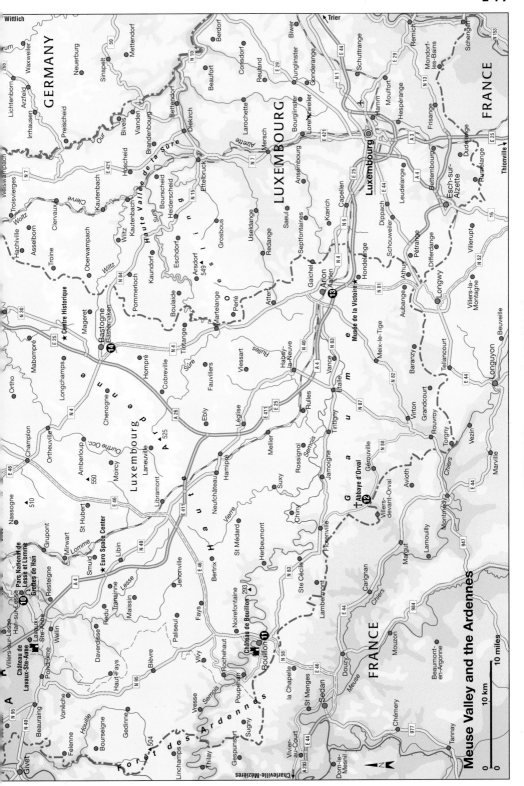

Meuse Valley and the Ardennes

THE MEUSE VALLEY

The Meuse has been a hard-working river for centuries,
supplying the power for weaving. It flows through enchanting
scenery and through ancient towns such as Liège and Namur

Map on pages 246–7

The Meuse Valley forms part of the industrial heartland of Belgium, but hidden amongst the machinery of production are some of the most interesting small towns, tucked into the river's rocky banks. And to the south of the broad valley you will find rural havens in the northern fringe of the Ardennes.

Our tour begins just to the east of the river valley in the town of **Eupen** ❶ (population 18,000), which is just within the mainly German-speaking district along the eastern border. The town's German culture reflects the fact that it only became part of Belgium in the 1920s.

Eupen lies at the edge of the Hautes Fagnes Nature Reserve (*see page 277*), one of the most beautiful and wild areas of the Belgian countryside. In the 14th and 15th centuries, Eupen experienced a tremendous flourishing thanks to an influx of weavers, who were attracted by the waters of the Vesdre river. The town's textile industry reached its peak in the 18th century.

Although Eupen suffered considerable damage in World War II, the old town of today is still characterised by numerous patrician buildings dating from the 17th, 18th and 19th centuries. Eupen's most famous building is the green-domed **church of Saint Nicholas**. Originally a chapel, it is first mentioned in documents of 1213; only in 1695 did it become a parish church. The city planner of Aachen, Laurenz Mefferatis, designed this baroque church; construction began in 1721. Ludwig von Fisenne, a well-known architect from Aachen, is responsible for the appearance of the western facade, which was built between 1896 and 1898. The front of the church is "defended" by two towers.

The **Municipal Museum of Eupen** (Gospert 52; open Sat & Sun; Wed 5–7pm only; entrance fee), housed in a building that is worth a look in itself, is devoted to the history of the area, which was compelled to change its political allegiance remarkably often over the years. The museum offers a complete restoration of a goldsmithy; in this workshop, three generations of Eupen goldsmiths toiled, and some of their remarkable handiwork is on display.

Carnival is celebrated with gusto in Eupen. The streets are alive with activity from the Thursday before Carnival weekend until the parade on the Monday before Lent, when the festivities culminate. Another event which attracts crowds of visitors every year is the **St Martin's Parade** held on 11 November, when citizens re-enact the story of St Martin. The saint is accompanied by his goose, Roman soldiers and lantern-bearing children. A massive bonfire concludes the festivities. In the summer, Eupen residents unwind at the **Stau See** (Dam Lake), the largest lake in Belgium, created at the confluence of the Vesdre and Getz by a dam 410 metres (1,340 ft) long.

PRECEDING PAGES: a roadside Virgin Mary in the Belgian countryside. **LEFT:** the bridge to the citadel, Namur. **BELOW:** the church of St Nicholas in Eupen.

Two visitors make a food stop in Liège.

BELOW: the "Fiery Elijah", a train that crosses the Hautes Fagnes region.

Metropolis in the East

Liège ➋ (Luik; population 250,000, or 500,000 including environs), located at the junction of the Meuse and the Ourthe rivers, is a bishopric, a university city, the centre of the Belgian steel industry and the capital of the province. The city of Liège grew from a simple chapel, which was erected on the Meuse in 558 at the behest of St Monulphe, the Bishop of Tongeren. One of the Bishop's successors, St Lambert, Bishop of Tongeren-Maastricht, was murdered in Liège in 705. St Hubert later had a church built in Lambert's memory, and transferred the seat of the bishopric to Liège.

The city experienced its first burst of development in the 10th century under Bishop Notker; his reign saw the construction of a cathedral, the Bishop's Palace, two cloisters, and seven monasteries. Liège in the Middle Ages was a city of craftsmen, particularly of goldsmiths, silversmiths and arms manufacturers. At the city limits stood the Fabrique Nationale d'Armes de Guerre, which was world-renowned for its hunting weapons in particular.

Liège was the first city in Europe to mine coal. The roads along which coal and steel were transported have remained, although the coal-mining industry eventually ground to a halt. But other industries persist, and Liège now has the third-largest inland port in Europe, after Duisburg and Paris.

The **marketplace** and adjoining **Place St-Lambert ➊** form the city's heart. A fountain, symbolising the city's freedom and its autonomous jurisdiction, dominates the marketplace, over which a shadow is cast by a large pedestal from the 13th century. The two-and-a-half storey baroque **town hall** from the early 18th century, which stands on the Place du Marché, has retained much of its original ornate furnishings: a double staircase, a lobby with eight marble Doric columns, fireplaces, and other artistic treasures.

To the left of the entrance, a bronze plaque commemorates the most famous citizen of Liège: **Georges Simenon**, the creator of Inspector Maigret. The plaque was put up in memory of the policemen who fell during World War I (the real Arnold Maigret was one such casualty). Rue Léopold 24 is the house in which Georges Simenon was born; he was a personal friend of Chief of Police Maigret, and later used him as the model for his fictional inspector.

The keys of St Hubert

From the Place Saint-Lambert, an open staircase leads to **Eglise St-Croix ➌** (church of the Holy Cross), which presents the visitor with the relatively rare spectacle of a church with three aisles of the same height. The church contains the keys of Saint Hubert, the first Bishop of Liège. Similar keys were once used in the church to cauterise bleeding wounds.

The **Palais des Princes-Evêques ➍**, (Palace of the Prince-Bishops) on Place St-Lambert, now houses the **Palace of Justice**. The building dates back to the reign of Bishop Notker, and the parts of the palace that have been preserved date from the 17th and 18th centuries. One of the most extensive collections of material pertaining to Belgian history can be found in the **Musée de la Vie Wallonne ➎** (open Tue–Sun; entrance fee; tel: (04) 223 6094). The museum is housed in the nearby Minorite Cloister, a building which dates from the 17th century. The Musée de la Vie Wallonne documents the history of the city's arts and industry and the folk customs, history, language and heritage of the Walloon people.

Since 1885, a neoclassical patrician house has been home to the **Musée d'Armes** (Museum of Weaponry) (Quai de Maestricht 8; open Wed–Mon; entrance fee). The elegant building was constructed by the Liège-born architect Barthélemy Digneffe. Containing some 12,500 different weapons, the museum is internationally recognised as one of the most important of its kind. Weapons of all kinds – for hunting as well as fighting – are on display.

The **Musée Curtius** ❻ (Quai de Maestricht; open Wed–Mon; entrance fee) is housed in a Renaissance palace dating from 1600, which was once the residence of the wealthy arms trader Jean Curtius. Today, the museum contains collections of Frankish and Gallo-Roman coins, furniture from Liège and porcelain, stoneware and woodcarvings from the Meuse area. Located in the same building, the **Musée du Verre** (Glass Museum) displays works by Phoenician, Moslem, Chinese, Venetian and Belgian craftsmen.

In 1794, the **Cathédrale St Hubert**, located on the square of the same name, was destroyed by Liège revolutionaries, although its foundations are still visible to this day. The city's most famous work of art – a bronze **Baptismal Font** by Renier van Huy – was fortunately saved from such a fate. The bronze font is now housed in the Romanesque **Eglise St Barthélemy** ❼ (St Bartholomew, open daily; entrance fee), which dates from the 10th to 12th centuries, and is also located in the historic city centre. The central image of the five baptismal scenes on the front is a depiction of John the Baptist baptising Christ.

**Maps:
Area 246
Liège 252**

TIP

To get a good overall view of the town, and see the winding course of the Meuse running through it, the citadel to the north of the city offers the best vantage point.

BELOW: a flower stall at the flea market in Liège.

One of the pretty, cobbled alleyways lined with cottages in Liège.

Side by side with the numerous modern industrial administration buildings are the churches of Saint Paul, Saint Jacques and Saint Jean (St John). The **Eglise St-Jean** (open daily; free) was built in the 10th century on the model of the Carolingian cathedral of Aachen. According to contemporary sources, the exterior of the original main building had 16 sides, while its interior was octagonal. In the middle of the 18th century a small round building, the side chapels and the choir were altered in accordance with the revived spirit of classicism. Located in the church is the famous Seat of Wisdom, the *Sedes Sapientiae*, or the throne of Christ.

Originally a collegiate church, **Cathédrale St-Paul** ❶ (Rue St-Paul; open daily; entrance fee for Treasury) was elevated to the status of a cathedral by the Concordat of 1801. It was founded in the 10th century, but restored and added to during the 19th century. The 16th-century stained-glass windows are worthy of note, as are the extraordinary 19th-century furnishings and *Christ in the Tomb* by Jean del Cour. Other treasures include carvings from the 11th century and a half-length reliquary of St Lambert – a gift from Charles the Bold.

Of the abbey church **Eglise St-Jacques** ❶ (Place St-Jacques 8; open Sun–Fri; free), founded in the 11th century, all that remains today is the western wing of limestone, with its ribbed vaulting and medallions. The rest of the building is a conglomeration of styles from Gothic to Renaissance. The interior contains a host of fascinating elements, including sculpture by del Cour, magnificent stained-glass windows from the 16th century and a rood screen of 1600.

BELOW: inner courtyard of the Palais des Princes–Evêques.

The **Aquarium** ❻ (Quai van Beneden 22; open daily; entrance fee) of the Zoological Institute of the University of Liège has all the latest technical equipment. It presents a fascinating record of the oceans' fauna.

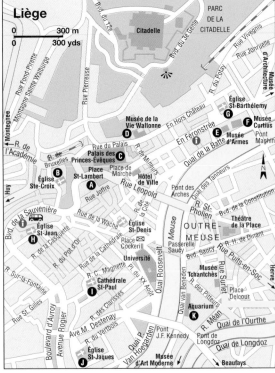

The two buildings in which the **Musée d'Architecture** is housed are typical of the building style popular in the Meuse valley in the 17th century. Exhibits include doors and woodcarvings (faithfully restored), fine panelling, fireplaces and mouldings. The museum's garden contains numerous porticoes, arcades, fountains, statues and bas-reliefs. The museum also houses a photo gallery and regularly holds exhibitions of modern art.

Late 19th- and 20th-century art is more thoroughly addressed in the **Musée d'Art Moderne** (Parc de la Boverie 3; open Tue–Sat p.m. only; entrance fee), which contains paintings and sculptures from 1850 to the present day. Among these are some 250 works by Marc Chagall, James Ensor, Paul Gauguin, René Magritte, and Pablo Picasso. The museum is located in the Parc de la Boverie, at some distance from the city centre.

Maps:
Area 246
Liège 252

Local folklore

On the other (east) bank of the Meuse, you will find the neighbourhood of **Outre-Meuse**, which is steeped in local tradition and folklore. Every year on 15th August it holds a fair, with lively church festivals and folkloric entertainment. The marionette Tchantchès, a figure central to the folklore hereabouts, is said to embody the spirit of the local inhabitants. Tchantchès was a character who spoke out plainly every time he saw an instance of injustice, and this upfront honesty is supposedly imbued in the local populace.

The composer **André Modeste Grétry** (1741–1813) was originally from Outre-Meuse. The house in which this man – dubbed the "father of comic opera" – was born has been converted into a museum; it is at Rue des Récollets 36. Another memorial to this artist stands in front of the opera house of Liège.

BELOW: view of Liège from the citadel.

Georges Simenon

When he created the figure of the pipe-smoking Inspector Maigret, Georges Simenon shaped one of the great detective characters of our time. Like Maigret, Simenon also rose to world fame, his prolific output unceasing for 34 years. Eventually he decided to forego a further episode of Maigret adventures, in order to "catch my breath", as he put it. But by the time he made this decision, there wasn't much time left for relaxation: in September, 1989, the author died in Lausanne aged 86.

As an author, Simenon broke many records in terms of output and popularity. In total, he had more than 300 published works, making him the most prolific writer since Balzac, and the fact that 500 million copies of his books have been sold to date makes him the most read author in the world. His many stories and novels have been translated into more than 50 languages. Some of his works also made it to the screen.

In the 1950s, Simenon selected Switzerland as his preferred country of residence. Here, after the suicide of his beloved daughter Mari-Jo, the former extrovert spent the last 10 years of his life as a recluse. At the same time, in keeping with his taste for the paradoxical, he exchanged his luxury villa near Lausanne for a modest house in the city.

Before these quiet later years, Simenon had had a reputation for living life to the hilt. In his *Intimate Memoirs*, for instance, he tells of having thousands of sexual affairs.

Simenon spent the first 19 years of his productive life in the Belgian city of Liège, where he was born on 13 February, 1903. "All of the feelings and impressions which we retain in later life have been collected by our 17th or, at the latest, 18th year," he was fond of saying. At 17, he was already a reporter for Liège's daily paper, *Gazette de Liège*. He wrote his first novel when he was 18; and he wasn't yet 20 when he signed a contract with the publishing house Fayard. The signing of this contract was, in effect, the official hour of Inspector Maigret's birth.

By the age of 26, the author Simenon was firmly established on the path of success. He began to lead an extravagant and nomadic life. At one time or another, he owned a ranch in Arizona, a villa in Cannes and a castle in Switzerland; altogether he moved 33 times in his life. Moving from Europe to the USA, from the canals of Belgium to the lagoons of Tahiti, Simenon travelled the world, eagerly gathering impressions and recording his adventures in the form of news reports.

The pace he set for his daily output was remarkable, and he is said to have written one of his novels in just three days. He generally used to shut himself up with six full pipes for six hours, and filled 100 pages every day.

Inspector Maigret lives on in the popular imagination as a figure comparable with Sherlock Holmes or Hercule Poirot. However, Maigret is a detective like no other, and does not use the methodology of pure logic, as does Sherlock Holmes, to solve his cases. In fact, Simenon never considered his books as detective stories; as he once said, he believed not in stories, but in people. ❏

LEFT: The beguiling pipe-smoking crime-writer Georges Simenon.

You can get a good view of the city and the Meuse from the old **citadel**. It has been destroyed many times, but always rebuilt anew. You can reach it by climbing 407 steps, although there is also a street which leads directly to it.

Liège has one of the largest pedestrian zones in Europe. Its total of more than 5,000 shops makes the whole city seem like one huge shopping centre. The abundance of shops is augmented by a great flea market, known as **la Batte**; it is one of the largest and most interesting in the country. The market is held every Sunday morning on the left bank of the Meuse, between Cockerill Square and the bridge Pont Maghin, between 9am and 2pm.

In the Walloon dialect of Liège, the word *batte* means embankment or river walk. Many such "battes" were erected over the centuries. This Sunday market has appropriated for itself the name used for the road running along the river. It originated in the 16th century, when the city administration decided to build an embankment along the Meuse and to open the land to trade. Cattle dealers and fruit and vegetable salesmen began to advertise their wares on the spot; it was here, too, that the first public theatrical performances took place in the city.

Along the Meuse

Two roads lead along the **Meuse valley** from Liège in the direction of Huy, and both present a perfectly good impression of the region. The landscape that unfolds is not a romantic, castle-filled valley such as one might find along the Meuse tributaries in the Ardennes, but rather a broad, wooded river valley packed with evidence of heavy industry. Metalworking plants, stone quarries, gravel and cement factories line the way. But if you turn off into one of the many smaller side valleys, birdsong soon overwhelms the drone of industry.

Maps:
Area 246
Liège 252

TIP

On Fridays in July and August there are river cruises across the border to Maastricht. The round trip takes about 10 hours, and departs from the centre of Liège.

BELOW: forsythia blooms in the Ourthe valley, near its confluence with the Meuse.

TIP

Huy straddles the river Meuse, and the tourist information office is situated on the south bank of the river, near the bridge at 1 Quai de Namur.

First mentioned in 636, **Huy** ❸ (population 15,000) is one of the oldest cities in Belgium, and in the Middle Ages it was a flourishing trade centre for pewter, copper and cloth. A **cable car** runs 70 metres (230 ft) upwards from Avenue Batta to Weiler La Satre, from which point you can look far out over the town and the Meuse valley; the view, from this perspective, is quite lovely. This is the site of Huy's **citadel** (open Jul & Aug daily; Sep–Jun Mon–Fri; entrance fee), which was built in 1818 on the site of a former castle. In the town centre, the **collegiate church of Our Lady** (open daily; free except for Treasury) has stood beside the bridge over the Meuse since 1377. The church is marked by a huge rose window on the west tower, 9 metres (30 ft) in diameter. The steeple of the tower, destroyed by a fire in 1803, has never been rebuilt. A series of 14th-century reliefs in the Bethlehem Portal, flanking the choir entrance to the church, depicts scenes from the birth of Christ.

The church treasury contains many valuable reliquaries, two of which come from the workshops of Godfrey of Huy. The **town hall** on the marketplace, which was built in 1799 in Louis XV style, was intended to symbolise the town's spiralling prosperity, as its majestic external double staircase demonstrates. The bell tower's complement of 36 bells regularly pealed out in celebration of the town's renown in trade – and, no doubt, the assured taxes to pay the town council. Another building which contributes to the harmonious appearance of the old town is the parish **church of St Mangold**, built as a simple chapel in the 15th century, but with some foundations dating from the 13th century.

Some 6 km (4 miles) south of Huy on the N641 is one of the most beautiful castles in Belgium, impressively located in the midst of a nature preserve of some 455 hectares (1,125 acres). Perched on top of a high rock wall, and commanding a

BELOW:
black cats in Huy.

magnificent view of the valley all the way to the little river of Hoyoux, stands **Château de Modave** ❹ (open Apr–mid-Nov daily; entrance fee). Containing 20 lavishly furnished rooms (open to the public), complete with sculptures, Brussels wall tapestries and colourful stuccowork by Jean Christian Hansche, the castle has, since 1673, been owned in succession by the Count de Marchin, Prince Maximilian of Bavaria, Cardinal Fürstenberg, Baron de Ville, the Duke of Montmorency and the families Lamarche and Braconnier. Although the main structure dates from the 17th century, the walls of the keep are 12th-century.

A trade route

Between Huy and Namur, the Meuse landscape is quite beautiful. Namur is a turning point in the course of the river, as the Meuse, which flows north out of the Ardennes, is intersected by the Sambre. From here, it follows the Sambre's original course eastwards. This stretch of the river serves as a shipping route for industry, part of an extensive network of waterways which, along with many canals, connects the west of the country with the Netherlands, and eventually leads right to the North Sea.

The Meuse is also a traffic route for barges south of Namur, flowing from the French border through Dinant, but many excursion steamers also ply this route. A trip along the river, passing between the high cliffs, castles and citadels, while enjoying cake and coffee, is highly recommended.

Namur ❺ (population 35,000) is the capital of the province and of the Walloon region, and because of its position at the confluence of the Meuse and Sambre rivers, amidst the foothills of the Belgian Ardennes, it is also the transportation hub of the region. Two major motorways, the E40 and E41,

Maps:
Area 246
Namur
258

BELOW: Namur's citadel at night.

The bicycle is a much loved means of transport everywhere in Belgium.

BELOW: the exterior of the Musée Felicien Rops.

intersect north of the city; these are, respectively, the historic link between Brussels and Luxembourg in the south and the East-West connection from Cologne through Aachen to Paris.

It's said that the name Namur harks back to a legendary dwarf who dwelt on the mountain where the castle now stands. People came to consult him for advice, and he gave a different answer to each of them. However, following the birth of Christ, the oracle remained mute. Later, the city which lay at the mountain's foot was named after the dwarf ("nain muet").

History offers a different account. The city was known in the days of the Romans as a point of military significance, due to its strategic position, and at that time it was called *Namurum Castrum*. The city's military status continued in the Middle Ages, when it became fortified. In 1559, Namur was made the seat of a new bishopric, but this brought no peace to the city. Between the 16th and 18th centuries, its inhabitants were subjected to repeated sieges and bombardments, which destroyed large sections of Namur.

In 1711, the city was made the capital of a small, independent country which encompassed the region of modern Namur, Luxembourg and parts of Hainaut. Nine years later, this state fell to the Netherlands. Under Dutch rule, broad boulevards were laid out within the city, and in 1794 Namur became the capital of the Department of Sambre-et-Meuse. In 1914, and again in 1940, the Germans seized the city, destroying substantial sections of it.

Namur is dominated by its mighty **citadelle** Ⓐ (open Jun–Sep daily; Oct–May Sat, Sun & public holidays; entrance fee includes museums), which has put in some 2,000 years of military service. The Celts first established a fortification here, and much later, as the fortress of the Counts of Namur, it was one of the

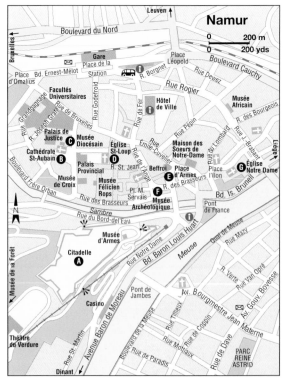

best-fortified castles of medieval Europe. Its appearance today is largely the re-sponsibility of the Dutch, who ruled here from 1815 to 1830. From Easter until October, a cable-car runs between the city and the citadel. Otherwise, you can take the *route merveilleuse*, a winding road that richly deserves its name: virtu-ally every point along it commands a marvellous view of the city.

There's not much left of the original fortress: a square with a small tower and a well 50 metres (163 ft) deep, and the bases of two towers. The citadel that you see today was built in 1692. Today, its 80-hectare (200-acre) grounds include parks, an open-air theatre, an amusement park, an observation tower and the Château de Namur, visible from afar and now operating as a hotel. A tourist "train" takes visitors slowly through the citadel's halls.

Located in two of the citadel's towers are the **Musée d'Armes** (Museum of Weaponry) and the **Musée de la Forêt** (Forest Museum). The Museum of Weaponry presents an overview of the military history and most important sieges of Namur, culminating with World Wars I and II. The museum also contains a range of African weapons, as well as some for hunting and fencing. Fauna and flora of the Ardennes are on display in the Forest Museum. Of special interest are the magnificent butterfly collection and the exhibits warning against environ-mental damage. Trees mainly indigenous to the Ardennes have been planted around the museum. They include chestnut and walnut trees, plane trees, oaks, beeches and birches, aspens, acacias, poplars, limes, willows and maples. The 3,500-seat open-air theatre in the citadel is Belgium's largest.

Namur's **Old City** stretches along the north bank of the Sambre and Meuse. The **cathédrale Saint-Aubain** Ⓑ (Place St-Aubain; open daily; free) was built during the middle of the 18th century by the Italian architect Gaetano Pizzoni.

Map on page 258

BELOW: half hidden by trees, a castle by the river's edge.

A bilingual post box ensuring fairness throughout the land.

Count Albert II of Namur had founded a collegiate church on the same site as early as 1047; the church's Gothic belfry is a remnant of this former building. Topped with a classical dome, the cathedral's interior is ornamented with statues by Laurent Delvaux. A plaque behind the main altar commemorates Don John of Austria, whose heart is interred here. This son of Charles V died of the plague in 1578 near Namur; he had beaten the Turks in the sea battle of Lepanto. Since 1579, his remains have lain in the Escorial, near Madrid.

On the right of the church, next to the choir, the **Musée Diocésain**  (open Apr–Oct Tue–Sun; Nov–Mar p.m. only), which contains the treasury of the cathedral, displays a Merovingian reliquary from Andenne, as well as the famous crown of Philip the Handsome. This is supposed to contain thorns from the crown of Christ, which Philip received from his brother, Emperor Henry of Constantinople. In addition, the museum displays treasures from churches and cloisters which were closed or destroyed during the French Revolution.

Near the cathedral, you can see the works of Namur artists and craftsmen in the **Musée de la Croix** (open Tue–Sun; entrance fee), the municipal and regional museum. The City Archive is located in the 17th-century **Palace of Justice**, which can be found just behind the cathedral.

Opposite the cathedral stands the **Provincial Palace**, which was built as the bishop's residence between 1726 and 1740. The Council of Namur Province meets in the chapel. A little to the east of the cathedral stands the **Eglise Saint-Loup** (church of St Loup), which was built by the Jesuit Huyssens between 1621 and 1645; the tower of this three-storey building was never finished. Black marble bases and red-brown columns support a vaulted sandstone ceiling, making the interior of this baroque church surprisingly colourful.

BELOW:
an old man and his dog in the Bergenbie Café, Dinant.

an old man and his dog in the Bergen-bie Café, Dinant.

Maps:
Area 246
Namur
258

The **Place d'Armes** , where the Stock Exchange is located, is the city's most popular square; behind it looms the bell tower **Tour St-Jacques**. The base of the tower is actually the remnant of the second city wall, which was erected in the 14th century. The bells in the tower's two smaller turrets were once rung to signal the opening and closing of the city gates.

In the city centre, the **Musée Felicien Rops** (Rue Fumal 12; open Jul & Aug daily; Sep–Jun Tue–Sun; entrance fee) holds an important collection of the works of this painter, printmaker, draughtsman and illustrator. Built in 1588, the former **butchers' hall**, the city's oldest extant secular building and a fine example of Meuse regional architecture, today houses the **Musée Archéologique** (Rue du Port; open Tue–Sun; entrance fee), which contains a treasure trove of prehistoric, Roman and medieval finds from the area.

A few minutes' walk northeast of the Archaeological Museum takes you to the **Eglise Notre Dame** (church of Our Lady, open Jan–Oct Tue–Sun; entrance fee), in which one of the city's most important works of art is housed: the **treasury of Hugo von Oignes**. This collection of work from the 13th century by the accomplished craftsman Hugo von Oignes has survived marauding French revolutionaries in 1794 and the air raids of 1940.

Medieval beer

Some 9 km (5 miles) west of Namur you'll find the **Floreffe Monastery** of the Premonstratensian order, founded by St Norbert in 1121. In the Middle Ages, the influence of its monks extended all the way to the Netherlands. The church occupies a prime spot high above the valley of the Sambre; the view over the broad expanse of forest is wonderful whatever the season.

BELOW: the citadel and Eglise Notre Dame, across the river in Dinant.

Once inside the monastery, the aroma of goats and cattle emanating from the agricultural buildings is immediately noticeable. Many of the farm buildings were converted in 1819 for the growing numbers of visitors, and now you can buy bread, cheese and hand-crafted pottery here. The income from the shops goes towards the maintenance of the monastery.

The **Brewery** can be seen as a monument to small business in the Middle Ages. Still operative today, it produces a fine blond beer, as well as several kinds of speciality beer, which you can sample in the adjacent pub. The beers are exported to Italy, France and Canada. The best accompaniment to these beers is the local strong bread, developed by Sister Marguerite at the beginning of the century. This bread continues to be baked according to her original methods. Blessed with their broad farmlands, the monks have never needed to worry about going hungry, even during the austerity and turmoil of the Middle Ages.

Flexibility is the distinguishing characteristic of these monks. Catering to the Belgians' tremendous proclivity for celebration, they organise large private parties on request; weddings at Floreffe, for example, are extremely popular in the region. Sometimes, the monastery itself arranges festivals, and children are particularly well catered for. At Easter they can hunt for eggs in the grounds, be entertained by clowns and devour an enormous chocolate cake.

A flower festival is held during the first two weeks of July, an open-air folklore festival in the middle of August, and all manner of toys are available at the children's fair that starts in the middle of November.

BELOW: houses in Impasse dela Couronne in Liège.

The main structural elements of the abbey church – the nave, choir and transepts – date from the 12th to 13th century, but the interior was transformed in the 18th century by Laurent Dewez, who applied stuccowork throughout.

Gardens of Annevoie

Heading south from Namur in the direction of Dinant, you'll see signs for the **Jardins d'Annevoie** ❼ (Apr–Oct daily; entrance fee). These gardens were created in the 18th century, and are not as severe as the gardens of the baroque period, or Versailles, which was planned in the 17th century. Charles-Alexis de Montpellier began working on Annevoie's gardens in 1758, and they have remained virtually unchanged since he completed his work in 1776.

Using only natural water pressure (no pump), absolutely clear water from four springs feeds the park's many fountains and waterfalls. Charles-Alexis drew inspiration from garden facilities he'd seen on his travels in France and Italy, and some of the fountains were based on Italian and French models

In bygone centuries, formal gardens didn't contain many flowers; coloured stones and green borders were more common. But, as tastes changed, a compromise solution was sought in the 1950s, the result of which was a new flower garden, complete with many fountains, at the edge of the formal garden.

These beautiful gardens are the private property of the Montpellier family, who emphasise the fact that they want to share with visitors their joy at being able to live in such splendid surroundings. They have taken great care to make visitors welcome; even the car park they have provided has an aesthetic charm.

Between rock and river

Built in its present form in 1820, **Dinant** ❽ (population 10,000) is a sliver of a town, squeezed between the Meuse and the steep cliffs. The town's outlying suburbs range themselves along this narrow ridge like links in a chain. Communities existed here even in prehistoric times, but the town of Dinant proper received its charter in 1152.

Because of its flourishing economy, the town was largely able to defend its independence against the archdiocese of Liège. It suffered greatly in the two world wars. Of its significant buildings, only the citadel and the early Gothic church of Our Lady, with its two incomplete towers, have been preserved. The citadel, which towers atop steep chalk cliffs to a height of 100 metres (330 ft), tells of the long military history of the town. Today, you can reach it by means of a cable car which leaves from the church beside the Meuse bridge; there's also a road up to the well-preserved fortification. You can prowl through its subterranean passageways into a mysterious past.

Since the Middle Ages, a main pillar of Dinant's economy has been the production of handcrafted objects for church and household use. Brass pulpits and chandeliers in the churches are souvenirs of a time when craftsmen with their Dinanderies travelled along the Rhine to Liège, Leuven, Bruges, Paris, Milan and London. Today, you can travel along the Meuse in the comfort of a steamer, or discover the Lesse under your own steam, travelling upstream by kayak to the Anseremme. Dinant's cave, "La Merveilleuse", lies on the other side of the Meuse, about a quarter of a mile from the bridge. Each cave has a distinct character; "La Merveilleuse" is notable for fine, light stalactites and underground waterfalls. ❑

Map on pages 246–7

TIP

From June to August there are river trips from Dinant to Namur each Saturday afternoon. Return journeys are not until the following morning, however, so you'll need to make arrangements for an overnight stay.

BELOW: running into the Meuse, the Ourthe valley.

THE ARDENNES

*The sparsely populated Ardennes is Belgium's hilliest
and most wooded region, providing some of the country's
most stunning scenery and wildlife*

Map
on page
246–7

The rolling landscape of the Ardennes is beautifully lush and almost Mediterranean in character, with houses of natural stone reminiscent of those in the south of France. The people are open and talkative and ever ready to dispense information and advice to visitors.

Sparsely populated, with 325 inhabitants per sq. km (125 per sq. mile) – the national average is about 800 – and predominantly agricultural because of its loamy, chalky soil, this region at the heart of Europe seems to have been overlooked by industry; the hilly, peaceful countryside with its friendly inhabitants is an ideal spot for holiday relaxation. However, even when the sun shines, temperatures in the mountains, which rise to heights of between 400 and 500 metres (1,300 and 1,600 ft), can be quite chilly at night. The Ardennes is not particularly well suited to winter sports; as in many other mountain areas in Central Europe, there has been little snow over the last few years.

PRECEDING PAGES: the deep forest near La Roche en Ardennes. **LEFT:** riverside pursuits in the Ardennes. **BELOW:** the beautifully poised Château Vêves.

Mediterranean mood

The lifestyle and temperament of this region has similarities to the ambience that prevails in Mediterranean countries. People here live at a leisurely pace. The mentality is evident in their tendency to stop and chat on a street corner rather than rush home and busy themselves with the chores of housework or gardening. Residents tend to overlook the first signs of rust or peeling paint on their property and, unlike most other inhabitants of these latitudes, are not as obsessed by their work.

About half of the land in the area is used for forestry. A characteristic feature of the region is its many grottoes: those in Hotton, Remouchamps, Han, Rochefort and Goyet, to name but a few. Many of the most popular caves are located directly on the through road (signs indicate where you should turn off). The caves have been formed over thousands of years by water containing carbonic acid carving a path through the chalky rock. The rivers Vesdre, Ourthe, Lomme, Lesse and Semois which flow through the region also contributed to the formation of the caves.

Our journey begins at Vêves Castle, a short distance south-west of Dinant (*see page 263*). Our route then takes a sweeping tour around the Ardennes, following Belgium's border with France and Luxembourg. From Bastogne, the route meanders to the resort of Spa and the ancient town of Theux.

Vêves Castle

Dinant has been described as the gateway to the Ardennes, and the densely forested countryside that surrounds the town is an indication of this. Rustic inns offering local or French cuisine, often with overnight

Freshly baked local pastries and pies, the wholesome cooking of the Ardennes.

accommodation as well, welcome travellers, and for many, the sight and aroma of smoke rising from the chimneys of stone houses brings about an appealing nostalgia for a long-forgotten past.

Château Vêves ❾ (open Apr–Oct Tues–Sun; entrance fee) is the stuff of dreams and fairy-tales, perched as it is on top of a rocky hill, with its four pointed turrets and surrounding moat. It is a truly idyllic spot. A stream rushes through the valley, birds twitter and you almost expect a maiden to appear in one of the lofty windows. In fact this could actually happen, as the castle is still inhabited by descendants of the Countess Liedekerke Beaufort. The elegant early 18th-century interiors are open to visitors.

Grotto of Han

On its southward path through the Ardennes, the E411 motorway crosses the Lesse River between exits 22 and 23. The forests that the roadway ploughs through are a kaleidoscope of green. Fields tenanted by grazing white cows and level, bald plateaus characterise the landscape. The nearer the motorway gets to the well-marked town of Han, the more picturesque the nature preserve of Lesse becomes. Stone farmhouses dot the landscape, their inhabitants hidden behind tiny windows.

Campsites, holiday cottages and an extensive but unobtrusive touristic infrastructure with many hotels and restaurants await visitors to **Han-sur-Lesse** ❿ (population 900). If you've made the long drive here in a single day you can be assured of a relaxing evening in Han. As well as the caves, Han offers a nature park, part of which is dedicated to the fauna of the Ardennes, and a **wildlife preserve** (open daily Mar–Dec; entrance fee), where you can see the animals which

BELOW: the dark mystery of the caves at Han.

once roamed freely in the region: bison, wild horses, aurochs and brown bears. Treasures from the caves are exhibited in a small museum. The caves of Han, particularly those near the entrance, have provided men with shelter since the dawn of the human race and have been a rich source of archaeological finds.

Kayak tours are offered along the Lesse; and to save aching arm muscles, the return journey can be made by bicycle. Mountain bikes, touring bicycles and tandems can be rented, while for those who want to learn about free-style rock climbing, there's a practice climbing wall. All these attractions draw some 300,000 visitors each year. The chief enticement is, of course, the **caves** (open daily Mar–Dec; entrance fee), which were discovered in 1771. You reach them on an old tram that runs from the centre of the village. Han is a place of superlatives: the largest of its many impressive caves, the "Cathedral", is 129 metres (422 ft) high.

Visitors come to the mouth of the caves by boat, and from there embark on a fantastic voyage along the Lesse, led through a forest of stalactites. Music and lighting effects enhance the two-hour tour, after which the hungry traveller is met by French-fry stands, a restaurant and a small animal zoo.

The Rochefort cave

Located 4 miles (6 km) further north, **Rochefort** (population 5,000) has its own **cave** (open daily Jul–Aug; Thur–Tue Apr–Jun and Sep–Nov; entrance fee). Discovered in 1865, and traversed by the Lomme river, this series of raw, wild caves includes the "Sabbath Room", the largest of the chambers. As well as the attraction of the cave, the small town of Rochefort has enough facilities to make it a good base from which to explore the surrounding countryside.

Map on page 246–7

BELOW: a suitably gothic sign for the Rochefort cave.

Southwest of Rochefort and Han, near the E411 motorway, is the **Château of Lavaux-Sainte-Anne** (open daily; entrance fee), located by the village of the same name. Dating from the 1190s, the castle is notable for its moated and turreted magnificence. Inside is a museum devoted to hunting, which has the slightly disingenuous name of the **Musée de la Chasse et de la Conservation de Nature** (Museum of Hunting and Nature Conservation). If the number of severed animal heads, deer racks and assorted horns that adorn the walls is anything to go by, the hunting element of the title would seem to carry more weight than the "conservation".

The village of books

Continuing south, route 40 will take you to **Redu**, famed in Belgium and further afield as the "village of books". It seems that just about every quaint little house in the village has been turned into a second-hand bookshop, or their supporting cast of arts and craft shops and artisanal producers of regional food specialities. Visually, Redu tends towards the twee, but the bookshops are pretty good and there are English books for sale as well as French, Dutch and German.

But if this seems pretty tame fare you can take yourself off to the **Euro Space Center** (Rue Devant les Hêtres 1; open mid-Feb–Nov daily; entrance fee) at nearby Transinne, close to the parabolic domes of a Belgacom satellite ground station. Although it is said to be the only one of its kind outside Houston, Texas, you can't actually take off into space here but you can tour exhibits on current and future manned and automatic space missions, including the Space Shuttle, the new International Space Station, colonies on Mars, etc. Enthusiasts can even take a week-long astronaut training course.

BELOW: visitors admiring the view near the entrance to the Château de Bouillon.

Medieval Bouillon

Bouillon ⓫ lies close to the French border in the southern Ardennes, amidst some wildly scenic country. It is a noted resort town and a place of gastronomic as much as historical pilgrimage. As well as a spectacular location in the plunging valley of the River Semois, Bouillon is the location of the country's finest medieval castle. Dating mostly from the 12th century, but with elements from the 10th, **Château de Bouillon** (open Mar–Nov daily; Dec–Feb Sat, Sun, and Mon–Fri pm only; Jan Sat, Sun only; entrance fee) crouches like a grey stone dragon on a cliff above the village. In medieval times it must have seemed awesome. It was from here in 1095 that Godfrey of Bouillon, the Duke of Lower Lorraine and lord of the castle, set out on the First Crusade to take Jerusalem from the Saracens. Today, tourists wander through its gloomy corridors, clamber up narrow stairways to its high-sited battlements and peer into dungeons and chambers, such as the one displaying state-of-the-art medieval torture instruments.

The adjacent **Musée Ducal** (open Apr–Oct daily; Nov–Dec and mid Jan–Mar Sat, Sun pm only; closed first two weeks Jan; entrance fee) includes the Musée Godefroid de Bouillon, with historical exhibitions, including artefacts, from Godfrey's life.

Beer and cheese from the monks

Continuing southeast along the French border, you will come to **Abbaye d'Orval** ⓬ (open daily; entrance fee), close to Florenville. The original abbey, founded around 1100 by the Cistercians, bit the dust thanks to the attentions of anti-clerical French revolutionaries in 1793. It wasn't until 1926 that the monks began to pick up the pieces here, but they have built a foundation that is noted

TIP

For up-to-the-minute information on local attractions and events, the tourist office can be found in Bouillon at the Porte de France.

BELOW: a restaurant beckons from across the river in Bouillon.

DUKE GODFREY OF BOUILLON

In 1096, Godfrey of Bouillon, 5th Duke of Lower Lorraine, sold up his lands and property in the Ardennes in order to finance his part in the First Crusade to the Holy Land. Fighting was fierce across the plains of Palestine, but by June 1099 Godfrey stood before the walls of Jerusalem at the head of the combined Crusader army. On 15 July of that same year, the flower of European chivalry took the Holy City by storm, and a massacre of its Moslem population ensued. Setting aside his armour after the battle, Godfrey put on a linen robe and, with bare feet, prayed at the church of the Holy Sepulchre.

When the dust of conquest settled he was offered the title King of Jerusalem, but refused it on the grounds that he "would not wear a crown of gold in the city where Our Lord had worn a crown of thorns". He accepted the title Defender of the Holy Sepulchre instead, which amounted to the same thing. Godfrey ruled Jerusalem for just one year, in which he began to extend the territory held by the Christians and successfully repelled an invasion by Egypt at Ascalon.

At the end of his year-long rule, Godfrey died. It is unclear whether his demise was the result of poisoning by his Muslim adversaries or an illness caught during the preceding years of the Crusaders' campaign.

Map on page 246–7

as much for its excellent beer and cheese as for religious devotion. The beer and cheese can of course be sampled on the premises. The ruins of the old abbey are lovingly tended by the monks and can also be visited.

Southern climes

You can taste Maitrank, a speciality of Arlon, at any time of the year. A slice of orange accompanies this apéritif made from Moselle wine.

Seen from the road to **Arlon** , the Ardennes present a broad, level and spacious aspect: here, there are no charming valleys, no steep cliffs. Large fields, and farm vehicle dealers at the side of the road, are indications that in this area farming, as well as raising animals and forestery, is the major occupation. In Arlon's town centre (population 23,000), red-brick houses alternate with white ones, all fronted with little balconies. There is a plethora of small speciality shops: one window contains only lovely cast- and wrought-iron pumps. Narrow alleyways and flights of steps are again reminiscent of the Mediterranean. The marketplace is used as a car park – an unfortunate custom, though not one reserved for the Ardennes, or indeed Belgium.

Up a steep staircase, past the statues of Roman legionaries and of Christ carrying his cross, and you come to the Roman Tower, once part of a 900-metre (3,000-ft) stretch of wall which the Gallo-Romans hoped would defend them against the Germanic hordes.

The town has been built on the site of an old Roman settlement. Roman legionaries controlled the roads here as early as the 1st century. With more than 400 sculptures from tombstones and secular buildings, the **Luxembourg Museum** (Rue des Martyrs; open Mon–Sat; entrance fee) contains the largest Roman collection in Belgium. Tools and cult objects of the early Franks are also displayed. Arlon also has the oldest church in the country, the remains of

BELOW: the ancient porch of the Abbaye d'Orval.

the **Roman Basilica** (Open daily May–Sep; free) in the old cemetery, which has been transformed into an archaeological park (Rue des Thermes Romains). Originally, the building was 125 metres (400 ft) long and some 12 metres (40 ft) wide. In the early Middle Ages, the Franks buried their dead here. Just next to it you can see all that's left of a 1st-century bath house. St Donatus church was built by Capuchin monks in 1626, over the remains of the castle of the Counts of Arlon. From the church tower, there is a panoramic view of three countries: Belgium, Luxemburg and France.

At the Hondelange service station on the E411/E25 motorway, near Arlon, a gigantic building houses the largest war museum in Belgium: the **Victory Memorial Museum** (open daily; entrance fee). The Allied victory over Germany, from North Africa to Berlin, is depicted with uniformed wax figures and more than 200 original vehicles, some unique. The brochure informs you that "because it is built on one level, the museum can be visited without difficulty by the handicapped. The guns, uniforms and equipment form the largest and most important collection in the world about this period of history." Veterans receive a reduction.

Proud to be European – a star-studded sign on the border of Belgium and Luxembourg.

Battle of the Ardennes

Further to the southwest, near the border of the Duchy of Luxemburg, the highest town in Belgium, **Bastogne** ⑭ (population 11,000), contains the Trier Gate (Porte de Trèves), a reminder of the area's historical link with the parts of Germany which were occupied by the Romans. Some of the city's 14th-century fortifications, built by John the Blind of Luxemburg, have been preserved in the town. Sixteenth-century ceiling murals in the church of St Pierre are signs of the region's Catholic heritage.

BELOW: father and son at A'Lestaminet café in Bouillon.

The town is relatively well preserved. In the marketplace at its centre, lined with lively street cafés, there's a Sherman tank, where young American tourists – striking the victory sign – pose for souvenir photos. Outside the town, and with parking facilities for at least three military companies, the **Historical Centre** (Mardasson Hall; open daily; entrance fee; tel: 061 211413) is a monument to the 77,000 American soldiers who were killed in the Battle of the Ardennes. The 7,000 Germans who fell here are buried in the cemetery of Recogne-Bastogne.

Bastogne's tourist brochure touts the "wonderful war museum" in which the visitor can look at the battle and the "war collection". In fact, this museum, rendered sepulchral by the darkened skies of its dioramas, seems more like a museum dedicated to military fashion. Small models of battle scenes are displayed alongside uniformed mannequins, including a suntanned General Baron Hasso Eccard von Manteuffel in a fur-lined winter coat, General "Ike" Eisenhower, who sports a "rare officer's jacket", and a grinning US Air Force pilot holding a bundle of French bills.

In a film and slide-show, the Ardennes battle is presented with commentary by the two opposing generals, discussing the military proceedings. Next to American flamethrowers and a comic book of the Ardennes offensive sold in the souvenir shop, is the

War relic – a tank left over from World War II now stands as a monument to the liberation of Belgium.

ominous presence of books such as *Hitler's Bodyguard*, a product of the right-wing German publishing house Viking.

At **Martelange**, mid-way between Arlon and Bastogne, you may well have noticed the sudden change of vista, as neon signs rise up dramatically before you. By the roadside an array of signs advertise petrol stations and oil companies: Shell, Elf, fina, Q8, Texaco. All of the major companies are represented, as well as some of the smaller ones, strung out along the entire left-hand side of the village. Oil wells in the Ardennes, you might think, but in reality the reason is simply down to the eccentricities of national borders and differing laws: the left side of the road belongs to Luxemburg, where the tax on petrol is lower.

A tank in every town

But heading north from Bastogne our route soon brings us to **La Roche** ⓯ (population 2,000). Around these parts, every town and every village displays its own tank – left-overs from World War II and reminders of the country's liberation. Before the war, La Roche was a flourishing holiday town which had retained its medieval flavour and had over 40 hotels. Two days after the German army had marched into Belgium, on 12 May 1940, the village was occupied. It was liberated by the Americans in September, 1944, but the Germans managed to win it back, albeit briefly, in December. Over 100 citizens were killed, and two-thirds of the houses were destroyed.

BELOW: flowers laid by a commemorative plaque in the town of Bastogne.

Occupying the figurative noman's land between the village's attempt to survive by means of tourism and its struggle with a history divided between Resistance fighters and collaborators, amidst ice-cream stores, cafés and billboards, the tank seems to be the forgotten remnant of a long-distant past. Along with the 11th-century castle ruins nearby, it is a favourite photographic subject of local, American and German tourists. Not far off, in the display window of a toy store, a video advertises toy tanks, rockets and space weapons, while an accompanying soundtrack blares through a loudspeaker into the shopping street of the peaceful old town.

The **War Museum** (Rue Chamont 5; open daily; entrance fee), a small exhibition in La Roche, presents bloodthirsty German soldiers in original uniforms next to French, English and Canadians in their land vehicles. The museum is an impressive collection of puppet soldiers and uniforms, but it doesn't begin to go into the history of the war or its causes.

Devoted to the pottery of the area, and open only in summer, the **Museum Poterie de Grès Bleu** (Rue Rompré 28; open Jul–Aug daily; Easter and Christmas holidays weekends only; entrance free) tends to be pushed into the background by the history of the war. However, it gives an insight into the serendipity of the locals and their fundamental link with the soil.

Grottoes à gogo

Further north, at the small town of Hotton, is the **Grottes de Hotton (grotto of a thousand and one nights)** ⓰. Thirty metres (100 ft) underground, this cave, with its red, white and pink stone strata, is the most beautiful underground grotto in Europe.

Particularly if you have toured elsewhere in Belgium, you will find the countryside of the Ardennes remarkably free of people and the landscape dramatic and wild. Many roads have barely been graded, the brooks haven't been channeled into canals, and the sun streams down into the pine forests with a kind of magical light. This area is a favourite haunt of racing cyclists, so watch out! Families picnic by the river and fishermen park their cars so close to the river that they could cast a rod from the driving seat.

Over the years, the flow of the Ourthe near **Barvaux** – mid-way between Hotton and Logne Fortress – has eroded a broad valley between the chalky cliffs. Not far from rock walls, ideal for climbing and topped by small castles and other fortifications, you will find a profusion of campsites and fields. It is a delightful region, in which the trees are in full bloom as early as the beginning of April. Take a river trip by canoe or kayak; both can be rented in Barvaux.

Château Logne ⓱ in Vieuxville was abandoned by its owners, the de la Marcks, who went by the nickname "the Wild Boars of the Ardennes". Today the fortress is a ruin, but it offers magnificent views over the Ourthe and the forested mountains around. A visit to the castle will lead you to the underground passageways, which, legend has it, contain medieval treasure.

Wilderness safari

To the north, in the direction of Remouchamps, the village of **Aywaille** ⓲ offers an entirely different kind of natural experience: a **Safari Park**, which you can visit by car or in an open-top tourist "train". Zebras, hippopotamuses, gorillas and elephants move freely across the landscape. The zoo houses lions and tigers, jaguars and bears. For children, there's a farmyard where domestic

Map on page 246–7

LEFT: Hotton caves.
BELOW: a forest stream at La Roche.

A shopkeeper at the counter of an Ardennes charcuterie.

animals, such as donkeys, goats and sheep, can be petted and fed. Children and nostalgic adults will also find plenty to entertain them en route to Aywaille, at the

Toy Museum in Ferrières. Open on weekend afternoons and during school holidays, it presents more than 1,000 objects from the end of the 19th century until 1950: wooden toys, dolls, dolls' houses and musical toys.

A short jaunt northward through the thick evergreen forests and the road brings you to **Remouchamps** (population 2,300) and its famous caves. In peak season, tours into the subterranean caverns start every eight minutes. The first inhabitants of these caves were Paleolithic hunters, who dwelt there some 8,000 years ago. They left behind them the skeletons of animals, thousands of stone tools, bone tools and jewellery, weapons, wall paintings and a calendar. Since 1829, the Stalactite Cave of Remouchamps has been open to the public; in 1912, while systematically developing the cave for visits by tourists, workers discovered the chamber which was to become its greatest attraction: the "Cathedral", 100 metres (330 ft) long and 40 metres (130 ft) high. The boat tour is highly recommended. Following the underground river, it winds through faults in the limestone. At one point it passes a spectacular pillar formed by the joining of a stalactite and a stalagmite. The tour lasts about one hour.

From Remouchamps, the road loops towards the valley of Malmédy. Here, small oriels ornament the slate-covered houses. The area has a pleasant relaxed ambience. Patrons of the numerous open-air cafés which line the marketplace engage in conversation until late into the evening. Their preferred refreshment is French fries, beer and the local mineral water.

The history of Malmédy began with St Remaclus, who founded a cloister

here in 648. At the same time, the **Stavelot Abbey** came into being; over the next millennium, this cloister took on a greater spiritual and cultural importance than Malmédy. Remaclus, the "Apostle of the Ardennes" who later became the Bishop of Maastricht, founded the double cloister of Stavelot-Malmédy in the spirit of St Benedict, at the behest of King Sigisbert III. Only the Gothic tower of the former abbey church remains today: originally some 100 metres (330 ft) in height, it now measures just 30 metres (98 ft). Its cornerstone was laid in August 1534 by Guillaume de Manderscheidt – laid upon a church which had originally been built in 1040 by the Abbot Poppon.

As a consequence of the secularisation attendant upon the French Revolution, the abbey was converted into a hospital for French soldiers, specialising in sexual diseases. The two-thirds of the tower which are missing today were used as building material to construct the houses in the well-preserved, narrow alleyways of the town of **Stavelot ⓳** (population 5,000). An edifice that appears to be a large greenhouse has been built in front of the tower to protect the ongoing excavation work, which has been partly carried out by lecturers and students.

At the entrance to the abbey premises, you'll stumble across a shining white monument which depicts a face with an oversized three-dimensional nose. This memorial is attributable to the monks. In 1499, Prince Abbot Guillaume de Manderscheidt forbade them from taking part in the town's carnival celebrations. The Stavelot monks mocked this command by participating in carnival festivities at Laetare, three weeks before Easter, dressed as white monks. This is the origin of the "Blanc Moussis" who, equipped with long red noses and ladders, represent the town as guests of honour at carnival celebrations in Düsseldorf, Cologne, Compiègne and Saint-Quentin each year.

Map on page 246–7

BELOW: a popular pastime of this verdant area, which is criss-crossed with rivers and streams.

HAUTES FAGNES NATURE RESERVE

To the northeast of Stavelot is Hautes Fagnes, Belgium's biggest nature reserve. This area of high boggy fenland owes its existence to the receding glaciers of the last Ice Age, and is valued today for the rarity of its flora and fauna. In a small country, preserving open spaces and wildlife habitats takes on added importance, and the Hautes Fagnes is vigorously protected. The reserve's director, Norbert Heukemes, believes that "tourism can be compatible with environmental protection, so long as it is managed properly." Part of this management is to ensure that in some 70 percent of the reserve, access is permitted only in the company of a guide. In the remaining 30 percent, access is free but visitors must stay on the wooden walkways or footpaths that criss-cross the moor. The reserve is closed completely during critical wildlife breeding periods.

Within the realm of the preserve, a piece of moorland, the Fagne de la Poleûr, has been laid out as an educational tour: its one- and two-hour round-trips make it attractive to casual walkers, while sparing more fragile areas from too much human interference. When the winter snows arrive, the Hautes Fagnes also has some of Belgium's most popular crosscountry skiing, although it is illegal to stray from the reserve's marked pistes.

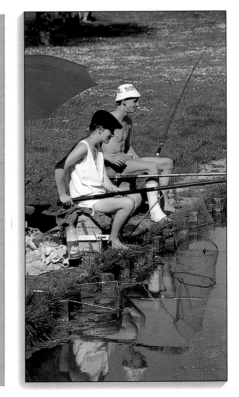

TIP

The Musée Religieux
Régional, situated in
one of the Stavelot
Abbey's refurbished
buildings, has many
interesting religious
art works, from a
portrait of Christ
attributed to Jean
Del Cour to some
medieval statuary.

Another part of the former abbey, the 1,000-year-old vaults, has been converted into a museum of the **Racetrack of Spa-Francorchamps** (open daily; entrance fee), which is located to the north of the town. It contains more than 80 vintage cars, Formula One racing cars and motorcycles. The ancient vaulted building provides a superb setting for the cars. Housed directly next door is a collection of artistic treasures of the Ardennes, concentrating in particular on the ancient art of leather-working in the region.

A reminder of Remaclus in the church of St Sebastian is the **Remaclus Shrine** of 1268, the product of 18 years of work by three master craftsmen. The ornate sarcophagus is based on the shrine of Mary and Charles in Aachen. On its gable, you can see an image of Saint Remaclus; opposite him is Saint Lambert, while the Apostles are depicted in an arcade of seven arches along the side.

In the town hall there is a small display which recalls the French poet and musician Guillaume de Machaut (1300–77). One of the creators of the harmonic art, he wrote a great many songs and ballads, as well as a considerable number of organ pieces. Geoffrey Chaucer is said to have been greatly influenced by *Le Livre du voir-dit*, written in the form of letters from the elderly poet to a girl. Perhaps Machaut would be celebrated more in Stavelot – where he stayed for three months – had he not made off without paying his bills.

International resort

Some 20 km (12 miles) to the north of Stavelot, the resort of **Spa** ❷⓿ is tucked just within the northerly range of Ardennes' forested hills. It is a landscape of austere beauty that surrounds the resort, as the slopes give way to meadows and heaths; the moorland landscapes are often shrouded by drifting fog, trapped

BELOW:
the invigorating
resort of Spa.

by the surrounding hills. This location has for centuries been the meeting place of the rich and famous of the European world, who have come to take the waters and reap the benefits of alkali mud baths containing iron – arteriosclerosis, heart trouble, varicose veins and rheumatism are all claimed to be helped by the medicinal waters and mud.

Spa has flourished without pause since the 16th century, and by the 18th century it was like a modern-day Cannes or Monte Carlo. Philip Thicknesse, visiting in 1786 had this to say: "You may easily imagine that a spot like this, visited by all the world, and where gaming is tolerated, nay, encouraged by the first magistrate of the principality, that it is not only the resort of invalids, and people of real fashion, but of the counterfeit nobility innumerable, and the outcasts, scum and refuse of both sexes, from every nation. So that what with the real, and the assumed badges of distinction, to be seen at Spa, a stranger would be apt to think all the crown heads in Europe had sent their courtiers to drink the Pouhon water".

A fin de siècle ambience is still in the air, albeit somewhat antiquated. The **Well-House of Peter the Great** is encircled by a traffic ring; however, able sprinters should have no trouble crossing the busy street to view the building.

In the 20th century, two events in particular have been responsible for the city's remaining in the limelight: on 8 November 1918, the town was the centre of world attention when Kaiser Wilhelm II, not far from the former German headquarters in Neubois Castle, took leave of his people and went into exile in Holland, to chop wood, as many of his detractors claimed. Two years later, Spa was the site of the conference of the same name, held to discuss the disarmament of Germany and its obligation to repay war debts.

Map on page 246–7

As well as the attraction of the healing waters, Spa also has some fine architecture, which dates from its turn-of-the-century hey-day. The neoclassical style is at its best in the Baths, the Casino and the town's pavilions.

BELOW:
the Casino at Spa.

Spa Water

Just as Dom Perignon brought champagne to fame, Bishop Remaclus succeeded in popularising the waters of Spa. The holy man of the Middle Ages had a reputation for performing miracles: he was able to cure seriously ill patients simply by prescribing a drinking cure. Of course, it was the water which was responsible for their recovery; and the water which the Bishop preferred came from the "holy springs" of the Ardennes. Whether a pilgrim was ailing physically or spiritually, a little Spa water was sure to wash the problem out of one's system.

But it is not only spiritual advisers who set such store by Ardennes water: purveyors of spirits value it equally. Bartenders around the world will all tell you that a good whisky should only be mixed – if mixed it must be – with low-salt mineral water, such as that from Spa.

Most visitors to Spa come for their health and for the world-renowned water, which even Peter the Great found increased his sense of physical well-being (one of the springs is named "Peter the Great"). Of course, not everyone who travelled to Spa was of his sublime rank; but the resort numbered among its guests many consequential figures on the European stage.

In its heyday, most of the guests seeking rejuvenation or cures came from Russia, Sweden and England. The fame of the springs' healing powers spread far and wide. In the end, "Spa" became a synonym for healing baths everywhere, and has been permanently incorporated into the English vocabulary.

The inevitable outcome of such success was a drive to export the precious water. By the end of the 18th century, some 150,000 bottles were being exported every year. They went to all corners of Europe and even further afield. Today, the company "Spa Monopole", which belongs to the Brussels firm Spadel, fills more than 300 million bottles annually.

Spa comprises a plethora of springs. "One hears everywhere the dull murmur of the fountains," wrote one literary resident of the town. Professor A. Monjoie, of the University of Liège, differentiates between four basic types of Spa water: "Pure", "Brisart", "Source", and the extremely variable "Pouhons".

For the purposes of export, only the first two types come into question: a bottle of "pure Spa", with a blue label, contains clear spring water without gas and virtually without metallic elements (even someone on a salt-free diet can drinbk it), while "Spa Brisart", with a pink label, is carbonated and contains some minerals.

Even if you're something of a layman when it comes to water, and do not study the list on the side of a bottle you may be surprised at the sodium content of "pure Spa" – three milligrams per litre. In international comparisons, this water stands at the low end of the scale. Perrier contains 14 milligrams per litre; Apollinaris, 500; and Vichy Celestins an astonishing 1,265.

Spa is synonymous with its water, and its name, which derives from the Latin *spagare* – meaning to bubble up – is still a considerable source of pride (and business) for the town's inhabitants.

LEFT: a poster of 1907 attracting visitors to the restorative aquatic charms of Spa.

Today, elegant villas in the town centre attest to Spa's former glory as an international resort, as do the baths and the casino. In the **Casino**, only the ballroom and theatre from 1763 are still standing. A building that was once a luxury hotel now houses the town hall. Although its former charms may have faded somewhat, Spa nonetheless continues to radiate a certain raffish attraction.

The baths, which are right next door to the Casino, have retained their grandeur, but if you want to make use of the water's healing properties you will have to book in advance.

Map on page 246–7

Early settlements

Just north of Spa, in the direction of Liège, the town of **Theux** ㉑ lies in the valley of Hoegne. Countless archeological finds of Gallo-Roman objects have been made in the area of the former settlement.

For a long time, Theux was the only town in the area, as Louis the Pious forbade his subjects to clear the wood or to build farms. In 1467, Theux received its city charter. Just 11 years later, the town was laid waste by the troops of Charles the Bold; some citizens had revolted against the Burgundian Duke, without success. Theux's **town hall** was built in 1770 by order of the Mayor of Liège, Barthélemy Digneffe.

The hall church of **St Hermès-et-Alexandre**, on the edge of Theux, is first mentioned in documents of 814; today it is a parish church. Excavations have shown that it is built on the foundations of an even older building; the parts of the church which we can see today date from the 11th century. The impressive gable roof spans the three broad aisles. Later additions are the choir, the chapels to the southeast of the main aisle, the sacristy and the entrance hall. ❏

Young travellers head for the hills.

BELOW: the blooms of a warm spring in the Ardennes.

BELGIUM'S CASTLES AND CHATEAUX

*The array of dramatic feudal castles and grand
classical châteaux and landscaped gardens
represents one of Belgium's best-kept secrets*

Wallonia and the Ardennes
represent perfect castle
country, with feudal fortresses
protecting former borders or
dominating the hills of Namur,
Liége and Belgian Luxem-
bourg. Conversely, the classical châteaux tend to be closer
to Brussels and Flanders.

The citadel of Namur,
wedged inside a two-river fork and reached by
cable car, charts both the country's checkered past
and the development of castle-building. There has
been a castle on this spot from the time of the
Celts to the Counts of Namur and subsequent
Spanish rule. As a result, the site embraces Celtic
earthworks, medieval ramparts, Spanish case-
mates and Dutch barracks. The military site was
reinforced in successive centuries and supplied
with gun emplacements.

ARCHITECTURAL SPLENDOURS

Belgian castles range from medieval fortresses to
models of Flemish Renaissance flamboyance or
French classicism. Bouillon castle in Belgian
Luxembourg is arguably the best-preserved
fortress, retaining an array of battlements, secret
passageways and dun-
geons. At the other end
of the scale is Beloeil,
in Hainaut province.
Known as the
Belgian Versailles,
this moated château
was remodelled
after a fire in 1900.
Closer to Brussels
are such beguiling
castles as the
medieval Beersel
and Gaasbeek, a
Flemish château
graced with a
richly furnished
interior.

△ **WATCHFUL EYE**
With its Louis XV watch-
tower, drawbridge and
dungeons, Bouillon fulfils
every castle cliché,
especially during an
atmospheric torchlit visit.

◁ **PRINCELY PALACE**
Beloeil, southwest of
Brussels, boasts the
grandest French gardens
and the most luxurious
château interior in
the country.

△ **FLEMISH JEWEL**
Château de Rixensart, set in
Brabant, is a 17th-century
Flemish Renaissance
treasure that has belonged
to the noble Mérode family
since the 18th century.

GARDENS OF THE CHATEAUX

French Classical, Flemish Renaissance and English Romantic are some of the eclectic styles of Belgian landscaped gardens. The residential districts south of Brussels conceal a number of châteaux with fine grounds: Château de Rixensart overlooks gardens supposedly designed by Le Nôtre (1613–1700), the great French landscape gardener; to the southwest, Château de Beloeil's classical gardens are lined with canals and dotted with statuary. Annevoie (above) is an 18th-century baronial château and its grounds are a blend of English and Italian styles, enhanced by fountains and waterfalls.

Château d'Hex, close to the Dutch border, was built in 1770 as a summer residence for the Prince of Liége, a passionate gardener. His China roses, exotic shrubs, kitchen gardens, underground fruit cellars and herds of Aberdeen Angus and Welsh black sheep still thrive on the estate today.

△ **CRUSADER CITADEL**
Bouillon castle, hewn out of the rocks of southern Belgium, was controlled by a succession of counts and crusader knights.

◁ **ARCH LOOK**
The vaulted Château de Warfusée, set in St Georges-sur-Meuse, is one of many charming minor châteaux in the lush Belgian Ardennes.

◁ **FINE ROMANCE**
Beloeil's classically French Le Nôtre-style gardens, with their lakes and statues, were anglicised during the 18th century in keeping with the Romantic spirit of the times.

ALONG THE DUTCH BORDER

In the past, this part of the country was merely a place for passing through en route to more exciting destinations, but in recent years the region has established itself as a holiday area in its own right

Map on page 288

T he area along the Dutch border belongs largely to the province of **Belgian Limburg**. Limburg belonged to the territory of the bishopric of Liège until 1784, and didn't become an independent province until 1815. Since 1839, Limburg has been divided into a Dutch section and a Belgian one. The core of the former duchy, containing the town of Limburg, is today still part of the province of Liège.

The area where tourists are made so welcome today was once far from hospitable. It was the Romans who built the area's first roads, to link up with their established settlements on the Rhine: the old Roman cities of Cologne, Koblenz, Aachen and Trier are not far away. But they probably wouldn't have gone to such lengths had they envisaged that from the 3rd century AD those same roads would be used by marauding Germanic tribes intent on attacking their empire.

Physically, the province of Limburg is remarkably attractive. Its territory is made up of a series of natural landscapes, successively moving from areas of heath to fens, and from dunes to forests and lakes. The flat, agrarian countryside, with a liberal sprinkling of camping sites, recreation and holiday centres, as well as nature preserves and well-marked trails, is ideal for lengthy walks and bicycle tours, particularly as the gradients are never too steep. There are special cycle paths everywhere, often well away from the main roads and always well maintained. Cycling is very popular in these parts, and as a consequence drivers are a good deal more considerate towards cyclists than elsewhere. Exploring Limburg by bike is a viable option even for the whole family.

Our tour begins in Tongeren, and proceeds counterclockwise along the Dutch border and back down through the province of Limburg to finish a mere 8 km (5 miles) from our starting point.

Belgium's oldest town

The fertile countryside in southern Limburg is characterised by fruit trees, fields and farmhouses. It's here that the most important old towns of Limburg can be found. The pristine town of **Tongeren ❶** (Tongres, population 35,000) is, in fact, the oldest town in Belgium. To make sure that the visitor doesn't forget this, there are signs advertising its venerable age along all roads going into town.

Belgium's first Christian town was founded in the 1st century AD, when it bore the name Aduatuca Tungrorum. In Roman times, Tongeren occupied a strategic position on the road from Bavai to Cologne. The town became the first bishop's see of the country in the 4th century. Like many other Belgian towns, in the Middle Ages Tongeren saw the flowering of a prosperous weaving and linen industry.

PRECEDING PAGES: cattle of the Belgian Limburg.
LEFT: the Begijnhof at St Truiden.
BELOW: Ambiorix, who led the struggle against the Romans.

A pastoral scene in this deeply agricultural area of the country.

The town contains a wealth of historic sites worth seeing, even though many of its very oldest buildings were destroyed by the Norman invasion of 881. The buildings one can see today are mainly Romanesque or Gothic in style.

Gallic uprising

A statue of **Ambiorix** stands proudly at the centre of the marketplace. The chieftain of the Eburon tribe, he was the first citizen of Tongeren. The memorial is a reminder of the year 54 BC, when Ambiorix plotted an uprising in Belgian Gaul in order to annihilate the legions of the occupying Romans, with the result that the latter were forced temporarily to abandon their attempts at conquering this part of the country of the Belgae.

Towering over this figure is the basilica of Our Lady, **Onze Lieve Vrouwe-basiliek** (open May–Sep daily; entrance fee), which, with its 90 metre (294 ft) high tower, presents an impressive sight. This basilica stands on the foundation of a 4th-century sanctuary to the Virgin Mary. While its choir, transept and nave

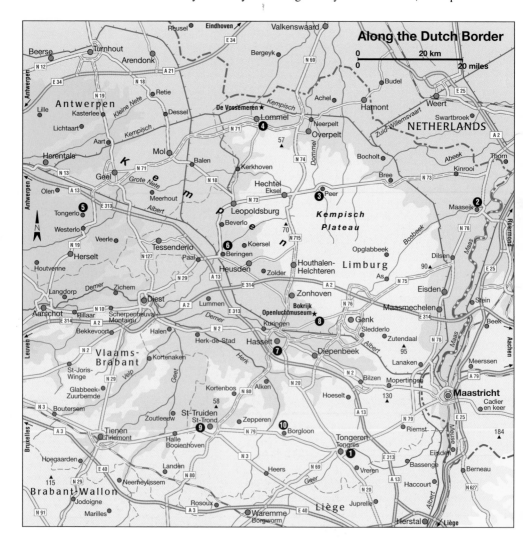

date from the 13th century, the building's western pillars and tower are products of a later time. The old windows from the middle of the 16th century have been preserved. The church's wealth of treasures is one of the richest in the country. One noteworthy item among the many wonderful objects is the *Head of the Dying Christ*, a woodcarving from the 11th century. Major concerts are given in the basilica every year as a part of the Festival of Flanders.

Roman fortifications

Tongeren was fortified by the Romans in the 2nd century AD with a double wall which ran around the town; the original outer wall was 5 km (3 miles) in length. These Roman protective walls served as a basis for the medieval fortifications, remnants of which can still be seen in the west of the town.

Only the 14th-century **Moerenpoort** among the gates survived. Its three storeys house the Museum of Military History. The old town hall fell victim to a fire in 1677, when the French troops of Louis XIV set the town ablaze. The new town hall, the **Stadhuis**, replaced it in the early 17th century. As well as containing a collection of 18th-century furniture from Liège, the town hall also has a collection of excellent paintings. The building is home to a **museum** (open daily; entrance fee), documenting the history of the town.

The Beguine convent, or **Begijnhof**, with its charming crooked streets and picturesque corners, is one of the largest and most beautiful in Belgium. It was founded in 1300, but the buildings and small church that you can see today weren't built until the 17th century.

As well as telling the story behind the Astérix comics, the **Gallo-Roman Museum** (open daily; entrance fee) is the province's Archaeological Museum.

Map
on page
288

BELOW: a water tap with coat of arms in Tongeren.

Boats, flowers and copper kettles

As you proceed toward the Dutch border, along routes 79 and 78, you come to **Lanaken**, which provides enthusiasts of watersports with a place from which to launch canoe trips down the Meuse. Around these parts, decorating windows with flowers, copper kettles, pots, figures, and small frilly curtains is a whole folk art, and when the cashier at the petrol station polishes the counter after you've picked up your change, you can be sure you're in Limburg.

Proceeding northward you eventually arrive at **Maaseik ❷** (population 20,000), tucked in the very northeast corner of Belgium. Its many old patrician buildings give an idea of the architectural style of the area. The "eik" in the village's name refers to the oak forest which used to surround the town. A monastery was founded here in the year 725 and it was from this that the present town developed. The square marketplace, the **Grote Markt**, is bordered by two rows of tall lime trees and surrounded by all the important buildings of the village: the registry office, the banks, hotels, the town hall with a typical stoop and, quite nearby, the church of Saint Catherine. Three museums shelter under one roof, in a complex known as **Museactron** (open Jul & Aug daily; Sep–Jun Tue–Sun; entrance fee). Here, you can see the Apothecary Museum; its sales rooms, where countless containers, scales and jars are on display, lead to the local Archaeological Museum, which has an extraordinary collection of items from prehistoric, Roman, medieval and modern times. The Baker's Museum contains a reconstructed bakery, complete with equipment.

About 10 km (6 miles) along route 762 is **Kinrooi**, which attracts primarily water-loving tourists, due to its plethora of water-related facilities, including two yacht marinas with capacity for about 1,300 boats.

Due to the relative dearth of public transportation, hitchhiking is common hereabouts. Even those of more advanced years rely on their thumbs and the brotherly love of passing drivers.

BELOW:
a monument to the van Eyck brothers in their home town of Maaseik.

THE VAN EYCK BROTHERS

Art historians now believe that the brothers Jan and Hubert van Eyck were originally from Maaseik, and accordingly a memorial in their honour has been erected in the town's marketplace. Jan was born here in about 1390, and his brother Hubert some 20 years earlier. Far more is known of Jan's life than Hubert's, who is rather an enigmatic figure in art historical terms. Jan worked in Holland and Lille during the 1420s, before settling in Bruges, where he lived until his death in 1441.

But it is only the work produced over the last 10 years of his life that can be accurately attributed to him. Earlier paintings, such as *The Crucifixion* and *The Last Judgment* (both c.1420–25) could be by either brother. Indeed, the greatest work of early Flemish painting, the Ghent Altarpiece (*see page 189*) is also a source of disputed authorship. An inscription suggests that it was begun by Hubert in the last year or two of his life, and completed by Jan seven years later, in 1432. The altarpiece is a complex work of some 20 panels, and it is fair to assume that Jan finished those his brother had started and added new panels of his own. But historians have been unable to detect sufficient deviation in the brushwork that would indicate which parts of the work could be attributed to Jan and which to Hubert.

A fistful of Belgian francs

Passing through the cosy town of **Bree**, whose church of St Michael, **St-Michelskerk**, contains impressive woodcarvings, you come to the first major holiday spot on our route: **Peer ❸**. The town's best tourist attraction is the **Pony Express Station**, named after the famous mail route of the American West. It offers a broad range of country & western activities, including a saloon, a stables and a workers' barracks. The most popular attractions are the tours, either on horseback "Western style" or in a covered wagon.

In the forested holiday area which lies to the north, around **Lommel ❹**, an attractive bungalow park, **De Vossemeren**, stretches between dunes and heath. This holiday resort offers a sub-tropical swimming pool, called "Aqua Sana", and various other vacation activities.

Heading west into the province of Antwerp, you will find **Tongerlo ❺**, just south of the E313. There are four windmills in Tongerlo, and one of these has been restored as a watermill and restaurant. The **Premonstratensian Abbey** of Tongerlo was founded in the 12th century, and is surrounded by a moat and stone walls. The avenue leading up to the arched entrance is lined with lime trees which are over 300 years old. The abbey buildings include mission houses and workhouses, a church with neo-Byzantine ornamentation, the bishop's residence, and a refectory, as well as farm buildings and a printing press.

Art exhibitions are regularly held in the monastery's 16th-century granary buildings. The **Leonardo da Vinci Fantasy Museum** (open May–Sep Sat–Thur, pm only; entrance fee) also belongs to the abbey. It includes a copy of Leonardo's *Last Supper* executed by Leonardo's student Andrea Solario shortly after the original had been painted.

Map on page 288

A sign for the abbey at Tongerlo.

BELOW: rather more pedestrian artwork for the gardens of Limburg.

Coal mining heritage

The forests, moors and purple-coloured heaths of the Kempen, in the northeast corner of Belgium, conceal many small lakes, home to a rich variety of birdlife, including crested grebes, rare kinds of woodpecker and pochards. The moors are known for their flora, including pipe-weed and carniverous sundew.

Visible traces of industrial buildings serve as reminders of the natural veins of coal underlying the area. For a time these veins were responsible for a rush of prosperity and a rapid increase of population in the region. But the coal was exhausted as early as 1910 and the industrial landscape was reclaimed to form holiday and hiking areas in the 1960s. In the mining town of **Beringen** ❻, the Mining Museum, **Mijnmuseum**, located directly at the entrance to the pits, is devoted to the history of Limburg's coal mines.

There are numerous recreation parks in the area to the east of Beringen, particularly around **Houthalen-Heichteren**. Hengelhoef, Kelchterhoef and Molenheide are all well endowed with hotels, vacation houses and campsites. The area includes a wildlife park, a water-slide complex, paddle-boat rentals, fishing ponds, and De Plas, a centre offering all manner of water sports.

Central Limburg

Hasselt ❼ (population 65,000), the capital of the Limburg province, lies in the middle of extensive fruit orchards. As well as many fruit-related businesses, the town contains the seat of the province's administration. Hasselt is a bustling, flower-filled shopping centre, serving the neighbouring communities, and a market is held every Tuesday and Friday on Kolonel-Dusart Square. In summer an art market is held behind the town hall every Saturday afternoon.

Between Beringen and Hasselt, you can see the Albert Canal, an important trading waterway that connects the Meuse to Antwerp and the sea.

BELOW:
the residential architecture that typifies the town of Hasselt.

The construction of **St-Quintinuskathedraal** (Saint Quentin's cathedral) was begun in the 11th century, but work continued on the building right up until the 19th century. As well as a Renaissance choir, a baroque chancel and many splendid paintings, the cathedral contains the oldest monstrance (1287) in the world. The cathedral tower houses the 42 bells of the famous **Hasselt Carillon**. Now restored, the bells regularly ring out in concerts during the summer months. In June campanologists from around the world rendezvous at the International Festival of Bell-Ringers held in the town.

The **Onze Lieve Vrouwekerk** (church of Our Lady), near the marketplace, was built in 1730, and restored in 1951. Among the church's many art objects, the one which particularly stands out is the image of the **Virga Jesse**, the Black Virgin, from the 14th century. A festival is held in her honour every seven years.

Hasselt has been the headquarters of the *jenever* (gin) industry since the 17th century and many folk customs have grown up over the years around this regional liqueur. The "Witteke" of Hasselt is most commonly served as an aperitif or with coffee but it is also valued as an essential ingredient in many local dishes. The **Nationaal Jenevermuseum** (Witle Nonnenstraat 19; open Tue–Fri, Sat & Sun pm only; tel: (011) 241144) offers the visitor a closer look into the long and rich jenever-making tradition of Hasselt.

The **Museum Stellingwerff-Waerdenhof** (Maastrichterstraat; open Tue–Fri, Sat & Sun pm only; entrance fee) offers a perspective on the County of Loon and, as well as a plethora of liturgical objects of veneration, the museum also contains some interesting art nouveau ceramics.

There are nine **nature trails** through this town of flowers, which has been awarded national and international prizes for its gardens and floral decorations.

Map on page 288

TIP

The Hazelaarroute, a 65-km (40-mile) long tourist route for motorists or cyclists, takes in the most beautiful spots in the area to the south and west of Hasselt.

BELOW: a novel advertisement for a town florist.

The main street in St Truiden with the church of Our Lady in the background.

To the east of Hasselt, on the road to Genk, you'll find the region's principal tourist attraction: the **Bokrijk Openluchtmuseum** ❽ (open-air museum, open daily; entrance fee; tel: (011) 224575). This is one of the largest and most scientific open-air museums in Europe; it's also an important centre of folk culture in Belgian Limburg. The museum offers a fascinating picture of the life of Flemish farmers living between 1500 and 1920.

The idea of building an open-air museum was first conceived in 1953, when a farmhouse from Lummen was moved to the area, at that time an unremarkable stretch of woodland. When the museum opened in 1958, and for a few years after that, it comprised a group of 20 houses. Today the museum covers 560 hectares (1,370 acres) and includes exhibits covering rural and urban themes. The museum's rural section depicts the daily life of the people in the different regions of Flanders. It's not only the houses that have been reconstructed: the entire environment in which people of earlier times lived and worked, including barnyards, interiors, furniture, kitchen utensils and equipment, has been recreated.

Among the buildings are mills, chapels, a 12th-century Romanesque church and a village school. There's also a bakehouse from Oostmalle, a peat-storage barn from Kalmthout and a blacksmith's from the village of Neeroeteren. The museum's urban section is a replica of part of the old city of Antwerp.

The three distinct sections of the museum are divided from one another by stretches of greenery. Approximately 100 buildings rescued from various villages and towns comprise this open-air museum; most of these buildings would have been ruthlessly torn down during the process of modernisation during the postwar recovery had they not been transported here. They have been carefully brought stone by stone and faithfully reassembled.

BELOW: Lambing season in Limburg.

As well as these structures, the grounds also contain an **arboretum** (containing over 3,000 species of shrubs and trees), a rose garden (**rosarium**), a deer park and a chicken yard, numerous ponds and, to the delight of all children, a first-rate playground.

The open-air museum is only a short distance from **Genk**, the geographic and economic centre of Limburg. Administrative buildings and industrial structures dominate the skyline of this centre, which, at the beginning of the 20th century, was a mere village. Today, the coal industry has transformed Genk into a modern city with a wealth of shopping centres and stores. But, other than for the practicalities of shopping, there is little to attract visitors.

Fruit gardens

Going back through Hasselt and diagonally through the surrounding orchards, you will come to **Sint Truiden** ❾ (population 37,000) in the southwest of the province. This city grew out of a Benedictine monastery, which was founded in the 7th century by St Trudo.

The slender **belfort** (bell tower), near the marketplace and the town hall, is visible from a long way off. While its pedestal dates from the 12th century, the bell tower itself was built in the 17th century. Its carillon is made up of 41 bells. The city's spacious marketplace, or **Grote Markt**, is the second-largest in Belgium. The elegant town hall was given its classical facade in 1750.

Right next to this, you can see the remains of the former **Benedictine monastery**. The steeple of the Romanesque tower burned down in December 1975, but the monumental entrance gate and the abbot's house with the Imperial Chamber have been preserved. The buildings of the **Begijnhof** date from the 17th and 18th centuries. The 35 wall paintings in the early Gothic **Onze Lieve Vrouwekerk** (church of Our Lady), which date from the 14th and 15th centuries, depict legends of the saints.

Opposite this church, the **Astronomical Clock** of K. Festraets is made up of more than 20,000 individual parts. At 6 metres (20ft) high and 4 metres (13 ft) wide, it is the largest clock of its kind.

Halfway between this city and Tongeren, the departure point of our excursion, lies the old town of **Borgloon** ❿, right at the centre of this fruit-growing area. In the Middle Ages, this was the capital of the county of Loon, which is today a part of the province of Limburg. The Renaissance town hall, the **Stadhuis**, which dates from the year 1680, is ornamented with an open arcade and a polygonal tower; the building contains a treasure chest that dates from the 12th century. Outside the town hall are the town stocks, for the punishment of miscreants.

Close to Borgloon is **Henk Palace**, one of the most splendid sights of the whole tour. It stands in the midst of wonderful gardens that are dotted with fountains. Unfortunately, this building is not open to the general public, but nevertheless, the view from without is good enough to provide the visitor with a lasting impression of the combination of invigorating freshness and undisturbed tranquillity – attributes that are the hallmark of Belgian Limburg. ❑

Map on page 288

TIP

If you are in St Truiden when the clock strikes the hour, look out for the 12 mechanical representatives of the medieval guilds that appear from the clock face; they are followed by Death, in the figure of a skeleton.

BELOW: the church from St Truiden's marketplace.
OVERLEAF: a view at Knokke.

INSIGHT GUIDES
Travel Tips

Insight Guides portray destinations in depth, providing the complete picture and the top photography

Insight Pocket Guides focus on the best choices for places to see and things to do and include large fold-out maps

Insight Compact Guides' portability makes them the perfect books to carry with you for on-the-spot reference

Three types of guide for all types of travel

INSIGHT GUIDES Different people need different kinds of information. Some want *background information* to help them prepare for the trip. Others seek *personal recommendations* from someone who knows the destination well. And others look for *compactly presented data* for on-the-spot reference. With three carefully designed series, Insight Guides offer readers the perfect choice. Insight Guides will turn your visit into an experience.

The world's largest collection of visual travel guides

CONTENTS

Getting Acquainted

The Place

Area: 30,520 sq. km (11,780 sq. miles).
Situation: Belgium lies in north-west Europe. It has borders with France to the west and south, Luxembourg to the south-east and Germany to the east. The Netherlands and the North Sea mark its northern border.
Capital: Brussels.
Highest point: Botrange 694 metres (2,272 ft)
Population: 10 million.
Language: Flemish, French and German.
Religion: Roman Catholic.
Time Zone: Central European Standard Time.
Currency: Belgian francs.
Weights & Measures: Metric.
Electricity: AC 220 volts; it is recommended that you bring an adaptor with you. Plugs are continental two-pin round.
International dialling code: 32

Topography

Belgium comprises 10 provinces: West Flanders, bordering the North Sea; East Flanders, Antwerp and Limburg to the north; Walloon Brabant, Flemish Brabant and the capital, Brussels, in the centre; Liège to the east; Hainaut to the south-west; Namur to the south and Luxembourg (not to be confused with the Grand Duchy of Luxembourg) to the south-east. The major commercial rivers Scheldt and Meuse trisect the country.

The north of Belgium, including the provinces of West and East Flanders, is mainly flat like the Netherlands. The North Sea coast,

site of Belgium's popular holiday resorts, is lined with sandy beaches, dunes and salt marshes.

To the south-east, in the Ardennes provinces of Namur, Liège and Luxembourg, the land becomes hilly and forested with deeply wooded valleys and high plateaux.

Brussels itself is situated upon several hills along the Senne, a small tributary of the Scheldt river. During the past century the river has been completely built over within the centre of the city. The city centre lies at about 15 metres (50 ft) above sea level and the Forest and Duden Parks at about 100 metres (335 ft). Corresponding to its hilly character, Brussels falls naturally into two parts: the Upper and Lower Cities, the latter of which includes the old part of the town.

Climate

Belgium enjoys a temperate maritime climate with relatively cool summers and mild winters. In summer the average temperature is about 16°C (61°F), in winter about 3°C (37°F).

Government

In accordance to the constitution of 7 February 1831, Belgium is a constitutional monarchy which is passed down through the House of Saxe-Coburg. The legislature is composed of the senate and the house of representatives, members of both being elected every four years. The monarch is the head of state; since 1993 this has been King Albert II. The executive branch of the government is in the hands of the prime minister and his cabinet. Constitutional reforms have created a federal state guaranteeing autonomy to the Dutch-, French- and German-speaking cultural communities.

Brussels is the capital city of Belgium. It is officially bilingual as it is situated only a few kilometres north of the "language border" between Flanders and Wallonia. However, in everyday discourse French is by far the most common

language used throughout the city. Greater Brussels, the "Bruxelloise", is comprised of 19 different districts. Formerly suburbs, these have expanded and merged to form a single, metropolitan area.

People

Belgium derives its name from the Belgae, the first recorded inhabitants, probably Celts. It was conquered by Julius Caesar and ruled in turn by Rome, the Franks, Burgundy, Spain, Austria and France. In 1815 Belgium was made part of the Netherlands and in 1831 it became an independent constitutional monarchy. Today Belgium has a population of 10,022,000; Brussels has 951,000 inhabitants and Antwerp 465,000.

The Flemings of northern Belgium (about 60 percent of the population) speak Dutch while French is the language of the Walloons in the south (40 percent). A German-speaking minority lives in East Belgium. This language difference has been an ongoing source of acrimony and while prosperity has shifted between the regions the French-speakers have traditionally represented the aristocracy and the Flemings the bourgeoisie. In the early 1980s parliament took steps to ease the tension by transferring power from central government to three regions, Wallonia, Flanders and Brussels, but the language divide still influences working life, education, politics and culture.

Economy

On the basis of its manufacturing industries alone, Belgium can be counted as a member of the leading European industrialised countries. The first industries to get under way were those based on coal and iron ore deposits. The most important industrial products manufactured in Belgium today include iron and steel, machinery, textiles, motor vehicles and chemical products. Diamond cutting, glassware and textile manufacture also play an important role. The chief crops are wheat, potatoes and sugar beet. Belgium's most significant trading partners are France, Germany, the Netherlands and Great Britain. In Europe, the port of Antwerp is second in importance only to Rotterdam. This harbour is primarily responsible for growing prosperity throughout the whole of Flanders. Tourism also plays a significant economic role along the Belgian coast, in Brussels and in many Flemish cities.

Brussels is the seat of the European Union as well as of NATO. The city is regarded as an international centre of high finance where dozens of multinational corporations maintain their headquarters. Business life is chiefly carried out in the old Flemish part of the city (referred to as the Lower City). The textile industry has enjoyed a special status in Brussels for hundreds of years. Wool, upholstery fabric and the world-famous "Brussels lace" are all manufactured here. International metal, electric and chemical companies have also been successful in establishing themselves in this thriving capital.

Public Holidays

1 January	New Year's Day
March/April	Easter Monday
1 May	Labour Day
May	Ascension Day and Whit Monday
21 July	National Holiday
15 August	Assumption of the Virgin Mary
1 November	All Saints' Day
11 November	Armistice Day
25 December	Christmas Day

If any of these holidays falls on a Sunday, the following Monday is taken in lieu.

For information about variable dates, contact the Chamber of Commerce of Belgium, which publishes a current calendar of festivals each year (see also Festivals, page 257).

Weights & Measures

The metric system is in use in Belgium, which means that units are measured in metres or kilograms and their derivatives. The following conversions may prove useful.

Weight/volume:
28 grams (g): 1 ounce (oz)
1 kilogram (kg): 2.2 pounds (lbs)
1 litre (l): 1.76 pints (pt)

Distance:
1 centimetre (mm): 0.39 inches (in)
1 metre (m): 3.28 feet (ft)
1 kilometre (km): 0.62 miles
8 kilometres: 5 miles

Business Hours

Banks: All the banks in Belgium will exchange foreign money. Most are open from 9am to noon and again from 2pm to 4pm, Monday–Friday. Some banks, however, do remain open at midday.

Shops: There is no official closing time for shops in Belgium. Most shops are open from 9am to 6pm, with grocery stores frequently remaining open until 9pm. Some shops close for a lunch break between noon and 2pm.

In large cities big department stores stay open late – until 9pm – once a week, usually on Fridays. You will also find a number of shops open round the clock, as well as on Sundays and holidays.

Post Offices: Generally post offices are open 9am–5pm; in smaller cities they are usually closed in the afternoons.

Museums: Most museums are open Tuesday–Saturday, 9am–4pm and sometimes on Sunday. They are closed on Monday. A number of museums are open from Easter to September only.

Planning the Trip

Visas & Passports

All visitors entering Belgium from countries which are members of the European Union or from Switzerland require a valid personal identity card or passport. Visitors from the United States, Australia, New Zealand and Japan need only a valid passport; no visa is required. Visas are still required for nationals of certain Commonwealth countries. Children under the age of 16 must be in possession of a child's identity card/passport if their names have not been entered in one of their parents' cards. For further information contact your local embassy or consulate or the Belgian Embassy, 103 Eaton Square, London SW1W 9AB, tel: 0171-235 5422.

Animal Quarantine

Travellers bringing in cats or dogs are required to have an official certificate issued by a vet stating that their pet has been vaccinated against rabies. The vaccination must have taken place at least 30 days prior to arrival and be no more than one year old (in the case of cats, six months).

Customs

There is no limit to the amount of foreign currency that can be brought into or taken out of Belgium. Items for everyday use and those frequently transported by tourists, such as cameras and sporting equipment, may be brought into the country duty-free.

European Union citizens: in addition to the above, visitors over 17 from European Union nations are not subject to restrictions on goods and consumable items for personal use.

Non-EU citizens: citizens from non-EU nations are permitted to bring the following into Belgium duty-free: 200 cigarettes or 50 cigars or 250 g tobacco; 2 litres still wine; 1 litre spirits or 2 litres sparkling or fortified wine; 50 g perfume and 0.25 litres toilet water.

Health

Visitors from the UK are not required to produce an international smallpox vaccination certificate or any other medical document.

Money Matters

The unit of currency in Belgium is the Belgian Franc (Bfr), with 100 centimes to 1 franc. There are 100, 200, 500, 1,000, 2,000, 5,000 and 10,000 Bfr notes, and 50 centimes, 1, 5, 20 and 50 Bfr coins.

Eurocheques can be cashed for a maximum of 7,000 Bfr a cheque. As a rule, exchange offices located in larger railway stations maintain longer hours than banks.

Most international credit cards are accepted in larger hotels, many gourmet restaurants, shops and boutiques, and at some banks and car rental agencies. Eurocheques, credit cards and many bank cards can be used to withdraw money from automatic cash dispensers, which are widely available.

If you should lose or have your Eurocheque or credit card stolen, report the loss immediately to your bank so that measures can be taken to freeze your account.

What to Bring

The Belgians are quite fashion-conscious. In large cities especially, people pay attention to presenting themselves in smart attire. However, visitors preferring to dress more casually will not feel conspicuous. When packing for a visit to Belgium, keep in mind that the weather is variable and select your travelling wardrobe accordingly.

Getting There

BY AIR

Brussels' international airport is located at Zaventem, 14 km (8 miles) north-east of the city centre. For information, telephone 02-722 31 11. International air services information is provided by Sabena (tel: 02-503 91 11). Being the seat of the European Union, Brussels is well served by international airlines. By air, it is one hour from the European cities of Paris, London, Amsterdam and Frankfurt. Sabena, the Belgian airline, has particularly good links with Africa. From the United States, three US airlines serve Brussels with daily flights: American Airlines flies daily from Chicago and Los Angeles, Delta Air Lines from Atlanta, and United Airlines from Washington DC. Sabena flies daily to Brussels from Boston, Chicago and New York JFK.

There is a tourist office in the arrivals hall (open 6.30am–9.30pm) which can book hotels (free of charge) and supply information on Brussels and Flanders. The Destination Belgium desk at the airport is not a tourist office but a private agency; it charges for booking some hotels. There is also a board near the exit to the arrivals hall with free direct phone connection to the hotels listed.

Getting into Brussels: An efficient train service connects with Brussels Gare Centrale. The journey takes about 20 minutes and costs under 100 Bfr. Tickets can be purchased from the train information desk (open daily 6.40am–10pm) before you go through customs, or from the ticket office in the station. The train also serves Gare du Nord and Gare du Midi. Unregistered taxis operate from the airport and charge much more than the official fares; it is better to use the official taxi rank outside the arrivals hall.

International airline offices in Brussels:
American Airlines, Grand'Place 12. Tel: 02-714 4916.
British Airways, Rue du Trône 98. Tel: 02-548 2111.
Delta Air Lines. Rue Colonel Bourg 128/B4. Tel: 02-730 8200.

Sabena. Brussels National Airport. Tel: 02-723 2323.
United Airlines. Avenue Louise 350. Tel: 02-646 5588.

Airlines with offices in the UK operating services to Brussels:
Sabena. Tel: 0181-780 1444.
British Airways. Tel: 0345 222111.
British Midland. Tel: 0345 554554.
Air UK. Tel: 0345 666777.
City Flyer Express (to Antwerp). Tel: 0345 222111.
Loganair. Tel: 0345 222111.

BY SEA

Ferry services between the UK and Belgium are operated by:
North Sea Ferries between Hull and Zeebrugge. Tel: 01482-377177.
P&O European Ferries between Dover and Calais and Zeebrugge. Tel: 0990-980980.
Sally Ferries between Ramsgate and Ostend. Tel: 0990-848848.

Arriving at Ostend: The ferry terminus is at Montgomerydok by the railway station, within walking distance of the town centre. The station information office has details of services; open Monday–Friday 7am–7pm and Saturday–Sunday 8am–7pm. Trams depart from beside the station: east to Knokke-Heist, west to De Panne.

Arriving at Zeebrugge: The ferry companies offer a free bus service from the docks to the railway station to coincide with sailings. Trains to Bruges depart hourly. There is a tourist kiosk on the sea front, open July–August daily 10am–1pm and 2pm–6pm.

BY TRAIN

The Belgian railway system maintains a well-developed railway network. There is a number of international railway lines crossing Belgium, connecting France and the Netherlands, Great Britain and Germany with one another. The capital's main railway stations are Brussels North (Nord), Brussels Central (Centrale) and Brussels South (Midi). Trains to Paris take 2 hours 27 minutes; to Cologne 2 hours 13 minutes; to Amsterdam 2 hours 55 minutes. Using the Thalys high-speed train can cut

journey times by about 30 minutes.
Belgium National Railways,
Premier House, 10 Greycoat Place,
London SW1P 1SB. Tel/fax: 0171-
233 0360. Tel: 0891 516444
(Premium Line).

P&O Ferries (Tel: 0990 980980), is
a reliable source of information
about boat trains to Brussels from
the UK.

Sally Ferries (Tel: 0990 848848),
train-boat-train services from London
to Bruges, Brussels, Ostend, Ghent
and Antwerp via Ramsgate.

In Brussels, rail information is
available on tel: 02-203 36 40.

The **Channel Tunnel**, opened in
1994, has shuttle trains with a
capacity of 120 cars, which take
about 10 minutes to load. From
Folkestone to Calais the journey
takes around 35 minutes and there
are up to four trains an hour, tel:
01303 273300 for bookings and
information. Eurostar passenger
trains connect London (Waterloo) to
Brussels (Gare du Midi) in three
hours; tel: 0990 186186 for reservations and information.

Apart from inevitable travelling, it
is best to avoid the depressed
immigrant area around the Gare du
Midi and the sleazy area around the
Gare du Nord, especially at night.
From stations other than the Gare
Centrale, either take the metro or a
taxi to your hotel. An exception can
be made for the lively Sunday
morning Midi market (Gare du Midi),
essentially a slice of working-class
Brussels life, with a North African
ethnic undertow.

BY BUS

Hoverspeed, tel: 01304-240241,
offers coach-Hovercraft-coach travel
from London or Dover to Brussels,
Mons and Antwerp. Buses stop in
the Place de la Bourse, Brussels.

Eurolines European Coach Travel,
tel: 0990 808080, coaches from
London to Antwerp, Brussels, Ghent
and Liège. In Brussels, buses stop
at Place de Brouckère.

BY CAR

Belgium is criss-crossed by international motorways which are toll-free.

Distances from Brussels to other

European cities: Amsterdam 232
km (144 miles), Paris 302 km (187
miles), Cologne 220 km (136
miles), Ostend 114 km (70 miles),
Luxembourg 216 km (134 miles).

If you are planning on entering
Belgium by car, you will need a
driver's licence, vehicle registration
papers and a nationality sticker
fixed to the rear of your vehicle. You
should carry a red triangle to
display in the event of a breakdown.
It is wise to take out additional insurance (Green Card) for full comprehensive cover. The minimum age
for driving in Belgium is 18 for cars
and motorcycles, 16 for mopeds.
Children under 12 are not allowed
in front seats if there is room in the
back. Seat belts must be worn.

Belgium drives on the right. In
towns the speed limit is 50 kph (31
mph); outside built-up areas 90 kph
(55 mph); motorways 120 kph (75
mph). There is a minimum speed on
motorways of 70 kph (45 mph). At
junctions, cars coming from the
right have priority unless otherwise
stated. Trams have priority, as do
their passengers when crossing the
road to board or alight.

For automobile associations and
breakdown services see page 238.

Information & route maps

Available in the UK from the AA
(tel: 0990 500600) and the RAC
(tel: 0800-550 550).

Many city names appear in both
Flemish and French. The most im-
portant of these are (Flemish/
French): Aalst/Alost; Antwerpen/
Anvers (Antwerp); Brugge/Bruges;
Brussel/Bruxelles (Brussels);
Dendermonde/Termonde;
Gent/Gand (Ghent); Hoei/Huy;
Ieper/Ypres; Kortrijk/ Courtrai;
Leuven/Louvain; Luik/Liège;
Mechelen/Malines; Bergen/Mons;
Namen/Namur; Oostende/Ostende
(Ostend); Oudenaarde/Audenarde;
Ronse/Renaix; Zinnik/Soignies;
Doornik/Tournai; Veurne/Furnes.

In Brussels, all road signs must
officially be in both Flemish and
French. Motorists need to note the
alternative spellings of districts on
road signs (Flemish/French): Grote-
Markt/Grand'Place; Ukkel/Uccle;

Elsene/Ixelles; and Vorst/Forest.
Given the bilingual nature of
Brussels, expect names to be
dissimilar: for instance, the main
Bruxelles-Midi station (French)
becomes Bruxelles-Zuid in Flemish.

The majority of hotels in Belgium
welcome and cater for babies and
small children. Most of them are
able to provide facilities such as
cots, high-chairs, special food and
baby-sitting services. Simply state
your requirements when making
reservations.

Booking Agencies

BTR **(Belgium Tourist Reservations)**, PO Box 41, 1000 Brussels
23. Tel: 02-230 5029, fax: 02-230
60 29. Provides hotel
accommodation and will make any
reservation for both single parties
and groups throughout Belgium.

Westtoer vzw, Kasteel Tillegem,
8200 Bruges 2. Tel: 050-38 02 92,
fax: 050-38 02 92. In the province
of West Flanders: reservations for
hotel accommodation, boat cruises,
guided tours, evening events and
entertainment, arrangements for
conventions and educational
courses.

**Toeristische federatie provincie
Antwerpen**, Karel Oomstraat 11,
2018 Antwerp. Tel: 03-216 28 10,
fax: 03-273 83 65. Province of
Antwerp: day excursions for groups,
weekend and short holidays trips.

**Provinciaal verbond voor toerisme in
Limburg**, Domein Bokrijk, 3600
Genk. Tel: 011-22 29 58,
fax: 011-22 60 86. In the province
of Limburg: day tours for groups,
bicycle excursions.

Practical Tips

Media

Newspapers & Magazines
As a result of the three different language communities, numerous newspapers are published in Belgium. The most important French papers are the Le Soir, La Libre Belgique and La Dernière Heure. The most popular Dutch newspapers are Het Laatste Nieuws, De Standaard and De Morgen, and the most read German newspaper is the Grenz-Echo. The weekly English-language newspaper, The Bulletin, keeps the many thousand members of the international community in Brussels informed and up-to-date regarding what is going on in Belgium. Foreign newspapers and magazines can be purchased at larger bookshops and supermarkets in the major cities.

Radio & Television
In addition to the many local stations, listeners can also tune into the national radio stations, the RTBF (broadcasts are in French), BRT (programmes delivered in Flemish) and the BRF (for German-speaking listeners). The television monopoly is shared by the RTBF and the BRT; in nearly all parts of the country it is also possible to receive foreign programmes transmitted by cable.

Postal Services

Post offices are generally open Monday–Friday, 9am–5pm; in smaller cities they are usually closed at lunchtime and sometimes in the afternoons. The post office located at Brussels South (Midi) Station is open every day around the clock. Post boxes are painted red.

Telegrams can be sent by dialling the number 1225 or via your hotel reception.

Telecommunications

You will find current calling rates posted in Belgian telephone booths. Booths from which it is possible to make international calls are designated by international flags. To make a call to another country, first dial 00, then the country code and finally the number of the party you are trying to reach (omit the 0 from the dialling code).

Telephones take Bfr 5, 20, 50 coins and cards, available from newsagents, post offices and railway stations, for Bfr 200, Bfr 500 or Bfr 1,000. Some post offices have booths from which you can call and pay afterwards.

City Dialling Codes

Antwerp	03
Bruges	050
Brussels	02
Ghent	09
Liège	041
Leuven	016
Namur	081
Ostend	059
Tongeren	012
Tournai	069

Tourist Offices

Belgian Tourist Office, 61 Rue du Marché aux Herbes. Tel: 02-504 03 90. Open: Monday–Saturday (January–May and October–December) 9am–6pm; (June–September) 9am–7pm; Sunday (January–March and November–December) 1–5pm; (April, May, October) 9am–6pm; (June–September) 9am–7pm.
Brussels Tourist Information, Town Hall (Hôtel de Ville), Grand'Place. Tel: 02-513 89 40. Open: Monday–Saturday, 9am–6pm, Sunday (in summer) 9am–6pm, (in winter) 10am–2pm. Closed: on Sunday, 1 December–28 February.

PROVINCIAL TOURIST OFFICES
Antwerp: Karel Oomsstraat 11, 2018 Antwerp. Tel: 03-216 2810, fax: 03-237 8365.
Brabant Walloon: Chaussée de Bruxelles 218, 1410 Waterloo. Tel: 02-351 12 00, fax: 02-351 13 00.
Hainaut: Rue des Clercs 31, 7000 Mons. Tel: 065-36 04 64.
Liège: Boulevard de la Sauvenière 77, 4000 Liège. Tel: 041-22 42 10.
Limburg: Thonissenlaan 27, 3500 Hasselt. Tel: 011-22 29 58, fax: 011-22 60 86.
Luxembourg: Quai de l'Ourthe 9, 6980 La Roche. Tel: 084-41 10 11.
Namur: Rue Pieds d'Allouette 18, 5100 Naninne. Tel: 081-40 80 10, fax: 081-40 80 20.
Oost-Vlaanderen: Koningin Maria-Hendrikaplein 64, 9000 Gent. Tel: 09-222 16 37, fax: 09-221 92 69.
West-Vlaanderen: Kasteel Tillegem, 8200 Brugge 2. Tel: 050-38 02 96, fax: 050-38 02 92.
Vlaams Brabant: Vanderkelenstraat 30, 3000 Leuven. Tel: 016-267620.

LOCAL TOURIST OFFICES
Antwerp: Grote Markt 15, 2000 Antwerp. Tel: 03-232 01 03, fax: 03-255 10 13.
Arlon: Place Léopold, 6700 Arlon. Tel: 063-21 63 60.
Blankenberge: Léopold III-plein, 8370 Blankenberge. Tel: 050-41 22 27, fax: 050-41 61 39.
Bruges: Burg 11, 8000 Bruges. Tel: 050-44 86 86, fax: 050-44 86 00.
Brussels: City Hall, Grand'Place (Grote Markt), 1000 Brussels. Tel: 02-513 89 40, fax: 02-514 40 91.
Dinant: Rue Grande 37, 5500 Dinant. Tel: 082-22 28 70.
De Panne: Gemeentehuis, Zeelaan 21, 8470 De Panne. Tel: 058-42 18 18, fax: 058-42 16 17.
Ghent: Stad Gent, Predikherenlei 2, 9000 Gent. Tel: 09-225 36 41, fax: 09-255 62 88.
Hasselt: Lombaartstraat 3 (Town Hall), 3500 Hasselt. Tel: 011-22 22 35, fax: 011-22 88 94.
Ieper (Ypres): Stadhuis, 8900 Ieper. Tel: 057-20 07 24.
Knokke-Heist: Lichttorenplein 660, 8300 Knokke-Heist. Tel: 050-63 03 80, fax: 050-63 03 90.

Kortrijk: Schouwburgplein, 8500 Kortrijk. Tel: 056-20 25 00.
La Roche: Place du Marché, 6980 La Roche. Tel: 084-41 13 42.
Liège: Féronstrée 92, 4000 Liège. Tel: 041-221 92 21, fax: 041-221 92 22.
Leuven: Naamsestraat 1A, 3000 Leuven. Tel: 016-21 15 39.
Mechelen: Stadhuis, Grote Markt, 2800 Mechelen. Tel: 015-20 85 11.
Mons: Grand'Place 20, 7000 Mons. Tel: 065-33 55 80.
Namur: Place de l'Europe Unie, 5000 Namur. Tel: 081-22 28 59, fax: 081-23 02 57.
Ostend: Monacoplein 2, 8400 Ostend. Tel: 059-70 11 99, fax: 059-70 34 71.
Spa: Place Royale 41, 4880 Spa. Tel: 087-79 53 53.
Tournai: Rue du Marché-aux-Poteries 14, 7500 Tournai. Tel: 069-22 20 45.

TOURIST INFORMATION ABROAD

Denmark: Nyropsgade 47, 5th Floor, DK-1602 Copenhagen V. Tel: 33-930357, fax: 33-934808.
France: Office Belge de Tourisme, 21, Boulevard des Capucines, 75002 Paris. Tel: 01-47 42 41 18.
Germany: Belgisches Verkehrsamt, Berliner Allee 47, 4000 Düsseldorf. Tel: 0211-864 84 40, fax: 0211-132 485.
Japan: Belgian Tourist Office, Tameike Tokyu Bldg 9 F 1-14, Askaka 1-chome, Minato-ku Tokyo. Tel: 03-586 7042.
The Netherlands: Belgisch Verkeersbureau, Herengracht 435-437, 1017 BR Amsterdam. Tel: 020-624 5953.
United Kingdom: Belgian Tourist Office, 29 Princes Street, London W1R 7RG. Tel: 0171-629 1988 (1300–1700 hrs Mon–Fri only); brochure request line 0891 887799 (calls cost 50 pence per minute).
USA: Belgian Tourist Office, 745, Fifth Avenue, New York 10151. Tel: 212-758 8130.

Tipping

You are not obliged to leave a tip. In cinemas and theatres it is nevertheless customary to pay a bit more in addition to the price of the programme. In hotels, all service tips are included in the room price, but here again it is usual to give a little something to the maid, doorman and porter when you depart if you've stayed for more than a couple of nights.

Where there is no charge for the use of a public lavatory, it is customary to leave between 10 and 15 Bfr for the attendant.

In restaurants, the service charge is usually added to, or included in, the bill so there is no need to tip although it is customary to leave any small change.

Embassies & Consulates

United Kingdom: Rue d'Arlon 85, 1040 Brussels. Tel: 02-287 62 11.
USA: Boulevard du Régent 27, 1000 Brussels. Tel: 02-508 21 11.
Canada: Avenue de Tervuren 2, 1040 Brussels. Tel: 02-741 06 11.
Australia: Rue Guimard 6, 1040 Brussels. Tel: 02-213 0500.
Ireland: Rue Froissart 89, 1040 Brussels. Tel: 02-230 53 37.

Medical Services

Visitors from EU countries should obtain a form E111 before leaving home. This entitles them to some free treatment, but does not cover all eventualities. Medical treatment must be paid for and the cost recovered when you return home. All visitors are, however, strongly advised to take out private medical insurance.

Chemists: After regular hours and during holidays you will find the name and address of the nearest chemist on night-duty posted at all chemists.

Loss of Belongings

Report any lost belongings immediately to the nearest police inspector's office, or at the police headquarters at Rue du Marché au Charbon in the centre of Brussels city, tel: 02-517 96 11, and ask for a certificate of loss for insurance purposes. If you lose your passport, contact your local embassy/consulate as soon as possible.

There is a lost and found office at Brussels airport, tel: 02-755 21 11. For articles lost or left behind on a train enquire at the nearest train station or at the Quartier Léopold Railway Station, Place du Luxembourg, Brussels, tel: 02-218 60 50. Otherwise items left on trains or buses may turn up at The Public Transportation Lost Property Office, Avenue Toison d'Or, Brussels. Tel: 02-513 23 94.

Security & Crime

The usual precautions are recommended:
• Don't keep all money, credit cards or traveller's cheques in one wallet or purse; disperse them so one theft won't leave you totally penniless.
• Make sure you hold bags closely and keep them fastened. Never leave them unattended.
• Have some form of identification in your wallet, because sometimes the thief will deposit your stolen wallet (minus the money, of course, but with all else intact) in a local mail box or drop it where someone might recover it and forward it on.

Smoking

Throughout Belgium, smoking is strictly prohibited in enclosed areas.

Emergency Numbers

Accident Aid and Fire Brigade, tel: 100.
Police, tel: 101.
In Greater Brussels **Emergency Services** can be contacted at any time, day or night, tel: 479 18 18 and 648 80 00.
Doctors on emergency call in Brussels, tel: 479 18 18 and 648 80 00.
Red Cross, tel: 105.
National Telephone Information, tel: 1207.
Time, tel: 1300.
Weather Report, tel: 702.

Getting Around

In Belgium, distances are fairly short and motorways serve most of the country, with the exception of the mountain regions of the Ardennes. Access to all roads is free; there are no toll roads. Belgium also has an extensive railway network; consequently, there are few long-distance bus services within the country.

Many travel agencies offer day excursions by rail to other cities in the country.

For the range of country and city maps available, see page 274.

Distances

The following are the distances from Brussels to some of the most important cities:

Antwerp: 48 km (30 miles)
Bruges: 97 km (61 miles)
Charleroi: 61 km (38 miles)
Ghent: 55 km (35 miles)
Liège: 94 km (59 miles)
Mechelen: 27 km (17 miles)
Mons: 67 km (42 miles)
Namur: 63 km (40 miles)
Ostend: 114 km (71 miles)
Tournai: 86 km (54 miles)

By Air

It is possible to fly from Zaventem Airport in Brussels to several cities in Belgium by air taxi.

By Bus

A bus service is operated by the European Railway Association and is referred to as the Europabus; this runs from various countries to Belgium during the summer months. It will deposit passengers in any of the larger cities.

By Train

For information regarding relatively inexpensive railway journeys within Belgium, consult the brochures available at any tourist information office. The "Benelux-Tourrail", whereby pass holders are able to travel on five days within a 17-day period using the complete railway network in any of the Benelux countries, is just one of the deals that are offered.

There are numerous international railway lines which pass through Brussels; many of these connect Belgium to France and Holland, and to Great Britain and Germany.

There are various discount ticket schemes. Three of the most popular ones are "A Weekend at the Seashore", "A Weekend in the Ardennes", and the popular "A Lovely Day in…" Considerable price reductions also apply to children's fares. Further information is available from the following or from Belgian railway stations.

Belgian National Railway Association, Rue France 85, 1000 Brussels. Tel: 02-525 21 11.
Germany: Generalvertretung der Belgischen Eisenbahnen, Goldgasse 2, 50668 Köln 1. Tel: 0221-13 47 61, fax: 0221-13 27 47.
France: Représentation Générale des Chemins de Fer Belges, Rue d'Alsace 13, 75010 Paris. Tel: 01-42 09 13 13, fax: 01-46 07 56 70.
UK: Belgian National Railways, Premier House, 10 Greycoat Place, London SW1P 1SB. Tel/fax: 0171-233 0360. Tel: 0891-516444.
Luxembourg: Représentation Générale des Chemins de Fer Belges, Rue du Fort Wallis 2, 3 Etage, Luxembourg (2714). Tel: 352-494 501, fax: 352-496 420.
Switzerland: Generalvertretung der Belgischen Eisenbahnen, Aeschen–vorstadt 50, 4010 Basle. Tel: 061-612 72 72 85, fax: 061-612 76 23 84.

Railway Traffic in Brussels

In Brussels there are four railway stations: **Gare du Nord (North Railway Station)**, Rue du Progrès; **Gare Centrale (Central Railway Station)**, located underground at the Boulevard de l'Impératrice; **Gare du Midi (South Railway Station)**, Boulevard de l'Europe; and **Gare du Luxembourg (Gare du Quartier Léopold)**, Place du Luxembourg.

All four railway stations are interconnected by means of a fast underground train network. Numerous international railway lines pass through Brussels; connections are especially good with France and the Netherlands, as well as with Great Britain and Germany. For information regarding timetables at all four Brussels railway stations, tel: 02-203 36 40. Reservations can be made in advance by calling 02-224 51 11. Those wishing to transport their vehicle by train should contact Schaerbeek Railway Station, tel: 02-525 31 87.

Brussels maintains a well-developed underground system complemented by bus and tram routes. Timetables can be obtained at the reception service, Rue du Marché aux Herbes/Grasmarkt 61, as well as at the TIB (Tourist Information Office) located in the Town Hall. Underground stations are easily recognised: look for the sign sporting a blue "M" (for Metro) on a white background. Bus stops are marked with red and white signs, tram stops with blue and white. At bus and tram stops with signs bearing the words "*sur demande*", waiting passengers can stop the bus or tram with a simple hand signal.

Information and tickets for the Belgian National Railway (SNCB/NMBS), the Regional Railway (SNCV/MIVB) and for the Brussels Passenger Transport Executive (STIB) can be obtained in the booking hall at the Gare du Midi. Information and tickets for SNCV are also available at Rue France 85, tel: 02-525 21 11, and for STIB on the 6th floor of the Galeries de la Toison d'Or, tel: 02-515 20 00, as well as at the Metro stations Porte de Namur, Rogier and Midi. You can also purchase train tickets in any of the larger Metro stations, at numerous newspaper kiosks and in the

Town Hall (TIB). Route maps are available free from the tourist office and information kiosks at Porte de Namur, Rogier and Midi.

There are several different types of tickets, including single-fare or multi-journey tickets, for five or 10 rides, and a 24-hour ticket to be used anywhere in the city centre.

For passengers travelling to any of the outlying districts it is necessary to get an additional "Z" ticket. There is no extra charge for transferring. Passengers caught riding without a valid ticket by one of the many roaming patrols can expect to pay a hefty fine.

The Brussels Passenger Transport Executive offers a variety of interesting excursions under the heading "Rose des Vents". Destinations include some of the more beautiful areas surrounding Brussels and are reached via metro, bus and tram.

Services run from 6am until midnight, with a sporadic night service.

Taxis

Taking a taxi in Belgium is not particularly expensive and can often present a practical alternative to using some form of public transport. The most convenient way to get a taxi is to ask the hotel reception to order you one.

The base rate is Bfr 95 and Bfr 170 after 10pm; for each additional kilometre there is a Bfr 38 charge within the city limits. For journeys extending beyond the city perimeter, this rate can be increased to as much as Bfr 76 per kilometre.

If you would like the taxi driver to wait for you, you can expect to pay around 600 Bfr for each hour. Some taxi companies charge reduced fares for the journey to Zaventem Airport. Ask for details of the fare before you set off.

Taxis in Brussels can be picked up from taxi stands, notably at Bourse, de Brouckère, Grand Sablon and Porte de Namur as well as at railway stations and hotels.

Taxis can be ordered from the central despatch service of the following companies:

ATR, tel: 02-647 22 22.
Autolux, tel: 02-512 31 23.
Taxis Bleus, tel: 02-268 10 10.
Taxis Verts, tel: 02-349 49 49.

By Waterway

Many boating companies cruising the waterways of Belgium offer excursions to different places. Tourist information centre agents will be happy to provide you with further information.

By Car

The fact that Brussels is situated in the very heart of Belgium definitely influences the country's traffic patterns. A ring-shaped motorway encircles the city, providing both direct access and the opportunity to skirt the city entirely.

Traffic Regulations

The maximum speed limit in Belgium within populated areas is 50 kph (31 mph); outside these areas it increases to 90 kph (55 mph). On motorways and other major thoroughfares of at least two lanes the speed limit is 120 kph (75 mph). The general rule is that those to the right of you have right of way. Wearing seatbelts is mandatory. It is illegal for children under the age of 12 to sit next to the driver if there is adequate space in the back of the vehicle. Motorcyclists and moped riders are required by law to wear helmets. Parking on yellow lines is not allowed. Trams always have the right of way. Foreign visitors caught transgressing regulations will be required to pay any fines on the spot.

In general terms, Belgium's road accident statistics are among the worst in Europe, and it is necessary to exercise caution at all times. Pedestrians should be careful on pedestrian crossings where their rights are often ignored by drivers.

Car hire

In Brussels you can reserve a rental car either in the capital itself, or in another city, by calling one of the following (7am–11pm):

Astral: Rue de Linthout 126, tel: 02-734 30 90, fax: 02-734 40 81.
Avis: Brussels Airport, Arrival Hall, Zaventem, tel: 02-720 09 44; Brussels Hilton, Boulevard de Waterloo 38, tel: 02-513 10 51, fax: 02-513 72 33.
Budget: Central Reservations Headquarters, tel: 02-721 50 97.
Eurodollar: Runwaypark, Vuurberg 42–43, Diegem, tel: 02-725-60-66, fax: 02-725 01 09.
Europcar: Brussels Airport, Zaventem, tel: 02-721 05 92; General reservations tel: 02-348 92 12.
Hertz: Brussels Airport, Zaventem, tel: 02-720 60 44; Boulevard Maurice Lemonier 8, tel: 02-513 28 86; Chaussée de Vleurgat 210, tel: 02-649 00 15.
Luxauto, Rue Defacqz 131, tel: 02-538 33 21, fax: 02-534 23 63.

Automobile Associations
Royal Automobile Club de Belgique (RACB), Rue d'Arlon 53, 1000 Brussels. Tel: 02-287 09 00.
Touring Club de Belgique (TCB), Rue Joseph II 25, 1000 Brussels. Tel: 02-233 22 11.
Vlaamse Automobilistenbond (VAB), Sint Jacobsmarkt 45, Antwerp. Tel: 03-253 63 63.

Breakdown Services
If you should have car trouble while on the motorway, call the Breakdown Patrol Service from the nearest emergency telephone. For breakdowns occurring on roads other than motorways, contact the **Touring Secours** central assistance number, tel: 070-34 47 77.

Cycling

Cycling in Belgium is one of the best ways of getting around. Some roads have bicycle lanes (especially those in Flanders in areas near the border with the Netherlands) and tourist offices can supply details and maps of local routes. For a charge you can take your bike on the train.
Rent-a-bike: You can rent bicycles from the 60 or so railway stations, open 7am–9pm, and return them to any station of your choice.

Belgium Railways Train & Vélo (*Trein & Fiets*) leaflet is available from the Belgian Tourist Office in London, tel: 0171-629 3977, fax: 0171-629 0454.

Hitchhiking

The Belgians are generally keen to give lifts to hitchhikers, but remember that hitchhiking on motorways is illegal.

Getting Around Brussels

In Brussels, the city boundaries are defined by a series of boulevards known as `le petit ring'. These connect with tunnels which ensure speedy access to the centre for residents but can cause confusion for visitors. Public transport is initially confusing but efficient, with an interlocking system of metro, overground trams and pre-metro (underground trams).

Unless wishing to explore the Brussels suburbs, it is best to leave the car (in the hotel or a multi-storey car park) and explore central Brussels by foot and public transport. Buy a day travelcard from the main metro stations, which represents good value. Request a metro map from any main station (and you may well be no wiser as to the routes).

Metro stations often seem unmanned, but always buy a ticket as there are severe penalties if you are caught without one. All tram and bus stops are request stops. Unless very confident of your route, avoid taking the city buses. Buses do, however, serve areas which are not covered by tram and metro lines. Taxis are only generally picked up at stands and vary greatly in reliability.

Much of the Upper Town can be enjoyably explored by tram, especially the Avenue Louise, Place Stephanie and Rue Royale districts. The Cinquantenaire and the European Quarter are reached by Schuman metro station while Avenue Louise is served by Louise metro station and numerous trams.

Where to Stay

Bed & Breakfast Agencies

One of the most enjoyable ways of discovering the country and its people is to stay in a family home for one night or even a few days. Bed and breakfast accommodation usually offers comfort and good value for money. Information booklets can be obtained from tourist offices or from:

Flanders: Taxistop, Onderbergen 51, B-9000 Ghent. Tel: 09-223 23 10, fax: 09-224 31 44.
Wallonia: Taxistop, Place de l'Université 41, 1348 Louvain-La Neuve. Tel: 016-45 14 14, fax: 016-45 51 20; Gites de Wallonie, Rue du Millénaire 53, B-6941 Villers-Sainte-Gertrude (Durbuy). Tel: 086-49 97 24, fax: 086-49 94 07.
Brussels: Promenade de l'Alma 57, 1200 Brussels. Tel: 02-779 08 46, fax: 02-779 08 32.

Camping

Bed & Breakfast Taxistop
Rue du Fossee-aux-Loups 28, Brussels.
Tel: 02-223 2231.
Fax: 02-223 2232.
Bed & Brussels
Rue V. Greyson 58, Brussels.
Tel: 02-646 0737.
Fax: 02-644 0114.
Windrose
Avenue Paul Dejaer 21a, Brussels.
Tel: 02-534 7191.
Fax: 02-534 7192.

Camping/Caravan Parks

These can be found throughout the country, and especially in such popular holiday areas as the Ardennes, the Kempen and along the coast. Site facilities range from fairly minimal services for campers, to those of Provincial Recreation Areas with chalets, tent and caravan zones, restaurants, bars, swimming pools, beaches, amusement centres, bicycle hire and entertainment. There are more than 500 licensed campsites in Belgium. They are classified into categories from one to four stars depending upon overall quality and the degree of comfort offered. The majority are one-star, but all are generally well-equipped. As a rule, you can check into a campsite any time after 2pm; check-out time is no later than noon. A leaflet is available from the Belgium Tourist Office.

Brussels: There are no campsites in the city itself. However, the following three sites are located nearby and are within easy reach by public transport:
Huizingen, 13 km (8 miles) south of Brussels, Provinciaal Domein 6. Tel: 02-380 14 93.
Neeerijse, 20 km (13 miles) east of Brussels, Kamstraat 46. Tel: 016-47 75 13.
Wezembeek-Oppen, 10 km (6 miles) east of Brussels, Warandeberg. Tel: 02-782 10 09.

Youth Hostels

There are several youth hostels in Belgium. Those in Flanders tend to be large and cater for parties, while those in Wallonia are smaller and more informal.

Booking in advance, especially in summer, is advisable. The two organisations in Belgium are:
Flanders: Vlaamse Jeugdherberg-centrale, Van Stralenstraat 40. 2060 Antwerp. Tel: 03-232 72 18.
Wallonia: Les Auberges de la Jeunesse de Wallonie, Rue Van Oost 52, 1030 Brussels. Tel: 02-215 31 00.

If you plan to stay in several youth hostels it is worth joining the Youth Hostel Association at home before you depart and obtaining a complete list.

England and Wales Youth Hostel Association: Trevelyan House, 8 St Stephen's Hill, St Albans, Herts AL1. tel: 01727-845047; 14 Southampton Street, London WC2, tel: 0171-836 1036.
American Youth Hostels Association, PO Box 37613, Washington DC 20005. Tel: 202-783 6161.
Australian Youth Hostels Association, Level 3, 10 Mallet Street, Camperdown, NSW. Tel: 02-565 1325.

BRUSSELS
Accommodation for Young People, Acotra, Rue de Madeleine 57, 1000 Brussels. Tel: 02-512 55 40 and 02-512 86 07.
Auberge de Jeunesse Jean Nihon, Rue de l'Eléphant 4. Tel: 02-410 38 58.
Breughel Youth Hostel, Heilige Geeststraat 2, 1000 Brussels. Tel: 02-511 04 36.

Choosing a Hotel

Hotel reservations can be made for you by the following tourist organisations:
Tourist Information Brussels
Hotel de Ville, Grand'Place, Brussels.
Tel: 02-513 8940.
Belgian Tourist Office
Rue du Marche-aux-Herbes 63, Brussels.
Tel: 02-504 0390.
Fax: 02-504 0270.
Belgian Tourist Reservations
Boulevard Anspach 111, Brussels.
Tel: 02-513 7484.
Fax: 02-513 9277.
Hotel Reservation Service
Gare Centrale, Brussels.
Tel/fax: 02-534 7040.

Hotels

ANTWERP
Luxury
Alfa de Keyser
De Keyserlei 66–70.
Tel: 03-234 0135.
Fax: 03-232 3970.
Located beside Centraal Station, this excellent hotel has a well-equipped health centre and a swimming pool.

Sofitel
Desguinlei 94.
Tel: 03-244 8211.
Fax: 03-216 4712.
In the south of the city beside a park, the Sofitel is a modern, business-oriented hotel with a good restaurant.

Moderate
Alfa Empire
Appelmansstraat 31.
Tel: 03-231 4755.
Fax: 03-233 4060.
Well placed for buying diamonds, with a location in the Diamond Quarter.
Alfa Theater
Arenbergstraat 30.
Tel: 03-231 1720.
Fax: 03-233 8858.
A modern hotel that is well placed for the downtown attractions.

Hotel Price Guide

Luxury	BFr 6,000 and over
Moderate	BFr 3,000–BFr 6,000
Budget	BFr 3,000 and under

These price ranges are based on a double/twin room, generally with private bathroom, although in some budget choices you will have to share.

Ibis
Meistraat 39.
Tel: 03-231 8830.
Fax: 03-234 2921.
A chain hotel whose lack of traditional character is made up for by its modern facilities.
Novotel
Luithagen-Haven 6.
Tel: 03-542 0320.
Fax: 03-541 7093.
A modern hotel with a near-harbour location and relatively low cost for the comfort on offer.

Budget
New International Youth Pension
Provinciestraat 256.
Tel: 03-218 9430.
Fax: 03-281 0933.
Cheap and cheerful kind of place for youthful backpackers.

Pension Cammerpoorte
Steenhouwersvest 55.
Tel: 03-231 2836.
Fax: 03-226 2864.
With a location overlooking the Cathedral, this is a convenient and user-friendly hotel for those on a fairly low budget.
Rubenshof
Amerikalei 115-117.
Tel: 03-237 0789.
Fax: 03-248 2594.
A little way out from the centre and a good-value small hotel.
Square Sleep-Inn
Bolivarplaats 1.
Tel: 03-237 3748.
Fax: 03-248 0248.
Low-cost rooms and studios.
Tourist
Pelikaanstraat 22.
Tel: 03-232 5870.
Fax: 03-231 6707.
Near Centraal Station and offers straightforward but comfortable accommodation.

BOUILLON
Luxury
Auberge du Moulin Hideux
Route de Dohan 1, 6831 Noirefontaine.
Tel: 061-467015.
Fax: 061-467281.
A very characterful country hotel 5 km (3 miles) from Bouillon.

Moderate
Aux Armes de Bouillon
Rue de la Station 9-15.
Tel: 061-466079.
Fax: 061-466084.
A fairly big, holiday-oriented hotel in the town centre.

BRUGES
Luxury
De Swaene
Steenhouwersdijk 1.
Tel: 050-342798.
Fax: 050-336674.
Built around an 18th-century guildhouse, this is a very special hotel, whose relatively few rooms do not stay vacant for long.

Sofitel
Boeveriestraat 2.
Tel: 050-340971.
Fax: 050-344053.
Big rooms and an atmospheric setting near the railway station make this hotel a good choice for families.

Moderate
Alfa Dante
Coupure 29.
Tel: 050-340194
Fax: 050-343539.
A modern and stylish hotel with a canalfront setting.

De Snippe
Nieuwe Gentweg 53.
Tel: 050-337070.
Fax: 050-337662.
Staying in one of the atmospheric rooms here you will have an easy choice of restaurant – De Snippe's is one of the best in Bruges.

Duc de Bourgogne
Huidenvettersplein 12.
Tel: 050-332038.
Fax: 050-344037.
One of the most characterful hotels in Bruges, with rooms furnished in antique style and a good restaurant.

Egmond
Minnewater 15.
Tel: 050-341445.
Fax: 050-342940.
Only eight rooms but loads of ambience in a villa-style building beside the Lake of Love.

Navarra
St-Jakobsstraat 41.
Tel: 050-340561.
Fax: 050-336790.
A royal residence in the 16th century – albeit "only" of a prince – this recently modernised hotel treats its guests like minor royalty.

Oud Huis Amsterdam
Spiegelrei 3.
Tel: 050-341810.
Fax: 050-338891.
A lovingly restored 15th-century canalfront building with lavishly furnished and equipped rooms, and a genuinely enthusiastic welcome.

Pandhotel
Pandreitje 16.
Tel: 050-340666.
Fax: 050-340556.

This is a good example of the Bruges style, with high-quality antique furnishings and a characterful location in an 18th-century mansion.

Ter Duinen
Langerei 52.
Tel: 050-330437.
Fax: 050-344216.
A good compromise between facilities and cost, modernity and old-fashioned looks.

Budget
Bauhaus International Youth Hotel
Langestraat 135–137.
Tel: 050-341093.
Fax: 050-334180.
Good, youth-oriented budget accommodation.

't Bourgoensche Cruyce
Wollestraat 41–43.
Tel: 050-337926.
Fax: 050-341968.
One of Bruges' little gems, with eight rooms in a perfect setting in the centre and a fine in-hotel restaurant.

Central
Markt 30.
Tel: 050-331805.
Fax: 050-346878.
Seven plain and simple rooms, with a location right in the heart of things on the Markt.

De Markies
't Zand 5.
Tel: 050- 348334.
Fax: 050-348787.
On the big square near the railway station, this hotel delivers good value for money in an atmospheric location.

Erasmus
Wollestraat 35.
Tel: 050-335781.
Fax: 050-334797.
The nine rooms here are all nicely furnished and the hotel is well situated for the centre.

Fevery
Collaert Mansionstraat 3.
Tel: 050-331269.
Fax: 050-331791.
Has a good central position and delivers good value for money.

Graaf van Vlaanderen
't Zand 19.
Tel: 050-333150.
Fax: 050-345979.
A good budget choice.

't Keizershof
Oostmeers 126.
Tel: 050-338728.
Owned by an enthusiastic young couple who make budget travellers welcome.

Leopold
't Zand 26.
Tel: 050-335129.
Fax: 050-348654.
Offers slightly more than budget-level accommodation in a good location.

Passage
Dweersstraat 26.
Tel: 050-340232.
Fax: 050-340140.
Good, youth-oriented budget accommodation.

Rembrandt-Rubens
Walplein 38.
Tel: 050-336439.
Fax: 050-336439.
Although this hotel has a minimalist style when it comes to facilities, its friendly nature and genuine Bruges style more than make up.

Ryelandt Hus
Predikherenrei 10.
Tel: 050-336184.
Fax: 050-336134.
Good, youth-oriented budget accommodation.

St Christophe
Nieuwe Gentweg 76.
Tel: 050-331176.
Fax: 050-340938.
Another of Bruges' budget gems, simple but clean and welcoming, with a garden at the back.

BRUSSELS
In the city's official hotel guide, available at the Reception Service, Rue du Marché aux Herbes (Grasmarkt) 61, and in the Town Hall (TIB), you will find a complete list, including addresses, of the 120 or so hotels in the capital. It is possible to book accommodation at both places. Ask about cheaper weekend and high-summer rates.

Luxury

Amigo
Rue de l'Amigo 1.
Tel: 02-547 4747.
Fax: 02-513 5277.
"Amigo" may be Bruxellois slang for "prison", but don't let that worry you. If this were the old prison that used to stand here, people would have been queueing up to get in.

Bristol Stephanie
Avenue Louise 91-93.
Tel: 02-543 3311.
Fax: 02-538 0307.
An ultramodern hotel with an indoor swimming pool on fashionable Avenue Louise.

Conrad
Avenue Louise 71.
Tel: 02-542 4242.
Fax: 02-542 4200.
All the style and glitter for which the Conrad chain is renowned, along with a prime position on Brussels' fanciest street.

Jolly Hotel Atlanta
Boulevard Adolphe-Max 7.
Tel: 02-217 0120.
Fax: 02-217 3758.
A fine location and a reliable reputation for consistent service are the main attractions of this Italian-owned hotel.

Metropole
Place de Brouckere 31.
Tel: 02-217 2300.
Fax: 02-218 0220.
More like a turn-of-the-century palace than a hotel, the Metropole is a fabulously elegant evocation of a vanished era, and a moderately priced hotel considering the style it offers. Its L'Alban Chambon restaurant and colourful Victorian Café Metropole, lit with gas lamps, are both fixtures on the city's see-and-be-seen list.

Pullman Astoria
Rue Royale 103.
Tel: 02-217 6290.
Fax: 02-217 1150.
A beauty that combines belle-epoque grandeur from its opening in 1909 in its public spaces with modern comfort in its rooms.

Royal Crown
Rue Royale 250.
Tel: 02-220 6611.
Fax: 02-217 8444.
Occupies a relatively green and tranquil location near Le Botanique and adds to this advantage with a certain style at reasonable rates.

Royal Windsor
Rue Duquesnoy 5.
Tel: 02-505 5555.
Fax: 02-505 5500.
A modern hotel with an old-fashioned sense of style and a location near the Grand'Place.

SAS Royal
Rue du Fosse-aux-Loups 47.
Tel: 02-219 2828.
Fax: 02-219 6262.
Impeccable top-flight hotel, incorporating part of Brussels' ancient city wall. Its Henry Jean's American bar and grill is both stylish and popular.

Hotel Price Guide

Luxury	BFr 6,000 and over
Moderate	BFr 3,000–BFr 6,000
Budget	BFr 3,000 and under

These price ranges are based on a double/twin room, generally with private bathroom, although in some budget choices you will have to share.

Stanhope
Rue du Commerce 9.
Tel: 02-506 9111.
Fax: 02-512 1708.
The Stanhope combines the facilities of a good city hotel with the style of a country house, and does so in an area that is noted for its upmarket shopping.

Moderate

Agenda
Rue de Florence 6.
Tel: 02-539 0031.
Fax: 02-539 0063.
A fine small hotel just off Avenue Louise.

Albert Premier
Place Rogier 20.
Tel: 02-203 3125.
Fax: 02-203 4331.
One of the grand old names in Brussels lodging, the Albert retains its cachet and has modernised to meet the changing ties.

Arlequin
Rue de la Fourche 17–19.
Tel: 02-514 1615.
Fax: 02-514 2202.
You have only to step out the hotel door to be in the heart of Brussels atmospheric city-centre dining area, the Ilot Sacre.

Bedford
Rue du Midi 135.
Tel: 02-512 7840.
Fax: 02-514 1759.
A modern hotel near the Grand' Place that achieves a harmonious mix of the old with the new.

Cascade
Rue Berckmans 128.
Tel: 02-538 8830.
Fax: 02-538 9279.
Cool and modern style, for those who are less concerned with local ambience and more with cleanliness and efficiency.

Clubhouse
Rue Blanche 4.
Tel: 02-537 9210.
Fax: 02-537 0018.
Another of the "upper town" hotels that offer country-house style combined with access to the action.

Dixseptieme
Rue de la Madeleine 25.
Tel: 02-502 5744.
Fax: 02-502 6424.
Graceful and elegant, the Dixseptieme is one of those places that generates a lot of repeat business thanks to customer loyalty and where early booking is advisable.

Ibis Sainte-Catherine
Rue Joseph-Plateau 2.
Tel: 02-514 0054.
Fax: 02-514 2214.
Moderate prices, consistent standards, and a location near the atmospheric Fish Market.

Lambermont
Boulevard Lambermont 322.
Tel: 02-242 5595.
Fax: 02-215 3613.
Conveniently located for making a quick getaway from Brussels by car.

Manos
Chaussee de Charleroi 100–104.
Tel: 02-537 9682.
Fax: 02-539 3655.
A highly individual and characterful hotel just off Avenue Louise.

New Hotel Siru
Place Rogier 1.
Tel: 02-203 3580.
Fax: 02-203 3303.
One of Brussels' most memorable hotels – each of its rooms is "decorated" with a work of art by a contemporary Belgian artist.

Vendome
Boulevard Adolphe-Max 98.
Tel: 02-227 0300.
Fax: 02-218 0683.
Only a short way from the heart of the city, this hotel offers modern comfort with a touch of tranquillity.

Budget
De Boeck
Rue Veydt 40.
Tel: 02-537 4033.
Fax: 02-534 4037.
Its big rooms and reasonable prices make it a good bet for budget group travellers.

George V
Rue 't Kint 23.
Tel: 02-513 5093.
Fax: 02-513 4493.
A friendly and good-value place located in an interesting if somewhat gloomy area not far from the centre.

Les Bluets
Rue Berckmans 124.
Tel: 02-534 3983.
Fax: 02-534 3983.
You'll feel like one of the family in this rambling place, whose decor revels in the eclectic.

Pacific
Rue Antoine-Dansaert 57.
Tel: 02-511 8459.
Fax: 02-511 8459.
Highly individualistic – not to say eccentric – hotel on a chic shopping street near the Bourse.

Sabina
Rue du Nord 78.
Tel: 02-218 2637.
Fax: 02-219 3239.
A good bet for those who like their comforts and a bit of individual style.

Welcome
Quai au Bois-a-Bruler 23.
Tel: 02-219 9546.
Fax: 02-217 1887.
Hotels don't get much smaller than one with six rooms, but nor do

Hotel Price Guide

Luxury	BFr 6,000 and over
Moderate	BFr 3,000–BFr 6,000
Budget	BFr 3,000 and under

These price ranges are based on a double/twin room, generally with private bathroom, although in some budget choices you will have to share.

guests get more personal service than at this little gem at the Fish Market which has a fine seafood restaurant attached.

DINANT

Moderate
L'Auberge de Bouvignes
Rue Fetis 112.
Tel: 082-611600.
More like a country house, with just six rooms in its riverside setting 3km (2 miles) from Dinant on the Namur road.

Hotel de la Couronne
Rue Adolphe-Sax 1.
Tel: 082-222441.
Fax: 082-222147.
A friendly hotel in the town centre.

Budget
Hotel de la Citadelle
Place Reine-Astrid 5.
Tel: 082-223543.
This is a straightforward kind of place, run with pride.

DURBUY

Luxury
Hostellerie le Sanglier des Ardennes
Grand' Rue 99.
Tel: 086-213262.
Fax: 086-212465.
The hotel restaurant stands out for the quality of its cuisine – in an area where outstanding restaurants are ten-a-penny.

Moderate
Le Clos des Recollets
Rue de la Prevote.
Tel: 086-211271.
Fax: 086-213685.
A very good little hotel.

Le Vieux Durbuy
Rue Jean-de-Boheme.
Tel: 086-213262.
Good value-for-money kind of place.

Budget
La Falize
Rue A. Eloi 1.
Tel: 086-212666.
A plain but very comfortable hotel furnished in traditional style.

GHENT

Luxury
Holiday Inn
Ottergemsesteenweg 600.
Tel: 09-222 5885.
Fax: 09-220 1222.
An out-of-town hotel with all the facilities for which Holiday Inns are known, including a swimming pool.

Sofitel
Hoogpoort 63.
Tel: 09-233 3331.
Fax: 09-233 1102.
One of the best hotels in the city, with guaranteed comfort and a location at the heart of things.

Moderate
Eden
Zuidstationstraat 24.
Tel: 09-223 5151.
Fax: 09-233 3457.
A characterful, reasonably good-priced hotel not far from the centre.

Europahotel
Gordunakaai 59.
Tel: 09-220 6071.
Fax: 09-220 0609.
A suburban location beside the river makes this a good choice for visitors who want to be close, but not too close, to the centre of the city.

Gravensteen
Jan Breydelstraat 35.
Tel: 09-225 1150.
Fax: 09-225 1850.
An elegant 19th-century mansion that has retained much of its former style combined with modern facilities.

Ibis Centrum Opera
Nederkouter 24–26.
Tel: 09-225 0707.
Fax: 09-223 5907.
This is a fairly new hotel that offers good value for money.

Novotel
Gouden Leeuwplein 5.
Tel: 09-224 2230.
Fax: 09-224 3295.
A bright and shiny hotel with a good city-centre location and a heated outdoor swimming pool.
Sint-Jorishof
Botermarkt 2.
Tel: 09-224 2424.
Fax: 09-224 2640.
This has been a lodging-house since the early 13th century, and its fine old style continues to attract visitors.

Budget
Carlton
Koningin Astridlaan 138.
Tel: 09-222 8836.
Fax: 09-220 4992.
Convenient for the railway station and a good budget option.

KNOKKE-HEIST
Luxury
La Reserve
Elizabetlaan 160.
Tel: 050-610606.
Fax: 050-603706.
A health-spa resort hotel, this is the deluxe end of the market.

Moderate
Lido
Zwaluwenlaan 18.
Tel: 050-601925.
Fax: 050-610457.
Brightly modern and located close to the sea.
Parkhotel
Elizabetlaan 204.
Tel: 050-600901.
Fax: 050-623608.
A tranquil atmosphere and elegant style are the attractions here.
Pauwels
Kustlaan 353.
Tel: 050-611617.
Fax: 050-620405.
A good upper-range hotel convenient for the beach and the stylish shopping.

Budget
Corner House
Hazegrasstraat 1.
Tel: 050-607619.
Low cost and comfort make up for a location far from the beach.

LIEGE
Moderate
Bedford
Quai St-Leonard 36.
Tel: 04-228 8111.
Fax: 04-227 4575.
This is a business-oriented hotel beside the Meuse that does good weekend packages.
Le Cygne d'Argent
Rue Beeckman 49.
Tel: 04-223 7001.
Fax: 04-222 4966.
Friendly, home-from-home style.
Holiday Inn
Esplanade de l'Europe 2.
Tel: 04-342 6020.
Fax: 04-343 4810.
Big modern hotel across the river from the centre.
Mercure
Boulevard de la Sauveniere 100.
Tel: 04-221 7711.
Fax: 04-221 7701.
A fine, business-oriented hotel with modern facilities and a good location.
Post House
Rue Hurbise 160.
Tel: 04-264 6400.
Fax: 04-248 0690.
Out-of-town, so best for car users, but a good exploring base.

Budget
Comfort Inn l'Univers
Rue des Guillemins 116.
Tel: 04-254 5555.
Fax: 04-254 5500.
Probably has the best quality/price ratio in Liège.
Hotel du Midi
Place des Guillemins 1.
Tel: 04-252 2004.
Fax: 04-252 1613.
You can't do much better pricewise, and the location is good.

MONS
Moderate
Infotel
Rue d'Havre 32
Tel: 065-356221.
Fax: 065-356224.
A modern hotel with comfort and facilities to match.

Budget
Saint-Georges
Rue des Clercs 15.

Tel: 065-311629.
Fax: 065-318671.
Fairly basic but comfortable place.

NAMUR
Luxury
Les Tanneurs
Rue des Tanneries 13.
Tel: 081-231999.
Fax: 081-229703.
There are big variations in room rates at this excellent hotel.

Moderate
Excelsior
Avenue de la Gare 4.
Tel: 081-231813.
Fax: 081-230929.
Not many rooms, but they are comfortable and good value.
Novotel
Chaussee de Dinant 1149, Wepion.
Tel: 081-460811.
Fax: 081-461990.
A modern hotel in the quaint surroundings of a riverside village 5 km (3 miles) from Namur.

Budget
Queen Victoria
Avenue de la Gare 12.
Tel: 081-222971.
Fax: 081-241100.
A simple but comfortable hotel.

ORVAL
Moderate
Hostellerie du Pieure des Conques
Route de Florenville 179, St. Cecile.
Tel: 061-411417.
Fax: 061-412703.
A superb country hotel that offers unrivalled value for money.

OSTEND
Luxury
Oostendse Compagnie
Koningstraat 79.
Tel: 059-704816.
Fax: 059-805316.
Once a royal villa, this famous hotel retains a kingly style.

Moderate
Andromeda
Westhelling 5.
Tel: 059-806611.
Fax: 059-806629.
You can't beat the location – right

beside the beach and the casino –
and the facilities are good too.

Bero
Hofstraat 1a.
Tel: 059-702335.
Fax: 059-702591.
This is a good resort hotel, with its
own swimming pool.

Danielle
Ijzerstraat 5.
Tel: 059-706349.
Fax: 059-706349.
This is typical of the good-quality mid-
range hotels in Ostend, and it has a
reasonable in-house restaurant.

Du Parc
Marie-Joseplein 3.
Tel: 059-701680.
Fax: 059-800879.
Another of the good mid-range
places in Ostend.

Old Flanders Hotel
Jozef II Straat 49.
Tel: 059-806603
Fax: 059-801695.
Old-fashioned public spaces
contrast with modern rooms here.

Prado
Leopold II Laan 22.
Tel: 059-705306.
Fax: 059-808735.
A modernly furnished hotel not far
from the beach.

Strandhotel
Visserskaai 1.
Tel: 059-703383.
Fax: 059-803678.
Looking out on the fishing boats and
ferries, well placed and comfortable.

Thermae-Palace
Koningin Astridlaan 7.
Tel: 059-806644.
Fax: 059-805274.
A taste of pre-war beach resort
style, and with one of Ostend's best
restaurants.

Hotel Price Guide

Luxury	BFr 6,000 and over
Moderate	BFr 3,000–BFr 6,000
Budget	BFr 3,000 and under

These price ranges are based on
a double/twin room, generally
with private bathroom, although
in some budget choices you will
have to share.

ROBERTVILLE

Moderate

Hotel des Bains
Lac de Robertville, Waimes.
Tel: 080-679571.
Fax: 080-678143.
Occupies a great position near the
shores of Robertville Lake.

SPA

Moderate

Dorint
Route de Balmoral 33.
Tel: 087-772581.
Fax: 087-774174.
A highly modern hotel above the
town, with excellent sports facilities.

Hotel la Heid des Pairs
Avenue Professor-Henrijean 143.
Tel: 087-774346.
Fax: 087-770644.
Leisurely style in a transformed
country villa.

L'Auberge de Spa
Place du Monument 4.
Tel: 087-774410.
Fax: 087-772179.
The price for rooms varies consider-
ably at this quality hotel in the centre.

TOURNAI

Moderate

L'Europe
Grand'Place 36.
Tel: 069-224067.
Fax: 069-235238.
A straightforward little hotel with a
prime location on the main square.

Budget

Aux Armes de Tournai
Place de Lille 24.
Tel: 069-226723.
Typical cosy little Tournai hotel.

Tour St-Georges
Rue St-Georges 2.
Tel: 069-225300.
Simple but attractive, this hotel
also has a popular restaurant.

YPRES

Moderate

Regina
Grote Markt 45.
Tel: 057-219006.
Fax: 057-219020.
Situated at the heart of Ypres' main
square, the Regina is small and
convenient enough to fill up quickly.

Where to Eat

The people of Belgium have a
reputation for especially fine
tastebuds; this is attested to by the
number of excellent restaurants,
particularly in Brussels.

The big meal of the day is usually
consumed in the evening. Nearly all
restaurants offer daily specials,
children's portions and complete
tourist menus.

In the centre of the capital along
the boulevards around the opera
house and stock exchange, as well
as around the Grand'Place, there
are numerous places to sit down
and enjoy a waffle, slice of pie or
cake, or a cold drink. The larger
hotels also serve various beverages
and snacks.

A "Gourmet" dining guide to
eating out in Brussels is available
from the Tourist Information Centre
(TIB); this booklet contains a list of
restaurants in the city along with
their addresses, hours, prices and
particular house specialities.

What to Eat

The numerous, relatively inexpensive gastronomic specialities of
Belgium are not the only dishes that
come highly recommended; the
plain, home-style fare served
throughout the country will probably
prove to be just as delicious. Along
the coast the culinary emphasis is
on seafood, while the cuisine on
offer in Brussels tends to be
international in flavour.

Brussels is world-famous for its
fresh mussels, oysters and lobster.
Fish dishes, made from sole, cod
and turbot, are prepared in a variety
of tasty ways. Belgian chicory also
enjoys an international reputation,
served frequently in a form of
casserole. Two more delicious

dishes which can be recommended are red cabbage prepared in the traditional Flemish style and asparagus from Mechelen.

Not to be missed while visiting Ghent and Antwerp is waterzooi – small pieces of chicken in chicken broth, served with a selection of vegetables and cream. In the forested regions, particularly in the Ardennes, adventurous diners will find a wide variety of game offered in local restaurants during the hunting season. Pheasant prepared in the old Brabant tradition is a particularly lauded dish. The Ardennes is also known for its hearty soups, cured ham and pâté.

Sweet rice cakes take the first prize among the wide assortment of baked goods and pastries. Waffles are another typical treat; in Brussels they are usually served with cream, in Liège with caramelised sugar.

Chocolate

Belgium is renowned for its chocolate – it is said that each Belgian consumes 12.5 kg (27.5 lbs) of chocolate annually – and a visit to a chocolatier is a treat. Godiva and Leonidas, among others, have shops in the main towns.

Drinking Notes

BEER

The Belgians' favourite drink is beer. It has been brewed in Belgium since the Middle Ages when a Benedictine monk, St Arnold, discovered that the noblemen had a considerably higher life expectancy than the common people because they were able to quench their thirst with beer rather than the often contaminated water. He exhorted his flock to drink beer and for centuries afterwards the art of brewing remained firmly in the hands of the various religious communities.

The craft has now become a major industry. Today there are no fewer than 400 breweries scattered across Belgium, producing 400 kinds of beer. It is usually served in

small glasses. Stella Artois from Leuven, Jupiler from Liège and Maes are the most common.

Local draught pilsner is relatively mild in flavour; the speciality beers, usually served by the bottle, tend to be strong. The Rodenbach Brewery in West Flanders brews a beer known as Dobbelen Bruinen which is stored in oak barrels and then filled into champagne bottles.

One unusual beer is Lambic, which also forms the basis for a number of other brews: Gueuze, Faro, Kriek and Framboise. Of the beers produced by Belgium's Trappist monasteries, Chimay, brewed in Hainaut, is the most widely available. Orval, from Luxembourg, is fruitier; Westmalle, from Antwerp is rich and malty.

WINE

Wines are widely available and generally imported from France. However, the southern province of Luxembourg produces very drinkable white wines from the banks of the Moselle.

SPIRITS

The Belgians' favourite chaser is jenever (juniper-flavoured gin). Be warned, however: jenever can cause a thundering hangover when consumed in quantity.

Restaurants

ANTWERP
Moderate
Beluga
Sint-Pietersvliet 3.
Tel: 03-226 1003.
Seafood specialities in a restaurant decked out like a liner.
De Manie
Hendrik Conscienceplein 3.
Tel: 03-232 6438.
Modern, French-style restaurant.
De Mergpijp
Vlaamsekaai 16.
Tel: 03-238 6197.
Very traditional Antwerp ambience.
De Peerdestal
Wijngaardstraat 8.
Tel: 03-231 9503.
Old-fashioned French-style restaurant.

In de Schaduw van de Kathedraal
Handschoenmarkt 17–21.
Tel: 03-232 4014.
The name means 'in the shadow of the Cathedral', exactly where this French-style restaurant is located.
La Perouse
Steenplein.
Tel: 03-231 3151.
Stylish floating restaurant that prepares Flemish specialities and seafood dishes to perfection.
La Terrazza
Wisselstraat 2.
Tel: 03-226 6658.
Down-home Italian food.
Rooden Hoed
Oude Koornmarkt 25.
Tel: 03-233 2844.
Flemish cooking mostly, mixed with a few regional specialities from neighbouring countries.
Sir Anthony Van Dyck
Oude Koornmarkt 16.
Tel: 03-231 6170.
Brasserie-style restaurant in the Vlaeykensgang courtyard.
't Vermoeid Model
Lijnwaadmarkt 2.
Tel: 03-233 5261.
As close to the Cathedral as possible, specialising in seafood.

Budget
Falafel Beni
Lange Leemstraat 188.
Tel: 03-218 8211.
Cheap 'n' cheerful falafel joint.
Panache
Statiestraat 17.
Tel: 03-232 6905.
Multiple choice, healthful sandwich-cum-deli place.
Pottenbrug
Minderbroedersrui 38.
Tel: 03-231 5147.
Basic but tasty Flemish fare at modest prices.

Price Guide

Luxury	BFr 5,000 and over
Moderate	BFr 2,000–BFr 5,000
Budget	BFr 2,000 and under

These price ranges are based on a three-course dinner for two accompanied by the house wine.

BOCHOLT

Moderate

Kristoffel
Dorpstraat 28.
Tel: 089-471591.
Gracefully old-fashioned restaurant near the Dutch border.

BRUGES

Moderate

Bistro De Stove
Kleine Sint-Amandsstraat 4.
Tel: 050-337835.
A lot less formal than many of Bruges' better restaurants but right up there in the taste stakes, with seafood a strong performer.

't Bourgoensche Cruyce
Wollestraat 41-43.
Tel: 050-337926.
One of the best and most atmospheric dining experiences in Bruges, in a beautiful hotel restaurant overlooking the canal.

De Gouden Meermin
Markt 31.
Tel: 050-333776.
Trade a little in terms of distinguished service for a great position on the Markt.

De Snippe
Nieuwe Gentweg 53.
Tel: 050-337070.
Flemish and French specialities served in a transformed 18th-century mansion.

De Visscherie
Vismarkt 8.
Tel: 050-330212.
With a name like this and a location in the Fish Market, it's no surprise that the speciality is seafood, and no one does it better.

Duc de Bourgogne
Huidenvettersplein 12.
Tel: 050-332038.
Another classic Bruges dining experience, with French-style dishes served in beautiful surroundings.

Kasteel Minnewater
Minnewater 4.
Tel: 050-334254.
This actually is a château, and if the prices are less than might be expected in such surroundings, the quality is not.

't Koffieboontje
Hallestraat 4.

Tel: 050-338027.
Bright and breezy modern restaurant that serves good seafood.

't Pandreitje
Pandreitje 6.
Tel: 050-331190.
Elegant and refined, this is one of the most considered choices for a special night out.

Budget

Brasserie Erasmus
Wollestraat 35.
Tel: 050-335781.
Great place for budget dining, and all the main dishes are prepared with beer.

't Dreveken
Huidenvettersplein 10–11.
Tel: 050-339506.
Comfortable and welcoming surroundings for Flemish and seafood dishes.

Graaf van Vlaanderen
't Zand 19.
Tel: 050-333150.
Straightforward budget bistro.

BRUSSELS

There are about 1,500 restaurants in Brussels and it's hard to find a bad one among them. Among prime areas to dine are the Ilot Sacré (Sacred Island) near Grand'Place: Rue des Bouchers, Petite Rue des Bouchers and the connecting streets are awash with restaurants with outdoor terraces; the Marché aux Poissons (Fish Market) in the Place Sainte-Catherine area, where seafood dishes are thick on the menus; the upper town around Avenue Louise, Place Stephanie and the Porte de Namur; the Ixelles district; ethnic restaurants in the Chaussée de Haecht and Chaussée de Louvain.

Luxury

Alban Chambon
Hotel Metropole, Place de Brouckére 31.
Tel: 02-217 2300.
Superbly classy restaurant that keeps a taste of the belle epoque alive in Brussels.

Comme Chez Soi
Place Rouppe 23.
Tel: 02-512 2921.
Master Chef Pierre Wynants, one of the world's great chefs, holds court in this French-style three Michelin star restaurant, whose name means "Just Like Home".

Maison du Cygne
Rue Charles Buls 2.
Tel: 02-511 8244.
With an unbeatable location overlooking the Grand'Place, this restaurant thoroughly deserves its high reputation.

Quatre Saisons
Royal Windsor Hotel, Rue Duquesnoy 5.
Tel: 02-511 4215.
Top-flight cuisine and service in what is a firm favourite with the Brussels' establishment.

Villa Lorraine
Chaussée de la Hulpe 28.
Tel: 02-374 3163.
French-style creations that surely outdo the best of France in taste and elegance of presentation.

Moderate

Aux Armes de Bruxelles
Rue des Bouchers 13.
Tel: 02-511 2118.
As genuinely Belgian as they come, and a highlight of the Ilot Sacré restaurant district.

Brasserie de la Roue d'Or
Rue des Chapeliers 26.
Tel: 02-514 2554.
The décor celebrates Magritte, and diners celebrate the firm commitment to the best of Belgium at this characterful location.

De l'Ogenblik
Galerie des Princes 1.
Tel: 02-511 6151.
Elegantly romantic French bistro-style ambience in the elegant surroundings of the Galeries Royales Saint-Hubert.

Falstaff
Rue Henri-Maus 23–25.
Tel: 02-511 9877.
A Brussels legend in its own lunchtime and dinnertime, Falstaff has art nouveau décor with typical Belgian cuisine and a reputation that attracts the young and modish.

Falstaff Gourmand
Rue des Pierres 38.
Tel: 02-512 1761.
The Falstaff's more restrained and refined cousin, just around the corner, where fine cuisine is served at remarkably reasonable prices.

Joueur de Flute
Rue de l'Epée 26.
Tel: 02-513 4311.
An excellent small restaurant whose owner-chef cooks whatever takes his fancy – and it's a fair bet that his customers won't be sorry.

Macon
Rue Joseph Stallaert 87.
Tel: 02-343 8937.
A standard-bearer of Belgian cuisine whose prices are notably "démocratique".

Marmiton
Rue des Bouchers 43.
Tel: 02-511 7910.
One of the best addresses in the Ilot Sacré, a consistently fine performer that treats its customers, regulars and visitors, with respect.

Pain et le Vin
Chaussée d'Alsemberg 812a.
Tel: 02-332 3774.
Mediterranean cuisine served in a fresh and breezy atmosphere that makes it a fun place to visit.

Paradiso
Rue Duquesnoy 34.
Tel: 02-512 5232.
Pasta and pizza just like mamma used to make them, in what is a hidden gem not far from the Grand'Place.

Passage to India
Chaussée de Louvain 223.
Tel: 02-735 3147.
Excellent Indian food at moderate prices served in an atmospheric and friendly restaurant.

Quincaillerie
Rue du Page 45.
Tel: 02-538 2553.
A wildly popular, and deservedly so, French-style restaurant whose premises used to be a hardware store. The seafood is particularly good.

Scheltema
Rue des Dominicains 7.
Tel: 02-512 2084.
Located just off the Grand'Place in an area awash with restaurants, few of which come even close to Scheltema's standards. Belgian specialities abound on the menu.

Shanti
Avenue Adolphe Buyl 68.
Tel: 02-649 4096.
Vegetarian food that takes a world of cuisine as its inspiration.

Sirène d'Or
Place Sainte-Catherine 1a.
Tel: 02-513 5198.
With a location at the Fish Market, you'd expect this to be a seafood specialist – and it is, one of the best in the city.

Stevin
Rue Saint-Quentin 29.
Tel: 02-230 9847.
Should you find yourself lost among the teeming bureaucrats and vast office blocks of Brussels' Euro-zone you can take refuge at this fine French-Belgian restaurant.

Table de l'Abbaye
Rue de Belle-Vue 62.
Tel: 02-646 3395.
Country-house style and fine French cuisine sit harmoniously together at this restaurant with a well-established reputation.

Truite d'Argent
Quai aux Bois-á-Bruler 23.
Tel: 02-218 3926.
Excellent seafood at this restaurant attached to the Welcome Hotel in Brussels' Fish Market district.

Budget
Auberge des Chapeliers
Rue des Chapeliers 1–3.
Tel: 02-513 7338.
Bistro-style restaurant near the Grand'Place that concentrates on Belgian specialities.

Au Trappiste
Avenue de la Toisond'Or 7.
Tel: 02-511 7839.
An excellent, low-cost Belgian-style restaurant in an area where high prices are otherwise as common as designer labels in the upmarket shops.

Au Vieux Bruxelles
Rue Saint-Boniface 35.
Tel: 02-513 0181.
Belgians are crazy about mussels, and you won't find them served any better than in this atmospheric brasseries dating from the 1880s.

Café Metropole
Hotel Metropole, Place de Brouckére 31.
Tel: 02-217 2300.
A fine place for snacks in the notably graceful surroundings of this hotel café.

In 't Spinnekopke
Place du Jardin-aux-Fleurs 1.
Tel: 02-511 8695.
This is also Brussels at its best, a traditional restaurant in everything from its looks to the quality of its downhome specialities.

't Kelderke
Grand'Place 15.
Tel: 02-513 7344.
You might think that a restaurant in the Grand'Place would be a tourist trap – 't Kelderke, located in a cellar, is Brussels at its best.

Mirabelle
Chaussée de Boondael 459.
Tel: 02-649 5173.
Low prices and good quality make this popular with students from the nearby university.

Paon Royal
Rue du Vieux-Marché-aux-Grains 6.
Tel: 02-513 0868.
A real favourite with locals in this area not far from the Fish Market. Serves Belgian standards.

BURG REULAND

Moderate
Val de l'Our
Burg Reuland.
Tel: 080-329009.
Fine good taste with Ardennes specialities at a reasonable price in one of the most attractive parts of the country.

DAMME

Moderate

De Lieve
Jacob van Maerlantstraat 10.
Tel: 050-356630.
Specialities of the season.
Pallieter
Kerkstraat 12.
Tel: 050-354675.
Characteristic of Damme's olde-
worlde style.

Budget

Gasthof Maerlant
Kerkstraat 21.
Tel: 050-352952.
Good value with a position on
Damme's main street.

DE PANNE

Moderate

Becassine
Rozenlaan 20.
Tel: 058-521100.
Great for North Sea shrimps and
has other seafood dishes also.
Le Fox
Walckierstraat 2.
Tel: 058-412855.
Good value for top-of-the-range
seafood dishes such as lobster.

DINANT

Moderate

Auberge de Bouvignes
Rue Fetis 112, Dinant-Bouvignes.
Tel: 082-611600.
Farmhouse-style restaurant beside
the River Meuse at Bouvignes near
Dinant.
Restaurant Thermidor
Rue de la Station 3.
Tel: 082-223135.
High standards are the norm for
mainly French specialities here.

DURBUY

Luxury

Le Sanglier des Ardennes
Grand' Rue 99.
Tel: 086-213262.
Among the most desirable
restaurants in Belgium, specialising
in fresh produce from the rolling
Ardennes.

EUPEN

Moderate

Alte Herrlichkeit
Gospertstrasse 104.
Tel: 087-552038.
Old fashioned and slightly severe
setting for traditional German–
Belgian cooking.

GHENT

Luxury

't Buikske Vol
Kraanlei 17.
Tel: 09-225 1880.
One of Ghent's favourite
owner/chefs puts his stamp on
Flemish and seafood dishes.

Moderate

Auberge de Fonteyne
Gouden Leeuwplein 7.
Tel: 09-225 4871.
Distinctively decorated restaurant
on an atmospheric square, with
mussels as a standard menu item.
The Ghost
Korenlei 24.
Tel: 09-225 8902.
Underground eating – in a crypt –
where the food is very traditional
Flemish.
Graaf van Egmond
Sint-Michielsplein 21.
Tel: 09-225 0727.
French and Flemish specialities
served in a very traditional setting
in the city centre.
Het Cooremetershuys
Graslei 12.
Tel: 09-225 0965.
There can be no better location
than a 14th-century guildhouse
overlooking this famous canal – and
the Flemish and French dishes are
pretty memorable too.
Jan Breydel
Jan Breydelstraat 10.
Tel: 09-225 6287.
Enthusiast owners ensure that
seafood and Flemish specialities
are nowhere done better.
Oranjerie
Corduwaniersstraat 8.
Tel: 09-224 1008.
Garden-style interior makes an airy
place for dining on Flemish and
French dishes.

Sint-Jorishof
Botermarkt 2.
Tel: 09-224 2424.
Restaurant of the hotel, a former
inn, that has been satisfying
customers since the 13th century.

Budget

Buddhasbelly
Hoogpoort 30.
Tel: 09-225 1732.
Vegetarian food whose high spiritual
value is matched by genuine taste.
Guido Meerschaut
Kleine Vismarkt 3.
Tel: 09-223 5349.
Top-flight, low-cost seafood from a
family restaurant steeped in the
fish business.

HASSELT

Luxury

Kasteel Sint-Paul
Lagendalstraat 1, Lummen exit 26
from the A2 near Hasselt.
Tel: 013-521809.
Not actually in Hasselt, but in
nearby Lummen, this is a country
chateau serving French cuisine.

KNOKKE-HEIST

Luxury

Ter Dijcken
Kalvekeetdijk 137.
Tel: 050-608023.
Upmarket elegance in Belgium's
most chic resort.

Moderate

Aquilon
Elisabethlaan 6.
Tel: 050-601274.
One of the best seafood bets in
Knokke.
Panier d'Or
Zeedijk 659.
Tel: 050-603189.
Another excellent seafood specialist.

Budget

Casa Borghese
Bayauxlaan 27.
Tel: 050-603739.
Italian and French cuisine – seafood
mostly – sit easily side by side.

LA ROCHE-EN-ARDENNE

Moderate

Claire Fontaine
Route de Hotton 64.
Tel: 084-411296.
Traditional country cooking.

LIEGE

Moderate

Au Vieux Liège
Quai de la Goffe 41.
Tel: 04-223 7748.
Seafood and Continental dishes served in an atmospheric house dating from the 16th century.

Brasserie as Ouhes
Place du Marché 21.
Tel: 04-223 3225.
Highly regarded locally for its Liègeoise specialities.

Chez Max
Place de la République Française 12.
Tel: 041 220859.
Cosy, unpretentious, cosy restaurant that serves excellent Belgian cuisine.

Dejeuner Sur l'Herbe
Rue des Begards 2.
Tel: 04-222 9234.
French-style restaurant in a light and airy location.

Mame Vi Cou
Rue de la Wache 9.
Tel: 04-223 7181.
Among the most atmospheric, romantic restaurants in Belgium, serving old Walloon specialities.

Rotisserie de la Sauvenière
Boulevard de la Sauvenière 100.
Tel: 04-221 7711.
French restaurant of the Hôtel Mercure, with a reputation that extends far beyond reception.

Budget

Brasserie du Midi
Place des Guillemins 1.
Tel: 04-252 2004.
Conveniently placed beside the station and a good budget choice.

Price Guide

Luxury	BFr 5,000 and over
Moderate	BFr 2,000–BFr 5,000
Budget	BFr 2,000 and under

These price ranges are based on a three-course dinner for two accompanied by the house wine.

Rotisserie l'Empereur
Place du 20-Aout 15.
Tel: 04-223 5373.
Popular and modestly priced, with a wide choice.

MONS

Moderate

Alter Ego
Rue de Nimy 6.
Tel: 065-355260.
Typical Belgian fare and a friendly atmosphere.

Devos
Rue de la Coupe 7.
Tel: 065-351335.
Seafood is recommended here, but there are plenty of other Belgian dishes on offer.

NAMUR

Moderate

Brasserie Henry
Place St-Aubin 3.
Tel: 081-220204.
One of the smartest places in Namur.

Chateau de Namur
Avenue de l'Ermitage 1.
Tel: 081-742630.
Dine like the aristocracy for a democratic price.

La Petite Fugue
Place Chanoine Descamps 5.
Tel: 081-231320.
An intimate and noteworthy little French restaurant.

Budget

Grand Café des Galeries Saint Loup
Rue du College 25.
Tel: 081-227146.
Fantastic quality in a memorable brasserie-style grand café.

OSTEND

Luxury

Au Vigneron
Koningstraat 79.
Tel: 059-704816.
Top-rated, French-style restaurant of the Oostendse Compagnie Hotel.

Gloria Restaurant
Westhelling 5.
Tel: 059-806611.
Restaurant of the Andromeda Hotel, with a strong line in seafood.

Villa Maritza
Albert I Promenade 76.
Tel: 059-508808.
Housed in an elegant old seaside mansion, with seafood top of the menu.

Moderate

Chopin
Alfons Buylstraat 1A.
Tel: 059-700837.
Surf 'n' turf gives plenty of choice at this fine mid-range restaurant.

Old Fisher Restaurant
Visserskaai 34.
Tel: 059-501768.
May be the best, moderately priced seafood restaurant in town, with a location beside the fishing harbour.

Budget

Le Basque
Albert I Promenade 62.
Tel: 059-705444.
Good seafood for those on tight budgets.

Villa Borghese
Van Iseghemlaan 65b.
Tel: 059-800876.
Try Italian for a change from wall-to-wall seafood.

ROCHEFORT

Moderate

Les Falizes
Rue de France 90.
Tel: 084-211282.
Offers a peaceful setting in which to enjoy the finest Ardennes specialities.

Sankt-Vith
Pip-Margraff.
Hauptstrasse 7.
Tel: 080-228663.
Highly popular in the German-speaking East Cantons.

SINT-MARTENS-LATEM

Luxury

Auberge du Pêcheur
Pontstraat 44.
Tel: 282-3144.
Highly regarded dining experience in an attractive riverside village south of Ghent.

SPA

Luxury

La Retraite de l'Empereur
Rue de Basse Desnie 841.
Tel: 087-376215.
Located in the nearby village of Deux la Reid, this is one of the best restaurants in the area.

Moderate

Larasserie du Grand Maur
Rue Xhrouet 41.
Tel: 087-773616.
French and Belgian specialities in a notably elegant setting.
Eurotaverne
Rue Royale 4.
Tel: 087-773926.
Although it's in Spa's Casino, you won't be gambling on good quality here for regional dishes.
La Fontaine du Tonnelet
Fontaine du Tonnelet.
Tel: 087-772603.
Fine Italian restaurant.

Budget

Chalet du Parc
Parc de Sept Heures.
Tel: 087-772284.
Straightforward but quick and tasty restaurant in the park.
La Geronstère
Fontaine de la Geronstère.
Tel: 087-770372.
Good place for snacks.
La Sauvenière
Fontaine de la Sauvenière.
Tel: 087-775168.
Farmhouse-style restaurant on the popular walking tour of the springs.

TOURNAI

Moderate

Charles Quint
Grand'Place 3.
Tel: 069-221441.
Perfectly positioned beside the Belfry, this is popular with locals as well as visitors.

Price Guide

Luxury	BFr 5,000 and over
Moderate	BFr 2,000–BFr 5,000
Budget	BFr 2,000 and under

These price ranges are based on a three-course dinner for two accompanied by the house wine.

Le Pressoir
Marché aux Poteries 2.
Tel: 069-223513.
A wide range of Continental dishes is on offer here.

YPRES

Moderate

Dikkebus Vijver
Vijverdreef 31.
Tel: 057-200085.
Out of town at Lake Dikkebus, serves seafood and Flemish dishes.

Bars & Cafés

ANTWERP

De Engel
Grote Markt 3.
Occupies an ideal position on the Grote Markt, where it serves up Antwerp's own De Koninck beer.
De Vagant
Reijndersstraat 25.
Some 150 kinds of *jenever* are sold at this specialist café.
Groote Witte Arend
Reyndersstraat 12–18.
Characterful café located in an old abbey.
Kulminator
Vleminckveld 32.
More than 500 different kinds of beer are on offer here.
Pelgrom
Pelgrimstraat 15.
Drink underground in a cellar lit by candles.

BRUGES

't Brugs Beertje
Kemelstraat 5.
The city's most popular traditional café.

BRUSSELS

A la Morte Subite
Rue Montagne-aux-Herbes-Potagères 7.
Traditional old café, popular with all walks of life.
Archiduc
Rue Antoine Dansaert 6.
Top of the line in terms of style, if not always of substance.
Au Bon Vieux Temps
Rue du Marché-aux-Herbes 12.
Characterful bar near the Grand'Place.
Cirio
Rue de la Bourse 18.
Genteel place popular with those of a certain age.
Falstaff
Rue Henri Maus 17.
Perhaps Brussels' most distinctive café, with art nouveau a big part of the attraction.
Fleur en Papier Doré
Rue des Alexiens 55.
Dates from 1846, a haunt of artist types.
Halloween
Rue des Grands-Carmes 10.
The devil is in the detail at this theme pub that celebrates the supernatural.
Le Cerceuil
Rue des Harengs 10.
Serenaded by funeral music, you sit at a coffin-lid table and drink beer from a pitcher in the form of a human skull.
Rick's
Avenue Louise 344.
A touch of American style.
Toone VII
Impasse Schuddeveld 6, Petite Rue des Bouchers 21.
A sophisticated puppet theatre is just one reason for visiting this wonderful old bar.
Ultieme Hallucinatie
Rue Royale 316.
Smart place a little too far out of the centre to be convenient, but well worth the tram journey.

GHENT

Dulle Griet
Vrijdagmarkt 50.
Popular local café with a tradition of selling the strong Kwak beer.

Galgenhuisje
Groentemarkt 5.
Tiny café where it is easy to meet local people.
Oud Middelhuis
Graslei 6.
More than 300 different kinds of beer on sale in a 17th-century alehouse.
't Dreupelkot
Groentenmarkt 12.
Specialises in *jenever*, serving it in an old café beside the River Leie.
Tolhuisje
Graslei 10.
On Ghent's most romantic canalside this used to be the Toll House.
Waterhuis aan de Bierkant
Groentenmarkt 9.
A very popular bar in a good location. Try Ghent's own Stropken beer here.

LIEGE

Pierre Levée
Rue de Serbie 62.
A cellar café with a huge range of beers on sale.
Vaudree II
Rue Saint-Gilles 149.
This place never closes and is popular with local students.

Culture

Belgium is a country rich in art, architecture and culture. Each of the towns has its own history, traditions and treasures. Antwerp is a lively city of Baroque elegance; the entire centre of medieval Bruges is a living museum; Ghent, with its canals and ancient architecture, has been compared to Venice; Brussels has the country's best art collections; Leuven is the seat of the oldest university in Belgium; Mons is surrounded by castles; Namur, gateway to the Ardennes, is dominated by its massive citadel, to name just a few places of interest. Museums and art galleries abound and performance art is thriving.

The daily newspapers contain information about events and entertainment. In Brussels, visitors can reserve tickets for the opera, concerts and theatre productions at the **Brussels Tourist Information Centre** (TIB). There are theatres in the capital which perform dramatic pieces in both the French and Dutch languages. Most of the important concerts take place in the **Palais des Beaux Arts**. Opera and ballet productions are performed at the **Théâtre Royale de la Monnaie** (the National Opera House), the most famous stage in Brussels. Puppet shows played out in the Brussels dialect have been performed at the **Théâtre Toone VII** since 1830.

Information Sources

The best source of "What's on" information in English is the weekly magazine *The Bulletin*. The cultural pages of newspapers such as *Le Soir* and *De Standaard* are also mines of information. Tourist offices publish information on upcoming events in their locality.

Classical Music

ANTWERP

DeSingel
Desguinlei 25.
Tel: 03-248 3800.
Also dance, opera and theatre.
Koningin Elisabethzaal
Koningin Astridplein 23-24.
Tel: 03-233 8444.
Also rock music and theatre.

BRUSSELS

Cirque Royal
Rue de l'Enseignement 81.
Tel: 02-218 2015.
Also theatre, dance, opera, jazz and rock.
Conservatoire Royal de Musique
Rue de la Régence 30.
Tel: 02-511 0427.
Chamber music.
Le Botanique
Rue Royale 236.
Tel: 02-218 3732.
Avant-garde music and theatre.
Palais des Beaux Arts
Rue Ravenstein 23.
Tel: 02-507 8200.
Home of the Orchestre National de Belgique.

LIEGE

Conservatoire Royal de Musique
Boulevard Piercot 27–29.
Tel: 04-222 0306.

Opera & Dance

ANTWERP

Koninklijke Vlaamse Opera
Frankrijklei 3.
Tel: 03-233 6685.
Home of the Vlaamse Opera.
Stadsschouwburg
Theaterplein 1.
Tel: 03-231 9750.
For the Koninklijk Ballet van Vlaanderen.

BRUSSELS

Théâtre Royal de la Monnaie
Place de la Monnaie.
Tel: 02-229 1211.
Home of the Opera Royal de la Monnaie and Anne Theresa de Keersmaeker's dance group Rosas.

CHARLEROI
Palais des Beaux Arts
Place du Manège.
Tel: 071-314420.
Home of Ballet Royal de Wallonie.

GHENT
Koninklijke Vlaamse Opera
Schouwburgstraat 3.
Tel: 09-225 2425.

LIEGE
Théâtre Royal
Rue des Dominicains 1.
Tel: 04-223 5910.
Home of the Opera Royal de
Wallonie.

Theatre

Most performances are in Dutch or
French, but occasionally English-
language productions are featured.

ANTWERP
Arenberg Theatre
Arenbergstraat 28.
Tel: 03-232 1114.
**Koninklijke Nederlandse
Schouwburg**
Theaterplein, Meistraat 2.
Tel: 03-231 9750.
Vancampens Puppet Theatre
Lange Nieuwstraat 3.
Tel: 03-237 3716.

BRUSSELS
Koninklijke Vlaamse Schouwburg
Rue de Laeken 146.
Tel: 02-217-69-37.
Mostly Dutch-language theatre.
Le Botanique
Rue Royale 236.
Tel: 02-218 3732.
Experimental French theatre.
Théâtre Royal des Galeries
Galerie du Roi 32.
Tel: 02-512 0407.
Théâtre Royal du Parc
Rue de la Loi 3.
Tel: 02-512 2329.
Mainstream theatre.
Théâtre du Résidence Palace
Rue de la Loi 155.
Tel: 02-231 0305.
Théâtre Toone VII
Impasse Schuddeveld 6, Petite Rue
des Bouchers.
Tel: 02-511 7137.

Folklore puppet theatre in a great
old Brussels bar.
Théâtre Varia
Rue du Sceptre 78.
Tel: 02-640 3550.
Modern theatre and dance.

Cinema

Most films are shown in their
original language with Dutch and
French subtitles.

BRUSSELS
Actor's Studio
Petite Rue des Bouchers 16.
Tel: 02-512 1696.
Two screens.
Arenberg/Galeries
Galerie de la Reine 26.
Tel: 02-512 8063.
Two screens.
Aventure
Galerie du Centre 57.
Tel: 02-219 1748.
Three screens.
Kinepolis
Boulevard du Centenaire 1,
Bruparck!
Tel: 02-474 2600.
No fewer than 29 screens, one of
which is an IMAX.
Musée du Cinema
Rue Baron Horta 9.
Tel: 02-507 8370.
Art house and historic films.
UGC Brouckère
Place de la Brouckère 38.
Tel: 0900-29930.
Eight screens.

Libraries

The **Albert I Royal Library**, Mont
des Arts, is located in Brussels.
Diverse manuscripts, prints and
book covers provide a good
overview of the history of books
from antiquity until the present
time. Hours are 2–5pm Monday,
Wednesday and Saturday. Other
libraries in Brussels:
Bibliotheca Wittockiana, Rue
Bernel 21. Tel: 02-770 53 33.
**Bibliothèque Régionale de Woluwe-
Saint-Lambert**, Rue Saint-Henri 62.
Tel: 02-735 28 24.
**Bibliothèques Publiques
Communales d'Uccle Centre**, Rue

du Doyenné 84. Tel: 02-345 86 00.
**Bibliothèque de l'Université Libre
de Bruxelles**, Avenue F. Roosevelt
50. Tel: 02-642 23 84.
Bibliothèque du Parlement, Palais
de la Nation, Place de la Nation.
Tel: 02-519 81 81.

Art Treasures

Most of the finest Flemish works
are naturally concentrated in the
major Flemish art cities of Antwerp,
Bruges, Brussels and Ghent. Given
the greatness of Flemish art and
the changing fortunes of the
country, it is hardly suprising that
some of the most celebrated works
are in galleries in London, Madrid
and Vienna. However, the country
has kept enough of its native
treasures to satisfy the most eager
art-lover. Moreover, Belgium is
particularly fortunate in preserving
many artists' homes, including
those of Brueghel, Rubens,
Memling and Magritte, which are
open to the public.

The Flemish art towns are
planning retrospectives of other
native artists to coincide with the
year 2000 and Brussels' turn as
Capital of Europe.

ANTWERP

The **Mayer van den Bergh Museum**
is a connoisseur's collection of art,
ceramics and tapestries displayed
in a merchant's house. Several
major works by Rubens are in
Antwerp Cathedral (including "The
Raising of the Cross") but to
appreciate his background it is best
to visit the **Rubenshuis**, the
mansion where Rubens lived and
worked. In addition, there is a self-
guided Rubens walk around the
16th- and 17th-century places
associated with the artist. This is
matched by an equally rewarding
van Dyck walk. The **Museum voor
Schone Kunsten** (Fine Arts
Museum) houses works by Van
Eyck, Van der Weyden, Memling,
Matsys, Jordaens, as well as Van
Dyck's "Lamentation" and a fine
collection of Rubens. Van Dyck's
"Crucifixion" in the Cathedral at
Mechelen, an historical town

between Antwerp and Brussels. However, most of his greatest portraiture is in England. The 400th anniversary of Van Dyck's birth, in 1999, is marked by a major retrospective in Antwerp and London.

BRUGES

The newly restored **Memling Museum** is a medieval hospice containing graceful and radiant works by the Flemish Primitives, notably Memling. The museum is a beguiling introduction to the late medieval world. The **Groeninge Museum** houses a fine collection of Flemish and Dutch paintings in a splendid setting, including milestones in medieval and modern art, and the Flemish Primitives. Apart from a powerful "Last Judgment" by Hieronymous Bosch and a naturalistic work by Pieter Brueghel the Younger, there are works by Van der Weyden, Van der Goes and Van Eyck. However, Van Eyck's "Arnolfini Betrothal" is in London.

BRUSSELS

The **Musée d'Art Ancien** represents an overview of Flemish art, with various different itineraries to follow. The collection contains works by Brueghel, including his masterpiece "The Fall of Icarus". Also on display are paintings by Bouts, Rubens, Van der Weyden, Memling and Bosch. The **Cinquantenaire Museum** houses a staggering display of world art, including Flemish sculpture, tapestry and furniture.

The **Palais des Beaux Arts** (Palace of Fine Arts) also stages impressive temporary exhibitions on modern painters, such as Magritte and Ensor. **Musée Wiertz** is one of the quirkiest museums in Brussels, housed in the former studio and home of Antoine Wiertz, a precursor of both Symbolism and Surrealism.

GHENT

Jan van Eyck's masterpiece in **St Baaf's (or Bavo's) Cathedral**, "The Adoration of the Mystic Lamb", is a richly symbolic work, sometimes called the first evolved landscape in

In Search of Surrealism

To celebrate the year of Surrealism in 1998, Belgium launched a series of rolling exhibitions and art trails. Brussels established Surrealist walks in the footsteps of the major painters in St-Gilles and Ixelles while Wallonia, French-speaking Belgium, responded with walks and guided tours of Charleroi and Chatelet, other Surrealist haunts. Brussels tourist office also has suggestions for a "Surrealist Weekend", from galleries to shopping and the influence of Surrealism on the comic strip.

The centenary of the birth of Magritte was celebrated in 1998 with the largest ever retrospective of his work, followed by the opening of a new **Magritte Museum** in Jette, north Brussels, in early 1999 (135 rue Esseghem; tel: 323-4496614).

This suburban house, Magritte's home for 25 years (1930–54), has been left much as it was in the artist's day and will contain a permanent collection of his work.

In Knokke, on the Flemish coast, the local casino is adorned with masterly Magritte murals. In Brussels, the **Musée d'Art Moderne** displays a fine selection of paintings by Magritte and Delvaux, matched by works created by the Belgian Symbolists and Expressionists. Also in the capital, the underrated **Musée Communal** d'Ixelles contains a collection of works by Magritte, Delvaux and Spilliaert. In Antwerp, the **Fine Arts Museum** contains works by Ensor and Delvaux.

The **Delvaux Museum** in St Idesbald (Koksijde, 25 km/15 miles from Ostend) is devoted to the distinguished local artist. Although he lived in Brussels, the Ardennes and Flanders, much of his work was composed in St Idesbald, a quiet Flemish resort buried by dunes. Delvaux's dreamy style is also visible in the murals he designed for **Ostend Casino**. Elsewhere, a Delvaux trail also leads to Spa and Louvain.

European painting. The **Museum voor Schone Kunsten** (Fine Arts Museum) displays Flemish works from the 14th century onwards.

OSTEND

Ostend has the **James Ensorhuis**, James Ensor's home, and also several museums featuring work by Ensor and Delvaux.

TOURNAI

The **Musée des Beaux Arts** (Fine Arts Museum) features several works by its most famous painter, Rogier van der Weyden (confusingly known as Roger de la Pasture in French). Tournai celebrates the 600th anniversary of his birth with a major retrospective in 1999. The museum also displays works by Jordaens, Rubens and Van Gogh.

EU Buildings

The main European Union buildings are located in Brussels in the Rond-

Point Schuman area. The EU Council of Ministers maintains offices in the Justus Lipsius building on Rue de la Loi, tel: 02-299 6111. The Commission currently has its headquarters at Rue Breydel 45 and an information office at Rue Archimède 73, tel: 02-295 3844. The European Parliament is at Rue Belliard 97-113, tel: 02-284 2111. Call for a tour or information.

Breweries

Contact the breweries direct for opening times and tours.
Oud Beersel, Laarheidestraat 230, 1650 Beersel. Tel: 02-380 33 96.
Straffe Hendrik Brewery, Walplein 26, 8000 Brugge. Tel: 050-33 26 97.
De Dolle Brouwers Brewery, Roeselarestraat 12b, 8600 Esen. Tel: 051-50 27 81.
Brasserie d'Achouffe, Rue W. Achouffe 32, 6660 Houffalize. Tel: 061-28 81 47/28 94 55.
Interbrew Brewery (Stella Artois),

Vaarstraat 94-96, 3000 Leuven.
Tel: 016-24 71 11.
Liefmans Brewery, Aalststraat 200,
9700 Oudenaarde.
Tel: 055-31 13 91.
Belle-Vue Brewery, Bergense-
steenweg 144, 1600 Sint-Pieters-
Leeuw. Tel: 02-377 03 12.
De Gouden Boom Brewery,
Lange–straat 45, 8000 Brugge.
Tel: 050-33 06 99.
Cantillon Brewery and Museum,
Gheudestraat 56, 1070 Brussels.
Tel: 02-521 49 28.
Floreffe Abbey (Mill Brewery), Rue
de Seminaire 7, 5750 Floreffe.
Tel: 081-44 53 03.
Domestic Brewery Domus,
Tiense–straat 8, 3000 Leuven.
Tel: 016-29 14 49.
Gouden Carolus Brewery, Guido
Gezellelaan 49, Krankenstraat 2,
2800 Mechelen. Tel: 015-20 38 80.
Du Bocq Brewery, Rue de la
Purnode 49, 5530 Purnode. Tel:
082-61 37 37, fax: 082-61 17 80.
Brasserie Fantome, Rue Preal 17,
6977 Soy. Tel: 086-47 75 86,
fax: 086-47 70 32.
**Musée de la Cervoise du Gruyt et
des Bières Médiévales**, Avouerie
d'Anthisnes, Avenue de l'Abbaye
19, 4160 Anthisnes.
Brewery and Malthouse Museum,
Verbrand Nieuwland 10, 8000
Brugge. Tel: 050-33 06 99.
Bier-o-Rama, Domein Kelchterhoef,
Kelchterhoefstraat 9, 3550 Hout-
halen.
Museum of Belgian Beers, Rue de
la Gare 19, 5170 Lustin.
Tel: 081-41 11 02.
Beer Museum, Rodt-Thommberg,
4780 Sankt-Vith.
Tel: 080-22 63 01.
Brewery Museum, Dorpsstraat 53,
3950 Bocholt. Tel: 089-47 29 80.
**Beer and Regional Museum 't
Nieuwhuys**, c/o Gemmentelijke
Dienst voor Toerisme,
Gemmenteplein 1, 3320
Hoegaarden. Tel: 016-76 61 11.
City Brewery Museum,
Naamsestraat 3, 3000 Leuven.
Tel: 016-22 69 06.
National Hop Museum, De Stads-
waag, Gasthuisstraat 71, 8970
Poperinge. Tel: 057-33 40 81.

Nature Reserves

Botrange Nature Park, situated in
the province of Luxembourg at the
highest point in Belgium, organises
walking and bicycle tours on
request and offers mountain bikes,
skis and boots for hire. Exhibitions,
nature films and a multivision slide
show can be viewed in the Park
Centre where there is a "Green
Shop" and cafeteria. Picnicking
facilities. Botrange Nature Park, B-
4950 Robertville. Tel: 080-44 57
81. Open: daily 10am–6pm, closed:
late November–early December.
Het Zwin Nature Reserve in West
Flanders is the largest salt marsh in
Belgium. Several thousands of birds
breed in the sanctuary. B-8300
Knokke-Heist, Het Zwin,
Ooievaarslaan 8. Tel: 050-60 70
86. Open: Easter–September
9am–7pm; October–Easter
9am–5pm, closed: Wednesday,
November–March.
Westhoek Nature Reserve southwest from De Panne in West
Flanders is an unspoilt stretch of
coastline and sand dunes with
marked footpaths for walking and
enjoying the local flora and fauna.
Maps available from the tourist
office in De Panne.
L'Eau d'Heure lakes at Boussu-lez-
Walcourt in Hainaut is a popular
centre for watersports (windsurfing,
sailing, fishing, waterskiing,
speedboat racing, jet-skiing, diving),
go-karting and walking. Other
attractions include guided visits to
the dam of Plate Taille and a film of
the history of the site, aquariums
and boat trips. The recreation
centre offers train rides, canoes,
pedalos, mini-golf, BMX track,
tennis, sandy beaches and a
cafeteria. Centre d'accueil de la
Plate Taille, B-6440 Boussu-lez-
Walcourt. Tel: 071-63 35 34.
The Virelles Lakes in Hainaut is a
250-acre nature reserve offering
guided tours on foot, observation
posts, restaurants, barbecue area,
children's games, pedalos and
boats. B-6200 Bouffioulx, rue E.
Hermant 20. Tel: 060-21 13 63.
Open: May–September daily 10am–
6pm; October–April Sunday only.

Beguine Convents

In the 13th century single women
were given the opportunity to live
together, well looked after, in
secular convents. These "worldly
nuns" could choose to leave the
Beguine Convent any time they
pleased. Most of these convents
remain well-preserved and are well
worth visiting. You'll find them in the
following cities: Aarschot, Antwerp,
Bruges, Brussels, Diest, Diksmuide,
Ghent, Kortrijk, Lier, Leuven.

Military Cemeteries

There are many war cemeteries in
Belgium, most centred on the World
War I battlefields around Ieper
(Ypres), and others dating back to
World War II in the Ardennes. For
information pertaining to war graves
contact:
War Graves Commission, 2 Marlow
Road, Maidenhead, Berkshire SL6
7DX, UK. Tel: 01628-634 221,
fax: 01628-771208.
**Volksbund Deutscher
Kriegsgräber–fürsorge**, Werner-
Hilpert-Strasse 2, 34117 Kassel,
Germany. Tel: 0561-700 90,
fax: 0561-700 92 11.

Tours

AROUND BRUSSELS

Tervuren is located only 13 km
(8 miles) from Brussels. Tervuren
Park is well worth visiting, as is St
Hubert's Chapel (built in the 17th-
century) and the Museum of Central
Africa (Musée Royal de l'Afrique
Centrale) with its impressive
collection of items dating back to
when Belgium was a colonial power.

The university city of **Leuven**
(Louvain) is also not far from
Brussels. While strolling through the
main market, be sure to take a look
at the town hall (Hôtel de Ville), and
St Peter's church. The university
itself was founded in the year 1425.

Children will have fun visiting the
town of **Wavre** (located 25 km
/15 miles) from Brussels. Young
and old alike are sure to enjoy a
day spent at "Walibi", Belgium's
largest amusement park.

The country's most frequently visited tourist attraction, the battlefield at **Waterloo**, is located in the province of Brabant, only 20 km (13 miles) south of Brussels.

Nivelles is situated 35 km (22 miles) away from Brussels; it's well worth your while to make an excursion to the St Gertrude Abbey, founded in the 7th century. Those who can't get enough of the Manneken Pis in Brussels should track down the "Jean de Nivelles Tower" in Nivelles, where the famous copper figure emerges to strike each hour.

The ruins of the Cistercian abbey of **Villers-la-Ville**, located east of Nivelles, make for an interesting excursion. The abbey was established in the 12th century.

There are many artistic treasures on view in the pilgrimage city of **Halle**, 15 km (9 miles) from Brussels, at the church of Our Lady.

The extensive park grounds in **Huizingen** positively invite the visitor to take time out for a relaxing stroll; the medieval **Beersel Castle** (a moated castle) is located close by. In **Anderlecht** tourists can admire St Peter's church, built in the 15th century, and the House of Erasmus (Maison d'Erasmus).

The city of **Mechelen** lies to the north of Brussels and is home to the almost 100-metre (333-ft) tall Rombout church tower with its exquisite carillon. Additional tourist attractions in Mechelen include the town hall (Hôtel de Ville) on the Grand'Place, the Palace of Justice and the church of St John.

Thanks to two of its citizens, the city of **Lier/Lierre** also enjoys a certain claim to fame: Felix Timmermans was both a writer and painter and Louis Zimmer invented the astronomical clock. The Timmermans-Opsomer House and the Zimmer Tower, the town hall (Hôtel de Ville), church of St Gummarus and the Wuyts van Campen-Caroly Museum are all worth visiting. In Lier you'll find the best-preserved Beguine convent in all of Belgium.

IN FLANDERS

Flandria Boat Tours. Excursions offered include a "Scheldt Tour", an "Extended Scheldt Tour" and a "Harbour Tour". Toeristisch Gebouw. Steenplein, 2000 Antwerp. Tel: 03-231 31 00.

Boat Cruises Along Antwerp's Canals. Departures from Rozenhoedkaai, Dijver and Mariaburg.

Boat Tours "De Lamme Goedzak". Excursions from Bruges to Damme and vice versa, from April until September. Dienst voor Toerisme Damme, Stadhuis Markt 1, 8340 Damme. Tel: 050-35 33 19.

Ghent by Boat. Korenlei, 9000 Ghent. Tel: 09-223 88 53.

Excursions on the Meuse around Marec. Maasdijk, 3640 Konrooi. Tel: 011-56 75 03.

Sea Tours and Sea Fishing. Fishing Center Vieren, Albert I-Laan 90, 8620 Nieuwpoort. Tel: 058-23 24 25.

Nightlife

Those who start their evening's clubbing too early may well find themselves facing locked doors. As in most major cities in Europe, the majority of Belgium's clubs and discothèques do not open until at least 10pm.

In Brussels, a stroll to the Place Brouckère will help to pass the time. The square is one of the centres of the city's nightlife and a good place to meet up with friends and enjoy a beer.

The bars and discos located in the Lower City are on the whole more relaxed and enjoyable than those in the Upper City. Prices at places in the latter are generally more expensive, and the clientele pays more attention to dressing stylishly.

Many of the clubs are private, but it is possible in some to obtain membership for one evening. Night spots in Brussels change hands frequently and are often in existence for a short time. It is wise to phone before you set your heart on a certain place.

Late-night Restaurants

La Grande Porte
Rue Notre-Seigneur 9, Brussels.
Tel: 02-347 4632
Open until 2am during the week and until 4am on the weekend.
Mok Ma Zwet
Rue des Carmélites, Brussels.
Tel: 02-344 0809
Open until 2am during the week and until 3am Friday and Saturday.
Le Mozart
Chaussée d'Alsemberg, Brussels.
Tel: 02-5128998
Open until 5am during the week and until 6am at weekends.

Cabaret & Nightclubs

Chez Flo
Rue au Beurre 25, Brussels.
Tel: 02-512 9496.
Transvestite show.
Show Point
Place Stephanie 14, Brussels.
Tel: 02-511 5364.
Glitzy place with sparsely clad floor-show.

Discos

ANTWERP
Café d'Anvers
Verversrui 15.
Tel: 03-226 3870.
Trend-setting disco.
Jimmy's
Van Ertbornstraat 12.
Tel: 03-233 3515.
Laid-back style.
New Casino
Kloosterstraat 70.
Tel: 03-237 8846.
A mature people's disco.
Paradox
Waalse Kaai 25.
Tel: 03-237 6458.
Located in the old docks area.

BRUSSELS
Cartagena
Rue Marché au Charbon 70.
Latin American.
L'Ecumes des Nuits
Galerie Louise 122a.
Tel: 02-513 5321.
Afro-Caribbean.
Le Garage
Rue Duquesnoy 16.
Tel: 02-512 6622.
Trendy and popular.
Mirano Continental
Chaussée de Louvain 38.
Tel: 02-218 5772.
Well-dressed kind of place.
New Portland
Place de la Chapelle 6.
For the trendy and well-heeled.
Vaudeville
Galerie de la Reine 15.
Tel: 02-512 4997.
Restrained and leisurely.

GHENT
Barney'z
Muinkaai 1.
Tel: 09-225 1069.
The height of fashion.
Boccaccio
Solariumdreef 5, Destelbergen.
Tel: 09-228 2414.
Expensively trendy place.
Champs Elysées
Citadellelaan 2.
Tel: 09-222 3250.
A touch of elegance.

LIEGE
La Chapelle
Place Saint-Denis.
Tel: 04-223 2685.
Student-oriented disco.
Palace Club
Place Saint-Paul 8.
Tel: 04-223 4053.
Golden oldies are its stock-in-trade.
Upside
Rue de la Wache 13.
Tel: 041 231488.
Exuberant and energetic disco.

Jazz, Rock & Blues

ANTWERP
De Muze
Melkmarkt 15.
Tel: 03-226 0126.
Jazz café.
Swingcafé
Suikerrui 13.
Tel: 03-233 1478.
Regularly features jazz.

BRUSSELS
Blues Corner
Rue des Chapeliers 12.
Tel: 02-511 9794.
Smoky, dark; atmospheric blues.
Forest National
Avenue du Globe 36.
Tel: 02-347 0355.
Belgium's main venue for mega rock concerts.
New York Jazz Club
Chaussée de Charleroi 5.
Tel: 02-534 8509.
Cool modern jazz.
Preservation Hall
Rue de Londres 3.
Tel: 02-511 0304.
For old-fashioned jazz enthusiasts.

LIEGE
Caves de Porto
En Feronstree 144.
Tel: 04-223 2325.
Le Lion S'en Vole
Rue Roture 11.
Tel: 04-242 9317.

Casinos

Blankenberge
Zeedijk 150.
Tel: 050-419393.
Dinant
Rue Grande 28.
Tel: 082-222374.
Knokke
Zeedijk-Albertstrand 509.
Tel: 050-606010.
Liège
Esplanade 1, Chaudfontaine.
Tel: 04-365 0753.
Namur
Avenue Baron de Moreau 1.
Tel: 081-220334.
Ostend
Oosthelling.
Tel: 059-705111.
Spa
Rue Royale 4.
Tel: 087-772052.

Festivals

Carnivals, religious processions and other traditional festivals are a big attraction in Belgium. One of Europe's most colourful carnivals takes place in the seemingly unremarkable town of Binche, and other cities, towns and villages have their own encounters with bouts of good-natured mayhem.

Brussels

January:
• Auto-Salon, every two years.
• Film Festival (Congress Palace).
February:
• Carnival (in the city centre).
• Antique Fair (Palace of Fine Arts).
March:
• Belgian Indoor Tennis Championships (Exhibition Park).
• Holiday, Tourist and Recreation Fair.
• International Book Fair (International Centre Rogier).
April:
• Son et Lumière at the Grand' Place.
May:
• Open door at the Royal Greenhouses (Laeken).
• Queen Elisabeth International Music Competition (Palace of Fine Arts).
• Foire Commerciale (Trade Fair).
• Petro-Mobile-Oldtimer-Rallye.
• International Comic Festival.
• Brussels Jazz Rally.
June:
• The 20-km Brussels Run.
• Re-enactment of the Battle of Waterloo, every five years (2000, 2005).
• Europe Festival.
July:
• Ommegang (Grand'Place). Orignally a 14th century religious procession, Today is like a Carnival.
• National Holiday (21 July, celebrations in city parks) and the Brussels Fair (Midi Quarter).
• Foire du Midi, big annual funfair.
August:
• Raising the Meiboom (Grand' Place).
• Brosella Folk & Jazz (Théâtre de Verdure).
• Carpet of Flowers (Grand'Place), held every two years.
• International Carillon Competition in Mechelen.
September:
• Eddy Merckx Grand Prix (Bois de la Cambre).
• Brussels Marathon.
• Brueghel Festival.
• Dressage and Team Competition (Bois de la Cambre).
• Food Fair, Eureka Hobby Fair (Exhibition Park).
• Ommegang (Grand'Place).
November:
• International Show Jumping Tournament (Exhibition Park).
December:
• Christmas Market (Sablon).
• Manger and Christmas Tree (Grand'Place).
• Arrival of St Nicholas, together with various processions and the giving of sweets to children, 6 December.

Other Places

Aalst:
• Carnival, February.
Binche:
• Carnival of the Gilles, February.
Bruges:
• Procession of the Holy Blood, May.
Diksmuide:
• Beer Festival, September.
Eupen:
• Carnival, including the Rosenmontag procession, February.
Fosse-la-Ville:
• Carnival of the Chinels, March.
Genk:
• Grand Procession, May.
Ghent:
• Flanders Festival, from mid-August to mid-September.
• Floralies of Ghent, International flower show in April.
Hasselt:
• Carnival, February.
Knokke-Heist:
• International Cartoon Festival, June–September.

Lembeke:
• Windmill Festival, May.
Leuven:
• International Folklore Festival, Easter weekend.
• Marktrock Rock Festival, August.
Liège:
• Outremeuse Folklore Festival (in the Outremeuse district), 15 August.
• Walloon Festival, the fourth Sunday in September.
Lier:
• Procession of the Pilgrims, October.
Malmedy:
• Carnival, February.
Mechelen:
• Handswijk Procession, May.
Mons:
• The Parade of the Golden Wagon and the "Battle Against the Dragon Lumecon", Trinity Sunday.
Moselle Valley:
• Wine Festivals, August–October.
Oostduinkerke
• Shrimp Festival, the second-to-last weekend in June.
Oudenaarde
• Adriaen-Brouwer Feest, beer festival, end of June.
Ostend:
• The Dead Rat Ball, Carnival on the first Sunday in March.
Poperinge:
• Hops Festival, first Sunday in September.
Stavelot:
• Carnival, March.
Theux:
• Medieval Fair at Franchimont Castle, August.
Tournai:
• The "Four Parades", the second Sunday in June.
• Procession of the Plague, the second Sunday in September.
Turnhout:
• The Peasants' Festival, the second weekend in June.
Verviers:
• International Costumed Parade, third Sunday in July.
Veurne:
• Procession of the Penitents, July.
Ypres:
• Cat Festival, the second Sunday in May (even-numbered years).
• The Procession of the Holy Cross and Our Lady of Succour, the Sunday following 8 September.

Sport

Spectator Sports

Information about local sporting events is available at tourist information agencies. The most popular spectator sports in Belgium include bicycle racing, soccer and equestrian events, especially galloping and trotting races.

CYCLING
Important annual cycling competitions are the Toer van Vlaanderen and the Flèche Wallonne in spring, the Tour of Belgium in August, and the Eddy Merckx Grand Prix in September.

HORSE RACING
There are three tracks in the Brussels area: Chaussée de la Hulpe 51, Boitsfort; tel: 02-660 2839; Sint-Jansberglaan 4, Hoeilaart; tel: 02-657 3820; and Du Roy de Blicquylaan 43, Sterrebeek; tel: 02-767 5475. Ostend also has one, the Wellington, Prinses Stefanieplein 41; tel: 059-803636.

MOTOR SPORT
Belgium's Formula One motor racing Grand Prix takes place at Spa-Francorchamps, set among the Ardennes hills and forests, usually in August each year.

SOCCER
Among the top clubs are FC Anderlecht from Brussels, FC Bruges and Standard Liège. International matches are generally played at Brussels' new Heizel Stadium in the north of the city. The Maison du Football, Avenue Houba de Strooper 145; tel: 02-477 1211, can arrange tickets for international soccer matches if you phone

Monday through Friday between 9am and 4.15pm.
Heizel Stadium, Marathonlaan 135, 1020 Brussels.
Royal Belgian Football Association, Wetstraat 43, 1040 Brussels.
Racing White Daring de Molenbeek, Charles Malisstraat 61, 1080 Brussels.
Royal Union Saint-Gilloise, Brusselse–steenweg 223, 1190 Brussels.
Sporting Club Anderlechtois, Thé Verbeecklaan 2 (Park Astrid), 1070 Brussels.

Local Sports

Vertical archery – picking off brightly coloured targets from high rigs – can be seen at some parks, such as Brussels' Parc Josaphat in Schaerbeek.

Participant Sports

Belgium's favourite sport is bicycle racing. This being the case, you can rent a bicycle anywhere in the country, even at railway stations. Most regions have marked cycle routes and maps are available from tourist offices. Facilities for athletic activities such as bowling, ice-skating, soccer, golf, mini-golf, roller-skating, tennis, swimming and squash can be found in every city and in many villages. The Belgian coastline provides excellent opportunities for sailing, surfing and fishing. A variety of boating companies offer excursions to other cities via the country's numerous waterways. Along the coastline sea tours are also available.

CYCLING
The flat landscape of Flanders and the rolling hills of the Ardennes make for different, but each in its own way enjoyable and challenging cycling possibilities. Bicycles can be hired from more than 50 railway stations, and mountain bikes are widely available for hire from private firms in the Ardennes. The Belgian National Tourist Office and the provincial tourist offices (see pages 234–235) publish brochures about cycling routes.

GOLF
Information on courses is available from the Fédération Royale Belge de Golf, Chemin de Baudemont 23, 1400 Nivelles. Tel: 067-220440.
Durbuy Golf Club
Route d'Oppagne, Barvaux.
Tel: 086-214454.
Royal Hautes Fagnes Golf Club
Balmoral, Spa.
Tel: 087-771613.
Royal Waterloo Golf Club
Vieux Chemin de Wavre 50, Ohain.
Tel: 02-633 1815.
Royal Tervuren Golf Club
Kasteel Ravenstein, Tervuren.
Tel: 02-767 5801.
Royal Het Zoute Golf Club
Caddiespad 14, Knokke-Zoute.
Tel: 050-601227.

HORSE-RIDING
There are extensive horse-riding facilities all around the country particularly in such areas as the Ardennes, the coast and the Kempen. Around Brussels, La Hulpe and the Foret de Soignes are particularly popular locations. Information is available from the **Fédération Royale Belge des Sports Equestres**, Avenue Houba de Strooper 156, 1020 Brussels; tel: 02-478 5056.

ICE SKATING
There is ice skating in Brussels from September to May at the following rinks:
Poseidon
Dapperenlaan 4.
Tel: 02-762 16 33.
Forêt National
Avenue du Globe 36.
Tel: 02-346 16 11.

SAILING
There are facilities at the coast and on rivers, lakes and canals. Information is available from the **Verbond van Vlaamse Watersportverenigingen**, Beatrijslaan 25, 2050 Antwerp. Tel: 03-219 6967.

SKIING
You can obtain a copy of the map "Ski Ardennes" from the Office de Promotion du Tourisme, Rue du Marché aux Herbes 61, 1000 Brussels.

Ski Areas

Spa–Francorchamps–Trois-Ponts.
Vielsalm.
Baraque de Fraiture–Plateau des
Tailles.
Plateau de Bastogne.
Anlier–Martelange.
Libramont–Champlon–Saint-Hubert.
Croix-Scaille.
Haute Fagnes–Cantons de l'Est.

SWIMMING

There is a wide variety of facilities –
local indoor pools, outdoor
swimming pools open in summer,
and water recreation parks – in all
parts of the country. In Brussels,
there is an Olympic-standard
swimming pool at the **Centre
Sportif de Woluwe-Saint-Pierre**,
Avenue Salome 2; tel: 02-773
1820.

TENNIS

There are indoor and outdoor tennis
courts all over the country.
Information is available from the
Fédération Royale Belge de Tennis,
Passage International 6, 1210
Brussels; tel: 02-217 2200.

Health Spas

There are three health spas in
Belgium:
Chaudfontaine: Thermal spring,
36.6°C, recommended for cases of
rheumatism and gout.
Ostend: Especially good for those
suffering from rheumatism, asthma,
neuralgia and hay fever.
Spa: Recommended for people with
rheumatism, heart and circulatory
troubles and metabolic disorders.

Shopping

What to Buy

Belgium enjoys an international
reputation for its fine dipped
chocolates, and chocolate in
general, crystalware, firearms,
diamonds and, of course, the world-
famous lace made in both Brussels
and Bruges. Most shops are open
9am–6pm, some close for a lunch
break between noon and 2pm, and
others remain open late.

You will find a variety of markets
which take place on certain days in
every city. A visit to any one of
these nearly always proves to be
well worth the effort.

Non-EU residents may be able to
claim back some of the tax they pay
on purchases. It is worth asking
about this in the main shopping
areas, especially if you are
spending a lot of money.

If you are looking for a bargain,
the magic words to look out for are
soldes and *solden*. Even better,
though rarer, are *liquidation totale*
and *totaal uitverkoop*, announcing
that "everything must go".

Belgian Specialities

BEER

More than 800 different kinds of
beer are produced in Belgium, each
one with its own mandatory glass,
and many of them the products of
artisanal breweries.

Lager beers such as Stella
Artois, Jupiler, Maes, Primus and
Eupener are the ordinary, everyday
beers. Among other beers well
worth tasting are Mort Subite,
Belle-Vue, De Koninck, Duvel, Kwak,
La Lunette, Hoegaarden,
Dentergems, Blanche de Namur,
Maredsous, Chimay, Orval and
Grimbergen and Verboden Vrucht.

CHOCOLATES

Handmade Belgian pralines (filled
chocolates) are the top-of-the-range
in chocolate. Look for names like
Wittamer, Nihoul, Neuhaus, Godiva
and **Leonidas**. Request *un ballotin
de pralines* (a box of chocolates)
from one of the better chocolatiers,
or make your own selection. They
are sold by weight and may come
beautifully wrapped. Pralines are
readily available all over Belgium.

CRYSTAL

Particularly, but not exclusively, that
produced by Val-Saint-Lambert,
whose workshop at Liege produces
hand-blown glass of outstanding
quality.

DIAMONDS

Antwerp's glittering Diamond
Quarter is the shopfront of
Belgium's $16 billion a year
diamond industry, but good-quality
stones can be bought all over the
country.

DINANDERIE

Hand-beaten copper or bronze
produced in and around the River
Meuse town of Dinant, as it has
been for centuries.

JENEVER/GENIEVRE

Called a *witteke* in Flanders and a
peket in Wallonia, this stiff grain-
spirit is served in brimful glasses,
some not much bigger than a
thimble. Belgium has more than 70
distilleries producing some 270
brands. Among the best are Filliers
Oude Graanjenever, De Poldenaar
Oude Antwerpsche, Heinrich Peket
de la Piconette, Sint-Pol, and Van
Damme.

LACE

Handmade Belgian lace has a
international reputation for quality
that is thoroughly merited. However,
most lace on sale is not handmade
and is often imported. If you want
the real thing, be sure to check,
and be prepared to pay the price.

PEWTER

Just downriver from Dinant is Huy, centre of the traditional pewter industry.

TAPESTRY

Tournai, Oudenaarde and Mechelen continue the art of Belgian tapestry, which once filled castles and the homes of aristocrats throughout Europe.

Shopping Areas

BRUSSELS

The main shopping districts detailed below sell speciality Belgian products, including lace, crystal, diamonds, chocolates, beers and foodstuffs such as cheeses, Ardennes hams and pâté.

Markets

Antwerp
Antiques Market
Lijnwaardmarkt. Easter–Oct, Sat.
Bird Market
Theaterplein. Sat, Sun.
A general market.
Friday Market
Vrijdagmarkt. Wed, Fri.
Antiques and household goods.
Rubens Market
Grote Markt. 15 Aug only.
Stallholders wear 17th-century costume.

Bruges
Antiques and Flea Market
Dijver. Apr–Sept, Sat, Sun.
Vrijdagmarkt
't Zand. Sat am only.

Brussels
Exotic market: Sunday morning, Gare du Midi.
Flower market: Saturday and Sunday mornings, Grand'Place.
Flea market: daily, Place du Jeu de Balle.
Junk markets: first Sunday in the month, Place St Lambert; Tuesday morning, Place Dailly, Schaarbeek.
Bird market: Sunday morning, Grand'Place.

Rue Neuve
What this area lacks in cool sophistication, it makes up for in popular prices. Beginning at Place Rogier, City 2 is a shopping mall on three floors offering everything under one roof with pizzerias, hot-dog stalls, ice-cream parlours, coffee stands and bar terraces. Especially notable are FNAC, Belgium's good-value books-magazines-CDs-computer-video-photo shop (where you can also buy concert tickets); Weyn's honey shop; Le Jardin d'Apollon, which specialises in bonsai trees; and Inno, Belgium's department store.

At the far end of Rue Neuve, past another entrance to Inno, are more department stores, C&A, Marks & Spencer, Peek & Cloppenburg (P&C) and Sarmalux, followed by two more malls, the Centre Monnaie and the Anspach Centre.

Antiques Market
Place du Grand-Sablon.Sat, Sun. Atmospheric market with many superb pieces for sales.
Crafts Market
Place de l'Agora. Sat, Sun.
All kinds of jewellery, trinkets, ornaments, etc.
Midi Market
Around the Midi Railway Station. Sun.
All kinds of stuff at amazingly cheap prices.

Leuven
Market day: Friday, Oude Markt.

Liege
Flea market "La Batte": Sunday morning.

Nieuwpoort
Fish market: early every morning.

Spa
Antiques Market
Galerie Leopold II. Sunday.
As much bric-a-brac as antiques, but still a worthwhile experience.

TONGEREN
Flea market and junk market:
Sunday morning.

The Centre
Here the pace slows down a little. On Rue des Fripiers are some small clothes boutiques and a charming toy shop, In Den Olifant. Samoka is a place to rest over a cup of freshly milled coffee or linden tea.

The Galerie du Centre attracts a regular clientele thanks in part to the Leonidas pralines shop, serving some of the best of Belgium's wonderful chocolates. One exit from the Galerie leads straight into Au Bon Vieux Temps, a typical Brussels bar.

Rue de Tabora sports the Nicolas wine shop and Le P'tit Normand cheeses. On Rue du Marché aux Herbes there is Michelangeli for perfumery and handbags; Dandoy for speciality biscuits; and Euro-lines, for every "euro-gift" you ever wanted. Rue du Midi has music shops and stamp and coin dealers.

Galeries Royales Saint-Hubert
Europe's first shopping mall, built between 1846 and 1847 in Italian neo-Renaissance style, the Galeries offer classy shopping, at a price. Here are Häagen-Dazs for ice-cream; Librairie des Galeries for art books; Tropismes for paperbacks; Ganterie Italienne for gloves; Oriande for crystal and jewellery; Delvaux for handbags and Neuhaus for chocolates.

Rue Antoine Dansaert
This is where some of the well-known designers have their boutiques – Della Spiga, Knokke, Stijl and Romeo Gigli to name a few.

Porte de Namur
This upmarket shopping district includes the nearby Avenue de la Toison d'Or; the Boulevard de Waterloo, Avenue Louise and Place Stéphanie. Well-known designers, including Gucci, Gianni Versace and Nina Ricci are located on Boulevard de Waterloo.

Opposite them gallery entrances lead to a glittering maze of shops. From Place Stéphanie there is Galerie Louise, Espace Louise, Galerie de la Toison d'Or (Gallery of the Golden Fleece) and Galerie Porte de Namur.

For Children

ANTWERP
Antwerp Zoo
Koningin Astridplein.
Tel: 03-202 4540.
Open daily; entrance fee.
A superb and well-managed zoo that presents a vast range of animals in an art deco setting.
Antwerpen Miniatuurstad (Antwerp Miniature City)
Hangar 15a, Scheldekaaien.
Tel: 03-237 0329.
Open daily; entrance fee.
Scale models that show how Antwerp developed into the city we see today.

BRUSSELS
Aqualibi
Wavre.
Tel: 010-414466.
Open Apr–Sept daily; Oct–Mar Tues–Sun pm only, closed Mon; entrance fee.
An aquatic theme-park attached to Walibi adventure park. You can swim here in tropical temperatures all year round.
Autoworld
Parc du Cinquantenaire.
Tel: 02-736 4165.
Open daily; entrance fee.
Displays a fine collection of classic and vintage cars, among them rare Belgian ones.
Belgian Comic Strip Centre
Rue des Sables 20.
Tel: 02-219 1980.
Open Tues–Sun, closed Mon; entrance fee.
A temple to the art of the comic strip, with the star of the show being Belgium's own Tintin, the creation of cartoonist Georges Remi, better known as Hergé.

Mini-Europe
Bruparck!
Tel: 02-478 0550.
Open Apr–Sept daily; entrance fee.
A miniature world that takes the European Union as its subject, and features famous buildings and places at 1:25 scale. See among others Big Ben, the Leaning Tower of Pisa, the Parthenon, the Arc de Triomphe and the Brandenburg Gate, as well as the Ariane rocket and the Channel Tunnel.
Musée des Enfants (Children's Museum)
Rue du Bourgmestre.
Tel 02-640 0107.
Open Sat, Sun, Wed, school hols, pm only; entrance fee.
Displays give an idea of how children's lives have changed over the years and how children in other countries live.
Musée du Jouet (Toy Museum)
Rue de l'Association 24.
Tel: 02-219 6168.
Open daily; entrance fee.
How children lived in the past and the toys they played with.
Musée des Sciences Naturelles (Natural History Museum)
Rue Vautier 29.
Tel: 02-627 4252.
Open Tues–Sun, closed Mon; entrance fee.
A first-rate museum that takes you on a magical journey into the natural world, now and in the past.
Musée du Transport Urbain (Public Transport Museum)
Avenue de Tervuren 364b.
Tel: 02-515 3108.
Open Apr–Oct, Sat, Sun, pub hols, pm only. Entrance and tram excursion fee.
Tells the story of Brussels' public transport and displays examples of the vehicles that carried the weight, including horse-drawn and electric trams. On some days vintage trams run between the museum and the Royal Museum of Central Africa in Tervuren.
Oceade
Bruparck!
Tel: 02-478 4320.
Open daily by 2pm; entrance fee.
One of those swimming pools with plastic beaches, palm trees, wave-

making machines, and a general illusion of being in some tropical paradise.
Walibi
Wavre.
Tel: 010-414466.
Open: Apr–Sept daily; entrance fee.
Probably Belgium's biggest, best and most exciting amusement park, with a commitment to thrilling rides. Walibi gets very busy thanks to its location near Brussels.
Bouillon
Crête des Cerfs (Stags' Crest)
1.5 km (1 mile) from Bouillon.
Tel: 061-466981.
Open daily; entrance fee.
Fawns, hinds, does and other animals wander around at this petting farm in a wooded area.
De Panne
Meli-Park.
De Pannelaan 68, Adinkerke.
Tel: 058-420202.
Open Apr–mid-Sept daily; Sept last two weekends; Oct Sun; entrance fee.
Honey bees are the theme at this theme park for smaller children. The rides and exhibits all have this busy bee as their motif.

HAN-SUR-LESSE
Ferme de Dry Hamptay (Dry Hamptay Farm)
Rue des Grottes 46.
Tel: 084-378231.
Open Apr to mid-Nov daily pm only; entrance fee.
One of the popular attractions at Han-sur-Lesse, the farm includes a children's playground. The farm is between the village and the Caves of Han.

KNOKKE-HEIST
Flindertuin (Butterfly Garden)
Bronlaan 14.
Tel: 050-610472.
Open Easter–mid-Oct, daily; entrance fee.
Located beside the entrance to the Zwin Nature Reserve, the butterfly garden is a magical place.

LEUVEN
't Zoet Water Recreation Park
Noesstraat 15, Oud-Heverlee (6 km/3 miles south of Leuven).

Tel: 016-477555.
Open Apr–Sept daily, entrance fee; Oct–Mar Sat, Sun, pm only, free.
An "adventure" park for small children, with rides and attractions that are appropriately sedate for that age group.

LIEGE
Monde Sauvage Safari Park
Fange de Deigne 3, Deigne-Aywaille (exit 45 from E25 south of Liège. Tel: 04-360 9108.
Open: mid-Mar to mid-Nov daily; entrance fee.
You can visit this safari park either in your own car, or on a little road-train that runs through it. One part, with less threatening animals than the lions and tigers of the main section, is accessible on foot.
Musée du Jouet (Toy Museum)
Route de Lognoule 6, Ferrieres 9 km (5 miles) from E25 exit 48 south of Liège).
Tel: 086-400198.
Open Sat, Sun, school hols, pm only; entrance fee.
Displays some 1,000 toys dating from the end of the 19th century to the 1950s.

MECHELEN
Speelgoedmuseum (Toy Museum)
Nekkerspoel 21.
Tel: 015-200386.
Open Tues–Sun pm only, closed Mon; entrance fee.
A vast range of antique toys is on display at Belgium's best toy museum.

STAVELOT
Telecoo
Coo village, between Stavelot and Trois Ponts.
A chairlift takes you to the top of a hill overlooking this park beside a waterfall on the scenic Ambleve river. The park itself has a variety of fairground attractions.

YPRES
Bellewaerde
Meenseweg 497 (outside Ypres).
Tel: 057 467491.
Open Apr–mid-Sept daily; last two weekends in Sept; entrance fee.
In the once shattered landscape outside that World War I place of sacrifice, Ypres, a children's amusement park provides firm evidence that life goes on.
The Kempen
Bobbejaanland
Lichtaart (exit 20 from E313).
Tel: 014-557811.
Open Apr–Sept daily; Oct Fri–Sun; entrance fee.
This theme park's owner is a fan of the Wild West, and music-and-dance performances at the park's theatre are based on Western themes. There are plenty of rides and other attractions as well.

Language

Learning the pronunciation of the French alphabet is a good idea. In particular, learn how to spell out your name.
a=ah, **b**=bay, **c**=say, **d**=day, **e**=er, **f**=ef, **g**=zhay, **h**=ash, **i**=ee, **j**=zhee, **k**=ka, **l**=el, **m**=em, **n**=en, **o**=oh, **p**=pay, **q**=kew, **r**=ehr, **s**=ess, **t**=tay, **u**=ew, **v**=vay, **w**=dooblahvay, **x**=eex, **y**=ee grek, **z**=zed

Even if you speak no French at all, it is worth trying to master a few simple phrases. The fact that you have made an effort is likely to get you a better response, even though many Francophone Belgians speak English. Remember to emphasise each syllable, but not to pronounce the last consonant of a word as a rule (this includes the plural "s") and always to drop your "h"s. Whether to use "vous" or "tu" is a vexed question; increasingly the familiar form of "tu" is used by many people. However it is better to be formal, and use "vous" if in doubt. It is very important to be polite; always address people as Madame or Monsieur, and address them by their surnames until you are confident first names are acceptable. When entering a shop always say, "*Bonjour Monsieur/ Madame,*" and "*Merci, au revoir,*" when leaving.

How much is it?	*C'est combien?*
What is your name?	*Comment vous appelez-vous?*
My name is...	*Je m'appelle...*
Do you speak English?	*Parlez-vous anglais?*

I am English/	Je suis anglais
American	americain
I don't understand	Je ne comprends
	pas
Please speak	Parlez plus
more slowly	lentement, s'il
	vous plaît
Can you help me?	Pouvez-vous
	m'aider?
I'm looking for...	Je cherche
Where is...?	Où est...?
I'm sorry	Excusez-
	moi/Pardon
I don't know	Je ne sais pas
No problem	Pas de problème
Have a good day!	Bonne journée!
That's it	C'est ça
Here it is	Voici
There it is	Voilà
Let's go	On y va. Allons-y
See you tomorrow	A demain
See you soon	A bientôt
Show me the	Montrez-moi le
word in the book	mot dans le livre
At what time?	A quelle heure?
When?	Quand?
What time is it?	Quelle heure est-il?
yes	oui
no	non
please	s'il vous plaît
thank you	merci
(very much)	(beaucoup)
you're welcome	de rien
excuse me	excusez-moi
hello	bonjour
OK	d'accord
goodbye	au revoir
good evening	bonsoir
here	ici
there	là
today	aujourd'hui
yesterday	hier
tomorrow	demain
now	maintenant
later	plus tard
right away	tout de suite
this morning	ce matin
this afternoon	cet après-midi
this evening	ce soir

On the Road

Where is the	Où est la roue de
spare wheel?	secours?
Where is the	Où est le garage
nearest garage?	le plus proche?
Our car has	Notre voiture est
broken down	en panne

I want to have	Je veux faire
my car repaired	réparer ma
	voiture
It's not your	Vous n'avez pas
right of way	la priorité
I think I must	Je crois que j'ai
have put diesel	mis le gasoil
in the car	dans la voiture
by mistake	par erreur
the road to...	la route pour...
left	gauche
right	droite
straight on	tout droit
far	loin
near	près d'ici
opposite	en face
beside	a côté de
car park	parking
over there	là-bas
at the end	au bout
on foot	à pied
by car	en voiture
town map	le plan
road map	la carte
street	la rue
square	la place
give way	céder le
	passage
dead end	impasse
no parking	stationnement
	interdit
motorway	l'autoroute

On Arrival

I want to get	Je voudrais
off at...	descendre a...
Is there a bus	Est-ce qui'il y a un
to the Grand'	bus pour la
Place?	Grand'Place?
What street is	A quelle rue
this?	sommes-nous?
Which line do I	Quelle ligne dois-
take for...?	je prendre
	pour...?
How far is...?	A quelle distance
	se trouve...?
Validate your	Compostez
ticket	votre billet
airport	l'aéroport
train station	la gare
bus station	la gare routière
Metro stop	la station de
	Metro
bus	l'autobus, le car
bus stop	l'arrêt
platform	le quai
ticket	le billet

toll	le péage
speed limit	la limitation de
	vitesse
petrol	l'essence
unleaded	sans plomb
diesel	le gasoil
water/oil	l'eau/l'huile
puncture	un pneu de crève
bulb	l'ampoule
wipers	les essuies-glace

Shopping

Where is the	Où est la banque/
nearest bank/	Poste/la
post office?	plus proche?
I'd like to buy	Je voudrai sacheter
How much is it?	C'est combien?
Do you take	Est-ce que vous
credit cards?	acceptez les
	cartes de credit?
I'm just looking	Je regarde
	seulement
Have you got?	Avez-vous...?
I'll take it	Je le prends
I'll take this one/	Je prends celui-
that one	ci/celui-là
What size is it?	C'est de quelle
	taille?
Anything else?	Avec ça?
size (clothes)	la taille
size (shoes)	la pointure

return ticket	aller-retour
hitchhiking	l'autostop
toilets	les toilettes
This is the hotel	C'est l'adresse
address	de l'hôtel
I'd like a (single/	Je voudrais une
double) room...	chambre (pour
	une/deux
	personnes)...
...with shower	avec douche
...with bath	avec salle de bain
...with a view	avec vue
Does that	Le prix comprend-
include	il le petit
breakfast?	déjeuner?
May I see the	Je peux voir la
room?	chambre?
washbasin	le lavabo
bed	le lit
key	la clef
elevator	l'ascenseur
air conditioned	climatisé

cheap	bon marché	Roman	romain
expensive	cher	Romanesque	roman
enough	assez	museum	le musée
too much	trop	art gallery	la galerie
a piece of	un morceau de	exhibition	l'exposition
each	la pièce (e.g. ananas, Bfr 15 la pièce)	tourist	l'office du
		information	tourisme/le
		office	syndicat d'initiative
bill	la note	free	gratuit
chemist	la pharmacie	open	ouvert
bakery	la boulangerie	closed	fermé
bookshop	la librairie	every day	tous les jours
library	la bibliothèque	all year	toute l'année
department store	le grand magasin	all day	toute la journée
		swimming pool	la piscine
delicatessen	la charcuterie/le traiteur	to book	réserver
fishmongers	la poissonerie		
grocery	l'alimentation/ l'épicerie		

Dining Out

Table d'hôte (the "host's table") is one set menu served at a set price. *Prix fixe* is a fixed price menu. *A la carte* means dishes from the menu are charged separately.

breakfast	le petit déjeuner
lunch	le déjeuner
dinner	le dîner
meal	le repas
first course	l'entrée/les hors d'oeuvre
main course	le plat principal
made to order	sur commande
drink included	boisson comprise
wine list	la carte des vins
the bill	l'addition
fork	la fourchette
knife	le couteau
spoon	la cuillère
plate	l'assiette
glass	le verre
napkin	la serviette
ashtray	le cendrier

tobacconist	le tabac
market	le marché
supermarket	le supermarché
junk shop	la brocante

Market shopping

In a market prices are usually by the kilo or by the piece, that is, each item priced individually. Usually the stall holder (*marchand*) will select the goods for you. Sometimes there is a serve yourself system – observe everyone else! If you are choosing cheese, for example, you may be offered a taste to try.

Sightseeing

town	la ville
old town	la vieille ville
abbey	l'abbaye
cathedral	la cathédrale
church	l'église
keep	le donjon
mansion	l'hôtel
hospital	l'hôpital
town hall	l'hôtel de ville/la mairie
nave	la nef
stained glass	le vitrail
staircase	l'escalier
tower	la tour
walk	le tour
country house/ castle	le château
Gothic	gothique

BREAKFAST & SNACKS

baguette	long thin loaf
pain	bread
petits pains	rolls
beurre	butter
poivre	pepper
sel	salt
sucre	sugar
confiture	jam
oeufs	eggs
...à la coque	boiled eggs
...au bacon	bacon and eggs
...au jambon	ham and eggs
...sur le plat	fried eggs
...brouillés	scrambled eggs
tartine	bread with butter
yaourt	yoghurt
crêpe	pancake
croque-monsieur	ham and cheese toasted sandwich
croque-madame	...with a fried egg on top
galette	type of pancake
quiche	tart of eggs and cream with various fillings
quiche lorraine	quiche with bacon

MAIN COURSES

la viande/meat

bleu	rare
à point	medium
bien cuit	well done
grillé	grilled
agneau	lamb
andouille/ andouillette	tripe sausage
bifteck	steak
boudin	sausage
boudin noir	black pudding
boudin blanc	white pudding
blanquette	stew of veal, lamb or chicken with creamy egg sauce
boeuf à la mode	beef in red wine with carrots, onions and mushroom
à la bordelaise	beef with red wine and shallots
à la Bourguignonne	cooked in red wine, onions and mushrooms
brochette	kebab
caille	quail
canard	duck
carbonnade	casserole of beef, beer and onions
carré d'agneau	rack of lamb

First Courses

An *amuse-bouche, amuse-gueule* or *appetizer* is something to "amuse the mouth", served before the first course.

assiette anglaise	**cold meats**
potage	**soup**

cassoulet	stew of beans, sausages, pork and duck	sanglier	wild boar
		saucisse	fresh sausage
cervelle	brains (food)	saucisson	salami
châteaubriand	thick steak	veau	veal
choucroute	Alsace dish of sauerkraut, bacon and sausages	viande	meat

poission/fish

anchois	anchovies
confit	duck or goose preserved in its own fat
anguille	eel
bar (or loup)	sea bass
barbue	brill
contre-filet	cut of sirloin steak
belon	Brittany oyster
bigorneau	sea snail
coq au vin	chicken in red wine
bercy	sauce of fish stock, butter, white wine and shallots
côte d'agneau	lamb chop
dinde	turkey
entrecôte	beef rib steak
bouillabaisse	fish soup, served with grated cheese, garlic croutons and rouille, a spicy sauce
escargot	snail
faisan	pheasant
farci	stuffed
faux-filet	sirloin
feuilleté	puff pastry
foie	liver
brandade	salt cod puree
foie de veau	calf's liver
cabillaud	cod
foie gras	goose or duck liver pâté
calmars	squid
colin	hake
cuisses de grenouille	frog's legs
coquillage	shellfish
coquilles Saint-Jacques	scallops
grillade	grilled meat
hachis	minced meat
crevette	shrimp
jambon	ham
daurade	sea bream
langue	tongue
fletan	halibut
lapin	rabbit
fruits de mer	seafood
lardon	small pieces of bacon, often added to salads
hareng	herring
homard	lobster
huître	oyster
magret de canard	breast of duck
langoustine	large prawn
limande	lemon sole
medaillon	round piece of meat
lotte	monkfish
morue	salt cod
moelle	beef bone marrow
moule	mussels
mouton navarin	stew of lamb with onions, carrots and turnips
moules marinières	mussels in white wine and onions
oursin	sea urchin
oie	goose
poissons	fish
perdrix	partridge
raie	skate
petit-gris	small snail
saumon	salmon
pieds de cochon	pig's trotters
thon	tuna
truite	trout
pintade	guinea fowl, peppers, onion

legumes/vegetables

porc	pork
ail	garlic
pot-au-feu	casserole of beef and vegetables
artichaut	artichoke
asperge	asparagus
poulet	chicken
aubergine	eggplant
poussin	young chicken
avocat	avocado
rognons	kidneys
bolets	boletus mushrooms
rôti	roast

In the Café

Settle the bill when you leave; the waiter may leave a slip of paper on the table to keep track of the bill.

celeri remoulade	grated celery with mayonnaise
champignon	mushroom
cepes	boletus mushroom
chanterelle	wild mushroom
cornichon	gherkin
courgette	zucchini
chips	potato crisps
chou	cabbage
chou-fleur	cauliflower
concombre	cucumber
cru	raw
crudités	raw vegetables
epinard	spinach
frites	chips, French fries
gratin dauphinois	sliced potatoes baked with cream
haricot	dried bean
haricots verts	green beans
lentilles	lentils
mais	corn
mange-tout	snow pea
mesclun	mixed leaf salad
navet	turnip
noix	nut, walnut
noisette	hazelnut
oignon	onion
panais	parsnip
persil	parsley
pignon	pine nut
poireau	leek
pois	pea
poivron	bell pepper
pomme de terre	potato
pommes frites	chips, French fries
primeurs	early fruit and vegetables
radis	radish
roquette	arugula, rocket
ratatouille	Provençal vegetable stew of aubergines, courgettes, tomatoes, peppers, olive oil
riz	rice
salade Niçoise	egg, tuna, olives, onions and tomato salad

salade verte	green salad
truffe	truffle

FRUITS/FRUIT

ananas	pineapple
cavaillon	fragrant sweet melon
cerise	cherry
citron	lemon
citron vert	lime
figue	fig
fraise	strawberry
framboise	raspberry
groseille	redcurrant
mangue	mango
mirabelle	yellow plum
pamplemousse	grapefruit
pêche	peach
poire	pear
pomme	apple
raisin	grape
prune	plum
pruneau	prune
Reine claude	greengage

SAUCES/SAUCES

aïoli	garlic mayonnaise
béarnaise	sauce of egg, butter, wine and herbs
forestière	with mushrooms and bacon
hollandaise	egg, butter and lemon sauce
lyonnaise	with onions
meunière	fried fish with butter, lemon and parsley sauce
meurette	red wine sauce
Mornay	sauce of cream, egg and cheese
Parmentier	served with potatoes
paysan	rustic style, ingredients depend on the region
pistou	Provençal sauce of basil, garlic and olive oil;
provençale	sauce of tomatoes, garlic and olive oil
papillotte	cooked in paper

DESSERTS/PUDDINGS

Belle Hélène	fruit with ice cream and chocolate sauce
clafoutis	baked pudding of batter and cherries
coulis	puree of fruit or vegetables
gâteau	cake
île flottante	whisked egg whites in custard sauce
crème anglaise	custard
pêche melba	peaches with ice cream and raspberry sauce
tarte tatin	upside-down tart of caramelised apples
crème caramel	caramelised egg custard
crème Chantilly	whipped cream
fromage	cheese
chèvre	goat's cheese

LES BOISSONS/DRINKS

coffee	café
...with milk or cream	au lait or crème
...decaffeinated	déca/décaféiné
...black/espresso	noir/express
...American filtered	coffee filtre
tea	thé
...herb infusion	tisane
...camomile	verveine
hot chocolate	chocolat chaud
milk	lait
mineral water	eau minérale
fizzy	gazeux
non-fizzy	non-gazeux
fizzy lemonade	limonade
fresh lemon juice	citron pressée
served with sugar	
fresh squeezed orange juice	orange pressé
full (e.g. full cream milk)	entier
fresh or cold	frais, fraîche
beer	bière
...bottled	en bouteille
...on tap	à la pression
pre-dinner drink	apéritif
white wine with	kir
cassis: blackcurrant liqueur	

kir with champagne	kir royale
with ice	avec des glaçons
neat	sec
red	rouge
white	blanc
rose	rosé
dry	brut
sweet	doux
sparkling wine	crémant
house wine	vin de maison
Where is this from?	De quelle region vient ce vin?
pitcher	carafe/pichet
...of water/wine	d'eau/de vin
half litre	demi-carafe
quarter litre	quart
mixed	panaché
after dinner drink	digestif
cheers!	santé!

Help!	Au secours!
Stop!	Arrêtez!
Call a doctor	Appelez un médecin
Call an ambulance	Appelez une ambulance
Call the police	Appelez la police
Call the fire brigade	Appelez les pompiers
Where is the nearest telephone?	Où est le téléphone le plus proche?
Where is the nearest hospital?	Où est l'hôpital le plus proche?
I am sick	Je suis malade
I have lost my passport/purse	J'ai perdu mon passeport/porte-monnaie
How do I make an outside call?	Comment est-ce que je peux téléphoner à l'extérieur?
I want to make an international (local) call	Je voudrais une communication pour l'étranger (une communication locale)
What is the dialling code?	Quel est l'indicatif?
I'd like an alarm call for 8 o'clock tomorrow morning	Je voudrais être réveille à huit heures demain matin

Who's calling?	*C'est qui a l'appareil?*
Hold on, please	*Ne quittez pas s'il vous plaît*
The line is busy	*La ligne est occupée*
I must have dialled the wrong number	*J'ai dû faire un faux numéro*
tasting	*la dégustation*
organic	*biologique*
flavour	*le parfum*
basket	*le panier*
bag	*le sac*
I am a vegetarian	*Je suis vegetarien*
I am on a diet	*Je suis au régime*
What do you recommend?	*Que'est-ce que vous recommandez?*
Do you have local specialities?	*Avez-vous des spécialités locales?*
I'd like to order	*Je voudrais commander*
That is not what I ordered	*Ce n'est pas ce que j'ai commandé*
Is service included?	*Est-ce que le service est compris?*
May I have more wine?	*Encore du vin, s'il vous plaît?*
Enjoy your meal	*Bon appetit!*

Numbers

0	*zéro*
1	*un/une*
2	*deux*
3	*trois*
4	*quatre*
5	*cinq*
6	*six*
7	*sept*
8	*huit*
9	*neuf*
10	*dix*
11	*onze*
12	*douze*
13	*treize*
14	*quatorze*
15	*quinze*
16	*seize*
17	*dix-sept*
18	*dix-huit*
19	*dix-neuf*
20	*vingt*

30	*trente*
40	*quarante*
50	*cinquante*
60	*soixante*
70	*septante*
80	*quatre-vingts*
90	*nonante*
100	*cent*
200	*deux cents*
500	*cinq cents*
1000	*mille*
1,000,000	*un million*

The number 1 is often written like an upside-down V, and the number 7 is crossed.

Days of the Week

Days of the week, seasons and months are not capitalised in French.

Monday	*lundi*
Tuesday	*mardi*
Wednesday	*mercredi*
Thursday	*jeudi*
Friday	*vendredi*
Saturday	*samedi*
Sunday	*dimanche*

Seasons

spring	*le printemps*
summer	*l'été*
autumn	*l'automne*
winter	*l'hiver*

Months

January	*janvier*
February	*février*
March	*mars*
April	*avril*
May	*mai*
June	*juin*
July	*juillet*
August	*août*
September	*septembre*
October	*octobre*
November	*novembre*
December	*décembre*

Saying the Date

20th October 1999	*le vingt octobre, dix-neuf cent quatre-vingt-dix-neuf*

Flemish Words & Phrases

How much is it?	*Hoeveel is het?/ Hoeveel kost dat?*
What is your name?	*Wat is u naam?*
My name is...	*Mijn naam is ... Ik heet ...*
Do you speak English?	*Spreekt u Engels?*
I am English/ American	*Ik ben Engelsman/ Amerikaan*
I don't understand	*Ik begrijp het niet*
Please speak more slowly	*Kunt u langzamer praten, alstublieft*
Can you help me?	*Kunt u mij helpen?*
I'm looking for...	*Ik zoek...*
Where is...?	*Waar is...?*
I'm sorry	*Excuseer/Pardon*
I don't know	*Ik weet het niet*
No problem	*Geen probleem*
Have a good day!	*Prettige dag nog!*
That's it	*Precies*
Here it is	*Hier is het*
There it is	*Daar is het*
Let's go	*Laten we gaan/ We zijn weg*
See you tomorrow	*Tot morgen*
See you soon	*Tot straks!*
Show me the word in the book	*Toon mij het woord in het boek, alstublieft*
please	
At what time?	*Hoe laat?*
When	*Wanneer?*
What time is it?	*Hoe laat is het?*
yes	*ja*
no	*neen*
please	*alstublieft*
thank you	*dank u*
(very much)	*(wel)*
you're welcome	*graag gedaan*
excuse me	*excuseer/ pardon*
hello	*hallo*
goodbye	*tot ziens!*
good evening	*Goeden avond!*
here	*hier*
there	*daar*
today	*vandaag*
yesterday	*gisteren*
tomorrow	*morgen*
now	*nu*
later	*later*
right away	*direct/onmiddellijk*
this morning	*vanmorgen*
this afternoon	*deze namiddag*
this evening	*vanavond*

On Arrival

I want to get off at...	Ik wil uitstappen in....
Is there a bus to the Grote Markt?	Is er een bus naar de Grote Markt?
What street is this?	Welke straat is dit?
Which line do I take for...?	Welke lijn moet ik nemen voor...?
How far is...?	Hoe ver is...?
Validate your ticket	Stempel uw ticket af
airport	de luchthaven
train station	het station
bus station	het busstation
Metro stop	de metrohalte
bus	de bus
bus stop	de bushalte
platform	het perron
ticket	het ticket

return ticket	een ticket retour
hitchhiking	liften
toilets	de toiletten
This is the hotel address	Dat is het adres van het hotel
I'd like a (single/double) room...	Ik wil graag een kamer (voor een/twee personen)
...with shower	...met douche
...with bath	...met bad
...with a view	...met zicht
Does that include breakfast?	Is het ontbijt inbegrepen?
May I see the room?	Mag ik de kamer zien?
washbasin	de wastafel
bed	het bed
key	de sleutel
elevator	de lift
air conditioning	airconditioning

one/that one	
What size is it?	Welke maat is het?
Anything else?	Iets anders?
size (clothes)	de maat
size (shoes)	de maat
cheap	goedkoop
expensive	duur
enough	genoeg
too much	te veel
a piece	een stuk
each	per stuk
bill	de rekening
chemist	de apotheek
bakery	de bakkerij
bookshop	de boekhandel
delicatessen	delicatessen
library	de bibliotheek
department store	het warenhuis
fishmongers	de viswinkel
grocery	de kruidenier
tobacconist	de tabakwinkel
markets	de markt
supermarket	de supermarkt
junk shop	curiosa/antiquiteiten

On the Road

Where is the spare wheel?	Waar is het reservewiel?
Where is the nearest garage?	Waar is de dichtstbijzijnde garage?
Our car has broken down	Onze auto is in panne
I want to have my car repaired	Ik wil mijn auto laten herstellen
It's not your right of way	U heeft geen voorrang
I think I must have put diesel in the car by mistake	Ik denk dat ik per ongeluk diesel in mijn auto heb gedaan
the road to...	de straat naar...
left	links
right	rechts
straight on	rechtstreeks
far	ver
near	nabij
opposite	tegenover
beside	naast
car park	de parkeerplaats
over there	daar
at the end	aan het eind
on foot	te voet
by car	met de auto
town map	het stadplan
road map	de (land)kaart
street	de straat
square	het plein

give way	geef voorrang
dead end	doodlopende straat
no parking	verboden te parkeren
motorway	de autosnelweg
toll	de tol
speed limit	de snelheids-beperking
petrol	de benzine
unleaded	loodvrij
diesel	de diesel
water/oil	water/olie
puncture	een lekke band
bulb	de lamp
wipers	ruitewissers

Shopping

Where is the nearest bank/post office?	Waar is de dichtstbijzijnde bank (het dichtstbijzijnde postkantoor)?
I'd like to buy	Ik zou graag ... kopen
How much is it?	Hoeveel is het?/Hoeveel kost dat?
Do you take credit cards?	Neemt u cretiet karten?
I'm just looking	Ik kijk alleen maar
Have you got?	Hebt u...?
I'll take it	Ik neem het
I'll take this	Ik neem dit/deze

Sightseeing

town	de stad
old town	de oude stad
abbey	de abdij
cathedral	de kathedraal
church	de kerk
keep	de slottoren
mansion	het hotel
hospital	het ziekenhuis
town hall	het stadhuis
nave	het schip
stained glass	het glasraam
staircase	de trap
tower	de toren
walk	de tour
country house/castle	het kasteel
Gothic	Gotisch
Roman	Romaans
Romanesque	Romaans
museum	het museum
art gallery	de galerij
exhibition	de tentoonstelling
tourist information office	het bureau voor toerisme (VVV)
free	gratis
open	geopend
closed	gesloten
every day	iedere dag

all year	het hele jaar
all day	de hele dag
swimming pool	het zwembad
to book	reserveren/ boeken

Dining Out

breakfast	het ontbijt
lunch	lunch/middageten
dinner	diner/avondeten
meal	de maltijd
first course	het voorgerecht
main course	het hoofdgerecht
made to order	op bestelling
drink included	dranken inbegrepen
wine list	de wijnkaart
the bill	de rekening
fork	de vork
knife	het mes
spoon	de lepel
plate	het bord
glass	het glas
napkin	het servet
ashtray	de asbak

BREAKFAST & SNACKS

boter	butter
boterham	bread with butter
brood	bread
broodjes	rolls
croque-monsieur	ham and cheese toasted sandwich
croque-madame (met een spiegelei)	... with a fried egg on top
eieren	eggs
...zachtgekookt	boiled eggs
...met spek	bacon and eggs
...met ham	ham and eggs
...spiegelei	fried eggs
...roerei	scrambled eggs
honig	honey
jam	jam
pannekoek	pancake
peper	pepper
quiche	tart of eggs and cream with various fillings
quiche lorraine	quiche with bacon
stokbrood	long thin loaf
yoghurt	yoghurt
zout	salt
zuiker	sugar

FIRST COURSE

charcuterie	cold meats
soep	soup

MAIN COURSES

vlees/meat

biefsteak	steak
bladerdeeg	puff pastry
brochette	kebab
carbonnade	casserole of beef, beer and onions
cassoulet	stew of beans, sausages, pork and duck, from southwest France
chateaubriand	thick steak
coq au vin	chicken in red wine
eend	duck
eendenborst	breast of duck
entrecote	beef rib steak
escargot	snail
everzwijn	wild boar
fazant	pheasant
foie gras	goose or duck liver pâté
gans	goose
gebraad	roast
gegrild	grilled
gegrild vlees	grilled meat
gehakt	minced meat
gestoofd vlees	beef stew with red wine, onions and tomatoes
gevuld	stuffed
goedgebakken	well done
goulash van lam	beef bone marrow
ham	ham
hersens	brains (food)
kalfslever	calf's liver
kalfsrib	rack of lamb
kalfsvlees	veal
kalkoen	turkey
kikkerbillen	frog's legs
kip	chicken
konijn	rabbit
kuiken	young chicken
kwartel	quail
lam	lamb
lamskotelet	lamb chop
lendestuk	sirloin
lendebiefstuk	cut of sirloin steak
lever	liver
medaillon	round piece of meat
niertjes	kidneys
parelhoen	guinea fowl
patrijs	partridge
pens	sausage
petit-gris	small snail

ragot	stew of veal, lamb or chicken with creamy egg sauce
rundvlees in rode wijn met wortelen, uien en champignons	beef in red wine with carrots, onions and mushroom
saignant	rare
saucijs	fresh sausage
spek	small pieces of bacon, often added to salads
stoofpot	casserole of beef and vegetables
sxvarken	pork
tong	tongue
varkenspoten	pig's trotters
witte pens	white pudding
worst/salami	salami
zuurkool in eigen vet ingemaakt vlees	duck or goose preserved in its own fat
zwarte pens	black pudding

vis/fish

ansjovis	anchovies
bouillabaisse	fish soup, served with grated cheese, garlic croutons and rouille, a spicy sauce
calamares	squid
daurade	sea bream
forel	trout
garnaal	shrimp
gezouten	salt cod puree
griet	brill
haring	herring
heilbot	halibut
kabeljouw	cod
koolvis	hake
kreeft	lobster
langoestine	large prawn
limande	lemon sole
lot	monkfish
mossel	mussels
mosselen in wijn en uien	mussels in white wine and onions
oester	oyster
paling	eel
rog	skate
saus van stokvis,	sauce of fish

boter, witte wijn en sjalotten — stock, butter, white wine and shallots
schaaldier — shellfish
sint-jakobsschelp — scallops
tonijn — tuna
tong met citroen — lemon sole
zeebaars — sea bass
zeeslak — sea snail
zeebrasem — sea bream
zeevruchten — seafood
zeeegel — sea urchin
zalm — salmon

Groenter/Vegetables

aardappel — potato
ajuin/ui — onion
artisjok — artichoke
asperge — asparagus
aubergine — eggplant
augurk — gherkin
avocado — avocado
biet — turnip
bloemkool — cauliflower
boon — dried bean
champignon — mushroom
cantharel (dooierzwam) — wild mushroom
chips — potato crisps
courgette — zucchini
erwt — pea
frieten/patat — chips, French fries
gemengde sla — mixed leaf salad
gratin — fries
groene bonen — green beans
groene sla — green salad
hazelnoot — hazelnut
komkommer — cucumber
kool — cabbage
linzen — lentils
look — garlic
mais — corn
noot/walnoot — nut, walnut
paprika — bell pepper
peterselie — parsley
peulvruchten — snow pea
pijnpitten — pine nut
prei — leek
radijs — radish
rauw — raw
rijst — rice
roquette — arugula, rocket
salade — raw vegetables
salade Niçoise — egg, tuna, olives, onions and tomato salad
selder in remouladesaus — grated celery with mayonnaise

spinazie — spinach
truffel — truffle
witte peen — parsnip

Vruchter/Fruit

aalbes — redcurrant
aardbei — strawberry
ananas — pineapple
appel — apple
citroen — lemon
(wijn)druif — grape
framboos — raspberry
grapefruit/kers — grapefruit
limoen — cherry
mango — lime
mirabel — mango
perzik — yellow plum
peer — peach
pruim — pear
vijg — prune
— fig

Sauzer/Sauces

béarnaise — sauce of egg, butter, wine and herbs
eieren en kaas — egg and cheese

geserveerd met aardappelen — served with potatoes

hollandaise saus — egg, butter and lemon sauce

landelijk (van de streek) — rustic style, ingredients depend on the region
looksaus — garlic mayonnaise

met uien — with onions
meunière — fried fish with butter, lemon and parsley sauce
provencalse saus van knoflook, basili- — Provençal sauce of basil, garlic and olive oil

rode wijn saus — red wine sauce
saus met champignons en spek — with mushrooms and bacon

Puddings

Belle Hélène — fruit with ice cream and chocolate sauce
caramelcreme — caramelised egg custard
clafoutis — baked pudding of batter and cherries
coulis — puree of fruit or vegetables
custardpudding — custard
gebak — cake
geitenkaas — goat's cheese

geklopt eiwit in custardsaus — whisked egg whites in custard sauce

kaas — cheese
pêche melba — peaches with ice cream and raspberry sauce
slagroom — whipped cream
tarte tatin — upside-down tart of caramelised apples

Dranken/Drinks

after dinner drink — pousse-café
beer — bier
...bottled — op fles
...on tap — van het vat
coffee — koffie
...with milk or cream — met melk of room
...decaffeinated — decafeine
...black/espresso — zwart/espresso
...American filtered — filterkoffie
dry — brut
fizzy lemonade — limonade

fresh lemon juice served with sugar — vers citroensap vers
sinaasappelsap
fresh or cold — koud

full (e.g. full cream milk) — volle melk
half litre — halve liter
hot chocolate — warme chocolademelk
house wine — huiswijn
milk — melk

mineral water	mineraalwater
...fizzy	spuitwater/Spa rood
...non-fizzy	plat water/ Spa blauw
mixed	bier met
neat	sec
pitcher	karaf
...of water/wine	water/wijn
pre-dinner drink	aperitief
quarter litre	kwart liter
red	rood
rose	rose
sparkling wine	schuimwijn
sweet	zacht
tea	thee
...herb infusion	kruidenthee
...camomile	kamille
white wine with cassis: black-currant liqueur	kir
white	wit
with ice	met ijs

Useful Phrases

Help!	Help!
Call a doctor	Bel een dokter
Call an ambulance	Bel een ziekenwagen
Call the police	Bel de politie
Call the fire brigade	Bel de brandweer
Where is the nearest telephone?	Waar is de dichtstbijzijnde telefoon?
Where is the nearest hospital?	Waar is het dichtstbijzijnde ziekenhuis?
I am sick	Ik ben ziek
I have lost my passport/purse	Ik ben mijn paspoort/ portemonnee kwijt/verloren passeport/porte-monnaie
How do I make an outside call?	Hoe krijg ik een buitenlijn?
I want to make an international (local) call	Ik wil naar het buitenland bellen?
What is the dialling code?	Wat is het zonennummer/ landnummer?
I'd like an alarm call for 8 o'clock tomorrow morning	Ik wil om 8 uur gewekt worden

Who's calling?	Met wie spreek ik?
Hold on, please	Blijf aan de lijn,alstublieft
The line is busy	De lijn is in gesprek
I must have dialled the wrong number	Ik heb een verkeerd nummer gedraaid
tasting	proeven
organic	biologisch
flavour	het aroma/de smaak
basket	de mand
bag	de zak
I am a vegetarian	Ik ben vegetarier
I am on a diet	Ik volg een dieet
What do you recommend?	Wat beveelt u aan?
Do you have local specialities?	Heeft u specialiteiten van de regio?
I'd like to order	Ik wil bestellen
That is not what I ordered	Dit is niet wat ik besteld heb
Is service included?	Is de dienst inbegrepen?
May I have more wine?	Mag ik nog een beetje wijn?
Enjoy your meal	Smakelijk!

Numbers

0	nul
1	één
2	twee
3	drie
4	vier
5	vijf
6	zes
7	zeven
8	acht
9	negen
10	tien
11	elf
12	twaalf
13	dertien
14	veertien
15	vijfteen
16	zestien
17	zeventien
18	achttien
19	negentien
20	twintig
30	dertig
40	veertig
50	vijftig
60	zestig
70	zeventig

80	tachtig
90	negentig
100	honderd
200	tweehonderd
500	vijfhonderd
1000	duizend

Days of the Week

Monday	maandag
Tuesday	dinsdag
Wednesday	woensdag
Thursday	donderdag
Friday	vrijdag
Saturday	zaterdag
Sunday	zondag

Seasons

Spring	de lente
Summer	de zomer
Autumn	de herfst
Winter	de winter

Months

January	januari
February	februari
March	maart
April	april
May	mei
June	juni
July	juli
August	august(us)
September	september
October	oktober
November	november
December	december

Further Reading

Books

Civilisation by Kenneth Clark, Penguin. Insightful commentaries on the major works of the Flemish Masters.

The Sorrow of Belgium by Hugo Claus, Viking. A novel charting the effects of the Nazi occupation of Flanders through the eyes of a young boy.

From Van Eyck to Bruegel by Max J. Friedlander, Phaidon. Definitive account of the Flemish Masters.

A New Guide to the Battlefields of Northern France and the Low Country by Michael Glover, Michael Joseph.

Battlefields of the First World War by T.&V. Holt, Pavilion.

History of the Belgians by A. de Meeiis. A colourful and wide-ranging history of the Belgians.

Bruegel by Gregory Martin. An introduction to the works of Pieter Bruegel.

The Renaissance and Mannerism Outside Italy by Alastair Smart.

Defiant Dynasty: The Coburgs of Belgium by Theo Aronson. A gossipy history of the kings of the House of Saxe-Coburg-Gotha from 1831 to 1950.

Twelve Cities by John Gunter. Includes a lively if dated essay on the temperament of Brussels and its citizens.

The Low Countries: 1780–1940 by E.H. Kossman. A thorough history.

Other Insight Guides

Nearly 200 Insight Guides cover the world, complemented by more than 100 Insight Pocket Guides and 100 Insight Compact Guides.

In more than 200 pages, **Insight Guide: Brussels** covers in comprehensive detail every aspect of the city: history, culture, people and places. It's the ideal companion.

For those on a tight schedule,

Insight Pocket Guide: Brussels sets out carefully crafted itineraries designed to make the most of your visit. It contains recommendations from a local expert and comes with a full-size fold-out map showing the itineraries.

Insight Compact Guides to **Belgium** and **Brussels** are ideal on-the-spot reference guides – in essence, mini-encyclopedias. Highly portable, each is packed with detailed text, photography and maps, all meticulously cross-referenced for ease of use.

Maps

Most good bookshops stock maps on Belgium. General maps to look out for are the AA Baedeker Map of Belgium (scale 1:250,000); RAC European Road Maps No. 3 Belgium, Netherlands and Luxembourg (1:500,000); Bartholomew Belgium and Luxembourg (1:300,000); Falk Benelux Countries (1:500,000); GeoCenter International Euro-Map Belgium-Luxembourg (1:300,000); Hallwag Euro-map Belgium-Luxembourg (1:250,000); Hildebrand's Belgium (1:250,000); Michelin Map No. 409 Belgie-Luxembourg (1:350,000); and Michelin Map No. 51 Calais-Lille-Brussels, No. 212 Brugge-Rotterdam-Antwerpen, No. 213 Brussels-Oostende-Liège (all 1:200,000).

Geocart and Falk both produce town plans of the major cities and the National Geographic Institute publishes topographic maps of Belgium itself, the Hautes Fagnes, Proven-Ieper-Ploegsteert and the Belgium Woods (Zoniëwoud/Forêt de Soignes) regions.

Online

For a complete listing of Belgian sites on the Internet, see: http://www.online.be/

ART & PHOTO CREDITS

Index

Numbers in italics refer to photographs

The World of Insight Guides

400 books in three complementary series cover every major destination in every continent.

Insight Guides

Alaska
Alsace
Amazon Wildlife
American Southwest
Amsterdam
Argentina
Atlanta
Athens
Australia
Austria
Bahamas
Bali
Baltic States
Bangkok
Barbados
Barcelona
Bay of Naples
Beijing
Belgium
Belize
Berlin
Bermuda
Boston
Brazil
Brittany
Brussels
Budapest
Buenos Aires
Burgundy
Burma (Myanmar)
Cairo
Calcutta
California
Canada
Caribbean
Catalonia
Channel Islands
Chicago
Chile
China
Cologne
Continental Europe
Corsica
Costa Rica
Crete
Crossing America
Cuba
Cyprus
Czech & Slovak Republics
Delhi, Jaipur, Agra
Denmark
Dresden
Dublin
Düsseldorf
East African Wildlife
East Asia
Eastern Europe
Ecuador
Edinburgh
Egypt
Finland
Florence
Florida
France
Frankfurt
French Riviera
Gambia & Senegal
Germany
Glasgow

Gran Canaria
Great Barrier Reef
Great Britain
Greece
Greek Islands
Hamburg
Hawaii
Hong Kong
Hungary
Iceland
India
India's Western Himalaya
Indian Wildlife
Indonesia
Ireland
Israel
Istanbul
Italy
Jamaica
Japan
Java
Jerusalem
Jordan
Kathmandu
Kenya
Korea
Lisbon
Loire Valley
London
Los Angeles
Madeira
Madrid
Malaysia
Mallorca & Ibiza
Malta
Marine Life in the South China Sea
Melbourne
Mexico
Mexico City
Miami
Montreal
Morocco
Moscow
Munich
Namibia
Native America
Nepal
Netherlands
New England
New Orleans
New York City
New York State
New Zealand
Nile
Normandy
Northern California
Northern Spain
Norway
Oman & the UAE
Oxford
Old South
Pacific Northwest
Pakistan
Paris
Peru
Philadelphia
Philippines
Poland
Portugal
Prague

Provence
Puerto Rico
Rajasthan
Rhine
Rio de Janeiro
Rockies
Rome
Russia
St Petersburg
San Francisco
Sardinia
Scotland
Seattle
Sicily
Singapore
South Africa
South America
South Asia
South India
South Tyrol
Southeast Asia
Southeast Asia Wildlife
Southern California
Southern Spain
Spain
Sri Lanka
Sweden
Switzerland
Sydney
Taiwan
Tenerife
Texas
Thailand
Tokyo
Trinidad & Tobago
Tunisia
Turkey
Turkish Coast
Tuscany
Umbria
US National Parks East
US National Parks West
Vancouver
Venezuela
Venice
Vienna
Vietnam
Wales
Washington DC
Waterways of Europe
Wild West
Yemen

Insight Pocket Guides

Aegean Islands★
Algarve★
Alsace
Amsterdam★
Athens★
Atlanta★
Bahamas★
Baja Peninsula★
Bali★
Bali Bird Walks
Bangkok★
Barbados★
Barcelona★
Bavaria★
Beijing★
Berlin★

Bermuda★
Bhutan★
Boston★
British Columbia★
Brittany★
Brussels★
Budapest & Surroundings★
Canton★
Chiang Mai★
Chicago★
Corsica★
Costa Blanca★
Costa Brava★
Costa del Sol/Marbella★
Costa Rica★
Crete★
Denmark★
Fiji★
Florence★
Florida★
Florida Keys★
French Riviera★
Gran Canaria★
Hawaii★
Hong Kong★
Hungary
Ibiza★
Ireland★
Ireland's Southwest★
Israel★
Istanbul★
Jakarta★
Jamaica★
Kathmandu Bikes & Hikes★
Kenya★
Kuala Lumpur★
Lisbon★
Loire Valley★
London★
Macau★
Madrid★
Malacca
Maldives
Mallorca★
Malta★
Mexico City★
Miami★
Milan★
Montreal★
Morocco★
Moscow
Munich★
Nepal★
New Delhi
New Orleans★
New York City★
New Zealand★
Northern California★
Oslo/Bergen★
Paris★
Penang★
Phuket★
Prague★
Provence★
Puerto Rico★
Quebec★
Rhodes★
Rome★
Sabah★

St Petersburg★
San Francisco★
Sardinia
Scotland★
Seville★
Seychelles★
Sicily★
Sikkim
Singapore★
Southeast England
Southern California★
Southern Spain★
Sri Lanka★
Sydney★
Tenerife★
Thailand★.
Tibet★
Toronto★
Tunisia★
Turkish Coast★
Tuscany★
Venice★
Vienna★
Vietnam★
Yogyakarta
Yucatan Peninsula★

★ = Insight Pocket Guides
with Pull out Maps

Insight Compact Guides

Algarve
Amsterdam
Bahamas
Bali
Bangkok
Barbados
Barcelona
Beijing
Belgium
Berlin
Brittany
Brussels
Budapest
Burgundy
Copenhagen
Costa Brava
Costa Rica
Crete
Cyprus
Czech Republic
Denmark
Dominican Republic
Dublin
Egypt
Finland
Florence
Gran Canaria
Greece
Holland
Hong Kong
Ireland
Israel
Italian Lakes
Italian Riviera
Jamaica
Jerusalem
Lisbon
Madeira
Mallorca
Malta

Milan
Moscow
Munich
Normandy
Norway
Paris
Poland
Portugal
Prague
Provence
Rhodes
Rome
St Petersburg
Salzburg
Singapore
Switzerland
Sydney
Tenerife
Thailand
Turkey
Turkish Coast
Tuscany

UK regional titles:
Bath & Surroundings
Cambridge & East Anglia
Cornwall
Cotswolds
Devon & Exmoor
Edinburgh
Lake District
London
New Forest
North York Moors
Northumbria
Oxford
Peak District
Scotland
Scottish Highlands
Shakespeare Country
Snowdonia
South Downs
York
Yorkshire Dales

USA regional titles:
Boston
Cape Cod
Chicago
Florida
Florida Keys
Hawaii: Maui
Hawaii: Oahu
Las Vegas
Los Angeles
Martha's Vineyard & Nantucket
New York
San Francisco
Washington D.C.
Venice
Vienna
West of Ireland